Heinrich Karl Brugsch

A History of Egypt under the Pharaohs

Vol. 2, Second Edition

Heinrich Karl Brugsch

A History of Egypt under the Pharaohs
Vol. 2, Second Edition

ISBN/EAN: 9783337127381

Printed in Europe, USA, Canada, Australia, Japan

Cover: Foto ©ninafisch / pixelio.de

More available books at **www.hansebooks.com**

EGYPT UNDER THE PHARAOHS

VOL. II.

LONDON: PRINTED BY
SPOTTISWOODE AND CO., NEW-STREET SQUARE
AND PARLIAMENT STREET

A

HISTORY OF EGYPT

UNDER THE PHARAOHS

DERIVED ENTIRELY FROM THE MONUMENTS

TO WHICH IS ADDED

A DISCOURSE ON THE EXODUS OF THE ISRAELITES

BY Dr HENRY BRUGSCH-BEY

PROFESSOR IN THE UNIVERSITY OF BERLIN
M.R.S.S. GÖTTINGEN
CORRESPONDING MEMBER OF THE R. ACAD. OF SCIENCES BERLIN, ETC.

TRANSLATED AND EDITED FROM THE GERMAN

(After the unfinished Translation by the late Henry Danby Seymour, F.R.G.S.)

BY PHILIP SMITH, B.A.

AUTHOR OF 'THE STUDENT'S ANCIENT HISTORY OF THE EAST'

SECOND EDITION

WITH A NEW PREFACE, ADDITIONS, AND ORIGINAL NOTES BY THE AUTHOR

IN TWO VOLUMES — VOL. II.

Maps and Illustrations

LONDON
JOHN MURRAY, ALBEMARLE STREET
1881

CONTENTS

OF

THE SECOND VOLUME.

CHAPTER XIV.

THE NINETEENTH DYNASTY.—THE PEOPLE OF THE KHITA.

B.C.		PAGE
	Review of the recent Schism	1
	Rise of the Khita, to the N.E. of Egypt	2
	They appear as early as Thutmes III.	2
	They are the Hittites of Scripture	2
	Their locality, and supremacy in Western Asia	3
	Mention of them and their gods in Egyptian inscriptions.	3
	Their kings, Sapalili, Maurosur, Mauthanar, and Khitasar, contemporary with Ramses I., Seti I., and Ramses II.	3
	Their deities, Sutekh and his warrior wife, Astartha-Anatha.	3
	Their towns, Daphne and Haleb, certainly fixed	3
	Their military array; *non-Semitic* names	4, 5
	List of their peoples and cities on the inscriptions	5-7
	Their supremacy in Western Asia before the Assyrians	7
1400.	I. RAMSES I.: his unknown relation to Dynasty XVIII.	8
	His reign neither long nor remarkable.	9
	Memorial of his coronation, at Karnak	9
	War and Treaty with the king of the Khita	9
	Monument at Wady Halfah. Tomb at Biban-el-Molouk	9, 10
1366.	II. MA-MEN-RA MINEPTAH I. SETI I. (SETHOS)	10
	Celebrated on the national temple at Thebes	10
	His Great Hall of Columns at Karnak	10
	Wars of Seti depicted on the N. outer wall	10
	Inroads of the E. border nations on the Delta	11
	War of his first year against the Shasu	12
	His route traced from Khetham to Kan'aan	12-14
	Inscriptions recording his victories	14-18

		PAGE
B.C.		
	Felling of cedars in Lebanon	18
	Celebration of his return home	19
	List of nations conquered by him	20
	His other campaigns in Asia	21
	His wars against the Libyans	21
	Record of prisoners and spoils, showing high art	22
	Connection of the Ruthen and the Khita	23
	Services of Seti to the temple of Amon	23, 24
	His wife, Tui, heiress of the old line of kings	24
	Worship of Baal-Sutekh by kings of XIXth Dynasty	24
	Association of Ramses II. as the legitimate heir	25
	Related in the inscriptions of Ramses II.	25, 26
	Wars with the countries of Kush and Punt	26
	Viceroys or 'King's Sons of Kush'	27
	Climax of Egyptian art. Works of Seti I.	27
	His tomb: its pictures and inscriptions	27, 28
	The 'Memnonium' in honour of Ramses I.	28
	The king's name of Usiri, in honour of Osiris	27, 28
	The temple of Osiris at Abydus, finished by Ramses II.	29, 30
	The *Table of Kings* at Abydus	29
	Temples at Memphis, Heliopolis, El-Kab, &c.	29, 31
	Records of the sculptor Hi and the painter Amen-uah-su	31
	Tributes and taxes. Gold mines in Egypt and Nubia.	32
	Road from the Nile to Coptos. Gold washing	32
	Inscriptions of the temple at Redesieh	32, 33
	Death and apotheosis of Seti I.	35
1333.	III. RAMESSU II. MIAMUN, RAMSES II., SESOSTRIS	35
	Vast number of his monuments over all Egypt	35
	Completion of the temple at Abydus.—Inscription	36-44
	Journey to Thebes for the feast of Amon	45
	Return to his royal residence at Zoan-Tanis	45
	Age of Ramses. His 60 sons and 59 daughters	46
	Inferiority of his buildings and sculptures	46
	His great war with the Khita, in his 5th year	46
	The heroic poem of Pentaur: its many copies	47-48
	First translation of it by E. de Rougé	48
	Pictures of the camps, armies, and battle of Kadesh	48-51
	Record of the battle on the temple walls at Karnak	52-54
	Pentaur's poem engraved on the temple walls	55
	Its style compared with that of Moses	55
	Translation of the poem of Pentaur	56-65
	Previous campaigns of Ramses against Kadesh	65
	Rock tablets of Beyrout; the 'Columns of Sesostris'	65
	War with Tunep—Inscription in the Theban Ramesseum	66
	Campaign in Canaan in his 8th year	66

B.C.	PAGE
Names of places—The storming of Askalon	67, 68
Lists of prisoners inscribed at Luqsor	69
Maritime wars proved by an inscription at Ibsamboul	70
Pressure of Semitic tribes upon Egypt.	70, 77
Treaty between Ramses II. and Khitasir of Khita	71
Its inscription on a silver tablet (comp. p. 410)	71, 74, 76
Ramses honoured as a god by the Khita	77
Ramses II. marries the daughter of the king of Khita	78
Pictures at Derr and Beit-el-Walli	78
Negro-hunting razzias and wars with Kush	78
Victories over the Marmaridæ and Phœnicians	79
Pictures of courts held after these victories	79, 80
Names of Ethiopian and Libyan tribes subdued	81
Names of viceroys of the South under Ramses II.	81
The Nubian gold-mines in the land of Akita	81
Well and gold-washing works of Ramses II.	82
Inscription about them at Kouban	83–87
Earlier wells in the valley of Hammamat	87
Temples built at Abydus, Thebes, and Memphis	87
The memorial tablet at Ibsamboul, 35th year of Ramses II.	88
Relations between Egypt and the Khita	88
Temple of Ptah at Memphis (near Qasrieh)	89
The great torso of Ramses at Mit-Rahineh	90
Labours of the *Apuirui*, i.e. Erythræans, *not Hebrews*	91
The architect Ameneman and his family	91
Probably the overseer of the Israelites in Egypt	91
Great works of Ramses II. at Thebes	92
At Karnak; the Hall of Columns completed	92
At Luqsor: the Temple of Amon, obelisks and statues	92
At Old Qurnah: sepulchral temple of Seti I.	92
The Ramesseum, with the greatest colossus of Ramses, said to have been thrown down by Cambyses	92, 93
Boast of Ramses, that 'he made Egypt anew'	94
Numerous temples and towns in Nubia	94
The great rock temple of Ibsamboul	94
Derivation of the name from Pimas (Greek, Psampolis)	96
Pictures on the walls	96
Ramesseum and obelisks at Heliopolis; the architect	98
Zoan-Tanis the special residence of Ramses II.	98
Its locality—the *key of Egypt* on the East	98
New temple-city built by Ramses to the gods of Egypt, with Baal-Sutekh, and himself	99
Memorial stone of the 400th year of king Nub	99
Present aspect of the '*field of Zoan*': ruins and inscriptions	99
Inscriptions in honour of Ramses II.	99

B.C.		PAGE
	New name of Zoan, *Pi-Ramessu*, the *City of Ramses* . .	100
	New capital of Egypt: 'here is the seat of the court' . .	100
	Vivid description in an old Egyptian letter	100–102
	It is the same as the 'temple-city' Raamses (Ex. i. 13) . .	102
	THE PHARAOH OF THE OPPRESSION IS NO OTHER, CAN BE NO OTHER, THAN RAMSES II.	103
	Absence of the name of the Israelites explained	103
	Importance of Zoan-Tanis in Egyptian history . . .	104
	Immense number of foreign prisoners in Egypt . . .	104
	Their various employments: soldiers; sailors; slaves .	105
	Semitic influence on religion, manners, and language . .	105
	Introduction of Semitic words by the scribes . . .	106
	Remarkable letter satirizing the new literature .	107–114
	Long reign of Ramses II., 67 years—His 30 years' jubilee .	114
	Family of Ramses: 60 sons and 59 daughters . . .	115
	His eldest son Khamus, and 14th son Mineptah . . .	116
	His daughters: Meri (Merris) probably the rescuer of Moses	117
	The name of Moses preserved in I-en-Moshé . . .	117
	Contemporaries of the king: especially Bekenkhonsu . .	117
	Inscription on his statue at Munich	118
	Seeds of trouble at the death of Ramses II.	119
	His tomb in the Biban-el-Molouk: a poor work . . .	119
1300.	IV. MINEPTAH II. HOTEP-HI-MA (MENEPHTHES) . . .	120
	Mean character of his architectural works	120
	He carved his own name on ancient monuments . . .	121
	His great inscription in the temple of Amon relating the invasion and defeat of the Libyans at Prosopis .	121–128
	The allies of the Libyans *Asiatic, not European* .	128, 129
	Names of Libyan tribes W. of the Delta	130
	Peaceful relations with the Khita or Canaanites .	130, 131
	Canaanites employed as bearers of official despatches . .	131
	Copies of such papers	131, 132
	Nomad Shasu received into the Delta	132
	MINEPTAH II. MUST BE THE PHARAOH OF THE EXODUS . .	133
	His special title, PIR'AO, 'great house, high gate'[1] . .	133
	The 'field of Zoan' (Ps. lxxviii. 43) his usual residence . .	133
	The '*Aper*,' *Apur'a*, or '*Aperiu* proved to be *not* the Hebrews	134
	Troubles of his reign: its end unrecorded	135
	His contemporaries: Mas, viceroy of Ethiopia . . .	135
	Pinehas; Lui (Levi), priest and chief architect . . .	136

[1] Dr. Brugsch identifies Mineptah II. with the *Pheron*, or *Pheros*, son of Sesostris, of Herod. ii. 111. It is a remarkable coincidence that this '*Pharaoh*' should be the one so called by the Egyptian informants of the historian.—ED.

B.C.		PAGE
	The ' Dirge ' of Mineptah : its reference doubtful . . .	136
	Men of letters under Ramses II. and Mineptah II. . .	137
1266.	V. SETI II. MINEPTAH III., son of Mineptah II. . . .	137
	Records of the first two years of his reign	137
	Zoan-Tanis still the capital—Royal road to the East . .	138
	Report concerning fugitive servants, an exact parallel to the Exodus (compare p. 389)	138
	Temple of Seti II. at Thebes.—Favour of the Priests . .	139
	The *Tale of the Two Brothers*, a parallel to the life of Joseph, written for him (*compare* Vol. I. p. 308)	139
	His magnificent sepulchre in the Biban-el-Molouk . . .	139
1233.	VI. SETNAKHT-MERER-MIAMUN II., son of Seti II. . .	140
	Time of trouble—The anti-king Mineptah Siptah . . .	140
	Inscriptions of Siptah's supporter, Seti	141
	Inscriptions of Siptah erased by Setnakht . . .	141, 142
	Usurpation of a Phœnician, Arisu or Alisu . . .	142
	Account of these troubles by Ramses III., son of Setnakht, in the great Harris Papyrus	143

CHAPTER XV.

THE TWENTIETH DYNASTY.

1200.	I. RAMSES III. HAQ-ON, i.e. ' Prince of Heliopolis ' . .	145
	Commonly called Ramessu-pa-nuti, 'Ramses the god,' the RHAMPSINITUS of Herodotus[2]	145
	Account of his reign in the Harris Papyrus . .	145
	Restoration of the several ranks in the state	146
	Punishment of the late invaders of Egypt	146
	Victory over the Sahir, the Seirites of SS.	147
	New war with the Libyan and Maxyan invaders . .	147
	Great fortress and well in the land of the Aperiu .	147, 148
	Fleet on the Red Sea—Voyages to the Indian Ocean . .	148
	Mines of 'Athaka and the peninsula of Sinai . .	148, 149
	Planting of trees : peace and security in Egypt . .	149
	Memorials in his Ramesseum at Medinet-Abou . . .	150
	Immense wealth in this ' treasury of Rhampsinitus ' . .	151
	Troubled state of Egypt at his accession	152
	Victory over the Libyans under kings Zamar and Zautmar	152, 153

[2] Dr. Brugsch identifies Ramses III. also with the king Proteus, named by several Greek authors, in whose reign Egypt was visited by Paris, Helen, and Menelaus (Herod. ii. 112, 118).—ED.

	PAGE
B.C.	
Great victory by sea and land at Migdol over the Carian-Colchian invaders from Cilicia and Armenia	153–155
Victory over the Maxyes under king Mashashal	155, 156
Detailed lists of slain, captives, and booty	156
Pictures and names of defeated kings, at Medinet-Abou	157, 158
Names of conquered cities and countries on the coasts and islands of Asia Minor	158, 159
Booty and captives devoted to the temples	160
List of the *Ramessea* of Ramses III. (Comp. *Additions*)	160, 161
Grand temple of Amon at Medinet-Abou, its reliefs	161, 162
The Egyptian calendar and holidays	162, 163
Other works at Thebes—*Ramessea* in foreign lands	163, 164
Remarkable account of a conspiracy at court	164–172
Foreign names of Ramses's chief wife and her father	172
His sons and the order of their succession	173
His rock-hewn tomb and its coloured pictures	174
1166. II. RAMESSU IV. MIAMUN III. (HAQ MAA or MAMA)	174
His expeditions to the rocky valleys of Arabian Egypt	174
Great memorial tablet at Hammamat	175–178
Insignificance of his architectural works	178
His rival and successor, III. RAMESSU V. AMUNHIKHOPESHEF, not of the family of Ramses III.	178
His inscribed rock-tablet at Silsilis	178–179
V. RAMESSU MIAMUN MERITUM (7th son of Ramses III.), probably viceroy of his brother, IV. RAMESSU VI.	180
Astronomical and chronological value of this king's tomb	186
Record respecting boundaries of lands in Nubia	181–182
The district of Wawa and its sun-city Pira (Dirr)	183
The Adon Penni, and Meri the viceroy of Kush	183
Historical importance of family records	184
Dominion S. of the tropic still maintained	185
VI., VII. RAMESSU VII. and RAMESSU VIII. insignificant	185
1133. VIII. RAMESSU IX.—Growing power of the priests of Amon	185
Inscription of the chief priest and architect, Amenhotep	186–189
Burglaries in the royal tombs at Biban-el-Molouk	189, 190
IX., X., XI. RAMESSU X., RAMESSU XI., and RAMESSU XII.	190
Their names in the oracle-temple of Khonsu	191
Curious inscription of Ramses XII.	191
His visit to Naharain, and marriage to the daughter of the tributary king of Bakhatana	191
The god Khonsu sent to cure the queen's demoniac sister	193
Agreement between the spirit and the god	193
Return of the ark of Khonsu to Thebes	194
Difficulty of identifying Bakhatana	194

B.C. PAGE
XII. RAMESSU XIII. apparently ends the Twentieth Dynasty:
but petty kings of the Ramessid family still under the
Twenty-first and Twenty-second Dynasties . . . 195
The temple of Khonsu the family chapel of the Ramessids . 195
Deposition of Ramessu XIII. by the priest Hirhor . . 196
Letter, (probable) *autograph* of Ramses XIII 196
Memorial of 27th year of Ramses XIII. at Abydus . 196, 197
List of Values and Prices about B.C. 1000 . . . 198–199

CHAPTER XVI.

THE TWENTY-FIRST DYNASTY.

THE PRIEST HIRHOR AND HIS SUCCESSORS.

1100–966. Usurpation of HIRHOR SI-AMON (son of Amon) . . 200
His previous high position at the court 200
The Ramessids banished to the Great Oasis 201
Rise of the Assyrian Empire in Mesopotamia 201
Alliance of its kings with the Ramessids 202
Marriage of Ramessu XVI. with an Assyrian princess . . 202
The Assyrians under King Nimrod invade Egypt . . 202
PINOTEM I. king, of the line of Hirhor 203
His son, Men-kheper-ra, recals the banished Ramessids . 203–6
Death of Nimrod (Naromath)—His burial at Abydus . 206
PISEBKHAN I., son of Hirhor, under-king at Tanis . . . 207
Shashanq, father of Nimrod, visits Thebes and Abydus . 207
Avenges the neglect of Nimrod's tomb 207
His inscription at Abydus: an historical revelation . 208, *f*
A real Assyrian conquest of Egypt, and a new foreign dynasty,
with Shashanq, son of Nimrod, as king . . 207 *and* 211
Statue of Nimrod in the Museum at Florence . . . 212
Karamat, wife of Shashanq I., an Egyptian princess . . 213
Inscription concerning her property in Egypt . . 213, 214

CHAPTER XVII.

THE TWENTY-SECOND DYNASTY.

Their names purely Assyrian 215
966. I. SHASHANQ I.—His royal residence at Bubastus . 207, 215
His good understanding with the Ramessids 215
Shashanq (Shishak) receives the fugitive Jeroboam . . 216

B.C.		PAGE
	His invasion of Judah recorded at Karnak	217
	Long list of conquered towns and districts	217
	Close relations of the Fenekh (Phœnicians) to the Hebrews	219
	Shashanq's 'Hall of the Bubastids' at Karnak . . .	219
	Record of its building preserved at Silsilis	219
	Its architect, Hor-em-saf, and his genealogy . . .	220
	Memorial tablet of Shashanq and his eldest son Auputh 221,	222
933.	II. USARKON I. (Sargon), son and successor of Shashanq I. .	223
	His second wife, daughter of the Tanite king, Pisebkhan II.	223
	Her son, Shashanq, high-priest of Amon	223
	Contest between Usarkon's two sons for the crown . . .	223
900.	III. Succession of the elder, THAKELOTH I. (Tiglath) . .	224
866.	IV. His son USARKON II., last king of the elder line . .	224
	His sons, Shashanq and Naromath, high-priests . . .	224
833.	V. SHASHANQ II., grandson of the high-priest Shashanq, the second son of Usarkon I.	225
800.	VI. THAKELOTH II. marries the priest Nimrod's daughter .	226
	Inscription of his son, the high-priest Usarkon . . .	226
	Record of an ominous eclipse of the moon	226
766.	Irruptions of the Ethiopians and Assyrians . . . 226–27
733.	VII., VIII., IX. SHASHANQ III., PIMAI, and SHASHANQ IV.	228
700.	Residence transferred from Bubastus to Memphis . .	228
	Four tombstones of an Apis bull under these kings . 229,	230
	Petty kings appearing as Assyrian satraps	231
	The supreme royal power confined to *Lower Egypt* . . .	231
	Upper Egypt under USARKON, king and high-priest of Amon	232
	Calculation of the life of the Apis	232
	The three kings of Dynasty XXIII., of Tanis . . .	233
	Note on BOCCHORIS, sole king of Dynasty XXIV. . . .	223

CHAPTER XVIII.

THE TWENTY-FIFTH DYNASTY.—THE ETHIOPIANS.

1000	The dethroned line of Hirhor retire to Ethiopia . . .	224
(*about*)	Loss of Egypt's dominion, but permanence of Egyptian civilization and religion, in Ethiopia	235
	Nap or Napata, at Mount Barkal, the new capital . .	235
	Piankhi, son of Hirhor: meaning of the name . . .	236
	Political and religious constitution on the Egyptian model .	236
	Distinguished position of the women of the royal house . .	236
	Extension of the kingdom to Upper Egypt, *Patoris* . .	237
	Petty kings in Lower Egypt, *Muzur*, under the Assyrians .	237
	Middle Egypt a 'march' between the two powers . .	237

B.C.		PAGE
	The Ethiopians the 'Princes of Noph' of Scripture . . .	237
766.	TAFNAKHTH (Tnephachthus), king of Saïs and Memphis, conquers the Ethiopian vassals in Middle Egypt . .	238
	List of petty kings and satraps in Lower Egypt . . .	239
	The great inscription of king PIANKHI at Mount Barkal, recording his conquest of Middle and Lower Egypt	240–257
	MIAMUN NUT, son (?) and successor of Piankhi . . .	257
	His dream, and campaign against Lower Egypt . . .	257
	His monument and inscription at Mount Barkal . .	258–263
	The success not lasting—Schism in Ethiopia . . .	264
	The three divisions of Patoris (Thebes), Takhont or Meluḫḫa (Nubia), and Kush (capital Napata)	264
700.	TAHARAQA, Tirhaka, Tearko, Tarkus, Etearchus . . .	265
	New light from the Assyrian cuneiform inscriptions . .	265
	Victory of Sennacherib at Altaku	265
	The ANNALS OF ASSURBANIPAL son of Sennacherib . .	266
	Conquest of Lower Egypt by Tirhaka, and its reconquest by Assurbanipal	267–270
	Assyrian list of the petty kings and satraps . . .	270
	M. Oppert's summary of the narrative	272
	Campaign against URDAMANEH or RUDAMON, the successor of Tirhaka, and twofold capture of Thebes by the Assyrians	272–275
	Review of events under Assarhaddon and Assurbanipal	275–277
	Important part played by Nikuu (Necho) grandson of Tafnakht, king of Memphis and Saïs, father of Psamethik I. .	277
	Obscurity of the succeeding period	277
	Taharaqa, Piankhi and his wife Ameniritis, Shabak (Sabaco), Shabatak (Sebichus), all contemporary . .	277
	Sitting statue of Shabatak, at Memphis	278
	Monuments at Thebes of Taharaqa and Monthemha . .	278
	Rudamon, stepson of Taharaqa, and an earlier Rudamon .	279
	Dynasty XXIV.: the BOCCHORIS of Manetho, discovered in Bek-en-ran-ef (in the Assyrian list, Bu-kur-ni-ni-ip) .	280
	Family relationships of Dynasties XXI.—XXVI. . . .	280
	Psamethik, of Saïs, unites the rival claims	281
	Statue and inscription of queen Ameniritis . . .	281–2
	Etymology of the Ethiopian proper names illustrated from the existing language of the Nubian Barabra . .	282–5

CHAPTER XIX.

DYNASTIES TWENTY-SIXTH TO THIRTY-FIRST.

B.C.   PAGE

666.   List of the Kings, with the Dates of their Accession   . 286, 287
Decline and fall of the Egyptian monarchy   . . . 287
Saïs succeeds to Thebes; Alexandria to Saïs . . . 288, 289
Causes of the fall of the Pharaohs 289, 290

§ I. THE TWENTY-SIXTH DYNASTY, OF SAÏS.

Character of its monuments : return to ancient models   . 291
Innovations in religion—Demons and magic 293
New historical light from the Apis Tablets   . . . 290
— of Psamethik I. : his additions to the Serapeum.   . 295, 296
— of Neku II. Uah-ab-ra (Apries), and Amasis .   . 296, 297
Care bestowed on the burial of the bulls   298
The Greek story of Cambyses and the Apis refuted   . 299, 300
Honour paid by Darius to the Apis   301
Khabbash, the Egyptian king, rival to Xerxes . . . 302
His sarcophagus intended for an Apis 302
356.   Latest Apis tablet of king Nakht-neb-ef 302

§ II. THE PERSIANS IN EGYPT. DYNASTY XXVII.

Readiness of Egyptian nobles to serve the Great King   . 303
Inscription of Uzahorenpiris, under Cambyses and Darius, on
    the statue called the Pastophorus of the Vatican   . 303–306
CAMBYSES placed in a new light   307
Egyptian learning fostered by DARIUS I.   307
His temple at Hibis (El-Khargeh) in the Great Oasis   . 307
Works and inscriptions of DARIUS II. at the temple   . 307, 308
Pedigree of the architect Khnum-ab-ra   . . . 308–310
Other inscriptions of the same architect 310
Inscriptions relating to the attempted Canal of Darius I.
    through the Isthmus of Suez 310, 311
Inscriptions of the Persian officers Ataiuhi and Aliurta   312–14
527.   The true date of the conquest by Cambyses . . . 315
XERXES I. and the anti-king Khabbash   315
311.   Inscription of the satrap Ptolemy, son of Lagus   . 315, 316

§ III. THE LAST PHARAOHS.

Dynasties XXIX. and XXX. at Mendes and Sebennytus. 316
358–340. The last Pharaoh, NAKHT-NEB-EF 317
280 (cir.) The sarcophagus of his grandson, Nahkt-neb-ef.   . 317

CHAPTER XX.

FALL OF THE KINGDOM OF THE PHARAOHS.

B.C. PAGE
332 Inscription of the priest Sam-taui Taf-nakht, under Darius
(cir.) III. and Alexander the Great 319
Its allusion to the victory of Alexander over Darius . . 320

SUPPLEMENTARY NOTE BY THE EDITOR.

HISTORY OF EGYPT FROM PSAMMETICHUS I. TO PTOLEMY I.

§ I. EGYPT'S RECOVERED INDEPENDENCE UNDER THE TWENTY-SIXTH
DYNASTY OF SAÏS: B.C. 666-527.
Trustworthiness of the history and chronology 321
666. 1. Reign of PSAMETHIK I., son of Neku, B.C. 666-612 . . 322
First commercial intercourse with the Greeks 322
His force of Greek mercenaries 322
Desertion of the Egyptian military caste 322
His fleet manned by Phœnician sailors 322
Long siege and capture of Azotus (Ashdod) . . . 322
612. 2. NEKU or NECHAO II.: PHARAOH-NECHO (SS.) B.C. 612-596. 322
Defeats and slays King Josiah at Megiddo 322
610. Conquers Western Asia as far as the Euphrates . . 322
605 Its reconquest by Nebuchadnezzar 323
604. His recal to Babylon and peace with Necho . . . 323
Necho's fleets: circumnavigation of Africa (?) . . 323
Attempt to reconstruct the canal of Sesostris . . . 323
596-1. 3. PSAMETHIK II., Psammis (Herod.), Psammuthis (Man.) . 323
War with the Ethiopians òf Napata 323
591. 4. UAHABRA, PHARAOH-HOPHRA (SS.), VAPHRES (Man.),
APRIES (Herod.) B.C. 591-572 324
His great prosperity and arrogance 324
Successful war with Sidon and Tyre 324
League with Zedekiah against Nebuchadnezzar . . . 324
586. Receives the Jewish remnant in Egypt 324
Prophecies of Jeremiah and Ezekiel fulfilled by Nebuchad-
nezzar's conquest of Egypt and the death of Apries . . 325
The Egyptian story of his fall 325
Invasion of Cyrene: revolt of Egyptian army . . 325
Amasis chosen king by acclamation 326
Defeat and death of Apries 326
Probable intervention of Nebuchadnezzar 326
572. 5. AMASIS: KHNUM-AB-R'A AAHMES SI-NEIT: B.C. 572-528 . 326
At first a vassal of Nebuchadnezzar 326
Babylonian marriage of the Princess Nitocris . . . 326
Amasis marries the daughter of Psamethik II. . . . 326

B.C.   PAGE

His personal habits and government 327
Encourages Greek commerce, settlers, and art . . . 327
Unexampled prosperity of his reign 327
His probable revolt against Nebuchadnezzar learnt from a
    Babylonian record 328
Navy of Amasis—Conquest of Cyprus 328
Relations with Greeks—The 'Ring of Polycrates' . . 328
Alliance with Lydia and Babylon against Cyrus . . . 328
Preparations of Cambyses against Egypt 329
527. 6. PSAMETHIK III.: the PSAMMENITUS of Herodotus . . . 329
     Defeated and put to death by Cambyses 329

§ II. EGYPT UNDER THE PERSIAN KINGS. DYN. XXVII. B.C. 527–414?

527. 1. CAMBYSES: KAMBATHET or KANBUZA: B.C. 529–522 . 329
     His respect for Egyptian institutions 329
522.   Aryandes, viceroy of Egypt 329
     Death of Cambyses in Syria 329
     (The Magian pseudo-Smerdis not in the list) . . . 329n.
521. 2. DARIUS I.: NTHARIUSH: B.C. 521–486 329
     His surname of SETTURA, Sesostris 329, 330
     Conciliates the Egyptians: promotes education . . . 330
     His temple of Amon in the Great Oasis 330
     Attempt to reopen the Red Sea Canal 330
     Story of his visit to Egypt, and piety towards an Apis,
        tested by the Apis-tablets 330, 331
     His claim to a statue at Memphis beside Sesostris . . . 331
487.   Revolt of Egypt under king KHABBASH 331
427. 3. XERXES I.: KSHIARSH or KHSHERISH: B.C. 486–465 . . 332
     Subdues the revolt: Achæmenes satrap 332
     Evidence of continued resistance 332
465. 4. ARTAXERXES I. ARTA-KHSHESESH: B.C. 465–425 . . 332
461.   Revolt under the Libyan Inaros 332
     He defeats and kills Achœmenes at Papremis . . . 332
     Aid from the Athenians—Siege of Memphis . . . 332
     Defeat of the allies by Megabyzus 332
455.   Amyrtæus, of Saïs, holds out in the marshes . . . 333
425. 5. XERXES II.: B.C. 425–4 333
424. 6. SOGDIANUS, usurper in Persia 333
424. 7. DARIUS II. NOTHUS: NTHARIUSH, B.C. 424–405 . . . 333
     His works at the temple in the Great Oasis . . . 333
     Successful revolt of Egypt 333

§ III. DYNASTY XXVIII., OF SAÏS.

505? AMYRTES or AMYRTÆUS: 6 years 333
     Questions relating to him 333, 334

§ IV. THE LAST NATIVE PHARAOHS: B.C. 399-340.

A. DYNASTY XXIX., OF MENDES: B.C. 399-378.

B.C.   PAGE
399. 1. NAIFAUROT I.: NEPHERITES I.: B.C. 399-393 . . . 335
       Alliance with the Lacedæmonians against Persia . . 335
       Naval defeat by the Athenians 335
393. 2. HAGAR or HAKORI: ACHORIS: B.C. 393-380 . . . 335
391. Alliance with Evagoras, tyrant of Cyprus 335
387. Peace of Antalcidas between the Greeks and Persia . . 335
       Egyptian preparations for defence 335
380. 3. PSAMUT: PSAMMUTHIS: B.C. 380-379 335
378. 4. NAIFAUROT II.: NEPHERITES II.: B.C. 379-8 . . . 335

B. DYNASTY XXX., OF SEBENNYTUS: B.C. 378-340.

378. 1. NAKHT-HOR-HIB: NECTANEBO I.: B.C. 378-360 . . . 336
376. Egypt invaded by Pharnabazus and Chabrias . . . 336
375. Complete failure of the attack 336
       Twenty-five years' peace—Last revival of Egyptian art . . 336
       Works of Nectanebo throughout all Egypt . . . 336
       Restoration of the temple of Anhur at Sebennytus . . . 337
364. 2. ZIHO: TEOS: TACHOS: B.C. 364-361 337
       Preparations against Artaxerxes II. 337
       Aid from Greeks under Agesilaus and Chabrias . . . 337
       Teos insults Agesilaus 337
       Leads his fleet and army against Phœnicia 337
       Revolt of Egypt and mutiny of the army 337
       Desertion of Agesilaus and the Greeks 337
       Teos flies to Artaxerxes 338
361. 3. NAKHT-NEB-EF: NECTANEBO II.: B.C. 361-340 . . . 338
       Victory over a rival prince of Mendes 338
360. Departure of Agesilaus and Chabrias 338
       Nectanebo's unwarlike tastes 338
       His fine monuments throughout Egypt 338
       Famed as a builder and magician 338
       First unsuccessful attack of Ochus (Artaxerxes III.) . . 338
       Desertion of Mentor and his mercenaries 339
       Invasion of Egypt by Ochus 339
340. Nectanebo, *the last of the Pharaohs*, flies to Ethiopia . . 339

§ V. DYNASTY XXXI., OF PERSIANS: B.C. 340-332.

340. 1. OCHUS (*reign in Egypt*), B.C. 340-338 339
338. 2. ARSES: B.C. 338-336 339
336. 3. DARIUS III. CODOMANNUS: B.C. 336-332 339
332. Egypt submits to Alexander the Great . . . 339

VOL. II.   a

§ VI. DYNASTY XXXII., OF MACEDONIANS: B.C. 332-311.

B.C.		PAGE
332.	1. ALEXANDER THE GREAT: B.C. 332-323	339
323.	2. PHILIP ARRHIDÆUS: B.C. 323-317	339
323.	3. ALEXANDER ÆGUS: B.C. 323-311	339
323.	Ptolemy son of Lagus, 'Satrap,' but in fact sovereign	340
306.	Assumes the crown as PTOLEMÆUS I. SOTER	340

§ VII. DYNASTY XXXIII., OF THE GREEK PTOLEMIES: B.C. 323-330.

323.	The years of PTOLEMY I. date from the beginning of his actual rule over Egypt	340
30.	Victory of Octavian and death of CLEOPATRA, the last of the line of the Ptolemies	340
,,	Egypt made a Roman Province	340

APPENDIX.

A.	LIST OF THE KINGS, WITH THEIR EPOCHS	341
B.	THE NOMES OF EGYPT, ACCORDING TO THE MONUMENTS	347
C.	TRANSCRIPTION OF THE ANCIENT EGYPTIAN NAMES	350
	SPECIMEN TEXT, WITH LITERAL AND FREE TRANSLATIONS	352

DISCOURSE ON THE EXODUS AND EGYPTIAN MONUMENTS . . 357

ADDITIONS AND NOTES CONTRIBUTED BY THE AUTHOR. . . 401

INDEX 433

LIST OF ILLUSTRATIONS.

Plan of the Great Temple of Amon at Thebes (Karnak)	11
Plan of the Temple of Seti I. and Ramses II. at Abydus	30
Plan of the Ramesseum, or Memnonium, at Thebes	93
Plan and Section of the Temple of Abou Simbel, or Ibsamboul	96
Tomb at Saqqarah, inscribed with the name of Psammetichus	318

GENEALOGICAL TABLES AND MAPS.
AT END OF THE VOLUME.

TABLE I.—Genealogy of a Distinguished Family, related to some Members of the Thirteenth Dynasty.

,, II.—Genealogy of the Ramessids.

,, III.—Genealogy of Amen-em-an, the architect of the city of Ramses.

,, IV.—Genealogy of Royal Families of Dynasties XX. to XXVI.

MAP OF LOWER EGYPT . . . . . . *At the end in Pocket*

Errata.

Page 20, line 25. *For* 'Ashur' *read* 'Asher.'
Pages 91-2. *For* 'a pictured family group' *read* 'a family group of many figures.'
Page 99, line 1. *For* 'united, &c.' *read* 'taken as a model, both in his likeness and his names.'
Page 100, note. It should have been stated that the letter of Panbesa is in the Papyrus Anastasi III.
Page 145, title. *Insert* 'I.' *before* 'RAMSES III.'
Page 153, note. The real meaning is that 'the peoples' touched by the invaders in their progress trembled with fear; 'and they (the invaders) came up,' &c.
Page 190, end. Before the names of the kings;
for VIII., IX., X., *read* IX., X., XI.
Page 192, foll. *For* 'Khonsu the oracular,' *read* 'Khonsu the administrator.'
Page 195, mid. *For* XI., *read* XII.
Page 225. Before names of kings; *for* IV. and V., *read* V. and VI.
Page 228. *For* VI., VII., VIII., *read* VII., VIII., IX.
Page 246, end. *For* 'Achnum' *read* 'Akhmun.'
Page 277, line 5. *For* 'son' *read* 'grandson.'
Page 287, lines 4 and 7. *For* 'Naif-an-rot' *read* 'Naif-au-rot.'
Page 327, note 9. *For* 298, *read* 297.
Page 336, line 2 and note 7. *For* 'Nakht-hor-ib' *read* 'Nakht-hor-hib.'
Page 365. To the references to *Exodus* for the stages, add Numbers xxxiii. 3-9.
Page 365, line 7; and 376, line 6. *For* 'Sea of Sea-weed,' *read* 'Sea of Weeds.'

Men-pehuti-ra.	Ma-men-ra.	Rauserma-sotepenra.	Hotep-hi-ma.

Ramses I.	Mineptah I., Seti I.	Ramses II., Miamun.	Mineptah II.

THE
HISTORY OF EGYPT.

CHAPTER XIV.

THE NINETEENTH DYNASTY.

THE PEOPLE OF THE KHITA.

AFTER the death of King Horemhib, the Eighteenth Dynasty ended its eventful history. The heretic king Khunaten had, by his novelties in the teaching about the being of the gods, somewhat diminished its splendour in the eyes of the orthodox priests and people, and had created a schism in the internal life of the nation, which the immediate successors of Khunaten found it difficult to heal. The new teaching, with its Semitic foundation, had at once gained many adherents among the susceptible Egyptians. Its banishment and extirpation, under the guidance of the Theban priests of Amon, whose power and influence were now for the first time used against the kings, formed the sad tenor of the internal events in the next portion of

VOL. II.   B

Egyptian history. How peace and reconciliation were brought about, it is now difficult to say; but Horemhib certainly appeared in the light of a happy mediator between the ruling adherents of the doctrine of Amon and the severely persecuted servants of the living god of the sun's disk.

While the kingdom was disturbed by such a schism, and the excitable spirits of the Egyptians were highly roused on each side of the question, a great nation had in the meantime been growing up, beyond the frontier on the north-east, to an importance and power which began to endanger the Egyptian supremacy in Western Asia.

Already, during the wars undertaken by Thutmes III. against the Syrian peoples and towns of that region, the Kheta or Khita had shown themselves on the scene of those yearly repeated and long-enduring struggles, under the leadership of their own kings, as a dominant race. The contemporary Egyptian inscriptions designate them as 'the great people,' or 'the great country,' less with respect to the space they occupied, than from their just reputation for those brave and chivalrous qualities, which the inhabitants of Khita, a race as noble as the Egyptians, were acknowledged even by their enemies to possess. We believe we are falling into no error if we persevere in our opinion, which recognises in these people the same Khethites (Hittites) about whom Holy Scripture has so much to tell us, from the days of the patriarch Abraham till the time of the Captivity. When Thutmes III. fought with them and conquered their towns, they were seated as an important people in the most northern parts of the land of Syria. At the commencement of the Nineteenth Dynasty, the power of the Khita had been extended over the whole of the surrounding nations. These predecessors of the Assyrian Empire held the first place in the league of the cities and kings of Western Asia. Their importance grew from year to year in such a way, that even the Egyptian inscriptions do not hesitate to mention the names of the kings of the Khita in a conspicuous manner, and to speak of their gods with reverence. When Ramses I. ascended the throne of Egypt, Sa-pa-li-li, Saplel, or Saprer, ruled as king of the Khita. He was followed by his son and heir in the empire, Maurosar, who after his death left two sons behind him, of whom the elder was that Mauthanar, who appears as a contemporary of Seti I. and an enemy of Egypt, while the younger, Khitasar or Khitasir, appears as the friend, ally, and father-in-law of the Pharaoh Ramses II. At the head of their divinities stood the glorious god of war, Sutekh (the Khethite counterpart of Amon), and his wife, the steed-driving queen of heaven, Astartha-Anatha.

Among the towns of the Khita, Tunep (Daphne) and Khilibu (Haleb) are two points certainly fixed by their definite position, and both with temples of the great Baal-Sutekh. On the other hand, the name of the country of Qazauatana points with infallible certainty to the region of Gozan (Gauzanitis) to the east of the Euphrates, between the towns of Circesium in the south and Thapsacus in the north. The situation of the places or countries of the Khita—Zaranda, Pirqa or Pilqa (Peleg, Paliga?), Khissap, Sarsu, Sarpina, Zaiath-khirra (hinder Zaiath)—and others named at the same time as those just mentioned, must be determined by future enquiries. Perhaps we may find an answer to these questions in the Assyrian inscriptions.

If it is allowable to form a judgment on the origin of this cultivated and powerful people from its outward bearing and appearance, it seems to us, under the guidance of the monuments, to be at least very doubtful whether we should reckon this chivalrous race among the Canaanites. Beardless, armed in a different manner, fighting three men on each chariot of war, arranged in their order of battle according to a well-considered plan previously laid down, the Khita present a striking contrast to their Canaanite allies. In the representations of the wars of Ramses II. against Khitasar, the prince of the Khita, the great foreign king appears surrounded by his generals and servants, who are mentioned by name, down to the 'letter-writer Khirpasar.' His warriors were divided into foot-soldiers and fighters on chariots, and consisted partly of native Khethites, partly of foreign mercenaries. Their hosts were led to battle by Kasans, or 'commanders of the fighters on the chariots,' by 'generals,' and Hirpits, or 'captains of the foreigners.' The nucleus of the army was formed of the native-born Khita, under the designation of Tuhir, or 'the chosen ones.' In the battle at Kadesh, 8,000 of these stood in the foremost rank, under the command of Kamaiz; while 9,000 others followed their king. In the same battle, the noblemen Thargannas and Pais led the chariots in the fight; Thaadar commanded the mercenaries of the Khita; Nebisuanna was at the head of the foreign warriors from Annas; another chief appears as the general of the mercenaries from Nagebus. Sapzar and Mazarima appear as brothers of the king of Khita; whether real brothers, or perhaps only allies. Among other names of Khethite origin, the following are mentioned: Garbitus, Thargathazas, Tadar or Tadal, Zauazas, Samarius, and that of the 'ambassador' Tarthisebu. It is evident at once that these names do not bear a Semitic, or at any rate not a pure Semitic stamp. The endings in s, r, and u, prevail. In the proper name Thargatha-zas, in which the ending *zas* plays the same part as in the proper name Zaua-zas, Thargatha seems to answer to the goddess called by the Greeks and Romans Atargates or Atargatis, Derketo and Dercetis, who possessed very celebrated temples in Askalon and Astaroth-Karnaim, as well as in the Syrian town of Hierapolis (Mabog).

The unmistakable peculiarities of the language, to which I have now called the attention of the reader, are for the most part found in that unexplained series of names of towns, which form the second division of the northern peoples, or northern cities, in the lists of the victories of Thutmes III. at Karnak. As examples, to show their foreign formation, let us cite the following names, which can be read with certainty, on the basis of M. Mariette's deciphering of the series:—

120. Pirkheta	185. Khatuma
121. Ai	186. Magnas
122. Amau	187. Thepkanna
124. Thuka	188. Thuthana (Susan ?)
125. Thel-manna	189. Nireb
126. Legaba	190. Theleb (Thalaba)
127. Tunipa (Daphne)	191. Atugaren
132. Ni	196. Nishapa (Nisibis)
134. Ar	197. Ta-zeker
135. Zizal	198. Abatha
136. Zakal	199. Ziras
139. Arzakana	200. 'Authir
140. Kharkakhi (or Kharkaka)	201. Natub
141. Bursu	202. Zetharseth
142. Lerti	203. Aithua
145. Unai	204. Sukaua
146. 'Aunfer	205. Tuaub
147. Ithakhab	206. Abir[na]th
148. Uniuqa	207. Shainarkai
150. Sakti	208. 'Aurma
151. Aubillina	212. Kainab
152. Zanruisu (Zarruisu)	213. Ares
153. Suka	214. Anautasenu
154. Pazalu	215. Azana
155. Sathekhbeg	216. Zetharsetha
156. Amarseki	217. Tulbentha
157. Khalros	218. Manthi
158. Nenuran'aantha	221. Atur
159. Shauirantha	222. Kartha-meruth
160. Mairrekhnas	223. A-sitha
161. Zagerel	224. Taniros
163. Kanretu	226. Athebena
164. Tauriza	227. Ashameth
166. Anriz	228. Athakar
167. A'ares	229. Tazet
168. Khazrezaa	230. Athrun
169. Arnir	231. Thukamros
170. Khatha'ai	232. 'Abetha
173. Thenuzuru	235. Anankeb
184. Anauban	236. Ares

THE PEOPLE OF THE KHITA.

237. Artha	290. Ann'aui
247. Farua	292. Thalekh
252. Sur	293. 'Aurna
253. Papaa	296. Papabi
254. Nuzana	306. Aiber
255. Zamauka	307. Kel-maitha (Khilmod)
259. Suki-beki	308. Amak
263. A-thini	309. Kazel
264. Karshaua	310. 'Aumai
265. Retama	311. Khalbu (Haleb)
271. Zazker	312. Piauanel (Pnuel)
272. Maurmar	315. 'Aukam
279. Khaitu	316. Puroth
280. Pederi (Pethor ?)	318. Aripenekha
281. Athrithan	320. Puqiu
282. Mashaua	322. Thinnur
283. A-anreka	323. Zarnas
284. Nepiriuriu (Nipur)	333. Iurima
285. Nathkina	338. Thethup.
286. Athetama	343. Shusaron
287. Abellenu	347. Thamaqur
288. Airanel	348. Retep (?) (Re-ap ?)
289. Airanel (sic)	349. Maurika

It is clear that this list exhibits in their oldest orthography the greater number of these towns, which are afterwards mentioned so frequently in the records of wars in Assyrian history, in the cuneiform inscriptions which have been deciphered. They are the old allied cities of those Khita, of unknown origin, who, long before the rise of Nineveh and Babylon, played the same part which at a later period the Assyrians undertook with success. Though we are not yet in a position to solve the obscure problem here suggested, yet future discoveries will doubtless afford convincing proofs, that the rule of the Khita in the highest antiquity was of an importance which we can now only guess at. This list of towns will therefore remain a monument of the greatest value, as a memorial of times and peoples long since vanished, whose lost remembrance is awakened to new life by the dead letters of these numerous names. With such a perception of their value, the reader may cast his eye over the long catalogue of those very ancient names which we have transcribed, even if his own science should not avail him better than ours for subjecting them to a comparative investigation. For in these names, so far as they are not demonstrably of Semitic origin, lies the key to their language. The right understanding of them offers, therefore, the surest means of fixing the place of the Khita in the life of the ancient nations.

I. MEN-PEHUTI-RA RAMESSU I. (RAMSES I.) 1400 B.C.

Although we possess no information from the monuments about the family ties which united the king, who was the head and founder of the Nineteenth Dynasty, with his predecessor Horemhib, there must have been nevertheless a close connection between them. Whether Ramses was the son, son-in-law, or brother of Horemhib, is as yet undecided. If I say the brother, I am led to this as a possible supposition by the testimony of the memorial stone of a contemporary family, which mentions the brothers Horemhib and Ramses among the sons of a certain Ha-Aai, an ' overseer of the cutters of hieroglyphs ' of his unnamed ' lord of the land ' (Ai? see Vol. I. c. xiii. near end).

The reign of Ramses I. seems to have been neither of long duration, nor to have been filled with remarkable deeds. His fame consists chiefly in the place he occupies in the historical series, as the father of a very celebrated son, and the grandfather of one who was covered with glory and sung of as a hero to the latest ages. His recognition as the legitimate king by the priests of Amon is authenticated by the representation of his solemn coronation on the entrance gate of the temple of Karnak.[1]

He had a war with the Khita, although we only learn this fact incidentally from the contents of the treaty of peace concluded by Ramses II. with the Khita.[2] His royal opponent Saplel had, after the end of the war, made an offensive and defensive alliance with Ramses I., and so the Khita and the Egyptians continued to exercise their sovereignty within their own boundaries, without molesting one another any further.

A memorial stone of the second year of his reign, found at the second cataract at Wady-Halfa (the place was then called Behani, and is the Boôn of Ptolemy), informs us, that king Ramses I. founded there a storehouse for the temple of his divine father Hor-khem, and filled it with captive men-servants and maid-servants from the conquered countries. Of

[1] For the better understanding of the frequent allusions in the following pages to the parts of the temple of Karnak, the reader may consult the description in Murray's *Handbook for Egypt*, p. 496. The plan of the temple is given on page 11.—ED.

[2] This treaty is translated in full under the reign of Ramses II. (See pp. 71, f.)—ED.

whatever consequence the fact thus recorded may have been to the ancient inhabitants of the temple at Behani, the history of his times gains little by it.

After his death, Ramses I. was laid in his own tomb-chamber in the valley of the kings' sepulchres, and he was succeeded in the kingdom by his son, to whom the monuments give the name of

II. MA-MEN-RA MINEPTAH I. SETI I. (SETHOS). 1366 B.C.

After a long interval, there rises again a brilliant star on the horizon of Egyptian history. The voice of the monuments begins anew to speak of the victories of Pharaoh, and to sing the glory of the empire. It is chiefly the great national temple at Thebes which records the honours of Seti by inscriptions and by pictures; for the king executed works to the glorious god Amon, the finished splendour of which is only surpassed by their extraordinary size. We refer to the building of that wonderful 'Great Hall' in the temple at Karnak, where 134 columns of astonishing height and circumference still attract the admiration of our fastidious age. As the description of this building does not come within the limits of our historical work, we are obliged to refer our readers to the excellent accounts of Egyptian travellers. The outer wall, however, on the north side of this hall, must have our full attention, since its representations stand in the closest connection with the wars of Seti, beginning with the first year of his reign.

These wars arose from the constant advances of the neighbouring peoples, to the east of Egypt, upon the Delta. The long duration of peace, as well perhaps as the weak reign of Ramses I., had induced these neighbours, and especially the Arabian Shasu, to take the bold resolve of pressing forward over the eastern frontier of Egypt, 'to find sustenance for themselves and their cattle on the possessions of Pharaoh.' Six battle paintings, ranged in a series, give us a view of the principal events of this campaign. We will endeavour, under the guidance of the inscriptions annexed to them, to put their contents faithfully before our readers.

The wars of Seti in the East began,

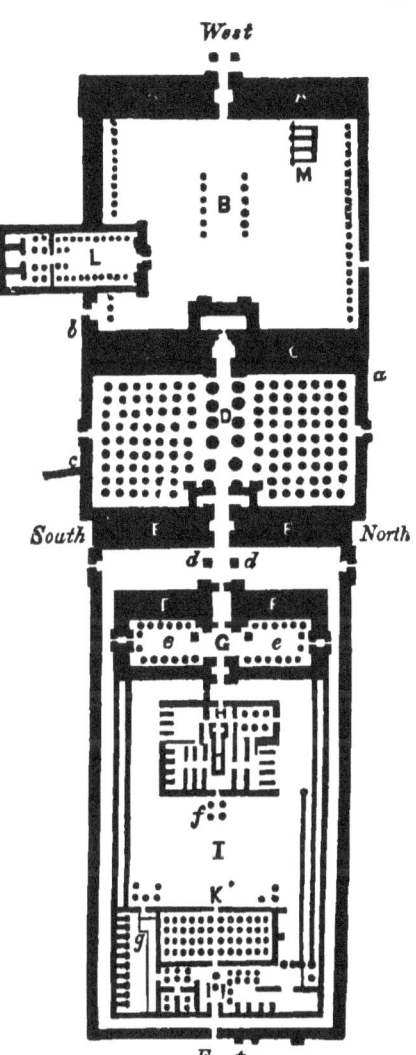

PLAN OF GREAT TEMPLE OF KARNAK.

A. First Propylon. B. Open Area, with corridors, and a single column erect. C. Second Propylon. D. Great Hall. E. Third Propylon. F. Fourth Propylon. G. Hall with Osirid figures. H. Granite Sanctuary and adjoining chambers. I. Open Court. K. Columnar Edifice of Thutmes III. L. Temple of Ramses III.

a. Sculptures of Seti I. *b*. Sculptures of Shishak. *c*. Sculptures of Ramses II. *d*. Small Obelisks. *e*. Large Obelisks. *f*. Pillars of Usurtasen I. *g*. Hall of Ancestors.

as we have already remarked, in the very first year of his reign. Their theatre was formed by the countries and fortresses in the region of the Shasu Bedouins, 'from the fortress of Khetam (the Etham of the Bible), in the land of Zalu (that is, the Tanitic nome), as far as the place Kan'ana or Kan'aan.' By these data the scene of the struggle is very closely fixed, and at the same time proof is afforded that the Shasu had pressed forward westward quite into the proper Egyptian territory, to make good their claims derived from the times of the Hyksos. The king assembled his army, put his chariots of war in array, and himself rode in his two-horse chariot against the invading Bedouins. The road which the Egyptian army took is clearly indicated by the pictures and the inscriptions.

The campaign was begun from the fortress of Khetam, which we have just mentioned, and which was situated on both sides of an arm of the Nile, swarming with crocodiles, and with banks covered with reeds. The king took thence the direction of the biblical 'road of the Philistines,'[3] and first reached the fortified but otherwise unknown place, Ta'a-pa-mau, 'the house of lions,' Leontopolis, near a small fountain of sweet water enclosed by a wall. His march was next directed to the Egyptian fortress of Migdol, mentioned in Holy Scripture, close to the

---

[3] Respecting this important road, and the localities by which its course is determined, see further in the author's *Discourse on the Exodus and the Egyptian Monuments* at the end of this volume.—ED.

springs in the country of Hazina or Hazian (the Kasion or Mount Casius of the ancients), and along the road to the 'north' fortress Uti (Buto, as the Greeks would write it), also near a spring. Uti denotes the fortified place where stood the often-mentioned temple on Mount Casius, in which a Jupiter (Amon) was worshipped, who was the Baal Zapuna of the Egyptian inscriptions, that is, the Baal Zephon of Holy Scripture. The army passed along the seashore to Ostracine, where there was a Bekhen, or tower, which the inscriptions designate as Pa-nakhtu, or 'the conqueror's tower' of King Seti. At this point the proper Egyptian boundary ended, and the territory of the land of Zahi, which was afterwards the land of the Philistines, began. The next halting-place on their territory was a fortified spot, newly built by King Seti, situated at the water of Absaqab. Two other fortresses lay on either side of the road. The one, which was also the larger, is called 'the town, which the king had built at the spring of . . . . tha.' It is called 'a strong place' in a second passage, and its water is designated as that of Ribatha, without doubt the Rohoboth of the Bible, to the south-west of Beersheba, in Negeb or the south country of Palestine. The smaller fortress stood near Takhnum-notem, that is 'the pleasant (or sweet) spring.' It is called 'A-nakhtu, that is, 'the fortress of victory.' Passing by a new fortress (the name is unfortunately destroyed), the end of the road was reached, and at the same time the eastern boundary of the land of the Shasu, marked by the hill-fortress of

Kan'aan,[4] near which a stream seems to have fallen into a lake.

We find ourselves here, as it appears, in the Arabah, and we have the choice between one or other of the fortresses situated there. In spite of many obscurities, the direction of the road is precisely determined. The king had taken possession of the land of the Shasu to its extremest boundary. The fortress of Kan'aan was stormed by Seti and his army, and thus Pharaoh became the lord of the whole of the Edomitish Negeb.

This first victory is celebrated by the following inscription :—

'In the first year of King Seti, there took place by the strong arm of Pharaoh the annihilation of the hostile Shasu, from the fortress of Khetam, of the land of Zalu, as far as Kan'aan. The king was against them like a fierce lion. They were turned into a heap of corpses in their hill country. They lay there in their blood. Not one escaped to tell of his strength to the distant nations.'

The warriors of the Shasu, driven out of their own land, attempted to make head against king Seti and his army, after they had marched on northwards, and had made a stand in the territory of the Phœnicians or Kharu. The king mounted his chariot of war, whose pair of horses bore the name, 'Amon gives him strength,' and dashed into the crowds of the scattered enemies, who were this time completely beaten and overcome. The inscription goes on as follows :—

[4] In the great Harris papyrus of the time of Ramessu III. Kan'aan is called a fortress 'of the land of Zahi.' Did this land then extend as far as the shores of the Dead Sea?

'In the first year of King Seti, they came to report to his Holiness that the hostile Shasu intended mischief, that the elders of their tribes had assembled together, and had made a stand in the territory of the Phœnicians (Khal). They were seized with the curse of discord, and slew one another. To those only who had not forgotten the orders of the royal court was the king gracious on that account.'

The prisoners were carried to Egypt by the king, as will be related more at length presently.

It seems to be indubitable that the population also of (southern?) Phœnicia did really assist the Shasu in their wars against this Pharaoh. But vengeance quickly overtook them also. In the furious encounter of the chariots of war, which were launched against one another on both sides, the Phœnicians succumbed in the battle at Inu'amu (Jamnia), and 'Pharaoh annihilated the kings of the land of the Phœnicians.'

From hence the Egyptian army turned against the inhabitants of the interior country, the Ruthen of Canaan. The kings of the several cities were successively overcome in many battles, in which a son of Seti fought by the side of his father, and the inhabitants were reduced under the Egyptian sceptre. Pharaoh himself took especial delight in the combat, for the inscription says that

'His joy is to undertake the battle, and his delight is to dash into it. His heart is only satisfied at the sight of the stream of blood when he strikes off the heads of his enemies. A moment of the struggle of men is dearer to him than a day of pleasure. He slays them with one stroke, and spares none among them. And whoever of them is left remaining finds himself in his grasp, and is carried off to Egypt alive as a prisoner.'

In his victorious campaign throughout the whole

land of Canaan, through which he was borne by his pair of horses named 'big with victory,' the great fortress of Kadesh, which had already played such an important part under Thutmes III., was reached by the Egyptian army. The inscription thus designates the campaign :—

'This is the going up of Pharaoh, to conquer the land of Kadesh in the territory of the Amorites.'

The arrival of the army was unexpected. The herdsmen were even pasturing their cattle under the trees which surrounded the city, when Pharaoh appeared on his war-chariot. Each seeks to save himself; the herds flee with their keepers; the warriors of Kadesh, as they sally out, are pierced by the arrows of Seti, and fall from their war-chariots. The defenders in the interior of the fortress fare no better. They also give way before the violent assault of the Egyptian army, and fortress and people fall into the hands of Pharaoh's warriors.

From Kadesh onwards, the land of the Khita lay open before the hosts of Pharaoh. The then king of the country, Mauthanar, had broken the existing treaties, which had been made between his predecessor and the Egyptians, and had given notice to Pharaoh of the termination of their alliance. Seti made no delay in falling upon the territory of the Khita, as the avenger of the broken treaties. Success crowned his enterprise. Although the well-ordered hosts of the beardless light-red Khita, on foot, on horseback, and on chariots, offered a determined resistance to the

Egyptians, yet for all this the Pharaoh triumphed. The inscription describes this victory in the brief words :—

'These are the miserable inhabitants of the land of the Khita; the king has prepared for them a great overthrow.'

And then the song of praise to Seti sounds forth with the most vigorous choice of phrases. Thus it is said of Pharaoh :—

'He is a jackal which rushes prowling through this land, a grim lion that frequents the most hidden paths of all regions, a powerful bull with a pair of sharpened horns.' 'He has struck down the Asiatics, he has thrown to the ground the Khita; he has slain their princes.' [5]

After the main battle had been fought, the king (whose pair of horses this time bore the name 'Amon gives him strength') had taken an immense number of prisoners, and prepared deliberately for his return home. Peace was concluded with the powerful Khita, and so the inscriptions could sing of him :—

'The king was victorious, great was his strength. His war-cry was like that of the son of Nut (that is, Baal-Sutekh). He returns home in triumph; he has annihilated the peoples, he has struck to the ground the land of Khita, he has made an end of his adversaries. The enmity of all peoples is turned into friendship. The terror of the king has penetrated them, his boldness has opened their hearts. The kings of the countries find themselves bound before him.'

On his return, which took place by the great royal highway through Kadesh, Seti made a diversion to

---

[5] An engraving of the picture at Karnak of Seti I. destroying the Khita in battle, is given in Wilkinson's *Ancient Egyptians*, 2nd ed. vol. i. p. 43, Plate IV.—ED.

the land of Limanon, the position of which answers exactly to the better known name of Mount Lebanon. The inhabitants of the country, Canaanites of the purest race, received the king in the most reverential manner, lifting up their hands to hail the conqueror. A short annexed inscription says :—

> 'The priests and elders of the land of Limanon, they speak thus, while they pray before the lord of the land to exalt his renown : "Thou appearest like thy father, the Sun-god, men live in thy glance."'

The king himself, as it appears, had made known certain intentions, for an Egyptian scribe assures him, 'All shall be accomplished as thou hast said.' The question related to the felling of cedars in the wooded mountain-region of Lebanon, for the building of a new great ship on the river of Egypt for the service of the Theban Amon, and for the fabrication of those tall masts which were wont to adorn the front of the propyla before the temples. In fact we see, in the lively representation here preserved, the Canaanites actively employed in felling the highest and straightest trees with their axes. An inscription, though half-destroyed, nevertheless enables us to understand clearly the object of their labours. It runs as follows (slightly filling up the parts wanting) :—

> '[The inhabitants of the land of] Limanon fell | [the trees for the building of a] great ship on the river | [in Thebes of the South], and in like manner for | [King Seti's] high masts at Amon's | [temple in Thebes].'

With this the deeds of Seti in the East had reached heir conclusion.

'He had smitten the wandering peoples (An), and struck to the ground the agricultural peoples (Menti), and had placed his boundaries at the beginning of the world, and at the utmost borders of the river-land of Naharain,'—'which the great sea encircles.'

His return took the form of a specially festive triumphal procession. Laden with rich booty from the land of Ruthen, with silver and gold, with blue, green, red, and other precious stones of the foreign country, accompanied by numerous captives of all lands, which he had again subjected to the supremacy of Egypt, Seti reached the plains of his home by the same road which had led him from Egypt into the foreign countries. At the frontier, near Khetam, the priests and great men of the land waited to meet him with rich gifts of flowers. The following inscription will give the best account of the object of this festive gathering :—

'The priests, the great ones, and the most distinguished men of South and North Egypt have arrived to praise the divine benefactor on his return from the land of Ruthen, accompanied by an immensely rich booty, such as never had happened since the time of the sun-god Ra. They speak thus in praise of the king and in glorification of his fame :

'" Thou hast returned home from the foreign countries which thou hast overcome. Thou hast triumphed over thy enemies which are subjected to thee. May the duration of thy life as king be as long as the sun in heaven! Thou hast quenched thy wrath upon the nine foreign nations. The Sun-god himself has established thy boundaries. His hand protected thee, when thy battle-axe was raised above the heads of all peoples, whose kings fell under thy sword."'

United with these representations, the richness of which we can only lay before our readers in a cursory description, are the lists of the nations conquered by

Seti. We will confine ourselves to those names, out of the whole number, that appear in the more distinct forms in which they are henceforward generally mentioned on the monuments:

1. Khita, the land of the Khita.
2. Naharain, the river-land (Mesopotamia).
3. Upper Ruthen, Canaan.
4. Lower Ruthen, Northern Syria.
5. Singar, the city and the land of Singara, the Sinear of Holy Scripture.
6. Unu, an unknown island or coast land.
7. Kadesh, in the land of the Amorites.
8. Pa-bekh }
9. Kadnaf } both names require to be more accurately defined.
10. Asebi, the island of Cyprus.
11. Mannus, the city and land of Mallos.
12. Aguptha, the land of Cappadocia.
13. Balnu, Balaneæ, to the north of Aradus.

To these we may add the names of the cities of Canaan mentioned in Seti's temple at Abydus (see below, p. 29), and which were conquered by Seti :—

Zithagael.
Zor or Tyre.
Inua'm or Jamnia.
Pa-Hir (Hil) Galilee? or Hali in the tribe of Ashur.
Bitha-'antha or Beth-anoth (in what was afterwards Judah).
Qartha-'anbu or Kiriath-eneb (in Judah).

That the wars and victories of the king in the East did not take place only in the first year of his reign is self-evident, and is sufficiently confirmed by several repetitions in the sculptures. The memorial wall at Karnak may be expected to unite together in one general representation everything glorious which the Pharaoh Seti had performed, as hero and favourite of the gods, up to the building of the great Hall of Columns. This is proved, not only by the wars against the Libyan peoples, which will be spoken of further on, but also by several inscriptions with dates later than his first year; as, for example, the historical record in the temple in the desert of Redesieh, which was built in the ninth year of the reign of Seti, and which cites the following names of the peoples which had then been conquered : 1. Sangar, i.e. Singara ; 2. Kadeshu ; 3. Makita, i.e. Megiddo ; 4. Ha . . . . . . ; 5. the Shasu Arabs of Edom ; 6. Asal or Asar, a name which we can hardly venture to identify with Assur.

Seti carried on his wars not only in the East but in the West, and in particular against the Libyan tribes, who now accordingly appear for the first time on the Egyptian monuments. The double plume on the crown of the head and the side locks of hair mark in the most striking manner these races, which the inscriptions designate by the name of Thuhi, Thuhen, or Thuheni—that is, ' the light or fair' people ; and they likewise denote by the same name the later Greeks, for the expression Marmaridæ, inhabitants of the country of Marmarica, always means these people. In this campaign Seti took his son and heir, Ramessu, among the company of his followers. The kings of the Marmaridæ were thoroughly beaten. In the battle itself Seti appears on a chariot, whose pair of horses bore the name, ' Victorious is Amon.' The campaign reached a mountainous country, full of caverns ; so, at least, the contents of the appended inscription lead us to conclude :—

'He (the king) utterly destroyed them, when he stood on the field of battle. They could not hold their bows, and remained hidden in their caves like foxes, through fear of the king.'

It may be well supposed that, after these extensive campaigns, which brought such a copious booty to Egypt, besides captives, Amon, the god of the empire, and his much venerated temple in Ape, would be the first to be remembered; and the memorial wall of the temple decisively confirms this supposition. The booty as well as the prisoners were solemnly dedicated to the god and to his wife Mut, and to the young son of Amon, Khonsu. In confirmation of this I may bring to the reader's knowledge, in an exact translation, a few of the inscriptions:—

'The king presents the booty to his father Amon, on his return from the miserable land of Ruthen, consisting of silver, gold, blue, green, red, and other precious stones, and of the kings of the peoples, whom he holds bound in his hand, to fill therewith the storehouse of his father Amon, on account of the victory which he has granted to the king.'

The following is added with regard to the prisoners:—

'The kings of the peoples which had not known Egypt are brought by Pharaoh in consequence of his victory over the miserable land of Ruthen. They speak thus to glorify his Holiness and to praise his great deeds:

'"Hail to thee! mighty is thy name, glorious thy renown. The people may well rejoice which is subjected to thy will; but he appears in fetters who oversteps thy boundaries. By thy name! We did not know Egypt; our fathers had not entered it. Grant us freedom out of thy hand!"'

Gold, silver, and precious stones, in purses, golden vessels, even to drinking-horns with wonderful handles in the shape of heads of animals and other ornaments full of taste, display to the spectator the generosity of the king towards the temple, and confirm afresh the remarks we made on the artistic excellence and skill of the Western Asiatic world. The inscriptions contribute their part to the explanation. Among others is the following :—

'The prisoners are presented by the divine benefactor to his father Amon, from the hostile kings of the nations which had not known Egypt—their gifts rest on their shoulders,—to fill therewith all the storehouses, as men-servants and maid-servants, in consequence of the victories which the god has given the king over all lands!'

The following inscription is remarkable, in relation to the connection between Ruthen and Khita :—

'The great kings of the miserable land of Ruthen are brought by the king in consequence of his victory over the people of the Khita, to fill with them the storehouse of his noble father, Amon-Ra, the lord of Thebes, because he has given him the victory over the southern world and the subjection of the northern world.

'The kings of the nations speak thus, to praise Pharaoh and to exalt his glory :

'" Hail to thee ! king of Kemi, sun of the nine peoples, exalted be thou like the gods !"'

In this tone the hieroglyphs describe with great fulness, as well as with the inevitable repetitions, the king's glory and his services to the temple of Amon of Thebes.

Seti I. must have proved his entire devotion to the Theban priests, or, to speak in official tone like the Egyptians, to the Theban Amon ; at least, the inscriptions leave this impression. His buildings, wonderfully beautiful creations of the unknown masters of his time, bespeak the efforts of the Pharaoh to express his gratitude for the distinguished position which the priests had allowed him. His rich presents complete the proof of the regard of the king for the temple at Ape. A special reason for this lay in the peculiar position of Seti with regard to the great question of the hereditary right to the throne.

The monuments name as the wife of the king, or rather as mother of his great son and successor Ramses II., the queen Tua or Tui, whose name at once reminds us of the family of the heretical Pharaoh, Khunaten. In genealogical succession, she was a granddaughter of that heretical king, whom the Theban priests had so bitterly excommunicated, although he belonged to the legitimate race of kings. But however hateful this connection might be to the priests, yet it was in accordance with the law of the hereditary succession. Her grandfather's blood flowed in her veins, although, on the other hand, there was entailed on her from her ancestress of the same name the curse of a foreign descent. The remembrance of this origin must further have appeared all the more distasteful to the priests, as king Seti and his race worshipped the foreign gods in the most obtrusive manner, and at the head of them all the Canaanitish Baal-Sutekh or Set, after whose name his father, Ramses I., had called him Seti—that is, 'the Setish,' or the 'follower of Set.' Thus he had to avoid an open breach, and to soothe the stubborn caste of the priests of Amon. As a conqueror Seti had done his part for Egypt, and he was bound to try to win over the priests as a benefactor and a generous king. And yet he seems to have had less success than he hoped, since at an early period he conferred the highest dignity of the empire on his infant heir, his son Ramessu, as associated king. In the great historical inscription of Abydus, Ramses II. relates the proceeding in his own words :—

'The lord of all himself nurtured me, and brought me up. I was a little boy before I attained the lordship; then he gave over to me the land. I was yet in my mother's womb, when the great ones saluted me full of veneration.[6] I was solemnly inducted as the eldest son into the dignity of heir of the throne on the chair of the earth-god Seb. And I gave my orders as chief of the bodyguard and of the chariot-fighters. Then my father presented me publicly to the people : I was a boy on his lap, and he spake thus: "I will have him crowned as king, for I desire to behold his grandeur while I am still alive." [Then came forward] the officials of the court to place the double crown on my head (and my father spake), " Place the regal circlet on his brow." Thus he spake of me while he still remained on earth, " May he restore order to the land; may he set up again [what has fallen into decay]. May he care for the inhabitants." Thus spake he [with good intention] in his very great love for me. Still he left me in the house of the women and of the royal concubines, after the manner of the damsels of the palace. He chose me [women] from among the [maidens], who wore a harness of leather.'

We stop here, for the above translation is quite enough to serve as a proof of our assertion. Ramses was, as a tender child, associated in the kingly office with his father, and a band of Amazons formed his court.

[6] In the Ramesseum at Medinet-Abou, 'there is a curious tableau representing the conception of Ramses, and even here he is represented wearing the crown of sovereignty. This difficult subject is in allegorical form; it is most delicately and ingeniously managed.' (Villiers Stuart, *Nile Gleanings*, p. 248.)—ED.

In another inscription of the times of Ramses II., the early reign of the king is mentioned in like manner by the writer in the following words :—

'Thou wast a lord (Adon) of this land, and thou actedst wisely, when thou wast still in the egg. In thy childhood what thou saidst took place for the welfare of the land. When thou wast a boy, with the youth's locks of hair, no monument saw the light without thy command; no business was done without thy knowledge. Thou wast raised to be a governor (Rohir) of this land when thou wast a youth and countedst ten full years. All buildings proceeded from thy hands, and the laying of their foundation-stones was performed.'

When Ramses II. ascended the throne, he may have been about twelve years old, or a little more. From this epoch we should count the years of his reign up to its sixty-seventh year, so that he was an old man of eighty when he left this mortal scene.

After Seti had assured the birthright of his race, in the manner we have described, by the joint elevation of his eldest son to the throne, it must have been easy for him to meet the reproach that he was not of royal descent. While he actually ruled the land as king, Ramses, his son, as legitimate sovereign, gave authority to all the acts of his father.

It seems to have been under their double reign that the wars took place, of which we have not yet spoken, and which were waged against the nations to the south of Egypt. When Seti, however, in the great list of conquered peoples, on his wall of victories at Karnak, mentions the countries of Kush and Punt, with all the great and small races of the southern lands of Africa, as the subjects of his crown, we must not forget that here, as so often on the monuments, the ancient usage was followed of exhibiting before the eyes of the vain Egyptians, in a renewed publication with more or less detail, the whole catalogue of those peoples, transcribed from the temple-books of the 'subjects of Egypt.' Nevertheless, several records of the time of Seti bear witness to campaigns of the Egyptian army beyond the frontier city of Syene (as those of Doshe and Sesebi). Egyptian viceroys, already well known to us under the name of King's sons of Kush, acted as governors in the place of Pharaoh in the south, and took care that the tributes imposed were regularly paid. As such are mentioned, in the joint reign of Seti and Ramses II., governors named Ani and Amenemape, a son of Pa-uër. The family of the latter, consisting of numerous members, will occupy us hereafter, for a special reason.

The reign of Seti belongs to that period in the history of the country, in which Egyptian art enjoyed the peculiar care and favour of the king, and, on the other hand, answered to this patronage in the most worthy manner by the creation of real masterpieces. The Hall of Columns of Karnak, in so far as it was carried out while Seti was alive, and the temple of Osiris, in the desert at Abydus, are master-works of the first order, the splendour of which consists, above all else, in the lavish profusion and beauty of the sculpture, even to the hieroglyphic characters. The celebrated tomb also of Seti (or, as the Pharaoh is there called, to avoid the hated name of Seti, Usiri) belongs to the most remarkable performances of Theban art, even to the variegated ornamentation in colours, which adds an abundance of rich life to the pictures and writing. It is the one called after the name of its discoverer, 'Belzoni's tomb,' which still to this day forms the chief point of attraction to all visitors to the Valley of the Kings at Thebes. Its artistic importance is enhanced by the rich abundance of pictures and inscriptions, which are for the most part of a mythological character, but which also involve a special significance in relation to astronomy, as do, above all, the very instructive roof-pictures of the so-called Golden Chamber. Unique in its kind is the mythological substance of a long text, which is found in a side chamber of the same tomb, and which (as M. Naville has lately proved)[7] has for its subject a description of the destruction of the corrupt human race, according to the Egyptian view.

As Seti had erected one of the most splendid works to the god Amon on the right bank of the Theban metropolis, so also at his command there rose on the western bank of the river that wonderful temple, which he dedicated to the memory of his deceased father Ramessu I. I mean the 'Memnonium' of Seti at old Qurnah. Again, in many places on this monument, which belonged to the West country and consequently to the realm of Osiris, the king avoids giving himself the name of Seti. He calls himself generally Usiri, or Usiri Seti (in the last phrase Seti is another word, and not the name of the god Set). The sanctuary bore the

---

[7] *Transactions of the Society of Biblical Archæology*, vol. iv. pp. 1, foll. 1875. [See also Villiers Stuart, *Nile Gleanings*, p. 260.—ED.]

designation, 'the splendid temple-building of king Mineptah Seti, in the city of Amon, on the western side of Thebes;' frequently also with the addition 'in sight of Ape' (namely, of the temple of Karnak). The temple, as has been remarked above, was dedicated to his deceased father, but also, moreover, to the gods of the dead, Osiris and Hathor, besides Amon and his company. The death of King Seti took place while the temple was in course of building. So we are told by the inscription which Ramses II. put up, as the finisher of the building, since it is there stated as follows :—

'King Ramses II. executed this work, as his monument to his father Amon-ra, the king of the gods, the lord of heaven, the ruler of Thebes; and he finished the house of his father King Mineptah (Seti). For he died, and entered the realm of heaven, and he united himself with the sun-god in heaven, when this his house was being built. The gates showed a vacant space, and all the walls of stone and brick were yet to be raised; all the work in it of writing or painting was unfinished.'

In similar expressions does the inscription of Ramses at Abydus describe the unfinished building of the temple in the desert of that city, which was dedicated to Osiris and his associate gods, Isis, Hor, Amon, Hormakhu, and Ptah. Seti also dedicated a special document to the memory of his royal ancestors in the temple of Abydus, namely, the very celebrated Table of the Kings, called that of Abydus, containing the names of seventy-six kings, up to the founder of the empire, Mena. (See Appendix, A.)

In Memphis and Heliopolis, king Seti I. raised temples, or added new parts to temples already existing,

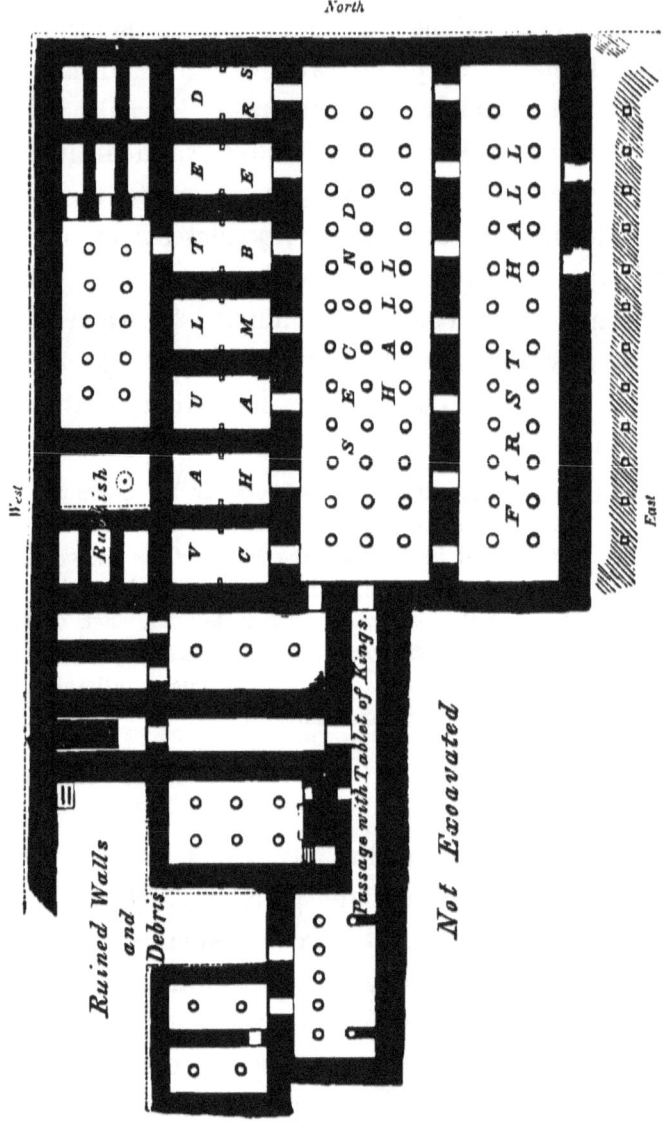

TEMPLE OF SETI I. AND RAMSES II. AT ABYDUS.

which are likewise designated as 'splendid buildings.' Even though their last remains have now disappeared from the earth without leaving a trace, nevertheless their former existence is most surely proved by the testimony of inscriptions. In the same way, at the foot of the mountain behind the old town of El-kab, he erected a special temple to the goddess of the South, the heavenly Nukheb, and a similar one, in the form of a rock-grotto, to the goddess Hathor, in her shape of a lioness, as Pakhith, in the cavern called by the ancients Speos Artemidos (the cave of Artemis).

On these and similar works, the Theban school of artists, who were in the service of the temple of Amon, and applied themselves to the highest style of art, were especially occupied. Among the sculptors of the time, the name of a certain Hi has been preserved; among the painters, Amen-uah-su is expressly celebrated as the 'first painter.'[8] Both worked by the king's order in the decoration of the tomb which was destined for the then governor of Thebes, by name Pa-uër, the son of the chief priest of Amon, Neb-nuteru surnamed Thera, and of the oldest among the holy wives of the god, Mer-amon-ra; and also for his brother Tathao.[9] Such records, which relate to the most important contemporaries of the kings, are useful and precious, for they frequently render good service in fixing the contemporary circumstances and events in Egyptian history nearly in their chronological order. They serve to keep open the sources which are destined

[8] Compare *Denkmäler*, iii. pp. 132, &c.   [9] Ibid.

sooner or later to bring the hidden stagnant waters of Egyptian chronology and the succession of the kings into a united current.

The tributes and the taxes, which under the third Thutmes were yearly contributed in rich abundance to the Pharaoh by the conquered nations and his own subjects, seem henceforward, from the reign of Seti, to have flowed in less abundantly, while the wants of the kings were the same, and the erection of costly buildings required a great expenditure. New sources must needs therefore be opened for the requisite means. So they began to devote special care to the regular working of the existing gold-mines in Egypt and Nubia, and, what was of the first importance, to give the needful attention to the formation of wells in the midst of the parched mountain regions, from which the gold was to be won. One of these regions was the extent of desert on the eastern side of the Nile, opposite Edfou, which at this day bears the name of Redesieh, and contains the remains of an old-Egyptian rock-temple. It marks the site of one of the resting-places on the great road of commerce, which in ancient days led straight through the desert from the town of Coptos, on the Nile, to the harbour of Berenice on the Red Sea. The inscriptions on the temple date from the times of Seti. They not only establish the existence of gold ore in the interior of the mountain, but also the position of a well (*hydreuma*, as the Greeks called it), made at the command of the king. They relate how, in the ninth year of king Seti, in the month Epiphi, on the 20th day, the Pharaoh undertook a journey to the solitary mountain region, as it was his wish to see for himself the gold-mines which existed there. After he had mounted up many miles, he made a halt, to take counsel with himself and to come to a conclusion upon the information he had received, that the want of water made the road almost impassable, and that travellers by it died of thirst in the hot season of the year. At a proper place a well was bored deep in the rocky ground, and a small rock-temple was made there, 'to the name of King Seti,' by the express order of the Pharaoh. Thereupon everything was done to carry on the gold-washing with success. The people who followed this laborious occupation were placed under the supervision of a hir-pit or 'overseer of the foreign peoples,' and all other measures were taken to ensure for all future time the keeping up of the temple and the worship of its divine inhabitants, Osiris, Isis, and Horus, besides the three great divinities of the country, Amon of Thebes, Ptah of Memphis, and Hormakhu of Thebes.

That the inhabitants of the country were highly pleased with this work is declared by the inscriptions on the temple:

'King Seti did this for his memorial for his father Amon-Ra and his company of gods, namely, he built anew for them a house of god, in the interior of which the divinities dwell in full contentment. He had the well bored for them. Such a thing was never done before by any king, except him, the king. Thus did King Seti do a good work, the beneficent dispenser of water, who prolongs life to his people; he is for every one a father and a mother. They speak from mouth to mouth, "Amon grant him (a long existence), increase to him an everlasting duration. Ye gods of the well! assure to him your length of life, since he has made for us the road to travel upon, and has opened what lay shut up before our face. Now can we travel up with ease, and reach the goal and remain living. The difficult road lies open there before us, and the way has become good. Now the gold can be carried up, as the king and lord has seen. All the living generations, and those which shall be hereafter, will pray for an eternal remembrance for him. May he celebrate the thirty years' jubilee-feasts like Tum; may he flourish like Horus of Apollinopolis; because he has founded a memorial in the lands of the gods,[1] because he has bored for water in the mountains.'

In the execution of the work, the utility of which the inhabitants of the country so frequently recognize, Ani, the King's son of Kush of that time, as well as commander-in-chief of the Mazai, was present as the directing architect. This fact is attested by rock-inscriptions, accompanied by pictorial representations, as for example that of the warlike foreign goddess Antha, the Anaitis of the ancients, who rides on horseback wielding a battle-axe and shield, like Bellona.

Whether, after all, the gold-mines yielded rich produce, whether the gold-washers delivered to the 'reckoner of silver and gold of the land of the country of Upper and Lower Egypt, Hi-shera,'[2] the shining grains of their laborious employment in satisfactory quantity, on these points the lay of the poet on the monuments is for ever silent.

As Seti's reign flows on parallel with that of his

---

[1] I will here call the attention of the reader to the fact, that in this and other places—for example, in the rock-inscriptions of Hammamât—the Arabian desert and the coast adjoining it, on the Red Sea, is designated as ' the land of the gods.'

[2] See Lieblein's *Dictionary of Proper Names*, No. 882.

great son Ramses, as king of the country, we will leave his end untouched, and suppose, with the ancients, that his soul suddenly flew up like a bird to the Egyptian heaven, to enjoy a better existence in the bark of the sun. His decease took place before his own tomb and his buildings in honour of the immortal ones were finished. The temples of Abydus and of old Qurnah have already afforded us proofs of this.

His son and associated king, Ramessu, bore the names—

III. RA-USERMA SOTEP-EN-RA RAMESSU II. MIAMUN I. (RAMSES MIAMUN). ABOUT 1333 B.C.

This is the king who above all others bears the name of honour of A-nakhtu, ' the Conqueror,' and whom the monuments and the rolls of the books often designate by his popular names of Ses, Sestesu, Setesu, or Sestura, that is, the ' Sethosis who is also called Ramesses ' of the Manethonian record, and the renowned legendary conqueror SESOSTRIS of the Greek historians.

The number of his monuments, which still to the present day cover the soil of Egypt and Nubia as the ruined remnants of a glorious past, or are daily brought to light from their concealment, is so great and almost countless, that the historian of his life and deeds finds himself in a difficulty where to begin, how to spin together the principal threads, and where to end his work. If to honour the memory of his father be the chief duty and the first work of a dutiful son—and we shall see that this was the persuasion of Ramses II.—the beginning is made easy for us, and we shall honour the king's memory in the worthiest manner by using the very words of the great Sesostris about his first acts on entering upon his sole reign.

King Seti had died. The temple of Abydus stood half finished. The first royal care of Ramses was to complete the work, and, in a long inscription on the left wall of the entrance, to record the intention with which his heart was charged, for the imitation of his contemporaries and of posterity.

'The lord of the land arose as king, to show honour to his father, in his first year, on his first journey to Thebes. He had caused likenesses of his father, who was king Seti I., to be sculptured, the one in Thebes, the other in Memphis at the entrance gate, which he had executed for himself, besides those which were in Nifur, the necropolis of Abydus. Thus he fulfilled the wish which moved his heart, since he had been on earth, on the ground of the god Unnofer. He renewed the remembrance of his father, and of those who rest in the under world, in that he made his name to live, and caused his portraits to be made, and fixed the revenues set apart for his venerated person, and filled his house and richly decked out his altars. The walls were rebuilt, which had become old in his favourite house, the halls in his temple were rebuilt, its walls were covered, its gates were raised up; whatever had fallen into decay in the burial-place of his father in the necropolis was restored, and [the works of art which] had been carried away were brought back into the interior.

'All this did the Conquering King Ramses II. for his father Seti I. He established for him the sacrifices in rich profusion, in his name and in that of the (earlier) kings. His breast had a tender feeling towards his parent, and his heart beat for him who brought him up.

'On one of these days, it was in the first year, on the 23rd day of the month Athyr,[3] on [his return home] after (the conclusion)

---

[3] The feast began on the 19th of Paophi. It lasted twenty-six

of the feast of the voyage of Amon to Thebes, then he went out, endowed with power and strength by Amon and by Tum, out of the city of Thebes. They had assured him a recompense through never-ending years, as long as the duration of the existence of the sun in heaven.—

'He raised his hand, which bore the incense-vessel, up towards the heavenly orb of light of the living god. The sacrificial gifts were splendid, they were received with satisfaction in all his . . . (?) The king (now) returned from the capital of the land of the South. [As soon as] the sun [had risen], the journey was commenced. As the ships of the king sailed on, they threw their brightness on the river. The order was given for the journey down the stream to the stronghold of the city of Ramessu, the Conqueror.

'Then the king, in order to behold his father, made the rowers enter the canal of Nifur, with the intention of offering a sacrifice to the beneficent god Unnofer with his choicest libations, and of praying to [the divinity] of his brother Anhur, the son of Ra in . . . as which he abides there.

'There he found the halls of the dead of the former kings, and their graves, which are in Abydus, hastening to the beginning of desolation. Their burial-places had become dilapidated from the foundations. [The stones were torn away] out of the ground, their walls lay scattered about on the road, no brick held to another, the hall " of the second birth " lay in ruins, nothing had been built up [for the father by his son], who should have been busied in preserving it according to his expectations, since its possessor had flown up to heaven. Not one son had renewed the memorial of his father, who rested in the grave.

'There was the temple of Seti. The front and back elevations were in process of building when he entered the realm of heaven. Unfinished was his monument; the columns were not raised on their bases, his statues lay upon the earth; they were not sculptured according to the corresponding measure of "the golden chamber" His revenues failed. The servants of the temple without distinction had taken what was brought in from the fields, the boundary marks of which were not staked out on the land.

---

days, and it ended on the 12th of Athyr. On the 17th of Athyr the feast of the fifth day after it took place; so that the journey of the king to Abydus is fixed precisely to the 23rd of Athyr.

'The king speaks to the chamberlain at his side: "Speak, that there may be assembled the princes, the favourites of the king, the commanders of the body-guards, as they are (i.e. all of them), the architects, according to their number, and the superintendents of the house of the rolls of the books."

'When they had come before the king, their noses touched the ground, and their feet lay on the ground for joy; they fell down to the ground, and with their hands they prayed to the king. They praised this divine benefactor, while they exalted his grace in his presence. They related exactly what he had achieved, and recited his glorious deeds as they had been done. All words that proceeded out of their mouths were employed to describe the deeds of the lord of the land in full truth. Thus they lay prostrate and touching the earth before the king, speaking thus:

'"We are come before thee, the lord of heaven, lord of the earth, sun, life of the whole world, lord of time, measurer of the course of the sun, Tum for men, lord of prosperity, creator of the harvest, fashioner and former of mortals, dispenser of breath to all men; animator of the whole company of the gods; pillar of heaven, threshold of the earth, weigher of the balance of the two worlds, lord of rich gifts, increaser of the corn, at whose feet the Ranen (the Egyptian Ceres) waits; thou former of the great, creator of the small, whose words engender the most splendid abundance; thou who watchest when other men rest, whose strength overshadows Egypt, conqueror of the foreigners, who hast returned home victorious, whose arm protects the Egyptians, who loves justice, in which he lives by his laws; protector of the land, rich in years; the conqueror whose terror has stricken down the foreigners; thou our Lord, our sun, by whose words out of his mouth Tum lives. Here we are all assembled before thee; grant us life out of thy hands, O Pharaoh, and breath for our nostrils; all men live, on whom he has risen (like the sun)."

'The king speaks to them after an interval: "I have called you because of a determination regarding that which I am about to do. I have beheld the houses of the Necropolis, the graves of Abydus. The buildings of them require labour from the times of their possessors down to the present day. When the son arose in the place of his father, he did not renew the memorial of his parent. In my mind I have pondered with myself the splendid occasion for good works for coming times (?). The most beautiful thing to behold, the best thing to hear, is a child with a thankful breast, whose heart beats for his father. Wherefore my heart urges me to do what is good for Mineptah. I will cause them to talk for ever and eternally of his son, who has awakened his name to life. My father Osiris will reward me for this with a long existence, like his son Horus. Let me do what he did; let me be excellent, just as he was excellent, for my parent, I, who am a scion of the sun-god Ra.

'"Let me speak to you of Seti. The lord of all, he himself nourished me and brought me up. I was a little boy before I attained to the government; then he gave over to me the country. I was yet in my mother's womb when the great ones greeted me with veneration. I was solemnly inducted as eldest son into the dignity of an heir of the throne, on the chair of the earth-god Seb. And I gave my orders as the chief of the life-guards and of the fighters on chariots. Then my father showed me publicly to the people, and I was a boy on his lap, and he spake thus: 'I will cause him to be crowned as king, for I will behold his excellence while I am yet alive.' [Then came forward] the officials of the court to place the double crown on my head (and my father spake): 'Place the regal circlet on his brow.' Thus he spake of me while he still remained on earth: 'Let him establish order in the land, let him raise up again what has fallen into decay, let him take care of the inhabitants.' Thus spake he [with kind intention] in his very great love for me; yet he left me in the house of the women and of the royal concubines, after the manner of the maidens of the palace. He chose for me women among the maidens, who wore a harness of leather. . . . It was the house of the women that took care of and nourished me.

'"Thus was I like the sun-god Ra, the first of mortals. The inhabitants of the South and of the North lay at my feet. [I gave orders for the buildings], I myself laid their foundation-stone to build [the work. I had an image] made of him who begat me, my father, of gold, quite new.

'"In the first year of my reign as king I had given orders to provide his temple with stores. I secured to him his fields, [and fixed their boundaries], and appointed him revenues for his worship, [and arranged the sacrifices of oxen and geese and bread] and wine and incense and other things. I planted for him groves to grow up for him. Thus was his house under my protection; I took upon myself all his buildings from the time that [I was crowned as king]. And thus I was a child [whose heart was full of thanks towards] his father who had exalted me.

'"I will renew the memorial. I will not neglect his tomb as children are accustomed to do, who do not remember their father. [Men shall speak of me] as of a son who did good, and shall estimate the strength of my father in me his child. I will complete it because I am lord of the land. I will take care of it because it is fitting and right.

'"I clothe the walls in the temple of my parent. I will commission the man of my choice to hasten the buildings for him, to build up again what was sunken of its walls, [and to raise up] his temple wings on the [front side], to clothe his house, to erect his pillars, and to place the blocks on the places of the foundation-stone. Beautifully shall the most splendid double memorial be made at once. Let it be inscribed with my name, and with the name of my father. As the son is, so was the father [who begat him]."

'The king's friends speak in answer to the divine benefactor: "Thou art the Sun-god, thy body is his body, no king is like to thee, thou alone art like the son of Osiris. What thou hast done is like his story. The mother Isis [never saw] such a king since the Sun-god, except thee and her son Horus. Greater is that which thou hast done than what he did when he ruled as king after Osiris. The laws of the land continue fixed. Such a son is dear to his father. The holy offspring [of Ra], who has formed him in the mother egg, [his heart] beats for him who brought him up. Glorious is he. None has done the deeds of Horus for his father up to the present day, except thou, O king! Thou loved one! Thou hast performed more than it was necessary to do; no permission for good [is necessary any more for thee. May such a king as thou be] our leader, whose word we may obey! Was not that which has just come to pass, to remember him, an example for thee? Thou didst refuse to forget [thy father]. Thy heart was true to thy father, King Seti, father of the divine one, the heavenly Mineptah.

'"Since the time of Ra, since kings have reigned, no other is to be compared to thee. Never was seen face to face, nor was heard of in story, [any other son] who has busied himself in renewing the memorial of his father. None who rose up would honour his father. Each one worked for his own name, except only thee alone and Horus. As thou hast done, so did the son of Osiris.

'"Therefore thou art a beautiful heir, like to him; his kingdom, thou guidest it in the same way. If any one does according as the god did, there will be to him a duration of life for that which he has done. The god Ra in heaven [is highly delighted], his company of gods is full of joy, the gods are friendly disposed towards Egypt, since thy rule as king of the land.

'" Noble is thy just disposition; it has reached as far as the heights of heaven. Thy upright wisdom pleases the sun-god Ra. Tum is full of delight [because of thy conduct]; Unnofer triumphs because of thy deeds, O king, for his name. He speaks thus: '[My dear son], let there be granted to thee the duration of heaven, the power of the gods, the secret of the lord of the depth, so long as thou shalt remain on earth, like the disk of the sun.'

'" Moved is the heart of Mineptah, his name lives anew; thou hast caused him to be made in gold and precious stones, [and thou hast set] up his [statues] of silver. [And his temple] thou hast built for him anew in thy name, and in the name of all the kings who are in heaven, and whose chambers need the work. No son has done what thou hast done since the time of Ra down to the [present day].

'" [That which thou hast determined], O king, do it. Remember that which was sunk in forgetfulness, renew the monuments in the Necropolis, and all the plans which were behindhand, execute them as is right and fitting.—Thou art now king of Upper Egypt and Lower Egypt. Do good even as thou willest. Let thy heart be satisfied in doing what is right. For that which is done for the honour of the gods, that will be accepted and [rewarded by the immortals] when thou hereafter shalt rise to heaven. When thy grace raises himself to the orb of light, then shall the eyes see thy glorious virtues in the sight of gods and men. Thus do thou! Renew memorial after memorial to the gods. Therefore shall thy father Ra command that thy name shall resound in all lands, beginning in the south with Khonti-hon-Nofer, northwards from the shores of the sea as far as the nations of Ruthen. The foreign fortresses and towns of the king and the cities, well guarded and occupied with their inhabitants, and [the dwellers in all places, they speak of thee], that thou art as a god for every one. They awake to offer incense to thee. Thus according to the will of thy father

Tum, the black land (Egypt), and the red land (the Erythræans), praise thee, O king."

'When [this speech] from the lips of the princes before their lord [was ended], then the king commanded, and gave commission to the architects, and separated the people of the masons and of the stone-cutters with the help of the graver, and the draughtsmen, and all kinds of artists, to build the most holy place for his father, and to raise up what had fallen into decay in the Necropolis, and in the temple of his father, who sojourns among the deceased ones.

'Then [he began] to have the statues of his father carved, from the first year. The revenues were doubled for his worship, his temple was enriched according to the number of its wants. He appointed its register of fields and peasants and herds. He named its priests according to their service, and the prophet, to raise in his hands [the incense-vessel], and he appointed the temple servants for the performance of the works for him. His barns were many, full of wheat [and his storehouses in all plenty]. His domain was immense in the South and in the North, and was placed under the administration of the superintendent of his temple. In such wise did King Ramses II. for his father, King Seti, under the protection of Unnofer.

'He repeated what he had done for his honour in Thebes, in On, and in Memphis, where his statues rested in their places, and in all the places of the granaries.

'These are the words of King Ramses II., [to sing] what he did for his father, the Osiris-king Seti. He speaks thus :

'"Awake, raise thy face to heaven, behold the sun, my father Mineptah, thou who art like God. Here am I, who make thy name to live. I am thy guardian, and my care is directed to thy temple and to thy altars, which are raised up again. Thou restest in the deep like Osiris, while I rule like Ra among men (and possess) the great throne of Tum, like Horus, the son of Isis, the guardian of his father. Beautiful is that which I have done for thee.—

'"Thou enterest on a second existence. I caused thee to be fashioned, I built thy house which thou didst love, in which thy image stands, in the Necropolis of Abydus forever. I set apart revenues for thee for thy worship daily, to be just towards thee. If anything is in my power, which seems to be wanting to thee, I do it for thee. Thy heart shall be satisfied, that the best shall be done for thy name. I appoint for thee the priests of the vessel of holy water, provided with everything for sprinkling the water on the ground, besides meat and drink. I myself, I myself am come here to behold thy temple near that of Unnofer, the eternal king. I urged on the building of it, I clothed [the walls], I did that which thou didst wish, that it may be done for thy whole house. I established thy name therein to all eternity. May it be done in truth, may it succeed according to my intention. I dedicated to thee the lands of the South for the service of thy temple, and the lands of the North, they bring to thee their gifts before thy beautiful countenance. I gathered together the people of thy service one and all, assigning them to the prophet of thy temple. All thy property shall remain in one great whole, to keep up thy temple for all time. I made presents to thy silver chamber; it is rich in treasures which are well pleasing to the heart, and I apportioned to thee the tributes at the same time. I dedicated to thee ships with their freight on the great sea, which should bring to thee [the wonderful productions] of the holy land. The merchants carry on their commerce with their wares, and their productions of gold and silver and bronze. I fixed for thee the number of the fields according to the proportion of the claims [of thy temple]. Great is their number according to their valuation in acres. I provided thee with land-surveyors and husbandmen, to deliver the corn for thy revenues. I dedicated to thee barks with their crews, and labourers for the felling of wood, for the purpose of building what is wanting in ships for thy house. I gave thee herds of all kinds of cattle to increase thy revenues, according to what is right. I fixed for thee the tribute of birds in the marshes for thy necessary sustenance. I [caused to be delivered to thee] living geese, to keep up the breed of the birds. I gave to thee fishermen on the river and on all the lakes, to feed the workmen who load the sea-going ships. I have provided thy temple with all kinds of guilds of my handi-[craftsmen]. Thy temple servants have been made up to their full number from the best people, and the peasants pay their taxes in woven stuffs for thy drapery. Thy men-servants and maid-servants work in the fields in all the town districts. Each man thus performs his service, to fill thy house.

'" Thou hast entered into the realm of heaven. Thou accompaniest the sun-god Ra. Thou art united with the stars and the moon. Thou restest in the deep, like those who dwell in it with

Unnofer, the eternal. Thy hands move the god Tum in heaven and on earth, like the wandering stars and the fixed stars. Thou remainest in the forepart of the bark of millions. When the sun rises in the tabernacle of heaven, thine eyes behold his splendour. When Tum (the evening sun) goes to rest on the earth, thou art in his train. Thou enterest the secret house before his lord. Thy foot wanders in the deep. Thou remainest in the company of the gods of the under world.

' " But I obtain by my prayers the breath (of life) at thy awaking, thou glorious one! and I praise thy numerous names day by day, I who love my father.—I let myself be guided by thy virtue. So long as I stay on earth, I will offer a sacrifice to thee. My hand shall bring the libations for thy name to thy [remembrance] in all thy abodes.

' " Come, speak to Ra [that he may grant long years] of life to his son, and to Unnofer, with a heart full of love, that he may grant length of time upon length of time, united to the thirty-years' feasts of jubilee, to King Ramses. Well will it be for thee that I should be king for a long time, for thou wilt be honoured by a good son, who remembers his father. I will be a [protector and] guardian for thy temple day by day, to have regard to the wants of thy worship in every way. If I should hear of any injury which threatens to invade it, I will give the order immediately to remove it in every way. Thou shalt be treated as if thou wert still alive. So long as I shall reign, my attention shall be directed continually to thy temple. My heart beats for thee; I will be thy guardian for the honour of thy name. If thou also remainest in the deep, the best, the very best shall be thy portion as long as I live, I, King Ramses." '

The reader will perhaps permit me to spare him the long answer of the father, Seti, as we can hardly cover the whole breadth, as well as go deep into the essential substance, of the old Egyptian records. In short, I will only mention this one point, that the spirit of the deceased king appears from the world below, to give the most satisfactory answer, in the way which was expected, to the vows of Ramses his son. To him, the son, all good fortune, all glory, health and joy, and whatever else a man, especially if he were an old-Egyptian Pharaoh, could wish besides, should be granted most richly by the gods, but above all, what Ramses most coveted, a very long term of life, to be measured as long as possible by the thirty years' feast of jubilee.

What gives this inscription its special value in relation to history, may be stated in a few words, although those who have hitherto interpreted the document seem to have been in the dark upon this point.

In the first year of his real reign as sole king, Ramses II. undertook with great splendour a journey to Thebes, to celebrate the customary great feast there to the god Amon. On his return to the city of Ramses, the biblical Raamses (Zoan-Tanis), where he had fixed his royal residence, the wish came upon him to travel to Abydus, to visit the temple and the tomb of his father Seti. Here he had to learn the melancholy news, that the buildings and service of the temple of his deceased father were in a very decayed condition, not to speak of the forgotten and dilapidated tombs of the former kings. (Here we may ask, Which kings?) Hence, Seti was first buried in Abydus, whose soil, impregnated with salt, is favourable to the preservation of the dead, and the position of his temple to Osiris quite agrees with this; but he was probably afterwards removed to the valley of the royal tombs at Thebes. We are here in presence of a riddle, which the documents known do not as yet suffice to explain.

It is scarcely worth while to relate what Ramses II. did for the buildings of his father at Abydus. In the course of his long reign the king completed the temple. When the great building was entirely finished, Ramses must have been already advanced in years, since not less than sixty sons and fifty-nine daughters of Ramses II. greeted in their effigies the entrance of the pilgrims at the principal gate.

In proportion as the works executed under Seti, the father, present to the astonished eyes of the beholder splendid examples of Egyptian architecture and sculpture, just so poor and inferior are the buildings which were executed under the reign of Ramses, and which bear the names of the Conquering King. The feeling also of gratitude towards his parent seems to have gradually faded away with Ramses, as years increased upon him, to such a degree that he did not even deem it wrong to chisel out the names and memorials of his father in many places of the temple walls, and to substitute his own.

As we wish to leave it to our readers to form their own opinion on the boastful Ramses, we will turn to another field of his activity, and follow him, in the 5th year of his reign, to the stream of the Orontes in Syria, the waters of which washed the fortress of Kadesh on all sides.

A great war had broken out between Egypt and the land of Khita. The king of the latter had assembled his allies to check the Egyptians. Kadesh was the rallying-place of the confederates. There appeared, besides the prince of Khita, the kings and peoples of Arathu (Aradus), Khilibu (Haleb), of the river-land of Naharain, of Qazauadana (Gauzanitis), of

Malunna, of Pidasa (Pidasis), of Leka (the Ligyes),[4] of the Dardani, or Dandani (Dardanians in Kurdistan),[5] of the Masu (the inhabitants of Mount Masius), of Kerkesh (the Girgesites?) or Keshkesh, of Qirqimosh (Carchemish), of Akerith, of Anau-gas (Jenysus), of Mushanath, all 'peoples from the extremest end of the sea to the land of the Khita.'

It was a slaughter of peoples, in the fullest sense of the word, that was prepared at Kadesh.

Since we prefer to follow the inscriptions themselves as the historians of the remarkable events which form the chief subject of the Egyptian record, we wish first to establish the fact that Ramses came out of the fight at Kadesh a doubtful conqueror, and had to thank his own personal bravery for his life and preservation, since ' he was all alone and no other was with him.' This heroic feat gave the occasion for poets, sculptors, and painters, to make the most of such fortunate materials, in order to immortalize in words and pictures the great deeds of the ' Conqueror '-king. The temple-scribe, Pentaur, a jovial companion, who, to the special disgust of his old teacher, manifested a decided inclination for wine, women, and song, had the honour, in the 7th year of Ramses II., to win the prize as the composer of an heroic song, of which we not only possess a copy in a roll of papyrus, but its words cover the whole surface of walls in the

---

[4] See Herodotus, vii. 72, where the Ligyes are mentioned as a people of Asia Minor, next to the Matieni and the Mariandyni, as allies in the Persian host.

[5] Compare Herodotus, i. 189.

temples of Abydus,[6] Luqsor, Karnak, the Ramesseum at Ibsamboul, in order to call the attention of the visitor, even at a distance, to the deeds of Ramses.

The fame of having for the first time brought to the knowledge of science in a complete translation this the oldest heroic song of the world, belongs with the most perfect right to the French scholar, E. de Rougé. If in our own translation, which we shall presently lay before the reader, we have in many places made essential corrections of the version of that master, we have herein only responded to the requirements of science, by giving effect to the latest acquisitions in the field of old-Egyptian decipherment, as applied to the interpretation of this heroic song.

From the poet we pass to the unknown painter and sculptor, who has chiselled in deep work on the stone of the same wall, with a bold execution of the several parts, the procession of the warriors, the battle before Kadesh, the storming of the fortress, the overthrow of the enemy, and the camp life of the Egyptians. The whole conception must even at this day be acknowledged to be grand beyond measure, for the representation sets before our eyes the deeds which were performed more vividly than any description in words and with the finest handling of the material, and displays the whole composition even to its smallest details.

Here in the camp of the Egyptians, which was laid out as a square, and was surrounded by an arti-

[6] The parts of this temple which were dug out have been again carefully covered up with sand.

ficial wall of the shields of the Egyptian warriors placed side by side, we see displayed the actions and life of the soldiers and the camp-servants, who rest on the ground by the side of the baggage and the numerous necessaries for a long journey. Among them wander asses, and even the favourite lion of the king has his place within the enclosure. The tent of Pharaoh is seen in the middle of the camp, and near it the movable shrine of the great gods of Egypt. Above the whole is placed the inscription :—

'This is the first legion of Amon, who bestows victory on King Ramses II. Pharaoh is with it. It is occupied in pitching its camp.'

Not far off the king sits on his throne, and receives the report of his generals, or gives the necessary orders to his followers. Important episodes are not wanting. Thus the Egyptians are dragging forward two foreigners, about whom the appended inscription thus informs us :—

'This is the arrival of the spies of Pharaoh; they bring two spies of the people of the Khita before Pharaoh. They are beating them to make them declare where the king of Khita is.'

There the chariots of war and the warriors of the king are passing in good order before Pharaoh : among them the legions of Amon, Ptah, Pra, and Sutekh. Then, after the gods, the hosts of the warriors are for the most part mentioned by name. Mercenary troops also are not wanting, for the Colchian Shardana, whose fine linen was well known to antiquity under the name of Sardonian, appear among the Egyptian allies. They are particularly distinguished by their helmets with horns and a ball-shaped crest, by their long swords and the round shields on their left arm, while their right hand grasps a spear.

The host also of the Khita and of their allies are represented with a lively pictorial expression, for the artist has been guided by the intention of bringing before the eyes of the beholder the orderly masses of the Khita warriors, and the less regular and warlike troops of the allied peoples, according to their costume and arms. The Canaanites are distinguished in the most striking manner from the allies, of races unknown to us, who are attired with turban-like coverings for the head, or with high caps such as are still worn at the present day by the Persians. Short swords, lances, bows and arrows, form the weapons of the enemies of the Egyptians. We have already made the necessary observations on the warlike and truly chivalrous appearance of the Khita, and must now particularly mention the Tuhir, or 'chosen ones,' who follow in the train of their king. Among these are the Qel'au, or slingers, who attended close about the person of their prince.

Wonderfully rich is the great battle-picture which represents the fight of the chariots before Kadesh on the banks of the Orontes. While the gigantic form of Ramses, in the very midst of the mass of hostile chariots, performs deeds of the highest prowess, to the astonishment of the Egyptians and of their enemies, his brave son, Prahiunamif, as the chief commander of the chariots, heads the attack on the chariots of the enemy. Several of his brothers, the children of Ramses, take part in the battle. The chariots of the Khita and their warriors are thrown into the river; and among them the King of Khilibu, whom his warriors have just dragged out of the water, and are endeavouring to restore to animation while the battle is raging. They hold their lord by the legs, with his head hanging down. The inscription by the side runs thus:—

'This is the King of Khilibu. His warriors are raising him up after Pharaoh has thrown him into the water.'

The battle, or rather its beginning, is described in the following manner in a short inscription annexed to the picture:—

'When the king had halted, he sat down to the north-west of the town of Kadesh. He had come up with the hostile hosts of Khita, being quite alone, no other was with him. There were thousands and hundreds of chariots round about him on all sides. He dashed them down in heaps of dead bodies before his horses. He killed all the kings of all the peoples who were allies of the (king) of Khita, together with his princes and elders, his warriors and his horses. He threw them one upon another, head over heels, into the water of the Orontes. There the king of Khita turned round, and, raised up his hands to implore the divine benefactor.'

The battle, or rather butchery, seems to have been as little agreeable to the people of the Khita as to their lords, for—

'The hostile Khita speak, praising the divine benefactor thus: "Give us freedom (literally, breath) from thy hand, O good king! Let us lie at thy feet; the fear of thee has opened the land of Khita. We are like the foals of mares, which tremble in terror at the sight of the grim lion."'

In the customary manner, as already described, the inscriptions sing the praise of their king :—

'The brave and bold conqueror of the nations, of the highest valour in the field of battle, firm on horseback, and glorious on his chariot, whom none can escape when he seizes his bow and arrows.'

A less poetical and ornate description of the great event, which is expressly stated to have happened before Kadesh, is preserved in a record repeated several times on the walls of the temple. We will not withhold it from our readers, if only because it shows with what clearness, in spite of their simple phraseology, the writers of thirty-two centuries ago were able to place before their contemporaries an historical description, in order to depict to their imagination, in true Homeric style, the fame and exploits of their hero.

'(1) In the 5th year, in the month Epiphi, on the 9th day, in the reign of king Ramses II., the Pharaoh was (2) in the land of Zahi, on his second campaign. Good watch was kept over the king in the camp of Pharaoh on the heights to the south of (3) the city of Kadesh. Pharaoh came forth as soon as the sun rose, and put on the (war) array of his father Monthu. And the sovereign went further (4) upwards, and came to the south of the town of Shabatun. There came to meet him two Shasu, in order to speak to (5) Pharaoh thus :

'" We are brothers, who belong to the chiefs of the tribes of the Shasu, which are (6) in the dominion of the king of Khita. They commanded us to go to Pharaoh, to speak thus: We wish to be servants (7) to the house of Pharaoh, so that we may separate ourselves from the king of Khita. But now (8) the king of Khita stays in the land of Khilibu, to the north of Tunep, for he fears Pharaoh, intending forwards (9) to advance."

'Thus spake the two Shasu. But the words which they had spoken to the king were vain lies; (10) for the king of Khita had sent them to spy out where Pharaoh was, so that the (11) soldiers of Pharaoh should not prepare an ambush in the rear, in order to fight with the king of Khita. For the king of Khita had (12) come with all the kings of all peoples, with horses and riders, which he brought with him in great numbers, and stood there ready (13) in an ambush behind the town of Kadesh, the wicked. And the king did not discover the meaning of their words.

'And Pharaoh went further downwards, and came to the region to the north-west of Kadesh, where he stayed to rest on (14) a golden couch of repose. There came in the spies, who belonged to the servants of the king, and brought with them two spies of the king of (15) Khita. When they had been brought forward, Pharaoh spake to them : " Who are ye ? " They said, " We belong to (16) the king of Khita, who sent us to see where Pharaoh is." Then spake to them (17) Pharaoh : " He, where stays he, the king of Khita ? For I have heard say that he is in the land of Khilibu." They said : " Behold (18) the king of Khita stays there, and much people with him, whom he has brought with him (19) in great numbers from all countries which are situated in the territory of the land of Khita, of the land of Naharain (20) and of all the Kiti.⁷ They are provided with riders and horses, who bring with them (21) the implements of war, and they are more than the sand of the sea. Behold, they stay there in ambush to fight behind the town of Kadesh, (22) the wicked."

'Then Pharaoh called the princes before him, that they might hear (23) all the words which the two spies of the land of Khita, who were present, had spoken. The king spake to them : " Behold the wisdom (24) of the governor and of the princes of the lands of the house of Pharaoh in this matter ! They stood there speaking daily thus to Pharaoh—(25) ' The king of Khita is in the land of Khilibu ; he has fled before Pharaoh since he heard say that he would come to him according to the words of Pharaoh daily.' (26) Now behold what I have had to hear in this hour from the two spies. The king of Khita is come up with much people, who are with him with horses and riders (27) as many as the sand. They stand there behind the town of Kadesh, the wicked. Thus has it happened that the governor and the princes knew nothing, to whom (28) the countries of the house of Pharaoh

---

⁷ Kiti means ' circle,' like the Hebrew Galil, Galilee.

are entrusted. (29) It was their duty to have said, They are come up."

'Then the princes who were before Pharaoh spake thus : " The fault (30) is great which the governor and the princes of the house of Pharaoh have committed, that they did not make enquiries (31) where the king of Khita stayed at each time, (32) that they might have given notice daily to Pharaoh."

'Then (33) was the commission given to a captain to urge on in haste the army of the king, which entered into the country (34) to the south of Shabatun, to direct them to the spot where (35) Pharaoh was. For Pharaoh had relied on the words of the princes, while in the meantime the king of Khita came up with much people that were with him, with riders (36) and horses. So exceeding great was the number of the people that was with him. They had passed over the ditch, which is to the south of the town of Kadesh, and they fell upon the army of Pharaoh, which entered in without having any information. And (37) the army and the horses of Pharaoh gave way before them on the road upwards to the place where the king was. Then the hostile hosts of the king of Khita surrounded the (38) followers of Pharaoh, who were by his side.

'When Pharaoh beheld this, he became wroth against them, and he was like his father Monthu. He put on his war array (39) and took his arms, and appeared like the god Baal in his time. And he mounted his horse, and hurried forth in a quick course. (40) He was all alone. He rushed into the midst of the hostile hosts of the king of Khita and the much people that were with him. (41) And Pharaoh, like the god Sutekh, the glorious, cast them down and slew them. And I the king flung them down head over heels, one after the other, into the water of the Arantha. I (42) subdued all the people, and yet I was alone, for my warriors and my charioteers had left me in the lurch. None of them stood (by me). Then the king of Khita raised his hands to pray before me.

'(43-44) I swear it as truly as the Sun-god loves me, as truly as my father, the god Tum, blesses me, that all the deeds which I the king have related, these I truly performed before my army, and before my charioteers.'

About two years after the events which we have

just described, Pentaur, the Theban poet, had finished his heroic song. The fact that it was engraved on the temple walls, and on the hard stone, may serve as a proof of the recognition which was accorded to the poet by the king and his contemporaries. And, indeed, even our own age will hardly refuse to applaud this work, although a translation cannot reach the power and beauty of the original. Throughout the poem the peculiar cast of thought of the Egyptian poet fourteen centuries before Christ shines out continually in all its fulness, and confirms our opinion that the Mosaic language exhibits to us an exact counterpart of the Egyptian mode of speech. The whole substance of thought in minds living at the same time, and in society with each other, must needs have tended towards the same conception and form, even though the idea which the one had of God was essentially different from the views of the other concerning the nature of the Creator of all things.

We cannot forego the opportunity of rendering with all fidelity, and laying before our readers in an (English) garb, the contents of this wonderful document, precious alike for its form and as a record. With this object, we have repeatedly compared with one another the copies extant on the monuments, and, as the foundation of all, we have given the preference to the well-known papyrus of the British Museum. Following the example of E. de Rougé, we have, however, transposed to a suitable place the little episode which relates to the charioteer Menna.

THE HEROIC POEM OF PENTAUR.[8]

'Beginning of the victory of king Ramses Miamun—may he live for ever!—which he obtained over the people of the Khita, of Naharain, of Malunna, of Pidasa, of the Dardani, over the people of Masa, of Karkisha, of Qasuatan, of Qarkemish, of Kati, of Anaugas, over the people of Akerith and Mushanath.

'The youthful king with the bold hand has not his equal. His arms are powerful, his heart is firm, his courage is like that of the god of war, Monthu, in the midst [of the fight. He leads] his warriors to unknown peoples. He seizes his weapons, and is a wall [of iron for his warriors], their shield in the day of battle. He seizes his bow, and no man offers opposition. Mightier than a hundred thousand united together goes he forwards . . . .
. . . . . . His courage is firm like that of a bull which seizes [the
. . . . . . He has smitten] all peoples who had united themselves together. No man knows the thousands of men who stood against him. A hundred thousand sank before his glance. Terrible is he when his war-cry resounds; bolder than the whole world; [dreadful] as the grim lion in the valley of the gazelles. His command [will be performed. No opponent dares] to speak against him. Wise is his counsel. Complete are his decisions, when he wears the royal crown Atef and declares his will, a protector of his people [against unrighteousness]. His heart is like a mountain of iron. Such is king Ramses Miamun.

'After the king had armed his people and his chariots, and in like manner the Shardonians, which were once his prisoners . . . .
. . . then was the order given them for the battle. The king took his way downwards, and his people and his chariots accompanied him, and followed the best road on their march.

'In the fifth year, on the ninth day of the month Payni, the fortress of Khetam (Etham) of the land of Zar opened to the king . . . . . As if he had been the god of war, Monthu himself, the whole world trembled [at his approach], and terror seized all enemies who came near to bow themselves before the king. And his warriors passed by the path of the desert, and went on along the roads of the north.

---

[8] A translation of this poem by Professor E. L. Lushington, is given in *Records of the Past*, vol. ii. pp. 65, foll.—ED.

'Many days after this the king was in the city of Ramses Miamun [which is situated in Zahi]. After the king had marched upwards, he reached ..... and arrived as far as Kadesh. Then the king passed by in their sight like his father Monthu, the lord of Thebes. He marched through the valley of the river Arunatha, (with him) the first legion of Amon, who secures victory to the king Ramses Miamun. And when the king approached the city, behold there was the miserable king of the hostile Khita (already) arrived. He had assembled with him all the peoples from the uttermost ends of the sea to the people of the Khita. They had arrived in great numbers : the people of Naharain, the people of Arathu, of the Dardani, the Masu, the Pidasa, the Malunna, the Karkish (or Kashkish), the Leka, Qazuadana, Kirkamish, Akarith, Kati, the whole people of Anaugas every one of them, Mushanath, and Kadesh. He had left no people on his road without bringing them with him. Their number was endless; nothing like it had ever been before. They covered mountains and valleys like grasshoppers for their number. He had not left silver nor gold with his people; he had taken away all their goods and possessions, to give it to the people who accompanied him to the war.

' Now had the miserable king of the hostile Khita and the many peoples which were with him hidden themselves in an ambush to the north-west of the city of Kadesh, while Pharaoh was alone, no other was with him. The legion of Amon advanced behind him. The legion of Phra went into the ditch on the territory which lies to the west of the town of Shabatuna, divided by a long interval from the legion of Ptah, in the midst, [in the direction] towards the town of Arnama. The legion of Sutekh marched on by their roads. And the king called together all the chief men of his warriors. Behold, they were at the lake of the land of the Amorites. At the same time the miserable king of Khita was in the midst of his warriors, which were with him. But his hand was not so bold as to venture on battle with Pharaoh. Therefore he drew away the horsemen and the chariots, which were numerous as the sand. And they stood three men on each war-chariot, and there were assembled in one spot the best heroes of the army of Khita, well appointed with all weapons for the fight. They did not dare to advance. They stood in ambush to the north-west of the town of Kadesh. Then they went out from Kadesh, on the side of the south, and threw themselves into the midst of the legion of

Pra-Hormakhu, which gave way, and was not prepared for the fight. There Pharaoh's warriors and chariots gave way before them. And Pharaoh had placed himself to the north of the town of Kadesh, on the west side of the river Arunatha. Then they came to tell the king. Then the king arose, like his father Month; he grasped his weapons and put on his armour, just like Baal in his time. And the noble pair of horses which carried Pharaoh, and whose name was 'Victory in Thebes,' they were from the court of King Ramses Miamun. When the king had quickened his course, he rushed into the midst of the hostile hosts of Khita, all alone, no other was with him. When Pharaoh had done this, he looked behind him and found himself surrounded by 2,500 pairs of horses, and his retreat was beset by the bravest heroes of the king of the miserable Khita, and by all the numerous peoples which were with him, of Arathu, of Masu, of Pidasa, of Keshkesh, of Malunna, of Qazauadana, of Khilibu, of Akerith, of Kadesh, and of Leka. And there were three men on each chariot, and they were all gathered together.

'And not one of my princes, not one of my captains of the chariots, not one of my chief men, not one of my knights was there. My warriors and my chariots had abandoned me, not one of them was there to take part in the battle.

'Thereupon speaks Pharaoh: "Where art thou, my father Amon? If this means that the father has forgotten his son, behold have I done anything without thy knowledge, or have I not gone and followed the judgments of thy mouth? Never were the precepts of thy mouth transgressed, nor have I broken thy commands in any respect. The noble lord and ruler of Egypt, should he bow himself before the foreign peoples in his way? Whatever may be the intention of these herdsmen, Amon should stand higher than the miserable one who knows nothing of God. Shall it have been for nothing that I have dedicated to thee many and noble monuments, that I have filled thy temples with my prisoners of war, that I have built to thee temples to last many thousands of years, that I have given to thee all my substance as household furniture, that the whole united land has been ordered to pay tribute to thee, that I have dedicated to thee sacrifices of ten thousands of oxen, and of all good and sweet-smelling woods? Never did I withhold my hand from doing that which thy wish required. I have built for thee propyla and wonderful works of stone, I have raised to thee masts for all times, I have conveyed obelisks for thee from the island of Elephantiné. It was I who had brought for thee the everlasting stone, who caused the ships to go for thee on the sea, to bring thee the productions of foreign nations. Where has it been told that such a thing was done at any other time? Let him be put to shame who rejects thy commands, but good be to him who acknowledges thee, O Amon! I have acted for thee with a willing heart; therefore I call on thee. Behold now, Amon, I am in the midst of many unknown peoples in great numbers. All have united themselves, and I am all alone; no other is with me; my warriors and my charioteers have deserted me. I called to them, and not one of them heard my voice. But I find that Amon is better to me than millions of warriors, than hundreds of thousands of horses, than tens of thousands of brothers and sons, even if they were all united together in one place. The works of a multitude of men are nothing; Amon is better than they. What has happened to me here is according to the command of thy mouth, O Amon, and I will not transgress thy command. Behold I call upon thee at the uttermost ends of the world."

'And my voice found an echo in Hermonthis, and Amon heard it and came at my cry. He reached out his hand to me, and I shouted for joy. He called out to me from behind: "I have hastened to thee, Ramses Miamun. I am with thee. I am he, thy father, the sun-god Ra. My hand is with thee. Yes! I am worth more than hundreds of thousands united in one place. I am the lord of victory, the friend of valour; I have found in thee a right spirit, and my heart rejoices thereat."

'All this came to pass. I was changed, being made like the god Monthu. I hurled the dart with my right hand, I fought with my left hand. I was like Baal in his time before their sight. I had found 2,500 pairs of horses; I was in the midst of them; but they were dashed in pieces before my horses. Not one of them raised his hand to fight; their courage was sunken in their breasts, their limbs gave way, they could not hurl the dart, nor had they the courage to thrust with the spear. I made them fall into the waters just as the crocodiles fall in. They tumbled down on their faces one after another. I killed them at my pleasure, so that not one looked back behind him, nor did another turn round. Each one fell, he raised himself not up again.

'There stood still the miserable king of Khita in the midst of his warriors and his chariots, to behold the fight of the king. He was all alone; not one of his warriors, not one of his chariots was with him. There he turned round for fright before the king. Thereupon he sent the princes in great numbers, each of them with his chariot, well equipped with all kinds of offensive weapons: the king of Arathu and him of Masa, the king of Malunna and him of Leka, the king of the Dardani and him of Keshkesh, the king of Qarqamash and him of Khilibu. There were all together the brothers of the king of Khita united in one place, to the number of 2,500 pairs of horses. They forthwith rushed right on, their countenance directed to the flame of fire (i.e. my face).

'I rushed down upon them. Like Monthu was I. I let them taste my hand in the space of a moment. I dashed them down, and killed them where they stood. Then cried out one of them to his neighbour, saying, "This is no man. Ah! woe to us! He who is in our midst is Sutekh, the glorious; Baal is in all his limbs. Let us hasten and flee before him. Let us save our lives; let us try our breath." As soon as any one attacked him, his hand fell down and every limb of his body. They could not aim either the bow or the spear. They only looked at him as he came on in his headlong career from afar. The king was behind them like a griffin.

'(Thus speaks the king):—

'I struck them down; they did not escape me. I lifted up my voice to my warriors and to my charioteers, and spake to them, "Halt! stand! take courage, my warriors, my charioteers! Look upon my victory. I am alone, but Amon is my helper, and his hand is with me."

'When Menna, my charioteer, beheld with his eyes how many pairs of horses surrounded me, his courage left him, and his heart was afraid. Evident terror and great fright took possession of his whole body. Immediately he spake to me: "My gracious lord, thou brave king, thou guardian of the Egyptians in the day of battle, protect us. We stand alone in the midst of enemies. Stop, to save the breath of life for us. Give us deliverance, protect us, O King Ramses Miamun."

'Then spake the king to his charioteer: "Halt! stand! take courage, my charioteer. I will dash myself down among them as the sparrow-hawk dashes down. I will slay them, I will cut them in pieces, I will dash them to the ground in the dust. Why, then, is such a thought in thy heart? These are unclean ones for Amon, wretches who do not acknowledge the god."

'And the king hurried onwards. He charged down upon the hostile hosts of Khita. For the sixth time, when he charged upon them, (says the king) "There was I like to Baal behind them in his time, when he has strength. I killed them; none escaped me."

'And the king cried to his warriors, and to his chariot-fighters, and likewise to his princes, who had taken no part in the fight, "Miserable is your courage, my chariot-fighters. Of no profit is it to have you for friends. If there had been only one of you who had shown himself a good (warrior?) for my country! If I had not stood firm as your royal lord, you had been conquered. I exalt you daily to be princes. I place the son in the inheritance of his father, warding off all injury from the land of the Egyptians, and you forsake me! Such servants are worthless. I made you rich, I was your protecting lord, and each of you who complained supplicating to me, I gave him protection in his affairs every day. No Pharaoh has done for his people what I have done for you. I allowed you to remain in your villages and in your towns. Neither the captain nor his chariot-horses did any work. I pointed out to them the road from their city, that they might find it in like manner at the day and at the hour at which the battle comes on. Now behold! A bad service altogether has been performed for me. None of you stood by, ready to stretch out his hand to me when I fought. By the name of my father Amon! O that I may be for Egypt like my father, the sun-god Ra! Not a single one of you would watch, to attend to what concerns his duty in the land of Egypt. For such ought to be the good kind of men, who have been entrusted with work for the memorial-places in Thebes, the city of Amon. This is a great fault which my warriors and chariot-fighters have committed, greater than it is possible to describe. Now behold, I have achieved the victory. No warrior and no chariot-fighter was with me. The whole world from afar beholds the strength of my arm. I was all alone. No other was with me. No prince was by my side, of the captains of the chariots, no captain of the soldiers, nor any horseman. The foreign peoples were eye-witnesses of this. They publish my name to the furthest and most unknown regions. All the combatants whom my hand left surviving, they stood there, turning themselves to wonder at what I did; and though millions of them had been there, they would not have kept their feet, but would have run away. For every one who shot an arrow aimed at me, his own weapon failed, which should have reached me."

'When now my warriors and my charioteers saw that I was named like Monthu of the victorious arm, and that Amon my father was with me, and the special favour he had done for me, and that the foreigners all lay like hay before my horses, then they came forward one after another out of the camp at the time of evening, and found all the people which had come against them, the best combatants of the people of Khita, and of the sons and brothers of their king, stretched out and weltering in their blood. And when it was light on the (next morning) in the plain of the land of Kadesh, one could hardly find a place for his foot on account of their multitude.

'Then came my warriors forward to praise highly my name, full of astonishment at what I had done. My princes came forward to honour my courage, and my chariot-fighters also to praise my strength.

'" How wast thou, great champion of firm courage, the saviour of thy warriors and of thy chariot-fighters! Thou son of Amon, who came forth out of the hands of the god, thou hast annihilated the people of Khita by thy powerful arm. Thou art a good champion, a lord of victory; no other king fights as thou dost for his warriors in the day of battle. Thou, O bold one, art the first in the fight. The whole world united in one place does not trouble thee. Thou art the greatest conqueror at the head of thy warriors in the sight of the whole world. No one dares to contend with thee. Thou art he who protects the Egyptians, who chastises the foreigners. Thou hast broken the neck of Khita for everlasting times."

'Thereupon the king answered his warriors and his chariot-fighters, and likewise his princes: "My warriors, my charioteers, who have not taken part in the fight, a man does not succeed in obtaining honour in his city unless he comes and exhibits his prowess before his lord, the king. Good will be his name, if he is brave in the battle. By deeds, by deeds, will such a one obtain the applause [of the land]. Have I not given what is good to each of you, that ye have left me, so that I was alone in the midst of hostile hosts? Forsaken by you, my life was in peril, and you breathed tranquilly, and I was alone. Could you not have said in your hearts that I was a rampart of iron to you? Will any one obey him who leaves me in the lurch when I am alone without any follower? when nobody comes, of the princes, of the knights, and of the chief men of the army, to reach me out his hand? I was alone thus fighting, and I have withstood millions of foreigners, I all alone.

'" 'Victory in Thebes,' and ' Mut is satisfied,' my pair of horses, it was they who found me, to strengthen my hand, when I was all alone in the midst of the raging multitude of hostile hosts. I will myself henceforth have their fodder given to them for their nourishment in my presence, when I shall dwell in the palace, because I have found them in the midst of hostile hosts, together with the captain of the horsemen, Menna, my charioteer, out of the band of the trusted servants in the palace, who stay near me. Here are the eye-witnesses of the battle. Behold, these did I find."

'The king returned in victory and strength; he had smitten hundreds of thousands all together in one place with his arm.

'When the earth was (again) light, he arranged the hosts of warriors for the fight, and he stood there prepared for the battle, like a bull which has whetted his horns. He appeared to them a likeness of the god Monthu, who has armed himself for the battle. Likewise his brave warriors, who dashed into the fight, just as the hawk swoops down upon the kids.

'The diadem of the royal snake adorned my head. It spat fire and glowing flame in the face of my enemies. I appeared like the sun-god at his rising in the early morning. My shining beams were a consuming fire for the limbs of the wicked. They cried out to one another, " Take care, do not fall! For the powerful snake of royalty, which accompanies him, has placed itself on his horse. It helps him. Every one who comes in his way and falls down, there comes forth fire and flame to consume his body."

'And they remained afar off, and threw themselves down on the earth, to entreat the king in the sight [of his army]. And the king had power over them and slew them without their being able to escape. As bodies tumbled before his horses, so they lay there stretched out all together in their blood.

'Then the king of the hostile people of Khita sent a messenger to pray piteously to the great name of the king, speaking thus: "Thou art Ra-Hormakhu. Thou art Sutekh the glorious, the son of Nut, Baal in his time. Thy terror is upon the land of Khita, for thou hast broken the neck of Khita for ever and ever."

'Thereupon he allowed his messenger to enter. He bore a writing in his hand with the address, "To the great double-name of the king" (and thus it ran):

'"May this suffice for the satisfaction of the heart of the holiness of the royal house, the Sun-Horus, the mighty Bull, who loves justice, the great lord, the protector of his people, the brave with his arm, the rampart of his life-guards in the day of battle, the king Ramses Miamun.

'"The servant speaks, he makes known to Pharaoh, my gracious lord, the beautiful son of Ra-Hormakhu, as follows:

'"Since thou art the son of Amon, from whose body thou art sprung, so has he granted to thee all the peoples together.

'"The people of Egypt and the people of Khita ought to be brothers together as thy servants. Let them be at thy feet. The sun-god Ra has granted thee the best [inhabitants of the earth]. Do us no injury, glorious spirit, whose anger weighs upon the people of Khita.

'"Would it be good if thou shouldst wish to kill thy servants, whom thou hast brought under thy power? Thy look is terrible, and thou art not mildly disposed. Calm thyself. Yesterday thou camest and hast slain hundreds of thousands. Thou comest to-day, and—none will be left remaining [to serve thee].

'"Do not carry out thy purpose, thou mighty king. Better is peace than war. Give us freedom."

'Then the king turned back in a gentle humour, like his father Monthu in his time, and Pharaoh assembled all the leaders of the army and of the chariot-fighters and of the life-guards. And when they were all assembled together in one place, they were permitted to hear the contents of the message which the great king of Khita had sent to him. [When they had heard] these words, which the messenger of the king of Khita had brought as his embassy to Pharaoh, then they answered and spake thus to the king:

'"Excellent, excellent is that! Let thy anger pass away, O great lord our king! He who does not accept peace must offer it. Who would content thee in the day of thy wrath?"

'Then the king gave order to listen to the words of him (the king of Khita), and he let his hands rest, in order to return to the south. Then the king went in peace to the land of Egypt with his princes, with his army, and his charioteers, in serene humour, in the sight of his [people]. All countries feared the power of the king, as of the lord of both the worlds. It had [protected] his own warriors. All peoples came at his name, and their kings fell down to pray before his beautiful countenance. The king reached the city of Ramses Miamun, the great worshipper of Ra-Hormakhu, and rested in his palace in the most serene humour, just like the sun on his throne. And Amon came to greet him, speaking thus to him : " Be thou blessed, thou our son, whom we love, Ramses Miamun ! May they (the gods) secure to him without end many thirty-years' feasts of jubilee for ever on the chair of his father Tum, and may all lands be under his feet!"'

Thus did the poet on the banks of the holy river sing the heroic deed of King Ramses before Kadesh. We are indebted to the Egyptian Homer for full information about this historical event, the knowledge of which was never transmitted by tradition to the memory of men.

The wars of the king in Syria and Canaan certainly did not begin in the fifth year of his reign, in which the great battle of Kadesh took place; but as early as the preceding years Ramses had extended his first campaign as far as these countries. The three celebrated rock-tablets in the neighbourhood of Beyrout—which were as well known to the Greek travellers in the fifth century before our era (they are the *stêlæ* of Sesostris mentioned by Herodotus II. 102), as they are still in our own day the goal of enquiring pilgrims in the land of Palestine—testify to the presence of king Ramses at this very place in the second year and first campaign, and in the fifth year and second campaign, of his reign.

After peace had been made with the Khita, their frontiers were henceforth spared, although several cities could not prevail upon themselves to acknowledge the Egyptian supremacy. In one of these, 'Tunep, in the land of Naharain,' where Ramses had set up his effigies as visible memorials of his campaigns against Khita, the opposition of the population assumed such a serious aspect, that Ramses saw himself obliged to lead his army and his chariots in person against Tunep. The memorial inscription preserved in the Ramesseum at Thebes, unfortunately destroyed in its upper part, describes this campaign in the following terms:—

'[There arose a new ?] war, which was against a city of Khita, in which the two statues of Pharaoh were set up. The king had reduced them [under his power. Then the king assembled] his warriors and his chariots, and gave orders to his warriors and his chariots [to attack] the hostile Khita, who were in the neighbourhood of the city of Tunep, in the land of Naharain. And the king put on his armour [and mounted his chariot]. He stood there in the battle against the town of the hostile Khita at the head of his warriors, and of his [chariots. His] armour was upon him. And the king came again to take his armour, and to put it on. [And he utterly smote] the hostile Khita, who were in the neighbourhood of the city of Tunep in the land of Naharain. After that he no more put on his armour.'

In the eighth year we again find the king on the soil of the land of Canaan, where, in the territory of what was afterwards Galilee, as well as in the neighbourhood of that ill-famed country, the inhabitants mocked at Pharaoh's highness, and at length tired out his patience. They were punished by the capture of their fortresses; and their kings and elders, together with the men capable of bearing arms, were carried away to the land of Kemi, after the Egyptian warriors had grossly insulted them, beaten them, and, in token of shame, had plucked out the long beards of the Canaanites. The representation of the conquest of the fortresses had its place on the northern flanking-tower at the corner of the west side of the temple of Ramses on the west side of Thebes. An inscription was annexed to every fortress, beginning with the words, ' This is the city which the king took in the eighth year,' to which the particular designation of the place was added. In what has been preserved we can make out the names: Shalama (that is the town of peace), the place Salem, or Salcim, to the south of Scythopolis; Maroma, that is Merom; 'Ain-'Anamim, that is, Anim or Engannim; ' Dapur in the land of the Amorites,' the well-known fortress on Mount Tabor; ' the town Kalopu, on the mountain of Beitha-Antha,' that is, the Bethanath of Scripture, in the land of Cabul.

That Ramses was the ruling lord ' of the foreign peoples of Singara and Khita,' that he had conquered, and probably also had occupied, the greater number of their cities, is proved especially by the names of the conquered places which the monuments of Ramses at Karnak exhibit, and the appearance of which entirely corresponds with the appellations of the places of the Khita in the list of nations of Thutmes III. I may adduce as examples Qa-sa-na-litha, Qa-li-pa, Khi-ri-za, Pa-rihi, Ab-el, Qa-ro-ma-na, Qa-si-ri-ba-na, Sha-ma-sha-na, Ri-hu-za, Sa-a-bi-tha, Ka-za-a, Qa-sa-ri-'a, Qau-zas, Ka-ri-ka, Qa-ma-sa-pui, A-zar or A-zal.

As in the north, so also in the south, the wars against the cities of Canaan called into play all the warlike activity of Ramses. Here above all the storming of As-qa-li-na, that is, Askalon, appeared to the Egyptians a great exploit, worthy of being perpetuated by a representation on the stone walls of the temple of Karnak.

The fortress of Askalon, which in the time of Joshua was counted among the five princely cities of the Philistines, lay on the Mediterranean Sea, in a fertile district. It was strongly fortified, and belonged sometimes to the Syrians and sometimes to the Egyptians, according as the one or the other held the supremacy of the lands and peoples of Western Asia. According to our Egyptian representation, it was situated on a height, and was inhabited by pure Canaanites, who outwardly differed in nothing from the rest of the inhabitants of Ruthen. The attack of Pharaoh, who, in his court-chariot, drawn by his pair of horses called 'Amon-neb-nakhto,' that is, 'Amon is the lord of victory,' personally directed his warriors, resulted in a speedy capture by storm. The warriors of Pharaoh mounted the walls of the city on ladders, and beat in the barricaded doors with bright axes. Men and women are trying to appease the victors by their prayers. The king of 'the miserable city' acknowledges his fault with the words: 'He rejoices, who acts according to thy will, but woe to him who transgresses thy boundaries. We will make known thy glory to all the nations who know not Egypt.'

Thus was Askalon punished for its revolt from Egypt, and again subjected to the sceptre of Pharaoh.

This seems to have been the only instance in the ancient history of Egypt, in which Askalon broke faith with the house of Pharaoh.

As a consequence of the wars of king Ramses in Western Asia, besides the booty (about which, however, the inscriptions are silent), a great number of prisoners were transplanted to the valley of the Nile. On the front wall of the temple of Luqsor, behind the obelisks and the splendid sitting figures of the king, there is a scene relating to this, with the superscription, ' Catalogue of the princes of the people of Khita, whom Pharaoh has brought back as living prisoners, to fill the house of his father Amon, and of the people of the Dardani, of Pidasa, and others.' As leaders of the band of the prisoners there appear the king's sons, who had taken part in the campaign against Khita, and had distinguished themselves at the storming of Tabor : Amon-hi-khopesh-ef, Kha-m-us, Miamun, and Seti. The foreigners are brought by the Pharaoh in person to the god Amon ; and, as usual, the action is designated as the 'bringing of the prisoners from all countries to which the king has come, to bind them, and whom the king has conquered. He brings their inhabitants with him as living prisoners, to fill with them the house of his father Amon.'

While Ramses in the representations and inscriptions, so far as they have escaped the destructive hand of man and the all-devouring tooth of time, appears before our sight as a champion of the first rank on land, fighting on his war chariot, represented in heroic form, with his warriors by his side, and his grown-up sons accompanying him,[9] in the face of a great confederacy of nations whose representatives belong to the most distant and unknown lands,—it is, on the other hand, beyond doubt that his campaigns were also carried on by water, and that his ships measured themselves in sea-fights with the most powerful maritime nations, for the dominion of the sea. A short but precious notice on the long rock-tablet (without date) on the outside of the temple of Abusimbel (or rather Ibsamboul), places this fact apparently beyond doubt. Unfortunately, the extant monuments contain no other indications which might serve as a further support for a fact of such historical importance.

The increasing movements of the nations, and the growing troubles in Canaan, the pushing forward of whole races in Western Asia, owing to the immigration of warlike tribes of foreign origin, seem to have attracted the serious attention of the kings of Khita, as well as of the Egyptian Pharaoh. The then lord of Khita, Khita-sir, was the first to make to his Egyptian friend the proposal, written on a tablet of silver, for an offensive and defensive alliance. Ramses II. was prudent enough not to refuse such a proposal, and a treaty was made, which laid the foundation of the intimate friendship, so often mentioned by the chroniclers of the time, between the two great empires of Asia and Africa.

---

[9] The presence of these grown-up sons will prove to a French scholar that Ramses II. could not have fought at Kadesh as *a boy of ten years old.*—[A bas-relief at Abusimbel, representing Ramses the Great in battle, followed by six of his sons on three

The historical account of this treaty has been handed down to us in a clear and intelligible manner, although with some breaks. The inscription concerning it, the translation of which we now give, will make our readers acquainted with the contents of this remarkable document better than any further explanation : [1]—

'OFFENSIVE AND DEFENSIVE ALLIANCE BETWEEN KHITA AND KEMI.

' In the year 21, in the month Tybi, on the 21st day of the month, in the reign of King Ramessu Miamun, the dispenser of life eternally and for ever, the worshipper of the divinities Amon-ra (of Thebes), Hormakhu (of Heliopolis), Ptah (of Memphis), Mut, the lady of the Asher-lake (near Karnak), and Khonsu, the peace-loving, there took place a public sitting on the throne of Horus among the living, resembling his father Hormakhu in eternity, in eternity, evermore.

' On that day the king was in the city of Ramses, presenting his peace-offerings to his father Amon-ra, and to the gods Hormakhu-Tum, the lord of Heliopolis, and to Amon of Ramessu Miamun, to Ptah of Ramessu Miamun, and to Sutekh, the strong, the son of the goddess of heaven Nut, that they might grant to him many thirty years' jubilee feasts, and innumerable happy years, and the subjection of all peoples under his feet for ever.

' Then came forward the ambassador of the king, and the Adon [of his house, by name . . . . . , and presented the ambassadors] of the great king of Khita, Khitasir, who were sent to Pharaoh to propose friendship with the king Ramessu Miamun, the dispenser of life eternally and for ever, just as his father the Sun-god [dispenses it] each day.

' This is the copy of the contents of the silver tablet, which the great king of Khita, Khitasir, had caused to be made, and which was presented to the Pharaoh by the hand of his ambassador Tar-

chariots, is engraved from a sketch by Mr. Villiers Stuart, *Nile Gleanings*, Pl. XIII. p. 176.—ED.]

[1] This treaty has been translated by Mr. C. W. Goodwin, in *Records of the Past*, vol. iv. p. 25, foll.—ED.

thi-sebu and his ambassador Ra-mes, to propose friendship with the king Ramessu Miamun, the bull among the princes, who places his boundary-marks where it pleases him in all lands.

'The treaty which had been proposed by the great king of Khita, Khitasir, the powerful, the son of Maro-sir, the great king of Khita, the powerful, the son of the son of Sapa-li-li, the great king of Khita, the powerful, on the silver tablet, to Ramessu Miamun, the great prince of Egypt, the powerful, the son of Mineptah Seti, the great prince of Egypt, the powerful, the son's son of Ramessu I., the great king of Egypt, the powerful,—this was a good treaty for friendship and concord, which assured peace [and established concord] for a longer period than was previously the case, since a long time. For it was the agreement of the great prince of Egypt in common with the great king of Khita, that the god should not allow enmity to exist between them, on the basis of a treaty.

'To wit, in the times of Mau-than-er, the great king of Khita, my brother, he was at war with [Mineptah Seti] the great prince of Egypt.

'But now, from this very day forward, Khitasir, the great king of Khita, shall look upon this treaty, so that the agreement may remain, which the god Ra has made, which the god Sutekh has made, for the people of Egypt and for the people of Khita, that there should be no enmity between them for evermore.

'And these are the contents :—

'Khitasir, the great king of Khita, is in covenant with Ramessu Miamun, the great prince of Egypt, from this very day forward, that there may subsist a good friendship and a good understanding between them for evermore.

'He shall be my ally; he shall be my friend :

'I will be his ally; I will be his friend : for ever.

'To wit, in the time of Mau-than-er, the great king of Khita, his brother, after his murder, Khita-sir placed himself on the throne of his father as the great king of Khita. I strove for friendship with Ramessu Miamun, the great prince of Egypt, and it is [my wish] that the friendship and the concord may be better than the friendship and the concord which before existed, and which was broken.

'I declare : I, the great king of Khita, will hold together with [Ramessu Miamun], the great prince of Egypt, in good friendship and in good concord. The sons of the sons of the great king of Khita will hold together and be friends with the sons of the sons of Ramessu Miamun, the great prince of Egypt.

'In virtue of our treaty for concord, and in virtue of our agreement [for friendship, let the people] of Egypt [be bound in friendship] with the people of Khita. Let a like friendship and a like concord subsist in such measure for ever.

'Never let enmity rise between them. Never let the great king of Khita invade the land of Egypt, if anything shall have been plundered from it (the land of Khita).[2] Never let Ramessu Miamun, the great prince of Egypt, overstep the boundary of the land [of Khita, if anything shall have been plundered] from it (the land of Egypt).

'The just treaty, which existed in the times of Sapa-li-li, the great king of Khita, likewise the just treaty which existed in the times of Mau-than-er, the great king of Khita, my brother, that will I keep.

'Ramessu Miamun, the great prince of Egypt, declares that he will keep it. [We have come to an understanding about it] with one another at the same time from this day forward, and we will fulfil it, and will act in a righteous manner.

'If another shall come as an enemy to the lands of Ramessu Miamun, the great prince of Egypt, then let him send an embassy to the great king of Khita to this effect : "Come! and make me stronger than him." Then shall the great king of Khita [assemble his warriors], and the king of Khita [shall come] and smite his enemies. But if it should not be the wish of the great king of Khita to march out in person, then he shall send his warriors and his chariots, that they may smite his enemies. Otherwise [he would incur] the wrath of Ramessu Miamun, [the great prince of Egypt. And if Ramessu Miamun, the great prince of Egypt, should banish for a crime] subjects from his country, and they should commit another crime against him, then shall he (the king of Khita) come forward to kill them. The great king of Khita shall act in common with [the great prince of Egypt].

'[If another should come as an enemy to the lands of the great king of Khita, then shall he send an embassy to the great prince of Egypt with the request that] he would come in great

---

[2] Mr. Goodwin has, 'to carry away anything from it (Egypt),' and so *vice versâ* in the next clause.—ED.

power to kill his enemies; and if it be the intention of Ramessu Miamun, the great prince of Egypt, (himself) to come, he shall [smite the enemies of the great king of Khita. If it is not the intention of the great prince of Egypt to march out in person, then he shall send his warriors and his two-] horse chariots, while he sends back the answer to the people of Khita.

'If any subjects of the great king of Khita have offended him, then Ramessu Miamun, [the great prince of Egypt, shall not receive them in his land, but shall advance to kill them] . . . . . . the oath, with the wish to say: I will go . . . until . . . Ramessu Miamun, the great prince of Egypt, living for ever . . . . their . . . that he may be given for them (?) to the lord, and that Ramessu Miamun, the great prince of Egypt, may speak according to his agreement evermore. . . . . .

'[If servants shall flee away] out of the territories of Ramessu Miamun, the great prince of Egypt, to betake themselves to the great king of Khita, the great king of Khita shall not receive them, but the great king of Khita shall give them up to Ramessu Miamun, the great prince of Egypt, [that they may receive their punishment.

'If servants of Ramessu Miamun, the great prince of Egypt, leave his country], and betake themselves to the land of Khita, to make themselves servants of another, they shall not remain in the land of Khita, [they shall be given up] to Ramessu Miamun, the great prince of Egypt.

'If on the other hand there should flee away [servants of the great king of Khita, in order to betake themselves to] Ramessu Miamun, the great prince of Egypt, [in order to stay in Egypt], then those who have come from the land of Khita in order to betake themselves to Ramessu Miamun, the great prince of Egypt, shall not be [received by] Ramessu Miamun, the great prince of Egypt, [but] the great prince of Egypt, Ramessu Miamun, [shall deliver them up to the great king of Khita].

'[And if there shall leave the land of Khita persons] of skilful mind, so that they come to the land of Egypt to make themselves servants of another, then Ramessu Miamun will not allow them to settle, he will deliver them up to the great king of Khita.

'When this [treaty] shall be known [by the inhabitants of the land of Egypt and of the land of Khita, then shall they not offend against it, for all that stands written on] the silver tablet, these are words which will have been approved by the company of the gods among the male gods and among the female gods, among those namely of the land of Khita, and by the company of the gods among the male gods and among the female gods, among those namely of the land of Egypt. They are witnesses for me [to the validity] of these words, [which they have allowed.

'This is the catalogue of the gods of the land of Khita:
 Sutekh, of the city] of Tunep (Daphne),
 Sutekh, of the land of Khita,
 Sutekh, of the city of Arnema,
 Sutekh, of the city of Zaranda,
 Sutekh, of the city of Pilqa,
 Sutekh, of the city of Khissap,
 Sutekh, of the city of Sarsu,
 Sutekh, of the city of Khilbu (Haleb),
 Sutekh, of the city of . . . . .
 . . . .
 Sutekh, of the city of Sarpina,
 Astartha, of the land of Khita,
 The god of the land of Zaiath-khirri,
 The god of the land of Ka . . . .
 The god of the land of Kher . . . .
 The goddess of the city of Akh . . . .
 [The goddess of the city of] . . . and of the land of A . . ua,
 The goddess of the land of Zaina,
 The god of the land of . . . nath . . . cr.

'[I have invoked these male and these] female [gods of the land of Khita, those are the gods] of the land, [as witnesses to] my oath. [With them have been associated the male and the female gods] of the mountains, and of the rivers of the land of Khita, the gods of the land of Qazauadana (Gauzanitis), Amon, Pra, Sutekh, and the male and the female gods of the land of Egypt, of the earth, of the sea, of the winds, and of the storms.

'With regard to the commandment which the silver tablet contains for the people of Khita and for the people of Egypt, he who shall not observe it shall be given over [to the vengeance] of the company of the gods of Khita, and shall be given over [to the vengeance] of the company of the gods of Egypt, [he] and his house and his servants.

'But he who shall observe these commandments, which the

silver tablet contains, whether he be of the people of Khita or [of the people of the Egyptians], because he has not neglected them, the company of the gods of the land of Khita and the company of the gods of the land of Egypt shall secure his reward and preserve life [for him] and his servants and those who are with him, and who are with his servants.

'If there flee away of the inhabitants [one from the land of Egypt], or two or three, and they betake themselves to the great king of Khita, [the great king of Khita shall not] allow them [to remain, but he shall] deliver them up, and send them back to Ramessu Miamun, the great prince of Egypt.

'Now with respect to the [inhabitant of the land of Egypt], who is delivered up to Ramessu Miamun, the great prince of Egypt, his fault shall not be avenged upon him, his [house] shall not be taken away, nor his [wife] nor his [children]. There shall not be [put to death his mother, neither shall he be punished in his eyes, nor on his mouth, nor on the soles of his feet], so that thus no crime shall be brought forward against him.

'In the same way shall it be done, if inhabitants of the land of Khita take to flight, be it one alone, or two, or three, to betake themselves to Ramessu Miamun, the great prince of Egypt. Ramessu Miamun, the great prince of Egypt, shall cause them to be seized, and they shall be delivered up to the great king of Khita.

'[With regard to] him who [is delivered up, his crime shall not be brought forward against him]. His [house] shall not be taken away, nor his wives, nor his children, nor his people; his mother shall not be put to death, he shall not be punished in his eyes, nor on his mouth, nor on the soles of his feet, nor shall any accusation be brought forward against him.

'That which is in the middle of this silver tablet and on its front side is a likeness of the god Sutekh . . . . surrounded by an inscription to this effect : " This is the [picture] of the god Sutekh, the king of heaven and [earth]." At the time (?) of the treaty, which Khitasir, the great king of Khita, made.' . . . . . .[3]

In such a form were peace and friendship made at Ramses, the city in Lower Egypt, between the two

[3] The two following lines of the conclusion are in fact too much destroyed to enable us to find out any connection between them and the parts which have been preserved.

most powerful nations of the world at that time, Khita in the East, and Kemi in the West. It was to be hoped that the new offensive and defensive alliance, which united the princes and countries in the manner thus described, would attain its end, and bridle the fermenting restless mass of the people of the Canaanites, which lay between them, and keep down every rising and movement of the hostilely disposed Semites, and confine them within the limits once for all fixed. For that a ferment existed, even in the inmost heart of the Egyptian land, is sufficiently proved by the allusion in the treaty to the evasions of evil-disposed subjects. We may perhaps read between the lines that the Jewish people are meant, who, since their migration into the land of Egypt, had increased beyond measure, and without doubt were already making preparations to withdraw themselves from the power of their oppressors on the banks of the Nile. But how? and when?—this was hidden in the councils of the Eternal.

The scribes at the court of Pharaoh at Ramses-Tanis,—and we must not forget that Ramessu Miamun had fixed his court there,—were full of joy at the great event of the conclusion of peace. Their letters, so far as a kind fate has preserved them for us, overflow with high delight that the war was at an end, and that Kemi and Khita had now become fraternal peoples. Their boasting rose to such a pitch of the wonted Egyptian pride, as to assert that king Ramessu had already assumed the position of a god for Khita, and for the regions of the heathen, namely Kati.

As we intend in a later portion of the history of Ramses to lay before our readers in a faithful translation some proofs of Egyptian vain-glory in such matters, we will first give additional confirmation of the proved fact, that Ramses lived in such friendly relations with the king of Khita of his time, that even family alliances were made between the two. According to a memorial tablet which was set up solemnly in the temple of Ibsamboul, and the long inscription on which begins with the date of the year 34 of the reign of Ramessu, the Egyptian king married the daughter of the king of Khita. The prince of Khita, clad in the dress of his country, himself conducted the bride to his son-in-law. After the marriage had taken place, the young wife, as queen, received the name of Ur-maa Nofiru-ra.

When we turn our glance to the West and to the South, we have there also to recognize the military activity of the king, whose successes are celebrated with their wonted fulness by the Nubian monuments, which are the real trophies of the famed Sesostris.

In the temple of Der (or Dirr, as I heard the name always pronounced by the Nubian inhabitants of the district) there is represented a razzia of the king against the poor negroes, whose wives and children behold the irruption of the Pharaoh with affrighted gaze.[4] In like manner the battle-pieces of the rock-grotto of Beit-el-Walli place before our eyes the victories of Pharaoh over the land of Kush, the

[4] Compare Villiers Stuart, *Nile Gleanings*, p. 156.

Thuhen (Marmaridæ), and the Syrian Khalu or Phœnicians. The date of these wars is nowhere given, and it is only the circumstances of the action, and the historical personages of those days, beginning with the king's children, that enable us to form a general conception as to the campaigns in the earlier or later years of the life of Ramessu.

We must imagine, from the written and pictorial testimony on the rock-walls of that temple grotto, that the king had just returned from his campaigns against the people of the South, and held a court in the midst of the temple. He was already covered with glory, for

'The deeds of victory are inscribed a hundred thousand times on the glorious Persea. As the chastiser of the foreigners, who has placed his boundary-marks according to his pleasure in the land of the Ruthennu, he is in truth the son of Ra, and his very likeness.'

Before the king, who is seated on his throne, appears 'the hereditary prince Amen-hi-unamif,' who presents to him a train of captive negroes, and the booty or tributes of leopards' skins, lions, giraffes, antelopes, gazelles, and of gold rings, ivory, and fruits, and other such productions of the South.

The then governor also of the South, the 'king's son of Kush, Amen-em-ape, a son of Pa-uër,' presents himself before his lord and master, in order to be decorated for his honest and successful services with the gold necklace of honour. For a campaign had just been brought to a close, which had subjected the revolted negro tribes anew to the sceptre of Egypt. In its principal battle, Ramses appeared high on his chariot. His son named above, and his pious brother Khamus, accompanied the king.

Here is another court of the king in the South. At his feet lies his faithful attendant, the lion Smam-kheftu-f, 'the tearer to pieces of his enemies.' Here again it is his son, the brave Aman-hi-unamif (i.e., 'Amon is on his right hand'), who, accompanied by Egyptian warriors, brings to the Pharaoh in Nubia some captive Khal-Phœnicians, without doubt for the purpose of being employed as workmen on the buildings which Ramses was erecting there.[5]

The Libyan land also must have yielded her captive children for the same buildings, since we admire the strength of the giant king, who is just giving a Thuhen the death-stroke with his scimitar, called Antha-em-nekh, 'Anaitis is the protector.' Prisoners of the Canaanite tribes are also seen employed on the same work, for the king had carried on wars against them. His own words declare of his victories, 'that henceforth sand is in their dwellings, instead of the fruits of the earth.' Accompanied by one of his sons, he took their chief city, the 'miserable king' of which declares to Sesostris, 'No other is to be compared to Baal as thou art. Thou, O king, art his true son for ever.'

Ramses seems to have subjugated only small tribes

[5] Excellent engravings of these scenes are given by Villiers Stuart, *Nile Gleanings*, Plates XLVI., XLVII., pp. 130, 138. There are casts from the sculptures of Beit-el-Walli in the British Museum. The fighting-lion of Ramses appears also at Der (see p. 78), where the leg of a captive negro in his mouth verifies his name.—ED.

of Ethiopia and Libya, in his campaigns into the interior of the African continent. We learn the names of these incidentally on several monuments: thus, for example, the above-mentioned memorial-stone of Ibsambul cites as conquered people of Africa the Auntom, Hebuu, Tenfu, Temuu, and Hetau (a sixth name is destroyed), whom the Memphian god Ptah-Totunen delivers as subjects into the hands of his son Ramses.[6]

The office of the viceroys of the South continued in full importance during the long reign of this king. The monuments mention to us as such, accompanied by the usual title of honour of 'King's sons of Kush,' the Egyptian lords Pa-uër, Amenemapi, son of Pa-uër, Setau-'an (who was entrusted also with the administration of the gold-mines), Amenemhib, Nakhtu, and Massui.

In order to increase his revenues and fill the treasury of the state, Ramses, following the example of his father Seti, turned his particular attention to the gold districts which had been discovered, and especially to the Nubian gold-mines of what is now the Wady-Alaki (Al-aki), anciently called Aki-ta. But water was wanting in the dreary sterile valleys of this mountainous country, and men and beasts died on the roads to the gold districts. By a curious accident, science is in possession of the old Egyptian map (at

[6] Compare above, the numbers 25, 28, 77, in the list of the tribes of the South under Thutmes III. (Vol. I. chap. xiii.) It is highly probable that the countries and peoples mentioned here scarcely extended beyond Napata. Maiu (No. 4, *ibid.*), for example, is mentioned as in Anibe, in the neighbourhood of Ibrim.

Turin), which enables us to recognize the situation of the mountain tracks, the roads, the places where the gold was found, the wells, and all the other appurtenances and buildings. Here, according to the annexed inscriptions, are 'the mountains out of which the gold was extracted; they are marked with a red colour;' there 'the roads which have been abandoned, leading to the sea:' here 'the houses of . . . . of the gold-washing,' the 'well,' and the 'memorial-stone of king Mineptah I. Seti I. :' there, 'the temple of Amon in the holy mountain.' Nothing is forgotten which could seem calculated to give the spectator an idea of the state of the region, even to the stones and the scattered trees along the roads. Seti I., the gold-seeker, had first worked the gold-mines, but without any remarkable success, as will be shown further on. He made the well named in the inscriptions, and erected near it the memorial-stone of which the inscription on the map speaks. The shaft of the well had a depth of more than 63 yards (120 Egyptian cubits), but the water soon became exhausted, and the mine was abandoned.

It was not till the third year of the reign of King Ramses that the works were opened, which are mentioned with such detail in the inscription given below. The inscription covers a stone which was found at the village of Kouban, opposite Dakkeh, on the eastern bank of the Nubian territory. Here was situated in ancient times a fortified place, provided with walls, trenches, and towers, destined by the Pharaohs for a bulwark against the irruptions of the Nubian tribes.

Inscribed blocks of stone, in the neighbourhood, mention the kings Thutmes III., Horemhib, and Ramses II. This place seems at the same time to have been the point of departure for the communication with the gold-mines, in which the prisoners of war and malefactors were forced to carry on their laborious works under the burning rays of a tropical sun. Even to the time of the Greeks, the remembrance was preserved of their cruel treatment and of the dreadful condition of those condemned to the gold-washings.

We now give the words of the stone inscription itself.[7]

'(1) In the year 3, in the month Tybi, on the fourth day, in the reign of king Ramessu Miamun, the dispenser of life eternally and for ever, the friend of the Theban Amon-Ra of Api.

'(2) A court was held on the throne of Hor (that is, of the king), among the living. Like his father, the everlasting Sungod, the divine benefactor, the lord of the south land, the radiant Hud-Hor, a beautiful golden sparrow-hawk, he has spread out his wings over Egypt, giving shade to the inhabitants in the protecting wall of the strong and victorious. When he goes forth thence diffusing terror, it is to (3) display his power for enlarging his boundaries. The glittering brilliancy of colour has been granted to his body by the victories of Monthu.[8] He is the lord of the two crowns of Hor and of Set. A shout of joy resounded in heaven on the day of his birth. The gods (spake) thus: We have begotten him; (4) the goddesses thus: He is born of us to govern the kingdom of Ra; Amon thus: I am he who formed him, to put truth in its place. The land was set in order, the heaven quieted, the company of the gods satisfied, through his piety.'

---

[7] This inscription is translated by Dr. Birch, in *Records of the Past*, vol. viii. pp. 75, foll.

[8] A very obscure and uncertain passage. The whole inscription is in high-flown and cumbrous language, which makes it difficult for the translator to keep hold of the threads of the description. The introduction is in a singularly bombastic style.

He is a mighty bull for the miserable land of Kush, who pushes back (5) the conspirators from the land of the negroes. His hoof crushes the An (the Kushites) and his horn gores them. He has made himself master of the land of Nubia, and his terror, it has reached the land of Kari. His name resounds in (6) all lands, because of the victories which his hands have achieved. The gold appears on the mountains at his name, as at the name of his father Hor, the lord of Baka, the well-beloved in the land of the south, as at the name of Hor in the land of Maama, the lord of Buhan (Boôn). (7) Thus is King Ramessu Miamun, the dispenser of life eternally and for ever, like his father the everlasting Sun-god.

'Then was the king in the city of Memphis to worship his fathers, the gods, and the lords of South and North Egypt, that they might grant him power and victory and a long duration of life of infinitely many (8) years. On one of these days it came to pass, that the king sat there on his great throne of gold, attired with the royal diadem, and with the ornament of the double plume, to consult about the countries from which the gold is obtained, and to consider the method and way of boring (9) wells on the roads, which are accursed for want of water, since he had heard that there was much gold existing in the land of Akita, but that the approach to it was accursed on account of the utter want of water. There were taken there some (10) gold-washers to the place where it was; but those who had gone thither had died of thirst on the road, together with the asses which were with them. They could not find what was required (11) for them to drink on their upward journey, unless it happened that the rain fell from heaven. So could no gold be obtained in this country, on account of the want of water.

'Then spake the king to his nobleman, who stood beside him: "Let the princes be called who are present. (12) I will take counsel with them about this land, as to what measures should be taken." As soon as they had been brought before the divine benefactor, they lifted up their hands to praise his name with speeches in his honour, and to pray before his beautiful countenance. And the king described to them the condition of this land, in order to take (13) their advice upon it, with the view of boring wells on the road. And they spake before the king: "Thou art like the sun. Everything succeeds with thee. What thy heart desires, that comes to pass. When thou conceivest a wish in the night, it is accomplished as soon as the earth becomes light (again). We have hastened to thee to do what there is to do, for (14) great is the number of thy astonishing works, since thou hast appeared as king in the country. We heard nothing, we saw nothing, and yet what is there, it was done just as it is. All the sayings of thy mouth are like the words of Hormakhu. Thy tongue is a balance; thy lips are a standard measure (15) according to the just scales of the god Thut. Where is that hidden which thou didst not know? Where is the wise man who might be like thee? There is no place found, which thou hast not seen; there is no land which thou hast not trodden. Everything excellent found an entrance into thy ears since (16) thou wast an Adon of this land. Thou didst act with wisdom when thou didst still sit in the egg. In thy time of childhood that happened which thou saidst, for the welfare of the land. When thou grewest up to boyhood with the lock of hair of youth, no memorial saw the light without thy command. (17) No business was carried out without thy knowledge. Thou wast raised to be an overseer (Rohir) of this land, when thou wast a youth and didst count ten full years. All buildings went forward under thy hand, and the laying of their foundation stones was carried out. When thou spakest to the water: Come upon the mountain, then appeared the rain (18) immediately at thy command. Thou art like the Sun-god. As the body of the Creator, so is that which he begets. Truly thou art the living likeness of Ra, the heir of thy father Tum of Heliopolis. Taste is on thy tongue, feeling is in thy heart. The place of thy tongue is the shrine of truth. The divinity sits on thy lips, and all thy words will be performed for ever. (19) What thy understanding has done is like the works of Ptah, the fashioner of the works of art. Thou art ever he whose intentions are all carried out, whose words are all fulfilled, thou our great lord and ruler! As regards the land of Akita, may a decision be made according to the counsel taken concerning it."

'Then spake the king's son of the miserable land of Kush, (20) saying thus before the king: "(The land) is in this state. It is accursed for want of water since the time of Ra. People die of thirst in it. All former kings wished to bore wells in it, but they were not successful. (21) King Seti I. also did the same, He had a well bored 120 cubits deep in his time, but they abandoned it, for no water made its appearance. If then now thou thyself wouldest speak to thy father, the Nile-god Hapi, (22) the father of the gods: 'Let the water come up on the mountain,' he will do all that thou sayest, yea, indeed, all which thou hast designed will be accomplished before us, and not only according to hearsay, because thy fathers the gods love thee more than all kings (23) which have been since the time of Ra."'

'Says the king to the princes: "If all is true that ye have spoken, and water has not been opened in that country since the time of the god, as ye have said, then I will bore a well there, to afford water perpetually, yea! that the well (24) may be under the command of the father Amon-Ra, the Theban god, and of Hor, the lords of the land of Nubia, that their heart may be fixed in love. I will therefore appoint that it be called after [their name." And the princes] (25) praised their lord and worshipped him, and fell prostrate before him (the king), and raised shouts of joy (26) to the heights of heaven.

'Then spake the king to a royal scribe [who was near him: "Prepare thyself and betake thyself to the] (27) road to the land of Akita. Let the second day of the month be the day on [which] thou shalt [carry out thy mission." The scribe did] (28) just as he was bidden. Behold, he assembled the people [which were skilful in boring, that they should work and form a well, which should furnish water to those who travelled] (29) the road to the land of Akita. Never was the like done since the earlier kings. [And of the water which streamed out brooks were formed, and] (30) fishermen from the islands in the neighbourhood of the lagoons of Natho enjoyed themselves, for they built [small boats and made use of the . . . . . .] (31) as a rudder with the wind.

'Then there came the bearer of a letter from the king's son of the miserable land of Kush [about the well, to say to the king : "All has in fact been done] (32) that thy Holiness has spoken with his own mouth. There has appeared water out of it 12 cubits deep. There were 4 cubits in it . . . . ? . . . . the depth . . . . (33) . . . . . . they . . . . out as was the intention of the work. The god has inclined his heart favourably through thy love. Never has such a thing happened [since the time of the god Ra]."

'(34) [And the inhabitants of] Akita made joyful music on great drums (?) Those who had diseased eyes [washed themselves with the water and were healed. They all sang: (35) "Hail] to the king! The water which is in the depth was obedient to him. He hath opened the water on the [mountain." And they offered thanks] (36) to him through the king's son, because of his mission. That was more pleasant to [the heart of the king than all else. Thus then were] (37) his plans well carried out. Beautiful was the acknowledgment which [the inhabitants of the district] uttered. [A road was made from] (38) this well to the well of Ramses Miamun, the conqueror [in the land . . . .].'

As early as the time of the Eleventh Dynasty we find clear traces of borings for water in the waste valleys of Hammamat. Twelve hundred years before the accession of king Ramses II., one of his ancestors, Sankh-ka-ra, had made four wells on the old road from Coptos to Qosseir, the remains of which can still be distinguished.[9] Thus did the ancients anticipate the enterprises of our later generations, and execute works, the utility and importance of which are still recognized and valued by travellers through the deserts of Africa in the present day.

From Ramses, the borer of wells, to Ramses the builder of temples and the founder of cities, is only a step. What he performed in this respect in the very commencement of his reign, the Pharaoh has himself narrated to us so explicitly, that it is almost impossible to forget it. Abydus was the first scene of his new erections, although we are incidentally informed that he had built two temple-gates in Thebes and Memphis to the memory of his father, at the entrance to which the statues of Seti kept a watch of honour.

Concerning the city of Memphis, and its buildings erected by Ramses, we have detailed information from

[9] See Vol. I. p. 137.

a conversation between Ramses II. and Ptah, the ancient god of the city and the great architect of the world. A stone has perpetuated this, and the curious reader may still at the present day listen to the words of the two, as inscribed near the second cataract.

On the memorial tablet of Ibsamboul, which bears at its head the date of the 35th year, and the 13th of Tybi, in the reign of Ramses II., we find first, in the conversation between the god and Ramses, very remarkable information on the relations between Egypt and Khita. The god begins his long address with the usual flatteries addressed to the king, from which I cite the following passage in a faithful translation. The god says :—

'I have given thee strength and might and the power of thy arm in all countries. Thou hast wounded the hearts of all peoples, which are placed under thy feet. When thou comest forth on each new day, the great kings of all nations lead to thee a captive people, to do homage to thee with their children. They are given into the power of thy strong arm, to do with them whatsoever pleases thee, O King Ramses II. I have placed in all hearts reverence for thee. The love of all peoples is turned towards thee. Thy manly courage is spread abroad over all the plains, and the fear of thee goes through the mountains. The kings tremble at the thought of thee, and thou art regarded as their established head. They come to thee with a prayer to entreat thy friendship. Thou allowest to live whom thou willest: thou killest whom it pleases thee. The throne of all peoples is with thee.'

Some lines further on is the passage which is of importance for us :—

'The people of Khita are subjects of thy palace. I have placed it in their hearts to serve thee, while they humbly approach thy person with their productions and the booty in prisoners of their king. All their property is brought to thee. His eldest daughter stands forward at their head, to soften the heart of king Ramses II.—a great inconceivable wonder. She herself knew not the impression which her beauty made on thy heart. Thy name is great and glorious for ever. Thou art the most complete example of strength and power. He is inconceivably great, who orders and does not obey. Since the times of the traditions of the gods, which are hidden in the house of the rolls of writing, from the times of the sun-god Ra down to thee, history had nothing to report about the Khita people, but that they had one heart and one soul with Egypt.'

The Pharaoh, moved by so much goodwill and kindness, does not want for an answer to his divine father. His reply is not less rich in images and ideas, which, thirty-two centuries before our day, furnish the tasteful expression of his thoughts. The king's answer touches especially on the most essential point of his gratitude towards the Memphian God, proved by the Ramses-buildings in the interior of the great temple-city of Memphis. We will not withhold from the eyes of the curious reader his statements on this subject, together with the accompanying introduction. He says, word for word :—

'Thou hast committed to me what thou hast created. I do and I will do again all good for thee, so long as I shall be sole king, just as thou hast been. I have cared for the land, in order to create for thee a new Egypt, just as it existed in the old time. I have set up images of the gods, according to thy likeness, yea, according to their colour and form, which hold possession of Egypt according to their desire. They have been formed by the hand of the artist in the temples. Thy sanctuary in the town of Memphis was enlarged. It was beautified by long-enduring works, and by well-executed works in stone, which are adorned with gold and jewels. I have caused a court to be opened for thee on the north, with a splendid double-winged tower in front. Its gates are like the heavenly orb of light. The people offer their prayers there. I have built for thee a splendid sanctuary in the interior of the walled enclosure. Each god's image is in the unapproachable shrine, and remains in its exalted place. I have provided them with priests and prophets of the land of Egypt, with arable land and herds of cattle. The account of the property of the temple in all things amounts to millions. All thy great thirty years' feasts of jubilee are celebrated. Thus has everything which thou hast commanded me been carried out in rich abundance according to thy wish. There are oxen and calves without end; all their sacrificial meat is provided, to the number of hundreds of thousands; the smell of their fat reaches to heaven; the heavenly ones receive it. I cause the whole world to admire the completeness of the monuments which I have dedicated to thee. I brand with a hot iron the foreign peoples of the whole earth with thy name. They belong to thy person for evermore. Thou hast in truth created them.'

According to this, Ramses had cared in a splendid manner for the temple of Ptah in Memphis. He had erected for him the whole northern court, together with the propyla belonging to it; and had built a temple within the surrounding wall, numerous remains of which have lately been discovered near the Arab village of Qasrieh. He had erected images of the gods, and had provided the necessary means for the divine service of the great Architect. There is no dearth of statues of Ramses II. and the members of his family. The most celebrated and most often visited is the great torso of Ramses, the property of the English nation, which, lying in a trench among the ruins of the very celebrated temple of Ptah near the present Arab village of Mitrahenne, in vain awaits its re-erection. Besides this, the smaller statues of the king, and of his wife and daughters, have been torn away from the surface of the grove of palm-trees at the same place. The wall of the temple at Abydus has already made us acquainted with the statues of king Seti. The king also raised in Memphis other temples and buildings to his name. The chief master of the house of Pharaoh and the leader of the Mazai (policemen), Hi, was also 'administrator of a Ramses-temple in Pi-neb-am, and the administrator of the sun-temple of Ramessu-Miamun in the southern part of Memphis.'[1] For the building of the last 'the people,' and the 'red-skins,' (Apuirui, *not* Hebrews but Erythræans)[2] were doomed to the laborious task of dragging over the heavy blocks of stone out of the quarries of the Trojan range of mountains on the other side of the river. These people were likewise employed as drawers of stone for the building of the great propylon called 'Meriu-ma,' which Ramses erected at the temple of Ptah, and for which a certain Ameneman had undertaken the office of architect and chief of the policemen.

The family of Ameneman plays too great a part in the Egyptian monumental history of this period, to be passed over in silence. We can the less do so, as the several members of the genealogical tree, which we lay before our readers as a separate table,[3] were invested with the most important offices in the land of the Pharaohs, and Ameneman himself was probably the immediate oppressor placed by Ramses II. over the children of Israel in Egypt. The genealogical tree has been compiled on the authority of a pictured

[1] See my Essay, 'A new City of Ramses,' in the *Aegyptische Zeitschrift*, 1876, page 69.
[2] On this interesting question of identification, see further below, p. 134.
[3] See Table III. at the end of this volume, 'Genealogy of Amen-em-an, the Architect of the City of Ramses.'

family group, which is preserved in the collection of antiquities at Naples,—a precious and rare memorial of ancient times.

Like Abydus and Memphis, so also the old capital of the empire, Thebes, was the object of the especial care of Ramses II. New temples were erected on both sides of the river, or those which already existed were enlarged. In the great sanctuary of Ape (Karnak), the king first completed the mighty hall of Seti I., by the erection of the fifty-four columns which were wanting on the south side, and of a stone wall to surround the whole temple on the east as far as the wall of the Hall of Columns just mentioned.[4] In Luqsor the temple of Amon, founded but not finished by Amenhotep III., was completed, the two splendid propyla were placed before it, and two beautiful obelisks[5] were erected beside the giant sitting statues of the king in granite, as guards of honour at the middle gate. On the western side, the temple of the dead built by Seti I. at Old Qurnah was finished, and on the south-western side of it a special temple of victory, called the 'Ramesseum,' was dedicated to the God Amon.[6] Here stood

[4] See the Plan on p. 11.

[5] One of these is now in Paris, where it occupies the centre of the Place de la Concorde.

[6] For a description of this edifice, which 'for symmetry of architecture and elegance of sculpture may vie with any other Egyptian monument,' see Murray's *Handbook for Egypt*, p. 457, 6th edit. It shows a very complete type of the plan of an Egyptian temple of the later and more complex form. It is commonly considered to be the building which the Greeks called the *Tomb of Osymandyas* and the *Memnonium*, or 'Temple of

also the largest statues of the king, which, according to tradition, Cambyses, on his visit to Thebes, threw down from their position.

We should be forced to overstep the limits of this work, were we even to attempt to describe the several parts of all these remarkable buildings, or to call attention to the remains of all the other edifices which still exist in Thebes, although only in their last ruins, and bear on their face the name of the great Sesostris. We should have to write a history of the monuments, and not a history of the Pharaohs.

We must likewise necessarily abstain from the attempt to mention even the names and situations of the buildings erected by the same king in the other parts of Egypt, whether we

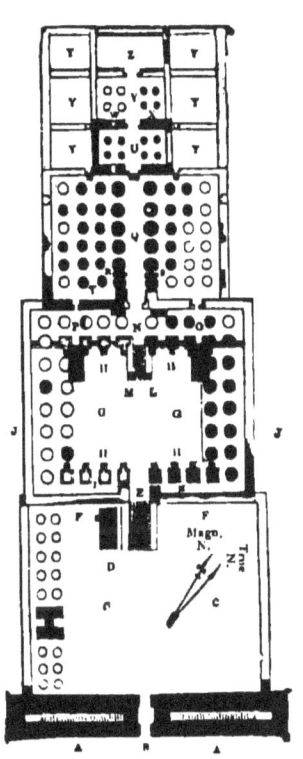

PLAN OF THE RAMESSEUM, OR MEMNONIUM.

A, A, Towers of Propylon. B, Entrance. C, C, Area. D, Broken granite statue of Ramses II. E, Entrance, between F, F, the Pylon. G, G, 2nd Area, with H, H, Osirid columns. I and J, Traces of Sculpture. K, Sculptures representing the wars of Ramses II. L and M, Sphinxes. N, O, P, Entrances into Q, The grand hall. R, S, Pedestals for statues. T, Sculptured battle scenes. U, Chamber with astronomical subject on ceiling. V, Another chamber, with w, x, Sculptured scenes. Y, Other chambers.

Memnon.' The latter name is thought to have sprung from the surname *Miamun* of Ramses II.; but the Greek myth of the Ethiopian or Egyptian Memnon still awaits fuller elucidation.— ED.

know them by trustworthy documentary records, or from the last remnants of them which still exist. The name of Ramses II. is thus everywhere to be found, and there appears from this point of view to be truth in his assertion, that ' he made Egypt anew.' (See above, p. 89.)

In Nubia, Ramses must be especially designated as a founder of temples and towns ' to his name,' for the works of Ramses put life into many formerly desert spots in these lonely regions of rocks. 'The Sun-town,' Pira, near Dirr, the Amon-town, Piamon, near Wady-Seboua, the Ptah-town, Pi-Ptah, near Gerf-Hussein, are works of Ramses, which still to the present day form points of attraction much visited by curious travellers, although the original plan of the buildings erected in the heart of the rocky mountain range seems to have been imperfectly carried out. But what shall we say, on the other hand, of the rock-temple of Ibsamboul, the wonderful façade of which surpasses everything which our imagination can conceive of grandeur in a human work? How small, how insignificant appear, in comparison with it, the pretty erections of our day, or the brick boxes full of windows, which serve for private use or for public purposes in the midst of our populous districts, and which have been erected with the help of steam and the most complete appliances of machinery! There in Nubia, in a solitary wall of rock, far removed from the dwellings of men, in hoary antiquity a temple was hewn to the great gods of the land of Egypt, Amon of Thebes, Ptah of Memphis, Hormakhu of Heliopolis, and, as a fourth united with these, the new god Ramessu-Miamun—hewn as if by *enchantment*—for this is the proper word—so bold, so powerful, so exceeding all human measure, as if giants had turned the bare rocks into a living work of art! Standing before this work, achieved by the hands of men, the thoughtful child of our modern age first feels the greatness of antiquity in its all-powerful might. It was not clever calculation, not profit, nor utility, but the most elevated feeling of gratitude to God, that caused such a work to be executed; a work worthy of and fit for the immortal inconceivable almighty Deity, to whom the ancients dedicated it in high veneration for the Everlasting and the Incomprehensible.[7]

The name of the place, as now expressed in the tongue of the Arabs, is Abou Simbel, that is 'father of the ear of corn.' None of the sitting figures, which stand out from the wall of rock like giant forms of the olden time, and with a disdainful smile upon their lips look down upon the pigmy race at their feet, carries any emblem in the hand, which can in the least degree be compared to an ear of corn. More correct, because there is a foundation for it, is the designation Ibsamboul,[8] for it has a direct relation to the ancient

[7] The construction of this temple is very clearly shown by the subjoined plan and section from Murray's *Handbook for Egypt*, p. 542, 6th edit. An excellent sketch of one of the enormous colossi of Ramses on its front is given by Mr. Villiers Stuart, *Nile Gleanings*, p. 164.—ED.

[8] It seems, however, that the first part of the Arabic name preserves the ancient appellation, which has been discovered by

name Psampolis, which in old Greek times travellers gave to this wonderful place; that is, the city (πόλις) of Psam. This last designation, again, came from the old Egyptian name of the place, Pimases or Pimas, Pimsa, from which the Greeks formed the more euphonious name of Psampolis.

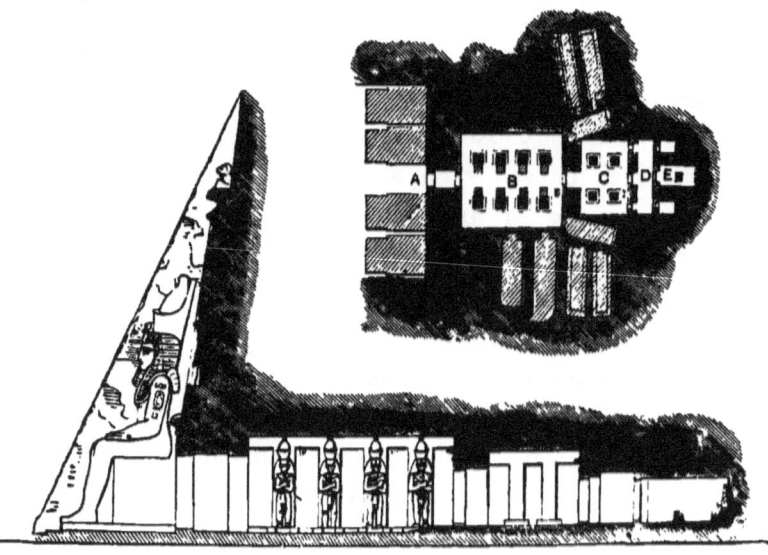

PLAN AND SECTION OF THE GREAT TEMPLE OF ABOU SIMBEL.

A, Entrance. B, Great Hall, supported by eight Osirid columns. C, Second hall, supported by four square columns, with religious subjects on the walls. D, Third hall, with similar subjects. E, Sanctuary, with an altar in the middle, and at the end four seated figures of Ptah, Amon, Horus, and Ramses himself.

We must refrain from entering the temple, to admire the wall-pictures in the freshest colours, and to see here the Khita, there the Libyans, here the

Mr. Villiers Stuart (*Nile Gleanings*, p. 169) on a newly cleared corner of the temple-frescoes in the form ⌒]̇ *Abbou*: another example of coincidence in *form* between Egyptian and Semitic words, which has been converted into a new *meaning*. In hieroglyphic texts, also, the place is called *Abushak* and *Abshak*. (Wilkinson, *Ancient Egyptians*, vol. iii. p. 116, 2nd edit.)—ED.

Negroes, there the Phœnicians, falling beneath the sword of Ramessu 'the god.' We must deny ourselves the pleasure of passing through the halls of the gods, and reading the inscriptions on the walls and pillars, and on the enormous memorial tablets. After long wanderings, we step out of the darkness of the primeval cave back into the bright light of day, silent, our thoughts turned within, confounded and almost overpowered by the indescribable impression of our own helplessness. We have experienced, in the gigantic tomb of a time long passed away, some portion of that nameless feeling, which moved our forefathers of old in their inmost being, at the sight of the most sublime of all dwellings made for the gods, the wonderful rock-temple of Ibsamboul.

Who was the architect?—who conceived the thought?—who laid down the plan?—who carried it out?—who were the artists that executed these gigantic works?—on such questions history keeps a deep silence. But whoever the forgotten author of this building may have been, he was a man full of enthusiasm, whose heart guided his hand, who sought not vain Mammon as his reward, but the eternal duration of his immortal and incomparable work.

Although Ramses raised his monuments in Thebes, and went up to the old capital of the empire to celebrate the festival of Amon;—though he held public courts in Memphis, to take counsel about the goldfields in the Nubian country;—though he visited Abydus, to see the tombs of the kings and the temple of the dead built by his father;—not to mention

Heliopolis, in which he dedicated a temple and obelisks to the sun-god;[9]—yet neither these nor other cities formed his permanent abode. On the eastern frontier of Egypt, in the low-lands of the Delta, in Zoan-Tanis, was the proper royal residence of this Pharaoh.[1]

We have often mentioned this city, and have come to understand its important position. Connected with the sea by its situation on the then broad and navigable Tanitic arm of the Nile, and commanding also the entrance of the great road, covered by 'Khetams,' or fortresses, which led to Palestine either in a north-easterly direction through Pelusium, or in an easterly direction through Migdol, on the royal road, Zoan-Tanis was, in the proper sense of the word, *the key of Egypt*. Impressed with the importance of the position of this 'great city,' Ramessu transferred his court to Zoan, strengthened its fortifications, and founded a new temple-city, the holy places of which were dedicated to the great gods of the country, Amon, Ptah, and Hormakhu, with whom as a fourth he associated the foreign Baal-Sutekh. With the newly established

[9] We obtain precise information on the name of the Ramesseum of Heliopolis, and on the person of its architect, from two inscriptions in the quarry to the north of the second pyramid of Gizeh, that of king Khafra. The smaller inscription runs, 'The architect of the city of the Sun (Pira), Mai:' the greater one, 'The architect of the beautiful temple of Ramessu Miamun in the great temple of the Ancient one (a surname of the sun-god Ra), Mai, a son of the architect Bok-en-amon of Thebes.' Below these, in like manner the sculptor from the life, Pa-uër, has immortalized himself. Mai, the son of Bok-en-amon, certainly belonged to that great family of architects, whose genealogy we shall hereafter lay before our readers. (The Table referred to is given below, Chap. XIX.)

[1] Compare Vol. I. pp. 160, 230, and the *Discourse on the Exodus*. (See Index, s. v. 'Zoan.')—ED.

divinities the king himself was united both by his effigy and his names, and there appeared in due order an Amon of Ramessu, a Ptah, a Hormakhu, and finally a Sutekh, of the same Pharaoh. The new temple-city had a superabundance of statues and obelisks, memorial stones, and other works. The most wonderful memorial must ever continue to be the stone, which has already been mentioned, with the date of the year 400 of king Nub. The inscription upon it, so far as it belongs to the historical scope of this work, has been translated, and its important bearing alike on Egyptian and Biblical chronology discussed, in the chapter on the Shepherd Kings.[2]

The plain covered with the ruins resembles a vast charnel-house, on which the dead remnants of stones, memorials of Ramses the Great, lie scattered broadcast, broken and worn, like the mouldering bones of generations slain long ago. From several inscriptions (not less than a dozen) on the obelisks and fragments of ruins at Tanis, we derive incidentally much important information of an historical and mythological character. One of these describes the king as

'Warrior (mohar) of the goddess Antha (Anaïtis),
Bull of the god Sutekh (Baal).'

Another calls him 'the bull in the land of Ruten' (sic); another again boasts of him, that he has made a great slaughter among the Shasu Arabs. Inscriptions on pillars say that 'he has prepared festivals for

[2] See Vol. I. pp. 296–7. We have transferred the translation, which Dr. Brugsch gives here, to the place where it seems much more appropriate.—ED.

the temples of the god Sutekh,' that 'he has conquered Kush and led into captivity the people of the Shasu ;' 'there, where he opened a road, he has taken them for his possession.' For the knowledge of these and similar records, which throw light on the history of the king and on the importance of Tanis, science is indebted to the researches of E. de Rougé.[3]

The hieratic rolls of papyrus, which have outlived the ravages of time, with one voice designate the newly founded temple-city (for the kings of the Eighteenth Dynasty had quite abandoned the old Zoan) as the central point of the court history of Egypt. Here resided the scribes, who in their letters have left behind for us the manifold information, which their life at the court, the ordinances of the king and of the chief officials, and their relations with their families in the most distant parts of the country, required them to give without reserve. Zoan, or, as the place is henceforth called, Pi-Ramessu, ' the city of Ramses,' became henceforward the especial capital of the empire.

It will be useful to the reader to hear in what manner an Egyptian letter-writer described the importance of this town on the occasion of his visit to it :[4]—

'So I arrived in the city of Ramses-Miamun, and I have found it excellent, for nothing can compare with it on the Theban land and soil. [Here is the seat] of the court.[5] It is pleasant to live

---

[3] Comp. *Mélanges d'Archéol. Egypt.* tome ii. p. 288, foll.

[4] This ' Letter of Panbesa, containing an account of the city of Rameses,' is translated by Mr. C. W. Goodwin, in *Records of the Past*, vol. vi. p. 11, foll.—ED.

[5] The Egyptian for court is *Pa-khennu*. The word means the residence of a king for the time being, as, for example, in the in-

in. Its fields are full of good things, and life passes in constant plenty and abundance. Its canals are rich in fish, its lakes swarm with birds, its meadows are green with vegetables, there is no end of the lentils; melons with a taste like honey grow in the irrigated fields. Its barns are full of wheat and durra, and reach as high as heaven. Onions and sesame are in the enclosures, and the apple-tree blooms (?). The vine, the almond-tree, and the fig-tree grow in the gardens. Sweet is their wine for the inhabitants of Kemi. They mix it with honey. The red fish is in the lotus-canal, the Borian-fish in the ponds, many kinds of Bori-fish, besides carp and pike,[6] in the canal of Pu-harotha; fat fish and Khipti-pennu fish are in the pools of the inundation, the Hauaz-fish in the full mouth of the Nile, near the "city of the conqueror" (Tanis). The city-canal Pshenhor produces salt, the lake-region of Pahir natron. Their sea-ships enter the harbour; plenty and abundance is perpetual in it. He rejoices who has settled there. My information is no jest. The common people, as well as the higher classes, say, "Come hither! let us celebrate to him his heavenly and his earthly feasts." The inhabitants of the reedy lake (Thufi) arrived with lilies, those of Pshenhor with papyrus flowers. Fruits from the nurseries, flowers from the gardens, birds from the ponds, were dedicated to him. Those who dwell near the sea came with fish, and the inhabitants of their lakes honoured him. The youths of the "Conqueror's city" were perpetually clad in festive attire. Fine oil was on their heads of fresh curled hair. They stood at their doors, their hands laden with branches and flowers from Pahathor, and with garlands from Pahir, on the day of the entry of king Ramessu-Miamun, the god of war Monthu upon earth, in the early

---

scription first deciphered by me, of the seventh year of Alexander II. (see *Aegypt. Zeitschrift*, 1871, p. 2, and below, Chap. XIX., *sub fin.*), it is related of Ptolemy I. that he made the city of Alexandria his *Khennu*, that is, his residence. It would lead to many errors to recognise this sense in the same appellation found in the quarries of Silsilis, as has been done, among others, by M. Maspero, and by Professor Lauth, of Munich, who has even made a high school in the midst of the quarries of Silsilis; but such errors are easily avoided by research into the real meaning of the inscriptions.

[6] I give this name conjecturally, as the Egyptian word is not yet explained.

morning of the monthly feast of Kihith (that is, on the 1st of Khoiak). All people were assembled, neighbour with neighbour, to bring forward their complaints.

'Delicious was the wine for the inhabitants of the "Conqueror's city." Their cider was like . . . . , their sherbets were like almonds mixed with honey. There was beer from Kati (Galilee) in the harbour, wine in the gardens, fine oil at the lake Sagabi, garlands in the apple-orchards. The sweet song of women resounded to the tunes of Memphis. So they sat there with joyful heart, or walked about without ceasing. King Ramessu-Miamun, he was the god they celebrated.'[7]

In spite of the unexplained names of the fishes and plants, the scribe could hardly have given a clearer or livelier account of the impression made on his susceptible mind by the new city of Ramses in its festal attire on the day of the entry of Pharaoh. We may suppose that many a Hebrew, perhaps Moses himself, jostled the Egyptian scribe in his wandering through the gaily dressed streets of the temple-city.

And this city of Ramses is the very same which is named in Holy Scripture as one of the two places in which Pharaoh had built for him 'arei miskenoth,' 'treasure cities,' as the translators understand it.[8] It would be better, having regard to the actual Egyptian word 'mesket,' 'meskenet,' 'temple, holy place' (as, for example, king Darius designates his temple erected

---

[7] Respecting the above translation I may be allowed to remark, that the versions of the document, as yet known to me, labour under the common fault of mistaking the connection of the several parts of the description given in the letter, or rather of not expressing it at all. One sentence follows another without any transition from the preceding to the succeeding.

[8] Exod. i. 13: 'And they built for Pharaoh treasure cities, Pithom and Raamses.'

in the great Oasis to the Theban Amon) to translate it 'temple-cities.' The new Pharaoh, 'who knew not Joseph,' who adorned the city of Ramses, the capital of the Tanitic nome, and the city of Pithom, the capital of what was afterwards the Sethroitic nome, with temple-cities, is no other, *can be no other*, than Ramessu II., of whose buildings at Zoan the monuments and the papyrus-rolls speak in complete agreement. And although, as it happens, Pitum is not named as a city in which Ramses erected new temples to the local divinities, the fact is all the more certain, that Zoan contained a new city of Ramses, the great temple-district of the newly founded sanctuaries of the above-named gods. RAMESSU II. *is the* PHARAOH *of the oppression, and the father of that unnamed princess, who found the child Moses exposed in the bulrushes on the bank of the river.*

While the fact, that the Pharaoh we have named was the founder of the city of Ramses, is so strongly demonstrated by the evidence of the Egyptian records both on stone and papyrus, that only want of intelligence and mental blindness can deny it, the inscriptions do not mention one syllable about the Israelites. We must suppose that the captives were included in the general name of foreigners, of whom the documents make such frequent mention. The hope, however, is not completely excluded, that some hidden papyrus may still give us information about them, as unexpected as it would be welcome.

We must again remark, and insist with strong emphasis on the fact, that from this time, and in the future history of the empire, the town of Zoan-Tanis is of great importance. On the wide plains before Zoan, the hosts of the warriors were mustered to be exercised in the manœuvres of battle; here the chariots of war rolled by with their prancing pairs of horses; the sea-going ships and their crews came to land at the harbours on the broad river. From this place Thutmes III. had started [9] in his war against Western Asia; it was to Tanis that Ramses II. had directed his return from Thebes; [1] here he had received the embassy of peace from the king of Khita; [2] and from hence, as we shall presently have to relate, Moses led the Hebrews out of the land of bondage to the land of promise, to give his people the milk and honey of the Holy Land in exchange for the flesh-pots of Egypt.

The numbers of prisoners, who, in the campaigns of the Egyptians, were transplanted to the Nile valley from foreign countries, and from whose best representatives, as the inscriptions expressly state, the gaps in the native population, caused by war and sickness, were filled up according to ancient usage, must under Ramses Sesostris have reached an unprecedented height. If we add to these the descendants of the foreigners transplanted to Egypt after former wars, a total number is reached, which certainly amounted to a third, and probably still more, of all the families of Egypt. So far as the contemporary information will allow us to judge, it was the custom to place the northern groups in the south, and the southern people

---

[9] See Vol. I. p. 368.   [1] Vol. II. p. 45.   [2] Vol. II. p. 71.

in the north, in order by this prudent measure to prevent any dangerous combination of neighbours related by blood.

The foreigners were employed in various services, according to their qualities and capacity. Those most active, and most experienced in war, were formed into foreign legions, the commanders of which, for the most part Egyptians, bore the name of Hir-pit ('captain of the foreigners'). Others, experienced in sea life, were enrolled in the Egyptian fleet. Others again were assigned to the service of the royal palace, or of the temples, or of distinguished personages, while no less a number were employed on the buildings, in the quarries, or in the mines. The king's name was branded upon them with a hot iron, to prevent their flight, and to facilitate their recapture. On the whole, the prisoners were treated with a certain mildness, for their captivity was not regarded as slavery in our sense of the word.

The influx of Semitic hostages and prisoners from Asia exercised a continually increasing influence on religion, manners, and language. The Egyptian language was enriched (we might almost say, for our profit) with foreign expressions, often indeed from mere whim, but more often for good reasons, in order properly to designate unknown objects by their native names. The letters and documents of the time of the Ramessids are full of Semitic words thus introduced, and in this respect they are scarcely less affected than the German language now, the strength and beauty of which are so much degraded by the borrowing of outlandish words. The learned court-scribes, especially, seem to have felt a sentimental craving for the use of foreign words without any necessity, in order to give themselves in the eyes of the public an air of learned culture. The Egyptian expressions for designating a 'hero' were supplanted by the words Mohar, or Ariel, borrowed from the Semitic; the Egyptian Nofer, 'a young man,' was changed for the Semitic name Na'ara-na; the army was in the same way called Zeba, and many other incongruous expressions were adopted.

The young Egyptian world, satiated with the traditions of the past thousands of years which had now vanished away, found a pleasure in the fresh and lively vigour of the Semitic spirit, to which a different and more attractive view of the universe gave a forward impulse. Besides all this, the long campaigns in foreign countries had paralysed the religious development in the native schools of the priests. The caste of the holy fathers itself counted many discontented persons in its ranks, who preferred the life abroad, and the adventures of a campaign, to the quiet contemplative existence within the temple walls; although the old teachers had used their utmost endeavours to put a ban upon the disinclination to scientific occupation, by epistolary warnings and even threatenings, some of which have been preserved to the present day. Among the young poets and historians within the temple walls there was awakened a desire hitherto unknown to set forth the warlike deeds of the Egyptian heroes in measured rhythm. It is to this impulse that we owe the heroic poem of the priest Pentaur, the beauty of which seems to have enchanted even the old masters of the language. Much mediocrity, on the other hand, was mingled with all this, and was for this reason alone rejected and condemned by the judgment of the cultivated priests. In order to give the reader a specimen of the views of the masters in this respect, we will lay before them the reply of one of them to his former pupil, who, as a scribe of Pharaoh, entertained the belief that, while portraying his hero in an artificial and confused composition, he had achieved a masterpiece. The answer of the priestly teacher is as biting and sharp, as it is scrupulously respectful. In placing a literal translation of the whole piece before my readers, I have endeavoured to represent the words borrowed from the Semitic by the French expressions answering to them. The reader of the translation will thus best form an idea of the impression which the original writing must have made on an admirer of the pure language of ancient Egypt, free from foreign words, at the epoch of B.C. 1300.

The whole contents of this letter were first made available for science, in the year 1866, by the united labour of two scholars, one French and the other English, both men of the highest merit in the pursuit of ancient Egyptian researches. We must express our regret that the judgment we formerly pronounced on the result of the labour of these two colleagues was such as to arouse much ill-feeling. Although we gave full praise to the rich fulness of the explanations of words in the old language which had been till then unknown or wrongly interpreted, we had the frankness to remark upon the less successful parts in the translation referred to, more particularly as to the conception of the meaning which lies at the foundation of the whole letter. The learned world may now examine the translation I offer, and compare it with the translation of those scholars, and after a scrupulous and minute examination may form their own judgment on the justice of our former assertions. We of course allow for the new advances which the science has made since the appearance of that remarkable work, and of which we have availed ourselves in our own translation. But even after making allowance for these aids towards the better understanding of this letter of the time of Ramses II., which is so remarkable in an historical sense, we can in no respect withdraw our former judgment, for in our opinion it is the simple truth, and we believe it to be the part of an honourable man under all circumstances to contend for the truth. And in having the courage to bear witness to this truth, according to the best of my knowledge and my conscience, without consideration for persons and circumstances, I believed that I was doing service, not to myself, but to science alone.[3]

[3] This curious composition is given in *Records of the Past* (vol. ii. pp. 107, foll.), under the rather strange title of 'Travels of an Egyptian,' from the translation of M. Chabas, which gave rise to much discussion between him and Dr. Brugsch. Much of the obscurity of the language is due to our ignorance of the literary exercise of which it seems to be a mock-heroic burlesque. If even the parodies of the 'Anti-Jacobin' lose half their relish

'Thy piece of writing has too much *glane*. It is a cargo of highflown phrases, the meaning of which may be the reward of those who seek for it; a cargo which thou hast laden at thy pleasure. I describe a *champion*, so sayest thou repeatedly; we on the other hand say, Is there truth in thy portraiture?

'Set out! examine thy yoke, the horses gallop like foxes; their eye is reddened; they are like the hurricane when it bursts forth. Put on the armour; seize the bow! We will admire the deeds of thy hand.

'I will portray for thee the likeness of a *champion*; I will let thee know what he does. Thou hast not gone to the land of Khita, neither hast thou beheld the land of Aupa. The appearance of Khatuma (Adama?) thou knowest not. Likewise the land of Igad'ai, what is it like? The Zor of Sesostris and the city of Khilibu (Haleb) is on none of its sides. How is its ford? Thou hast not taken thy road to Kadesh and Tubikhi, neither hast thou gone to the Shasu with numerous foreign soldiers, neither hast thou trodden the way to the Magar (Migron), where the heaven is darkened in the daytime. It is planted with maple-trees, oaks, and acacias, which reach up to heaven; full of beasts, bears, and lions; and surrounded by Shasu in all directions. Thou hast not gone up to the mountain of Shaua (Shawah), neither hast thou trodden it; there thy hands hold fast to the [rim] of thy chariot; a jerk has shaken thy horses in drawing it. I pray thee, let us go to the city of (Hi-?) Birotha. Thou must hasten to its ascent, after thou hast passed over its ford, in front of it.

'Do thou explain the relish for the *champion*! Thy chariot lies there [before] thee; thy [strength] has fallen lame; thou treadest the backward path at eventide. All thy limbs are ground small. Thy [bones] are broken to pieces. Sweet is the [sleep]. Thou awakest. There has been a time for the thief in this unfortunate night. Thou wast alone, in the belief that the brother would not come to the brother. Some grooms entered into the stable; the horse kicks out, the thief goes back in the night; thy clothes are stolen. Thy groom wakes up in the night, he sees what has happened to him, he takes what is left, he goes to the evil-doers, he mixes himself up

---

in the absence of their forgotten originals, who can hope to detect the *points* of a parody written in old Egyptian more than thirty centuries ago?—ED.

with the tribes of the Shasu. He acts as if he were an Amu. The enemies come, they [feel about] for the robber. He is discovered, and is immovable from terror. Thou wakest, thou findest no trace of them, for they have carried off thy property.

'Become (again) a *champion*, who is fully accoutred. Let thy ear be full of that which I will relate to thee besides.

'The town "Hidden," such is the meaning of its name Kapuna, what is its state? Its goddess (we will speak of) at another time. Thou hast not visited it. Be good enough to look out for Birotha (Berytus), Ziduna (Sidon), and Zareptha (Sarepta). Where are the fords of the land of Nazana? The land of Authu (Avathus), what is its state? They speak of another city in the sea, Zor (Tyrus), the lake is her name. The drinking water is brought to her in boats. She is richer in fishes than in sand. I tell thee of something else. Dangerous is it to enter into Zar'au-na (Zareah).[4] Thou wilt say, it is burning with a very painful sting! *Champion*! come! Go forwards on the way to the K'aikana. Where is the road of 'Aksapu (Achsib)? Towards no city. Pray look at the mountain of User. How is its crest? Where is the mountain of Ikama? Who can surmount it? *Champion*! whither must you take a journey to the city of Huzor (Hazor)? How is its ford? Let me (choose) the road to Hamatha (Hamath), Dagana (Beth-Dagon), and Dagal-ael (Migdal-El?). Here is the place where all *champions* meet. Be good enough to spy out its road, cast a look on I'ana (Ijon). When one goes to Adamin (Adumim), to what is one opposite? Do not draw back, but instruct us! Guide us! that we may know, thou leader!

'I will name to thee other cities besides these. Thou hast not gone to the land of Takhis, to Kafir-Marlena, Thamnah (Thimnah), Kadesh (Kedes), Dapur (Tabor), Azai, Hairnemma (Horonaim), nor hast thou beheld Qairtha-Anbu (Kiriath-eneb) near Bitha-Thupail (Tophel), nor dost thou know Adulma (Adullam), Zidiputha (Jotapata), nor dost thou know any better the name of Khaan-roza, in the land of Aupa,[5] the bull on its frontiers. Here is the place, where all the mighty warriors are seen. Be good enough

---

[4] Zareah means in Hebrew 'to beat,' 'to sting,' particularly with relation to Zir'eah, hornets, wasps; hence the play upon the name of the city.

[5] The country of Aupa or Aup formed the northernmost boundary of the Khalu or Phœnicians.

to look and see how Sina is situated, and tell me about Rehobu. Describe Bitha-Sheal (Bethshean), and Tharqa-ael. The ford of Jirduna (Jordan), how is it crossed? Teach me to know the passage in order to enter into the city of Makitha (Megiddo), which lies in front of it. Verily thou art a *champion*, well skilled in the work of the strong hand. Pray, is there found a *champion* like thee, to place at the head of the army, or a *seigneur*, who can beat thee in shooting?

'Drive along the edge of the precipice, on the slippery height, over a depth of 2,000 cubits, full of rocks and boulders. Thou takest thy way back in a zigzag, thou bearest thy bow, thou takest the iron in thy left hand. Thou lettest the old men see, if their eyes are good, how, worn out with fatigue, thou supportest thyself with thy hand. *Il est perdu, le chameau, le champion. Eh bien!* Make to thyself a name among the *champions* and the knights of the land of Egypt. Let thy name be like that of Qazailoni,[6] the lord of Asel, because he discovered lions in the interior of the balsam-forest of Baka, at the narrow passes, which are rendered dangerous by the Shasu, who lie in ambush among the trees. They measured 14 cubits by 5 cubits. Their nose reached to the soles of their feet. Of a grim appearance, without softness, they ceased not for caresses. Thou art alone, no stronger one is with thee, no *armée* is behind thee, thou findest no *lion de dieu* (ariel),[7] who prepares the way for thee, and gives thee counsel on the road before thee. Thou knowest not the road. The hair of thy head stands on end; it bristles up. Thy soul is given into thy hands. Thy path is full of rocks and boulders, there is no way out near, it is overgrown with thorns and thistles, with creepers and wolf's-foot. Abysses are on one side of thee, the mountain and the wall of

---

[6] This word seems to be connected with Kislon (i.e. strong), which was the name, for example, of the father of Elidad, the prince of the tribe of Benjamin (see Numbers xxxiv. 21).

[7] A very remarkable word, which shows a full knowledge of Semitic in the writer. In Hebrew also, *arel* or *ariel*, 'the lion of God,' means a hero. In 2 Sam. xxiii. 20, it is related of Benaiah, of Qabzeel (the name sounds uncommonly like Qazail-oni), that he, the commander of the bodyguard of David, slew two Moabitish *ariel*, i.e. heroes ('lion-like men of Moab,' A.V.); killed a lion snowed up in a pit, and overcame an Egyptian in full armour with only a staff.

rock on the other. Thou drivest in against it. The chariot, on which thou art, jumps. Thou art troubled to hold up thy horses. If it falls into the abyss, the pole drags thee down too. Thy *ceintures* are pulled away. They fall down. Thou shacklest the horse, because the pole is broken on the path of the narrow pass. Not knowing how to bind it up, thou understandest not how it is to be repaired. The *essieu* is left on the spot, as the load is too heavy for the horses. Thy courage has evaporated. Thou beginnest to run. The heaven is cloudless. Thou art thirsty; the enemy is behind thee; a trembling seizes thee; a twig of thorny acacia worries thee; thou thrustest it aside; the horse is scratched, till at length thou findest rest.

'Explain thou (to me) thy relish for the *champion*!

'Thou comest into Jopu (Joppa). Thou findest the date-tree in full bloom in its time. Thou openest wide the hole of thy mouth, in order to eat. Thou findest that the maid who keeps the garden is fair. She does whatever thou wantest of her. She yields to thee the skin of her bosom. Thou art recognized, thou art brought to trial, and owest thy preservation to the *champion*. Thy girdle of the finest stuff, thou payest it as the price for a bad rag.[8] Thou sleepest every evening with a rug of fur over thee. Thou sleepest a deep sleep, for thou art weary. A thief takes thy bow and thy sword from thy side; thy quiver and thy armour are cut to pieces in the darkness; thy pair of horses run away. The groom takes his course over a slippery path, which rises before him. He breaks thy chariot in pieces; he follows thy foot-tracks. [He finds] thy equipments, which had fallen on the ground, and had sunk into the sand; it becomes again (i.e., leaving only) an empty place.

'Prayer does not avail thee; even when thy mouth says, "Give food in addition to water, that I may reach my goal in safety:" they are deaf, and will not hear. They say not yes to thy words. The iron-workers enter into the smithy: they rummage in the workshops of the carpenters; the handicraftsmen and saddlers are at hand; they do whatever thou requirest. They put together thy chariot; they put aside the parts of it that are made useless; thy

---

[8] An expression with a double meaning, intelligible to those who know the secondary sense at the present day of the oriental word 'rags,' in Arabic Sharmutah.

spokes are *façonné* quite new; thy wheels are put on, they put the *courroies* on the axles, and on the hinder part; they splice thy yoke, they put on the box of thy chariot; the [workmen] in iron forge the . . . . ; they put the ring that is wanting on thy whip, they replace the *lanières* upon it.

'Thou goest quickly onward to fight on the battle-field, to do the works of a strong hand and of firm courage.

'Before I wrote I sought me out a *champion*, who knows his power (*lit.* hand), and leads the *jeunesse*, a chief in the *armée*, [who goes forward] even to the end of the world.

'Answer me not, "That is good, this is bad;" repeat not to me your opinion. Come, I will tell thee all which lies before thee, at the end of thy journey.

'I begin for thee with the city of Sesostris. Thou hast not set foot in it by force. Thou hast not eaten the fish in the brook. . . . . Thou hast not washed thyself in it. With thy permission I will remind thee of Hazina; where are its fortifications? Come, I pray thee, to Uti, the strong fortress of Sesostris User-maa-ra, to Sabaq-Ael and Ab-saqabu. I will inform thee of the position of 'Aini, the customs of which thou knowest not. Nakhai and Rehoburotha thou hast not seen, since thou wast born, O *champion*! Rapih (Raphia) is widely extended. What is its wall like? It extends for a mile in the direction of Qazatha (Gaza).

'Answer quickly. That which I have said is my idea of a *champion* in reply to thee. I let the people keep away from thy name, I wish them a *seigneur*. If thou art angry at the words which I have addressed to thee, yet I know how to estimate thy heart in every way. A father chastises, but he knows the right measure a hundred thousand times. I know thee. To put on armour is really beyond thy ability. No man whose hand and courage is warlike makes himself famous in my esteem. I am open and clear, like the spring-water of the god Monthu. It matters very little what flows over thy tongue, for thy compositions are very confused. Thou comest to me in a covering of misrepresentations, with a cargo of blunders. Thou tearest the words to tatters, just as it comes into thy mind. Thou dost not take pains to find out their force for thyself. If thou rushest wildly forward, thou wilt not succeed. What comparison is there between one who does not know the goal that he wishes to reach, and one who reaches it?

Now, what is he like? I have not gone back, but I have reached (my goal). Soften thy heart, let thy heart be cheerful; may the way to eat cause thee no trouble!

'I have struck out for thee the end of thy composition, and I return to thee thy descriptions. What thy words contain, that is altogether on my tongue, it has remained on my lips. It is a confused medley, when one hears it; an uneducated person could not understand it. It is like a man from the lowlands speaking with a man from Elephantiné.[9] But since thou art the scribe of Pharaoh, thou resemblest the water for the land, that it may become fertile. Take my meaning kindly, and do not say, "Thou hast made my name to stink before all other men." Understand me as having wished to impart to thee the true position of a *champion*, in doing which I have visited for thee every foreign people, and placed before thee in a general view the countries, and (every) city according to its special character. Acquaint us kindly, that thou so understandest it. If thou findest that the remarks upon thy work are apposite, thou wilt be for us like the famous Uah.'

Ramses II. enjoyed a long reign. The monuments expressly testify to a rule of sixty-seven years, of which probably more than half must be assigned to his joint reign with his father. His thirty-years' jubilee as (sole?) Pharaoh was the occasion for great festivities throughout the whole country, of which we have frequent mention in the inscriptions at Silsilis, El-Kab, Bigeh, Sehêl, and even upon several scarabæi. The prince and high priest of Ptah of Memphis, Khamus, travelled through the principal cities of the land, in order to make the necessary preparations, through the governors, for celebrating this great feast of joy in honour of his father in a proper manner.

The return of this jubilee seems to have been cal-

---

[9] This is the passage referred to at Vol. I. p. 19.—ED.

culated according to a fixed cycle of years, perhaps when the lunar and solar years coincided [1] at short intervals of three or four years, in the same manner as the festivals. In the 30th year Khamus celebrated the feast under his own superintendence, according to usage and prescription, in Bigeh and in Silsilis, where at that time Khai was governor of the district, while at El-Kab the governor Ta conducted the festivities. The recurrence of the succeeding jubilees took place —the second in the 34th year, the third in the 37th year, and the fourth in the 40th year, of the reign of Ramses II.

Great in war, and active in the works of peace, Ramses seems also to have enjoyed the richest blessings of heaven in his family life. The outer wall of the front of the temple of Abydus displays the effigies and the names (only partially preserved) of 119 children (60 sons and 59 daughters); which gives ground for supposing a great number of concubines, besides his lawful wives, already known to us, namely, his favourite wife Isenofer, the mother of Khamus, the queen Nofer-ari,[2] Mienmut, and the daughter of the king of Khita.

[1] Comp. Vol. I. pp. 121-2.
[2] The small temple at Ibsamboul, specially dedicated to queen *Nofer-ari Mer-en-shat* ('the good consort beloved of Amon'), contains some interesting pictures of the family of Ramses, of which Mr. Villiers Stuart gives engravings (*Nile Gleanings*). Among them is a splendid coloured portrait of the queen, and another representing her in a group with the goddess Anke. In the same temple Ramses is represented with his family between his knees and at his feet. Mr. Villiers Stuart also gives coloured and other engravings from the pictures at Ibsamboul, representing

Among his sons, Khamus held a fond place in his father's heart. He was high priest of Ptah in Memphis, and in that character did his best to restore the decayed worship of the holy Apis-bulls, which were regarded as the living type of Ptah-Sokari, and to invest it with the greatest splendour. His buildings in Memphis, and in the so-called Serapeum, the burial-place of the holy bulls, are celebrated by inscriptions as splendid works of the age, and their author is overwhelmed with praises. From all that the monuments tell us about Khamus, in words more or less clear, the king's son seems to have been a learned and pious prince, who devoted himself especially to the holy service of the deity, and remained in the temple of Ptah at Memphis, keeping himself more estranged from state affairs than was altogether pleasing to his royal father.

The elder sons, including Khamus, died during the long reign of their father. The fourteenth in the long list of children, by name Mineptah, 'the friend of Ptah,' was chosen by destiny to mount at last the throne of the Pharaohs. He had already taken part in the affairs of government during the lifetime of his aged father, and in this capacity he appears on the monuments of Ramses II., by the side of his royal parent.

Of the daughters of the king, the monuments

Ramses on his chariot attended in battle by his fighting lion; also followed by six of his sons in three chariots; also in a duel with a Libyan foe; also a portrait of his eldest son, Amen-hi-khop-sanef; also a colossal statue of his daughter Ba-ta-anta.—ED.

name, during the lifetime of the Pharaoh, as real queens and wives of Egyptian kings (perhaps sub-kings or brothers), his favourite daughter, called by the Semitic name of Bint-antha, 'the daughter of Anaïtis,' and Meri-amon, and Neb-taui. A much younger sister of the name of Meri deserves to be mentioned, since her name reminds us of the princess Merris (also called Thermuthis), according to the Jewish tradition,[3] who found the child Moses on the bank of the stream, when she went to bathe. Is it by accident, or by divine providence, that in the reign of Ramses III., about 100 years after the death of his ancestor, the great Sesostris, a place is mentioned in Middle Egypt, which bears the name of the great Jewish legislator? It is called I-en-Moshé, 'the island of Moses' or 'the river-bank of Moses.' It lay on the eastern side of the river, near the city of the heretic king Khu-n-aten. The place still existed in the time of the Romans; those who describe Egypt at that time designate it, with a mistaken apprehension of its true meaning, as Musai, or Musôn, as if it had some connection with the Greek Muses.

The list of contemporaries during the long reign of the king, about whom the monuments furnish us with information, is almost innumerable. It were a labour which would repay the cost, to collect together their names and families, so as to form a general view of their generations under Ramses II. Among them, a distinguished place was held by that Bekenkhonsu,

[3] Joseph. *Antiq.* ii. 9, § 35; Artapanus, *ap.* Euseb. *Præp. Evang.* ix. 27.

upon whose statue (in Munich) the following notice of his career is handed down to the latest generations :—

'(1) The hereditary lord and first prophet of Amon, Bekenkhonsu, speaks thus: I was truthful and virtuous towards my lord. I undertook with pleasure that which my god taught me. I walked in his ways. I performed acts of piety within his temple. I was a great architect in the town of Amon, my heart being filled with good works for my lord.

'O ye men, all of you altogether, of reflecting mind, (2) ye who remain now upon the earth, and ye who will come after me for thousands and later thousands of years, according to your age and frailty, whose heart is possessed by the knowledge of virtue, I give you to know what services I performed on earth, in that office which was my lot from my birth.

'I was for four years a very little child. For twelve years (3) I was a boy. I was the superintendent of the office for the sustenance of the king Mineptah Seti. I was a priest of Amon for four years. I was a holy father of Amon for twelve years. I was third prophet of Amon for sixteen years. I was second prophet of Amon for twelve years. He (the king) rewarded me, and distinguished me because of my deserts. He named me as first prophet of Amon for six years. I was (4) a good father for my temple servants, in that I afforded sustenance to their families, and stretched out my hand to the fallen, and gave food to the poor, and did my best for my temple. I was the great architect of the Theban palace for his (Seti's) son, who sprang from his loins, the king Ramses II. He himself raised a memorial to his father Amon, (5) when he was placed upon the throne as king.

'The skilled in art, and the first prophet of Amon, Bekenkhonsu, speaks thus : I performed the best I could for the temple of Amon as architect of my lord. I erected for him the wing-tower "of Ramessu II., the friend of Amon, who listens to those who pray to him," (thus is he named) at the first gate of the temple of Amon. I placed obelisks at the same made of granite. Their height reaches to the vault of heaven. A propylon is (6) before the same in sight of the city of Thebes, and ponds and gardens, with flourishing trees. I made two great double doors of gold. Their height reaches to heaven. I caused to be made double pairs of great masts. I set them up in the splendid court in sight of his temple. I had great barks built on the river for Amon, Mut, and Khonsu.'

Although the day of the death of Bekenkhonsu is not given in the inscription, yet it is clear that he must have departed this life while priest of Amon, after having completed sixty-six years.[4] We can therefore divide his whole life of sixty-six years into the following sections :—

		Years.
Bekenkhonsu was a little child	4 years	1–4
A boy, and at last official of the palace	12 „	5–16
Priest of Amon	4 „	17–20
Holy father of Amon	12 „	21–32
Third prophet of Amon.	16 „	33–48
Second prophet of Amon	12 „	49–60
First prophet of Amon.	6 „	61–66

It is hardly probable that the great Sesostris died leaving his earthly empire in peaceful circumstances. A large family of sons and grandsons were ready in his advanced years to dispute the inheritance of their father. The seeds of stormy and unquiet times were sown. The historical records in the sequel justify these anticipations in the most striking manner.

The body of Pharaoh was laid in his sepulchral chamber in the rocky valley of Biban-el-Molouk. The son of Seti, so full of gratitude to his father, notwithstanding the large number of his children, had not left

---

[4] Champollion has briefly described the extensive but much-ruined sepulchre of this man, on the west side of Thebes, in his *Notices Descript.* tome i. p. 538. On its second door the French hierogrammatist read the following inscription :—' The hereditary lord and president of the prophets of Amon-ra, the lord of Thebes, the first prophet of Amon, Bekenkhonsu, the blessed.'

one descendant who prepared for him a tomb worthy of his deeds and great name, a tomb which might even be compared with the splendid sepulchre of Seti. The tomb of Ramses is an insignificant structure, of rather tasteless work, seldom visited by travellers in the Nile valley, who scarcely imagine that the great Sesostris of Greek legend can have found his last resting-place in these mean chambers. At his death, Pharaoh might have said of himself, 'I stood alone, no other was with me,' as formerly in his struggle against the Khita.

IV. MINEPTAH II. HOTEP-HI-MA (MENEPHTHES). B.C. 1300.

We must still retain our judgment, which we expressed in the first [French] edition of our History of Egypt, upon the insignificant character of the works of this king. In opposition to the opinion of a learned colleague, who never set his foot on Egyptian soil, we must be permitted again to affirm, with all decision, as the result of the most minute examination of the monuments, that Mineptah II. does not rank with those Pharaohs who have transmitted their remembrance to posterity by grand buildings and the construction of new temples, or by the enlargement of such as already existed. A glance at the detailed architectural plan of the temple of Karnak, which M. Mariette has recently published, with the names of all the royal builders, is alone sufficient to prove that Mineptah did as good as nothing for the great temple of the empire at Api. With the exception of small works, hardly worthy of being named, the new Pharaoh contented himself with the cheap glory of utilizing, or rather misusing, the monuments of his predecessors, as far back as the Twelfth Dynasty and not excepting even the works of the Hyksos, as bearers of his royal shields; for in the cartouches of former kings, whence he had chiselled out their names, he unscrupulously inserted his own, without any respect for the judgment of posterity. Short, unimportant, badly executed inscriptions, for the most part during the first years of his reign, commemorate merely his existence, without any further information of historical value. We must make an exception in favour of that single important record, which Mineptah caused to be chiselled on the inner side-wall of one of the southern forecourts of the great temple of Amon at Api, to call to the remembrance of the Thebans his great friendship with the gods.

The contents of this inscription, unfortunately injured in its upper portion, are extremely important, for it announces to us the irruption of the Libyan peoples and their allies into Egypt, and their repulse by the victorious Egyptian army. We lay before our readers the most important part of this inscription in an accurate translation, and we do not hesitate to give the completion of the parts that are wanting, as they must necessarily be supplied from the connection of the whole and of the several parts: [5]—

---

[5] This inscription is translated by Dr. S. Birch, in *Records of the Past*, vol. iv. pp. 39, foll. The variations in the spelling of the names are faithfully preserved from Dr. Brugsch's German.—ED.

'(1) Catalogue of the peoples which were smitten by the king: ....] -i the A-qa-ua-sha, the Tu-li-sha, the Li-ku, the Shair-dan, the Sha-ka-li-sha, peoples of the North, which came hither out of all countries.

'(2) [In the year V., in the month ...., in the reign of the lord of the diadem] to whom his father Amon has given power, the king of Upper and Lower Egypt, Mineptah Hotephima, the dispenser of life, the divine benefactor, was [in the town of Memphis, to thank the god Ptah] (3) [for] his [benefits]. For all gods protect him, all peoples were in fear of his glance. The king Mineptah (4) [received at that time a message, that the king of the Libyans had fallen upon the towns of the country] and plundered them, and turned them into heaps of rubbish; that the cowards had submitted to his will; that he had overstepped the boundaries of his country, that he had gained the upper hand.

'(5) [Then the king caused the towns to be fortified, and measures to be taken] in all directions for the protection of the breath of life. He gave it back to the inhabitants who were without it, sitting still in (their) hiding-places. Powerful was his might to (6) [attain his end. He had entrenchments drawn] to protect the city of On, the city of the sun-god Tum, and to protect the great fortress of Tanen (i.e. Memphis), and to extend [the works for the protection of other cities] in great numbers.

'(7) [For the foreign peoples had long since made inroads also from the East, and had pitched] their tents before the town of Pi-bailos (Byblus, Bilbeïs); they found themselves (already) on the canal Sha-ka-na, to the north of the canal Ao (of Heliopolis), (8) [so that the adjoining land] was not cultivated, but was left as pasture for the cattle on account of the foreigners. It lay waste there from the times of our forefathers. All the kings of Upper Egypt sat in their entrenchments (9) [and were occupied in building themselves memorials], and the kings of Lower Egypt found themselves in the midst of their cities, surrounded with earthworks, cut off from everything by warriors, for they had no mercenaries to oppose to them.

'Thus had it been (10) [until the day when king Mineptah] ascended the throne of Horus. He was crowned to preserve life to mortals. He was brought in as king to protect men. There was the strength in him to do this, because he was the likeness of the [beautiful] faced (11) [god (Ptah). And the king sent messengers to the land of Ma?]-bair. The choicest of his mercenaries were equipped; his chariots were assembled from all directions; and his spies [betook them to the road to keep him informed. Thus had he] prepared [everything] for his equipment in (12) [a short time. And thus was he armed for the approaching struggle. For he is a hero]; he takes no count of hundreds of thousands (of enemies) on the day of the turmoil of battle. His life-guards marched forward; there came on the most powerful warriors; and beautiful was the sight at the entrance of the mercenaries for all the inhabitants [of Egypt].

'(13) [And they came to announce to the king : " In . . . .] month of the summer has it happened, that the miserable king of the hostile land of Libu, Mar-ajui, a son of Did, has made an irruption into the land of the Thuhennu (the Marmaridæ) with his foreign mercenaries, (14) [the catalogue of whom is as follows : the Sh]airdan, the Shakalsha, the Qauasha, the Liku, the Turisha : since he has sought out the best of all combatants, and of all the quick runners of his country. He has also brought with him his wife and his children; (15) [besides there are come with him the princes] and the captains of the host. He has reached the boundaries of the west land at the fields of the town of Pi-ar-shop (Prosopis)."

'Then his Majesty was enraged against them like a lion, (16) [and he assembled the princes and leaders of his host and spake thus :] " Listen to the sayings of your lord. I give you [to know] what you have to do at my word. For I am the king, your shepherd. My care is to enquire (17) [what tends to the good of the land. Who among] you is like him, to keep life for his children ? Should they be anxious like the birds ? You do not know the goodness of his intentions." No answer (was made to this) on the part of (18) [the princes. And the king continued : " It is not my intention to await the enemy, so that the land] should be wasted and abandoned at the advance of all foreign peoples, to plunder its boundaries. The enemies (19) overstep them daily. Each takes [what he pleases, and it is their intention] to plunder the frontier cities. They have already advanced into the fields of Egypt from the boundary of the river onwards. They have gained a firm footing, and spend days and months therein. [They have] settled themselves (20) [near the towns. Others of them] have reached the mountains of the Oasis, and the lands in sight of the nome of Taahu.[6] It was a privilege ever since the kings of Upper Egypt, on the ground of the historical records of other times. But no one (21) knows [that they ever came in large numbers] like vermin. Let no more be granted to them than their belly requires. If they love death and hate life, if their temper is haughty to do (22) [what they wish, then let them apply to] their king, let them remain on (their) ground and soil, and go to the battle, so as always to fill their bodies. They have come to Egypt to seek sustenance for their mouth. They [direct] their mind (23) [to this, to fill] their belly [with] my property, just like the fishermen. Their king is like a dog, a bragging fellow. His courage is naught. Having arrived, he sits there planning (24) [a treaty, to carry out with him] the people of the Piti-shu, whom I allowed to take away wheat in ships, to preserve the life of this people of Khita, because I, the king, am he whom the gods have chosen. All plenty, (25) [all sustenance, lies] in my hand, the king Mineptah, the dispenser of life. In my name are laid [the supporting columns] of my [buildings]. I act as king of the country. [All] happens (26) [in my name in the land of Egypt]. What is spoken in Thebes pleases Amon. He has turned himself away from the people of the Mashauasha (Maxyes), and (he) looks [no more] on the people of the Thamhu, they are (27) [lost."

'Thus spake the king to] the leaders of the host, who stood before him, that they should destroy the people of the Libu. They went forth, and the hand of God was with them. Amon was at their [side] as a shield. The news reached the [people] of Egypt, (28) [namely, that the king in his own person would take part] in the campaign on the fourteenth day. Then his Majesty beheld in a dream as if the statue of Ptah, which is placed at the [gate of the temple,] stepped down to Pharaoh. It was like a giant. (29) [And it was] as if it spoke to him: "Remain altogether behind," and, handing to him the battle sword, "Mayest thou cast off the lazy disposition that is in thee." And Pharaoh spoke to it: "Behold! (30) [thy word shall be accomplished]."

'And my warriors and the chariots in sufficient number had prepared an ambush before them in the high land of the country of the nome of Prosopis.

'Then the miserable king of (31) [the hostile Libu caused his

---

[6] Called Touho by the Copts, in Middle Egypt.

warriors and his mercenaries to advance] in the night of the first of Epiphi, when the earth became light enough for the encounter. When the miserable king of the hostile Libu had arrived, about the time of the 3rd of Epiphi, he had brought (32) [with him all his hosts. But] they held back. When the warriors of his Majesty had charged forward, together with the chariots, then was Amon-Ra with them, and the god Nub reached out to them his hand. Each (33) [man fought bravely. A great defeat was inflicted on them, and they lay there in] their blood. No man was left remaining of them, for the foreign mercenaries of his Majesty had spent six hours in annihilating them. The sword gave (34) [no mercy, so that] the land was [full of corpses.]

'While they thus fought, the miserable king of the Libu stood there full of fear, his courage deserted him; then fled (35) [he in quick flight, and left] his sandals, his bow, his quiver, in his haste behind him; and [all other things] which he had with him. He, in whose body there was no timidity, and whose form was animated by a great manly courage, (36) [he fled like a woman. Then the mercenaries of his Majesty took what he had left] of his property, his money which he had gathered in, his silver, his gold, his vessels of iron, the ornaments of his wife, his chairs, his bows, his weapons, and all other things which he had brought (37) [with him. All was allotted to the] palace of the king, whither it was brought together with the prisoners. When in the meantime the miserable king of the Libu had hurried forth in his flight, then there [followed] him a number (38) [of the people of his nation, since they had escaped] destruction by the sword. Then did the cavalry who sat upon their horses spring forward to pursue them. [The enemy] fell in (39) [their flight into their hands, and great destruction was inflicted on them]. No [man] had seen the like in the historical records of the kings of Lower Egypt, at the time when this land of Egypt was in their [power], when the enemy maintained their ground firmly, at the time when the kings of Upper Egypt (40) [would afford no assistance]. But [all] this was done by the gods from love to their son who loves them, to preserve the land of Egypt for its ruler, and to protect the temples of the land of Ta-Mera, in order to exalt (41) [the glory of the king to the latest generations.

'Then the governor] of the frontier garrisons of the west land sent a report to the royal court to the following effect: "The enemy Mauri has arrived in flight; his body trembled; he escaped far away only by favour of the night. (42) [His flight, however, does no harm, for] want [will be his fate.] He has fallen. All the gods are for Egypt. The promises which he had made are become vain, and all his words have rolled back on his own head. His fate is not known, whether he is dead, (43) [or whether he is living. Thou, O king!] leave him his life. If he is alive, he will not raise himself up any more. He has fallen down, and his people have become hostile (to him). Thou wilt be the man who will undertake it, by giving orders to kill (44) [the rebels among the inhabitants] in the land of the Thamhu, and [of the Libu]. Let them set up another in his place, one of his brothers, who took part in the battle. He will be obliged to acknowledge him, since he is himself despised by the princes as a (45) [monster without an equal."

'Then the king gave the order that there should return home] the leaders of the foreign mercenaries, the life-guards, the chariots of war, and all the warriors of the army whose service was ended. But those who were of the young men, in full force, (46) [received the command to drive] before them the asses which were loaded with the (cut off) members of the uncircumcised people of the Libu, and with the (cut off) hands of all the peoples which were with them, like foals in the clover, and with all things (47) [which the warriors of Egypt had taken as booty from] the enemy, to their own country. Then the whole land rejoiced to the height of heaven; the towns and villages sang the wonderful deeds that had been done; the (48) [river resounded with the joyful shouts of the dwellers on its banks, and they] carried the booty under the window of the palace in order that his Majesty might behold their conquests.

'This is the catalogue of the prisoners, who were carried away out of this land of the Libu, together with the foreign peoples, whom they had brought with them in great numbers, likewise of the things (49) [which had been taken from them] and brought to the magazines of king Mineptah; (who was called) "the Annihilator of the Thuhennu," in the town of Prosopis, and to the upper towns of the country from the place called "of Mineptah" (50) [to the city . . . .].

'1. *Members of the uncircumcised*—
   Of king's children and brothers of the king
      of the Libu   6

their members were cut off and delivered
over.
[Of leaders and people] of the Libu. Their
members were cut off and delivered over.   6359 men
Making together: of king's children, leaders
'(51) [and common people of the Libu, whose
members were cut off and delivered
over . . . .   6365 men]

'(52) [2. *Hands of the circumcised:* namely, of the
Tulisha, the Shar]dina, the Shakal-sha,
and the Aqáiuasha of the lands of the
sea :
'(53) Shakalsha : 242 men, number of the hands .   250
Tulisha : 750 ,, ,, ,, ,, .   790
'(54) Shairdana [x . . . . . . x]
Aqaiuasha, who were circumcised, and
whose hands were cut off and delivered
over, though they were circumcised.
[Number of the hands : $1040+x$]

'(55) [The members and hands were stored up in] heaps. The members of the uncircumcised were brought to the place where the king was. Their number, of 6,111 men, amounted in all to . . . . x pieces

'(56) [Of the circumcised the number] of their hands [amounted to], of common men (namely) 2370

'3. *As living captives,* there were delivered
of the Shakalsha and Talisha, who
had come with the hostile tribes of
the Libu . . . .   [9146] men
'(57) [Further of the . . . . and] Libu . .   218 ,,
Of the women of the king of the hostile Libu, whom
he had brought with him, living women . . .   12
So that altogether those who were delivered over [of
the enemy as living prisoners, the (58) number
amounted to] of men and women   9376

'4. *Other booty.*
Weapons that were in their hands, or that had been
taken from the prisoners :
Bronze swords of the Mashuasha   .   9111 pieces

'(59) [Swords, daggers, and other weapons of the] land [of the Libu] . . . . 120,214 pieces

'Pairs of chariot-horses, which had been driven by the king of the Libu, and the children [and brothers] of the king of the Libu, and which were delivered over alive . . . . 113 pairs

'(60) The objects [which were otherwise taken as booty] with the Mashuasha [were given as a present to the warriors] of the king, who had fought against the hostile Libu:

Of cattle of various sorts	1308 head
Of goats	[x] ,,
Of various [. . . .]	[54] ,,
Silver drinking-cups	x pieces
Other vessels	x ,,
Swords	104 ,,
. . . bronze armours and daggers, and many other implements	3174 ,,

'(61) When [the booty, as the number has been written above,] was placed apart, fire was set to the camp, to their tents of skins, and to all their baggage.'

Such was the great battle of Prosopis, in the 5th year[7] of the reign of Mineptah, by which the threatening irruption of the Libyans (Libu) and their allies upon Egypt was repulsed. With the Libyans, who were held in contempt by the Egyptians as uncircumcised, were joined mercenary troops of the Caucaso-Colchian race, who in these times had migrated into Libya,[8] and rendered military service for pay, partly in Egypt and partly in Libya. In the times of Ramses III. they appeared again on the scene of Egyptian

[7] This regnal year is determined once for all by a monument which I have discovered at Cairo. See also my work, in the press, *On the Libyan Peoples in the Fourteenth and Fifteenth Centuries before Christ.*

[8] May they have been revolted prisoners of war, whom Ramses II. (Sesostris) had brought from Asia to Egypt in his military expeditions?

history, increased by names of peoples and races, some of which have been preserved among the Greeks in the exact equivalent forms. We annex the list of them, in order that we may here at once dispose of the question as to the origin of these tribes, who were highly esteemed by the Egyptians as being circumcised :—

1. Qaiqasha : the Caucasians.
2. Aqaiuasha : the Achæans of the Caucasus.
3. Shardana : the Sardones, Chartani.
4. Shakalsha : the people of Zagylis.
5. Tursha : the Taurians.
6. Zakar, Zakkari : the Zyges, Zygritæ.
7. Leku : the Ligyes.
8. Uashash : the Ossetes.

To identify these *circumcised* tribes, as some have done, with the Achæans, Sardinians, Siculi, Etruscans, Teucrians, Lycians, and Oscans, of classical antiquity, is to introduce a serious error into the primitive history of the classic nations.

We ought to give all credit to the assurances of the inscriptions on stone and the writings on papyrus, when they tell us how, after her deliverance from such dangerous enemies as the Libyans and their allies, Egypt again took breath with joyful courage, and the people, feeling themselves freed from a pressing incubus, gave loud and jubilant utterance to their joyous sense of victory. The chief share in this rejoicing must have belonged to the Egyptian lowlanders of the Delta, whose cities and villages touched, to the west, on the borders of the enemies, and especially on the Colchian group and the Carian immigrants, whom we shall again meet with presently when we come to describe the wars of Ramses III. against the Libyans. In what was afterwards called the Mareotic nome, the Danau were settled in the district named by the geographer Ptolemy Teneia, or Taineia. Their next neighbours were the Purosatha, the Prosoditæ of the same writer; while onwards along the coast, as far as the great Catabathmus, the last remnant of the Shakalsha still remained at the time of the Romans in the village of Zagylis; and the descendants of the Shardana and the Zakkar were perpetuated in the small tribes of the Chartani and the Zygritæ. The whole coast beyond, as far as Cyrene, appears to have been a gathering-ground of warlike adventurers of the Colchio-Cretan tribes, up to the Dardani,[9] whose name again is faithfully reflected in that of the city of Dardanis.

The officials and priests at the court of Mineptah were not backward in extolling their Pharaoh to the heavens. The fragments, which happen to have been preserved, of the writings and epistolary communications of some of these officers, display a poetical enthusiasm in lauding the king, whom they commonly introduce under his throne name of Bi-n-ra (or Bi-n-pra, 'soul of Ra'), as an invincible conqueror; and they exhaust themselves *usque ad nauseam* in the most flattering descriptions of his exploits.

The relations which Mineptah maintained with the Khita, towards the East, were of the most friendly nature, in consequence of the old treaty of peace.[1] His

[9] See p. 46.   [1] See p. 71.

contribution of corn to the people of the Khita, already mentioned,[2] gives the most striking confirmation of this view. The fortresses and wells, which the kings Thutmes III. and Ramses II. had established in Canaan, and had provided with Egyptian garrisons, still existed under Mineptah. With them, as well as with the inhabitants of Gaza, who were dependent on Egypt, a constant intercourse was regularly maintained, and messengers went to and fro as bearers of the king's orders, or to carry tidings to the court from the East. The official bearers of despatches belonged mostly to the people of the Canaanites, as their names fully prove. We cite, as an example, with some corrections, the records of despatches inscribed on the back of the papyrus Anastasi III. (first deciphered by M. Chabas), which was written in the third regnal year of king Mineptah:—

'In the year 3, Pakhons, day 15. There have gone up (i.e. departed) from Gaza the servant Ba'al .... son of Zapur, who is bound for Khal (Phœnicia); two government despatches of miscellaneous contents. The messenger of the controller (?) Khaa; one despatch. The prince (king?) of Zor (Tyrus), Ba'al-ma-rom-ga-bu; one despatch.'

'In the year 3, Pakhons, day 27. There have arrived the leaders of the foreign legion of the fountain of Mineptah-Hotephima, in order that these overseers might vindicate themselves in the fortress of Khetam (the Etham of the Bible), in the district of Zor (the Tanitic nome).'

'In the year 3, Pakhons, day 28. There have departed from Gaza the servant Thut, son of Za-ka-li-man, the Maza (?) Duin, son of Sha-ma-Ba'al, from the same place; Sutekh-mes, son of 'Aper-degar, from the same place; who have gone to the king; the steward of the controller (?) Khaa. Replies: one despatch.'

---

[2] See p. 124.

'There have departed from the tower of Mineptah-Hotephima (Ostracine), the servant Nekh-amon, son of Zor, who goes to the land of Zarduna,³ and who is bound for Khal (Phœnicia); two despatches of miscellaneous contents. The steward of the controller (?), Pen-amon; one despatch. The temple-overseer, Ramessu, from this city (i.e. Tanis); one despatch. The town-reeve, Zani, from the city of Mineptah-Hotephima, which is situated in the district of Amor, who are going to the king; two despatches of miscellaneous contents. The steward of the controller (?) Pr'a-em-hib; one despatch. The .... (?) .... Pr'a-em-hib; one despatch.'

'In the year 3, Pakhons, day 25. There has departed the commander of the war-chariots, An-ua-uu, of the administration of the court of the king Bi-n-ra Miamun.'

In this list of officers, departing and arriving, we have to recognize nothing more than the business-entries of some scribe, to serve as his memoranda on future occasions.

The nomad tribes of the Edomite Shasu—who under Seti I. still regarded the eastern region of the Delta, up to the neighbourhood of Zoan, the city of Ramses, as their own possession, until they were driven out by that Pharaoh over the eastern frontier—bestirred themselves anew under Mineptah II., but now in a manner alike peaceful and loyal. As faithful subjects of Pharaoh, they asked for a passage through the border fortress of Khetam, in the land of Thuku⁴ (Sukoth), in order to find sustenance for themselves and their herds in the rich pasture-lands of the lake district about the city of Pitum (Pithom).

On this subject an Egyptian official makes the following report:—

³ The Hebrew Zarthon, Zaretan in the A.V. (Josh. iii. 16).
⁴ So *here* in the German. See the note to Vol. I. p. 233.—ED.

'Another matter for the satisfaction of my master's heart. We have carried into effect the passage of the tribes of the Shasu from the land of Aduma (Edom), through the fortress (Khetam) of Mineptah-Hotephima, which is situated in Thuku (Sukoth), to the lakes of the city Pi-tum, of Mineptah-Hotephima, which are situated in the land of Thuku, in order to feed themselves and to feed their herds on the possessions of Pharaoh, who is there a beneficent sun for all peoples. In the year 8 . . . . Set, I caused them to be conducted, according to the list of the . . . . for the . . . . of the other names of the days, on which the fortress (Khetam) of Mineptah-Hotephima is opened for their passage.'[5]

As Ramses-Sesostris, the builder of the temple-city of the same name in the territory of Zoan-Tanis, must be regarded beyond all doubt as the Pharaoh under whom the Jewish legislator Moses first saw the light, so the chronological relations—having regard to the great age of the two contemporaries, Ramses II. and Moses—demand that Mineptah II. should in all probability be acknowledged as the PHARAOH OF THE EXODUS. He also had his royal seat in the city of Ramses, and seems to have strengthened its fortifications. The Bible speaks of him only under the general name of PHARAOH, that is, under a true Egyptian title, which was becoming more and more frequent at the time now under our notice. PIR-'AO—'great house, high gate'—is, according to the monuments, the designation of the king of the land of Egypt for the time being. This does not of itself furnish a decisive argument; but then, besides, the incidental statement of the Psalmist, that Moses wrought his wonders *in the field of Zoan* (Psalm lxxviii. 43), carries us back again

[5] Pap. Anastasi VI., pp. 4, 5.

to those sovereigns, Ramses II. and Mineptah, who were fond of holding their court in Zoan-Ramses.

Some scholars have recently sought to recognize the Egyptian appellation of the Hebrews in the name of the so-called 'Aper, 'Apura, or 'Aperiu, the Erythræan people in the east of the nome of Heliopolis, in what is known as the ' red country' on the ' red mountain;' and hence they have drawn conclusions which—speaking modestly, according to our knowledge of the monuments—rest on a weak foundation. According to the inscriptions, the name of this people appears in connection with the breeding of horses and the art of horsemanship. In an historical narrative of the time of Thutmes III. (unfortunately much obliterated),[6] the 'Apura are named as horsemen or knights (*senen*), who mount their horses at the king's command. In another document, of the time of Ramses III., long after the Exodus of the Jews from Egypt, 2,083 'Aperiu are introduced, as settlers in Heliopolis, with the words, 'Knights, sons of the kings and noble lords (Marina) of the 'Aper, settled people, who dwell in this place.' Under Ramses IV. we again meet with 'Aper, 800 in number, as inhabitants of foreign origin in the district of 'Ani or 'Aini, on the western shore of the Red Sea, in the neighbourhood of the modern Suez.

These and similar data completely exclude all thought of the Hebrews, unless any one is disposed to

---

[6] Translated for the first time by Mr. Goodwin in the *Transactions of the Society of Biblical Archæology*, vol. iii., part i., pp. 342, foll.

have recourse to suppositions and conjectures against the most explicit statements of the biblical records. On the other hand, the hope can scarcely be cherished that we shall ever find on the public monuments—rather let us say in some hidden roll of papyrus—the events, repeated in an Egyptian version, which relate to the Exodus of the Jews and the destruction of Pharaoh in the Red Sea. For the record of these events was inseparably connected with the humiliating confession of a divine visitation, to which a patriotic writer at the court of Pharaoh would hardly have brought his mind.

Presupposing, then, that Mineptah is to be regarded as the Pharaoh of the Exodus, this king must have had to endure serious disturbances of all kinds during the time of his reign :—in the West the Libyans, in the East the Hebrews, and—we have now to add—in the South a spirit of rebellion, which declared itself by the insurrection of a rival king of the family of the great Ramses-Sesostris. The events which form the lamentable close of his rule are passed over by the monuments with perfect silence. The dumb tumulus covers the misfortunes which befel Egypt and her king.

In casting a glance over the most eminent contemporaries of this king, we are reminded especially of his viceroy in Ethiopia, the 'king's son of Kush,' named Mas,—the same who had been invested with this high office in the southern province under Ramses II. His memory has been perpetuated in a rock-inscription at Assouan. We may further make mention—instructed by a record in the quarries of Silsilis—of the noble Pinehas, an Egyptian namesake of the Hebrew Phinehas, the son of Eleazar, son of Aaron. In conclusion, let us not forget the very influential highpriest of Amon, Roi or Loi, Lui (i.e. Levi), who under Mineptah held the command of the legion of Amon, administered the treasury of Amon, and, according to the custom of the time,[7] was chief architect to Pharaoh. To be sure this must have been an easy office for him, since there was not much building, except perhaps the royal sepulchre, which the drowned Pharaoh probably never entered.[8]

The more troublous the times, the less thought

[7] See our account of the life of his predecessor, Bek-en-khonsu, pp. 117–19.

[8] Without discussing the Author's view, which is beyond an Editor's province, it will suffice to say that writers of high authority, both Biblical scholars and Egyptologists, hold that it is not a *necessary* inference from the Scripture narrative that Pharaoh *himself* was drowned in the Red Sea, and it is difficult to suppose that this was Mineptah's end, unless we impute to the Egyptians an elaborate fiction about his death and burial. Besides his splendid tomb, we possess a papyrus (*Anastasi* IV.) containing a highly eulogistic 'Dirge of Mineptah' (as it is entitled by the translators), in which the Pharaoh is congratulated on having been blessed by Amon with 'a good old age,' after a lifetime of pleasure 'and a most prosperous reign,' ending : 'Thou hast gone before the gods, the victor, the justified.' The piece has been translated by M. Chabas (*L'Egypte aux temps de l'Exode*), and by Dr. Birch (*Records of the Past*, vol. iv. pp. 49, foll.), who observes that the *titles* do not exactly correspond with those of Mineptah, and that the dirge *may* refer to his son Seti II. M. Maspero holds that the composition is copied almost word for word from a song of triumph dedicated to Mineptah II. and appropriated to Seti II. by a mere substitution of names (*Histoire ancienne des peuples de l'Orient*, p. 255). The same high authority places the Exodus under Seti II., but for reasons which do not seem very decisive (p. 259).—ED.

was there of heroic expeditions, and the greater was the attention paid to the pursuit of elegant knowledge under a learned priesthood. The worthy Thebans have left us many specimens of their works. History, divinity, practical philosophy, poetry and tales,—all that unbent the mind from the anxieties of worldly business was brought within the sphere of their activity. The following temple-scribes are among the brilliant stars of this galaxy of writers : Qa-ga-bu, Hor, Anna, Mer-em-aput, Bek-en-ptah, Hor-a, Amon-masu, Su-an-ro, Ser-ptah. If we add to these the name, belonging to the earlier time, of Pentaur, the author of the epic of Ramses-Sesostris, also of Amen-em-ant, the director of the Theban library, as well as those of Amon-em-api and Pan-bas, we have completed the cycle of the lights of learning in those times from Ramses II. downwards.

Mineptah II. was succeeded in his dominion by his son and heir—

V. SETI II. MINEPTAH III.,

with the official name of

USER-KHEPERU-RA. B.C. 1266.

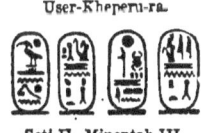

User-Kheperu-ra.

Seti II. Mineptah III.

Already during the lifetime of his royal father, Seti II. enjoyed a special distinction, inasmuch as, with reference to his future dignity as Pharaoh, the son is frequently designated, and that with unmistakable emphasis, as crown prince of the empire. We possess records of the first two years only of his reign, which at that time extended over all Egypt, in inscriptions scattered here and there as far to the south as Ibsamboul. The Ramses-city of Zoan-Tanis remained, as before, the special residence of the court, whence were issued the king's orders to his officers, especially with regard to the administration of the Egyptian posts in Western Asia. As in the preceding time, special attention was devoted to the fortresses eastward of Tanis, which covered the entrance from Syria. Here was the old royal road, which offered fugitives the only opportunity of escaping from the king's power, though not without danger. That such attempts were often made, is proved by the following report of a scribe, who had gone out upon the road from the city of Ramses, in order to retake two fugitive servants of the court :—

'I set out (he says) from the hall of the royal palace on the 9th day of the month Epiphi, in the evening, after the two servants. I arrived at the fortress of Thuku (Sukoth) on the 10th of Epiphi. I was informed that the men had resolved to take their way towards the south. On the 12th I reached Khetam (Etham). There I was informed that grooms, who had come from the neighbourhood [of the 'sedge-city,' had reported] that the fugitives had already passed the rampart (i.e. the Shur of the Bible, Gerrhon of the Greeks) to the north of the Migdol of king Seti Mineptah.'[9]

Notwithstanding the apparent shortness of his reign, in consequence of the power of one or two anti-kings, of whom we shall have to speak further,

[9] On the striking light which this letter throws on the passage of the Israelites out of Egypt, see the author's *Discourse on the Exodus and the Egyptian Monuments*, printed at the end of this volume.—ED.

Seti II. found the time and means to erect a special sanctuary to his father Amon in the great temple of the empire at Api. This is the small temple, consisting of three chambers, to the north-west of the great front court;[1] an insignificant building, which merely attests the official acknowledgment of the king on the part of the priestly guild of Thebes. Loi (Levi), the high-priest of the god Amon, was friendly to the king, as was also his son and successor in office, Roma. Both were declared adherents of the king, whose affection for the pious fathers of Amon shows itself also in other forms in the extant papyri. It was for him, while he was still crown prince, that a temple-scribe composed that wonderful tale of 'The Two Brothers,' the translation of which, by the late master of Egyptology, E. de Rougé, gave such an unexpected surprise to the learned world.[2]

The sepulchre of this king, in the rocky valley of Biban-el-Molouk, is really princelike and magnificent. In it also we have a new proof of the priestly recognition of his sovereignty over the land of Egypt.

After his death the sovereignty passed in regular succession to his son—

[1] Marked L on the plan of Mariette-Bey.
[2] The first part of this beautiful tale, which contains a wonderful parallel to the history of Joseph, has been already given in Vol. I. pp. 309-11.—ED.

VI. SETNAKHT MERER MIAMUN II., B.C. 1233, called by his official surname—

USER-KHA-RA MIAMUN SOTEP-EN-RA.

Userkhara Miamun.

Setnakht.

All that we are able to say of him can be condensed into a few words; that he was the father of a great illustrious king, and that he lived in times full of disturbance and trouble. As his father had, in all probability, been opposed by a rival king, Amenmessu, so had the son of the latter, Mineptah Siptah, become a dangerous successor against Setnakht. Siptah, the husband of that queen Ta-user,—whose grave obtained a very distinguished position in the valley of the kings at Thebes, in the midst of those of the men,—seems to have been favoured by a number of adherents in the city of Amon, and to have owed his elevation to the throne to the help of an Egyptian noble, named Bi. This latter held the office of one of the first confidential servants of the king, and he declares on his own behalf that 'he put away falsehood and gave honour to the truth, inasmuch as he set the king upon his father's throne—he, the great keeper of the seal for all the land, Ramessu-kha-em-nutern-Bi.' Among the remaining adherents of the anti-king, no insignificant part was played by his governor of the southern lands, Seti, whose memory has been perpetuated by an inscription on the south wall of the rock-temple of Ibsamboul. In that representation, this official exhibits himself as a zealous worshipper of the Theban Amon, and there is appended an inscription of four lines, giving the following explanation :—

'(1) Worship offered to Amon, that he may grant life, prosperity, and health, to the person of the king's envoy into all lands, the companion (2) of the lord of the land, of the friend of Hor (i.e. the king) in his house, the first commander of the war-chariots of his Majesty, (3) who understood his purpose, when the king came, to exalt (him) the king's son of Kush, (4) Seti, upon his throne (or, the throne of his father ?) in the first year of the lord of the land, Ramessu Siptah.'

On the summit of a group of rocks on the island of Sehêl, in the neighbourhood of Philæ, there remains the following inscription of the same Seti, annexed to the name of his king :—

'In the year 3, Pakhons, day 21. Honour to thy name, O king ! May it attest the acknowledgments of the person of the commander of the chariots, and the King's son of Kush, and the governor of the southern lands, Seti !'

Underneath is an inscription nearly to the same effect :—

'The hereditary prince, bearer of the fan, King's son of Kush, governor of the southern lands, Seti—'

We cannot tell what other historical information the inscriptions and papyrus-rolls of those rival and anti-kings might have been ready to give us (i.e. if they had not been cancelled by their successful rivals). On the last visit which we paid at Thebes, a year ago, to the grave of 'the great queen and lady of the land, the princess of Upper and Lower Egypt, Ta-user,' we were able again to corroborate the fact, that the names of her husband Siptah are seen at its entrance, while in the interior, on the piece which has been laid on to cover the names of the queen, the royal shields of Setnakht meet the spectator in a re-engraving. Setnakht took possession of his predecessor's sepulchre, or rather that of his wife, without in a single case replacing the feminine grammatical signs in the inscriptions by the corresponding masculine forms. His rival having been driven out, Setnakht could deal with the tomb at his pleasure.

Nor was it only against native claimants of the throne, that Setnakht had to maintain a conflict for the double crown : foreigners also contributed their efforts to turn Egypt upside down. A certain Khal, or Phœnician, had seized the throne, maintained himself on it for some time, driven the Egyptians into banishment, and grievously oppressed those left in the land. This is that Arisu or Alisu, Arius or Alius, whom the great Harris papyrus first made known to us. We conclude with a translation of the part of this record which refers to the Nineteenth Dynasty, while we regret our inability to suppress the remark, that the translations hitherto put forth by several scholars have completely mistaken the sense of the document just in its most important passages.[3]

King Ramses III., the son of Setnakht, gives, by

[3] The most recent translation of the 'Great Harris Papyrus,' by Professor Eisenlohr and Dr. Samuel Birch, is given in the *Records of the Past*, vols. vi. and viii. The historical part here referred to, forming the last five of the seventy-nine leaves into which the papyrus was divided by Mr. Harris (Plates 75-79 of the British Museum publication), begins at vol. vi. p. 45 (see Dr. Brugsch's mention of the B. M. edition in his Preface).—ED.

way of introduction to his own reign, the following summary of the events immediately before his accession to the throne :—

'Thus says king Ramessu III., the great god, to the princes and leaders of the land, to the warriors and to the chariot soldiers, to the Shairdana, and the numerous foreign mercenaries, and to all the living inhabitants of the land of Ta-mera:—

'Hearken! I make you to know my glorious deeds, which I have performed as king of men.

'The people of Egypt lived in banishment abroad. Of those who lived in the interior of the land, none had any to care for him. So passed away long years, until other times came. The land of Egypt belonged to princes from foreign parts. They slew one another, whether noble or mean.

'Other times came on afterwards, during years of scarcity. Arisu, a Phœnician, had raised himself among them to be a prince, and he compelled all the people to pay him tribute. Whatever any had gathered together, that his companions robbed them of. Thus did they. The gods were treated like the men. They went without the appointed sin-offerings in the temples.

'Then did the gods turn this state of things to prosperity. They restored to the land its even balance, such as its condition properly required. And they established their son, who had come forth from their body, as king of the whole land on their exalted throne. This was king Setnakht Merer Miamun.

'He was like the person of Set when he is indignant. He took care for the whole land. If rebels showed themselves, he slew the wicked who made a disturbance in the land of Ta-mera.

'He purified the exalted royal throne of Egypt, and so he was the ruler of the inhabitants on the throne of the sun-god Tum, while he raised up their faces. Such as showed themselves refusing to acknowledge any one as a brother, were locked up.[4]

---

[4] Literally, walled up. That this punishment was sometimes inflicted by the kings, I can prove by the testimony of my own eyes. When Mariette-Bey opened the sepulchres of the Apis-bulls in the Serapeum, in 1850, there was found in one of the walls the skeleton of a culprit who had been walled up in ancient times.

'He restored order to the temples, granting the sacred revenues for the due offerings to the gods, as their statutes prescribe.

'He raised me up as heir to the throne on the seat of the earth-god Seb, to be the great governor of the Egyptian dominions in care for the whole people, who have found themselves united together again.

'And he went to his rest out of his orbit of light, like the company of the celestials. The (funeral) rites of Osiris were accomplished for him. He was borne (to his grave) in his royal boat over the river, and was laid in his everlasting house on the west side of Thebes.

'And my father Amon, the lord of the gods, and Ra, and Ptah with the beautiful face, caused me to be crowned as lord of the land on the throne of my parent.

'I received the dignities of my father amidst shouts of joy. The people were content and delighted because of the peace. They rejoiced in my countenance as king of the land, for I was like Horus, who was king over the land on the throne of Osiris. Thus was I crowned with the Atef-crown, together with the Uræus-serpents; I put on the ornament of the double plumes, like the god Tatanen; thus I reposed myself on the throne-seat of Hormakhu; thus was I clothed with the robes of state, like Tum.'

King Ramses, the third of the name, opened the long series of Pharaohs of the succeeding dynasty. With him also we begin a new chapter of our History of Egypt.

User-ma-ra Miamun.

Ramses III.

CHAPTER XV.

THE TWENTIETH DYNASTY.

RAMSES III. HAQ-ON. B.C. 1200.

As this king's official name was User-ma-ra Miamun, he is only distinguished from Ramses II. by the title Haq-On, that is, 'Prince of Heliopolis.' Among the people, as is proved by the monuments, he bore the appellation of RAMESSU-PA-NUTER, or PA-NUTI, that is, 'Ramses the god,' from which the Greeks formed the well-known name of Rhampsinitus.[1] And, as his name, so also his deeds—nay even his wealth in the blessing of children—remind us of Ramses Sesostris, whom he evidently honoured as the ideal type and model of a great Pharaoh.

The miserable state of Egypt before his accession could not be better described than in his own words, cited in the last chapter. The same Harris papyrus, which has enabled us to lay before our readers such valuable information on the condition of the land of the Pharaohs at the time referred to, proceeds to give a general view of the 'glorious deeds' of this Ramses. It is a comprehensive outline of his eventful life, of

[1] Herod. ii. 121.

which, following the king's own words, we propose to set forth in order the chief occurrences.²

The first care of king Rhampsinitus, after his accession, was for the restoration and demarcation of the several castes, which he arranged in their descending degrees, as follows: The Ab en Pir'ao, 'counsellors of Pharaoh,' an office with which we have seen Joseph invested at the court of Pharaoh:³ the 'great princes,' evidently the governors and representatives of the king in the several nomes: 'the infantry and chariot-soldiers;' the mercenaries of the tribes of the Shardana and the Kahak: and, lastly, the lowest classes of the officers and servants.

He was next occupied with wars against foreign nations, who had invaded the borders of Egypt, and for whose punishment he prepared severe blows in their own land. The Danau were pursued by Pharaoh to the Cilician coast, and were there defeated; so in Cyprus were the Zekkaru (Zygritæ), and the Perusatha (Prosoditæ); while the Colchio-Caucasian Shardana (Sardones), and the Uashasha (Ossetes), on the other hand, were exterminated in their settlements west of the Delta, and were transplanted to Egypt in great masses, with their families. They were compelled to settle in a Ramesseum, a fortress still unknown to us, and to pay every year, according to the custom of the country, a tribute of woven stuffs and corn to the temples of Egypt.

---

² See the *Harris Papyrus*, Plates 76–79; *Records of the Past*, vol. viii. pp. 47–52.—ED.

³ See Vol. I. p. 307.

On the east of Egypt, the arms of the king achieved a like success against the Sahir, the Seirites of Holy Scripture, who are clearly recognized as a branch of the Shasu. The king plundered their tents and the dwellers in them, seized their possessions and effects, with their cattle, and carried off the people as prisoners to Egypt, to give them as special slaves to the temples.

A new war was kindled by the Libyans and Maxyes. In like manner as had already happened under the reign of Mineptah II., these nomad and warlike tribes of the West had made an inroad into the Delta, and occupied the whole country which stretched along the left bank of the Canopic branch of the Nile, from Memphis as far as Carbana (Canopus). In the neighbourhood of the latter place, along the seashore, lay the district of Gautut, the cities of which they had held for many years. They and their allies were defeated by the Pharaoh, and among the latter the king mentions by name the Asbita (Asbytæ), the Kaikasha (Caucasians), the Shai-ap (who cannot be more closely defined), the Hasa (Ausees), the Bakana (Bakaloi). The king of the Libu, his family, and the whole people, together with their herds, were transplanted as captives to Egypt, where some were placed in the fortified 'Ramessea,' and others branded with hot iron 'in the name of the king' as sailors. A magnificent gift was made of their herds to the temple of Amon at Thebes.

For the protection of the eastern frontier towards Suez, the king formed a great well, and surrounded it with strong defences, in the country of 'Aina or 'Aian (the home of the 'Aperiu, or Erythræans). The walls had a height of thirty Egyptian cubits (nearly sixteen mètres, 52½ English feet). In the harbour of Suez, and therefore in close proximity to the fortress of the well, Ramses III. built a fleet of large and small ships, to make voyages on the Red Sea to the coasts of Punt and ' the Holy Land.' The bringing of the costly productions of those distant regions, and especially of incense, is expressly set forth as the immediate purpose of their construction. Connected with these objects was the establishing of trade relations with the kings and princes of the countries on those coasts, and a caravan trade by land was established on the road from Kosseir to Coptos on the Nile. In a word, Ramses III. opened a direct intercourse by land and sea with the rich countries on the shores of the Indian Ocean, which in later times was renewed by the Ptolemies, with great advantage to the commerce of the whole world.

Not less important for Egypt, which above all things required copper for a variety of objects of industrial activity, was the despatch of a mission by land (on asses!), and on ships by sea, for the discovery of the rich copper mines of 'Athaka (in the neighbourhood of the gulf of Akaba?); and the metal, shining like gold, and in the form of bricks, was brought from the smelting-houses in those parts and laden on the ships.

The king also turned his attention anew to the treasures of the peninsula of Sinai, which from the times of king Senoferu[4] had appeared to the Egyptians so desirable. Laden with rich presents for the temple of the goddess Hathor, protectress of the Mafka peninsula, distinguished officials went thither on the king's commission, to bring to the treasuries of Pharaoh the much-prized greenish-blue copperstone (Mafka turquoises?).

In the whole land of Egypt (thus the king concludes his remarkable account) he planted trees and shrubs to give the inhabitants rest under their cool shade. The benefit which he conferred on his country by this measure will be fully appreciated by those who have passed long years of their life in the valley of the Nile. The planting of trees has likewise been undertaken in the most recent times by the Khedive Ismael Pasha, and complete success has attended this beneficent work.

In a beautiful poetic effusion of rhetoric, Rhampsinitus concludes by extolling the peaceful condition of the whole country. The weakest woman could travel unmolested on all the roads.[5] The Shardana and the Kahak remained quietly in their cities. Kush had ceased to annoy Egypt with its attacks. The Phœnicians let their bows and arrows rest in peace.

In a prolonged strain of praise to himself, the king enumerates his benefits towards gods and men, to-

[4] See Vol. I. p. 80.
[5] We are irresistibly reminded of Bede's description (*E. H.* ii. 16) of the security established in Britain by Edwin of Northumbria, 'ut, sicut usque hodie in proverbio dicitur, etiam si mulier una cum recens nato parvulo vellet totam perambulare insulam a mari ad mare, nullo se lædente valeret.'—ED.

wards poor and rich; and finally, in the 32nd year of his reign, he recommends his son Ramses IV., whom he had raised to the throne as joint king with himself, to the recognition and obedience of his fortunate subjects.

We have thus placed clearly before the eyes of our readers a short sketch of the deeds of this Egyptian Pharaoh during his reign of thirty-two years. In so far as the sure guidance of the monuments does not fail us, we will endeavour to fill up this broad outline of his deeds with more definite facts. The material for our work is supplied by the Ramesseum at Medinet-Abou; that enormous building which, lying to the west of the city of Thebes, and to the south-west of the gigantic statues of Memnon, was turned from a treasure-house into a complete temple of victory. The 5th, 8th, and 11th years of the reign of Ramses III. designate the period of time occupied in the gradual completion of the plan laid down for the buildings, from west to east.[6] The treasure-

[6] From a hieratic inscription on the rock of the quarry of Silsilis, put up in the month Pakhons of the 5th year of Ramses III., it is clearly ascertained that, at the date named, the king had given to his court-official, Seti-em-hib, the treasurer of the temple about to be founded anew, the commission to quarry stones at that place for the building. Here is the translation of this record:

'In the year 5, in the month Pakhons, under the reign of the king and lord of the land, User-ma-ra Miamun, the son of Ra and lord of the crowns, Ramses Haq-An, the friend of all the gods, the dispenser of life for ever and ever, the command of his royal Majesty was issued to the treasurer Seti-em-hib, at the temple of many years' duration of King User-ma-ra Miamun in the city of Amon, to put into execution the monumental works at the

chambers, on the southern side of the hindmost hall, are now empty. Pictures and words alone replace the ' mammon ' which is now gone. If it be true, as the inscriptions clearly and distinctly declare, that the treasures once hoarded here were dedicated by Rhampsinitus as gifts to the Theban Amon, the king of the gods had no reason to complain. Gold in grains, in full purses up to the weight of 1000 lbs., from the mines of Amamu in the land of Kush, of Edfou (Apollinopolis Magna), of Ombos and of Koptos; bars of silver; whole pyramids of blue and green stones, besides the much-prized bluestone of Tafrer (the land of the Tybarenes?), and the real greenstone of Roshatha; copper ore; lead; precious sorts of incense from Punt and from the Holy Land; moreover gold and silver statues, images of animals, vases, chests, and other ornaments, down to the seal-rings with the name of the king upon them;—all these and many other things a hundred-thousandfold did the Pharaoh dedicate to show his gratitude to the god, of course with an elaborate address:[7]—

'I dedicate this to thee as a memorial for thy temple, consisting of clear raw copper, and raw gold, and [of all works of art], temple of many years' duration of King User-ma-ra Miamun in the city of Amon on the west side of Us (Thebes).

[Catalogue] of the people who were under his command: men	2,000
Hewers of stone: men	200
The crews of 40 broad ships of 100 cubits long (?) and of 4 pairs of ships with beaks	800
Making together individual heads	3,000 '

[7] Concerning the details of these offerings, see below, p. 160.—ED.

which have come forth from the workshops of the sculptor. The productions of the land of Ruthen shall be brought to thee as gifts, to fill the treasury of thy temple with the best things of all lands.'

Again :—

'Thou hast received gold and silver like sand on the [sea] shore. What thou hast created in the river and in the mountain, that I dedicate to thee by heaps upon the earth. Let it be an adornment for thy Majesty for ever. I offer to thee blue and green precious stones, and all kinds of jewels in chests of bright copper. I have made for thee numberless talismans out of all kinds of valuable precious stones.'

In truth Rhampsinitus was in this respect no niggard, and if we may be allowed from the costliness of his gifts to draw a safe conclusion as to the position of the donor, Ramses III. must have enjoyed enormous wealth. We shall not omit the opportunity presently, on the authority of information contained in the Harris papyrus, to set in a clear light the boundless generosity of the king, not only towards the temple of Amon, but also towards the sanctuaries of the great national gods, Ptah of Memphis, and Ra of Heliopolis.

When Ramses III. came to the throne, things looked bad for Egypt, as well in the East as in the West.

'The hostile Asiatics and Thuhennu robbers (the Libyan Marmaridæ) showed themselves only to injure the state of Egypt. The land lay open before them in weakness since the time of the earlier kings. They did evil to gods as well as to men. No one had so strong an arm as to oppose them, on account of their hostile intentions.'

In the 5th year of his reign the enemies prepared a fresh attack on Egypt from the West.

'The people of the Thamhu assembled together in one place. The tribes of the Maxyes prepared themselves for a raid out of their own country. The leaders of their warriors had confidence in their plans.'

As in former times the Libyan kings, Didi, Mashakan, and Mar-aju, were the prime movers of hostilities against Egypt, so now the kings Zamar and Zautmar of Libya appear as instigators and leaders in battle. Their last great place of reunion was the country of Libya in the narrower sense of the word. The victory of the king over the enemy was very decisive. It took place in the neighbourhood of the Ramses-fortress of Khesef-Thamhue. The defeat of the enemy, both circumcised and uncircumcised tribes, was tremendous; for 12,535 members and hands, which were cut off from dead enemies, were counted over before the proud victorious king.

Three years after this event, which gave occasion for great festivities in Egypt, a warlike movement broke out against Egypt from the North, caused by the migrations of the Carian and Colchian tribes which, from Cilicia and the mountains of Armenia, partly by land through Asia Minor, and partly by water on the Mediterranean, made a formidable campaign against Egypt, only to be at last utterly defeated in a naval engagement at Migdol, at the mouth of the Pelusiac branch of the Nile. The inscriptions of the temple of victory relate to us this great event in the following manner:—

'A quivering[8] seized the people in their limbs: they came up

---

[8] Not of fear, but of eager agitation, as it is said below of the war-horses (p. 154).—ED.

leaping from their coasts and islands, and spread themselves all at once over the lands. No people stood before their arms, beginning with the people of Khita, of Kadi (Galilee), and Karchemish, Aradus, and Alus. They wasted these countries, and pitched a camp at one place in the land of the Amorites. They plundered the inhabitants and the territory as if they had been nothing. And they came on (against Egypt), but there was held in readiness a fiery furnace before their countenance on the side of Egypt. Their home was in the land of the Purosatha, the Zakkar, the Shakalsha, the Daanau, and the Uashuash. These nations had leagued together; they laid their hand on the double land of Egypt, to encircle the land. Their heart was full of confidence, they were full of plans. This happened, since such was the will of this god, the lord of the gods (Amon of Thebes). An ambush was prepared to take them in the snare like birds. He (Amon) gave me strength, and granted success to my plans. My arm was strong as iron when I broke forth. I had guarded well my boundary up to Zah (Philistia). There stood in ambush over against them the chief leaders, the governors, the noble marinas, and the chief people of the warriors. [A defence] was built on the water, like a strong wall, of ships of war, of merchantmen, of boats and skiffs. They were manned from the forepart to the hindpart with the bravest warriors, who bore their arms, and with the best life-guards of the land of Egypt. They were like roaring lions on the mountain. The knights were of the swiftest in the race, and the most distinguished horsemen of a skilful hand. Their horses quivered in all their limbs, ready to trample the nations under their hoofs. I was like the war-god Monthu, the strong. I held my ground before them. They beheld the battle of my hands. I, king Ramessu III., I went far forward in the van, conscious of my might, strong of arm, protecting my soldiers in the day of battle. They who had reached the boundary of my country never more reaped harvest. Their soul and their spirit passed away for ever. They who had assembled themselves over against the others on the great sea, a mighty firebrand lightened before them, in front of the mouths of the river. A wall of iron shut them in upon the lake. They were driven away, dashed to the ground, hewn down on the bank of the water. They were slain by hundreds of heaps of corpses. The end was a new beginning. Their ships and all their possessions lay strewn on the mirror of the water. Thus have I taken from the nations the desire to direct their thoughts against Egypt. They exalt my name in their country; yea, their heart is on fire for me so long as I shall sit on the throne of Hormakhu.'

Such was this great battle by sea and land against those invaders, of whom numerous inscriptions, some longer, some shorter, tell us so much in eloquent language. I will give here two examples:—

'A trembling seized the inhabitants of the northern regions in their body, because of the Purosatha and the Zakkar, because they plundered their land. If they went out to meet them, their spirit failed. Some were brave people by land, others on the sea.[9] Those who came by way of the land, Amon-ra pursued them and annihilated them. Those who entered into the mouths of the Nile were caught like birds in nets. They were made prisoners.'

Again :—

'It came to pass that the people of the northern regions, who reside in their islands and on their coasts, shuddered in their bodies. They entered into the lakes of the mouths of the Nile. Their noses snuffed the wind:[1] their desire was to breathe a soft air. The king broke forth like a whirlwind upon them, to fight them in the battle-field, like all his heroes. Their spirit was annihilated where they stood, their soul was taken from them; a stronger than they came upon them.'

But few years of peace and rest had passed by, when, in the 11th year of Rhampsinitus, a new struggle threatened the safety of the country from the West. The Maxyes attacked Egypt under the leadership of their king Mashashal (Massala), a son of Kapur, in great force, in order to obtain possession of the

[9] How it was possible to translate so simple a sentence, in opposition to the first rules of grammar, by 'they were brave people of another country,' appears absolutely incomprehensible.

[1] This phrase is used here as, in our translation of the Bible, of the wild ass (Jeremiah ii. 24, xiv. 6).—ED.

rich districts on the banks of the Canopic mouth of the Nile. A great battle was fought about the month of Mesori in the same year, and the enemy were utterly defeated. The number of the enemy who were killed was very considerable, and as they were circumcised, only their hands were cut off. Not less was the number of the prisoners, and the amount of the spoil, of which a detailed list has been handed down to us. I will here give the translation of the remarkable document relating to these details:—

'Total number of hands (cut off) . . . 2175

Prisoners of war of Pharaoh belonging to the nation of the Maxyes:

Commander-in-chief.	1	
Commanders .	5	
Maxyes: Men .	1205	
Youths	152	
Boys .	131	
Total .		1494
Their wives	342	
Girls	65	
Maid-servants .	151	
Total .		558

Total number of prisoners of war of Pharaoh, without distinction, heads .	2052
Maxyes, whom the king killed on the spot .	2175

Other things (as spoil):

Cattle—bulls .	$119+x$
Swords, 5 cubits long[2] .	115
Swords, 3 cubits long[2] .	124

---

[2] So in the German, *Ellen*; but a measure answering to the *foot* would seem more reasonable. Be this as it may, the *two*

Bows	603
Chariots of war	93
Quivers	2310
Spears	92
Horses and asses of the Maxyes . .	183'

This list seems to deserve special attention, as it gives the impression of being a faithful and complete account.

That the campaigns thus described were not the only ones conducted by the king on the blood-stained field of honour during his reign, appears from many inscriptions and tablets of victory. We know that he undertook expeditions on the south of Egypt, and conquered the negroes (Nahasi), the Thiraui, and the Amarai or Amalai. We are also informed from the same sources that, besides the Purosatha, the 'Tuirsha of the sea' were numbered among his enemies, and that the Khal (Phœnicians) and the Amorites received a severe chastisement from the Egyptian king.

Of very special value are the effigies of the conquered foreign kings and leaders, which the Pharaoh Ramses III. caused to be sculptured in a long series, one after the other, in his palace, or Ramesseum, by the side of the temple of Amon at Medinet Abou, and that, as appears to us, in a portraiture quite true to life. So far as this has been preserved, we will give at least the translation of the inscriptions which are appended to the figures of the several persons in succession:—

lengths have a parallel in the swords found by Dr. Schliemann at Mycenæ, the *long* ones being perhaps swords of state.—ED.

' 1. The king of the miserable land of Kush (Ethiopia).
2–3. Destroyed.
4. The king of the Libu (Libya).
5. The king of Turses (land of the Negroes).
6. The king of the Mashauasha (Maxyes).
7. The king of Taraua (land of the Negroes).
8. The miserable king of Khita (Hethites) as a living prisoner.
9. The miserable king of the Amori (Amorites).
10. The leader of the hostile bands of the Zakkari (Zygritæ).
11. The people of the sea of Shairdana (Chartani).
12. The leader of the hostile bands of the Shasu (Edomites).
13. The people of the sea of Tuirsha (Taurus).
14. The leader of the hostile bands of the Pu[rosatha] (Prosoditæ).'

The campaign of vengeance which Ramses III. undertook against several of the nations above named, in order to attack them in their own homes, by land and sea, must have been far more instructive than the detailed descriptions of the wars on African soil. That this campaign actually took place, we have all reasonable assurance in the names of the conquered foreign cities and countries, which cover one side of the pylon of the temple of Medinet Abou, and which we will now give in an exact translation. The reader cannot fail to share our astonishment at recognizing among them names well known to classical antiquity, in the form in which they were written 1200 years before the Christian era : [3]—

' 1. Ma . . .
2. Poro . . .

3. Puther . . . . (Patara ? in Lycia).

---

[3] A translation of this list is also given, with the rest of the inscription, by Dr. Birch in *Records of the Past*, vol. vi. pp. 17, foll.—ED.

NAMES FROM ASIA MINOR.

4. Zizi . . .	23. Kabur (Cibyra in Cilicia).
5. Tharshka (Tarsus in Cilicia).	24. Aimal (Myle in Cilicia).
6. Khareb.	25. U . . . lu (Ale in Cilicia).
7. Salomaski (Salamis in Cyprus).	26. Kushpita (Casyponis in Cilicia).
8. Kathian (Citium in Cyprus).	27. Kanu (comp. Caunus in Caria).
9. Aimar (Marion in Cyprus).	
10. Sali (Soli in Cyprus).	28. L . . . aros (Larissa).
11. Ithal (Idalium in Cyprus).	29. Arrapikha.
12. (M)aquas (Acamas in Cyprus?).	30. Shabi.
	31. Zaur (Zor-Tyrus in Cilicia).
13. Tarshebi.	32. Kilsenen (Colossæ? in Phrygia).
14. Bizar.	
15. A . . . si.	33. Maulnus (Mallus in Cilicia).
16. Aman (Mons Amanus).	34. Samai (Syme, a Carian island).
17. Alikan.	
18. Pikaz.	35. Thasakha.
19. . . . ubai.	36. Me . . . ari.
20. Kerena, Kelena (Cerynia in Cyprus).	37. I-bir-, I-bil.
	38. Athena (Adana in Cilicia).
21. Kir . . . (Curium in Cyprus).	39. Karkamash (Coracesium in Cilicia).
22. Aburoth.	

Even if some of the parallel names should receive rectification hereafter, yet still on the whole the fact remains certain, that, in this list of the conquered towns, places on the coast and islands of Asia Minor were intended by the Egyptians. In making the comparison we must at once set aside the idea, that the succession of the names corresponds to the situation of the towns and countries; since even the lists of the better-known towns, as for instance those of Canaan, are thrown together on the monuments in inextricable confusion. Even the assumption, which has lately found favour, of different campaigns having been made in different directions, does not help us to get completely over the difficulty of the totally irregular succession of the towns. In the case before us, we may assume as certain, that the places enumerated were the seats of Carian peoples in Asia Minor and on the neighbouring islands, and especially in Cilicia and Cyprus. I am happy to have been able first to point out this fact to the learned world.[4]

The rich spoil, which the king carried off in his campaigns from the captured cities and the conquered peoples, enabled him to enrich most lavishly with gifts, not only the sanctuaries in Thebes, but also the temples of Heliopolis, Memphis, and other places in Egypt, to adorn them with buildings 'in his name,' which are called 'Ramessea,' and to devote the prisoners of war as slaves to the holy service of the gods in Upper and Lower Egypt. The presents and buildings, for which the gods were indebted to their grateful son Ramses III., are all set forth according to their situation, number, and description, in the great Harris papyrus, which from this point of view has all the value of an important temple archive. We would have laid before our readers the catalogue contained in it, if only in a general summary, if this comprehensive document, which has never yet been published, had been brought to our knowledge in its full extent.[5]

---

[4] In last September's sitting of the Royal Society of the Sciences at Göttingen (1877), I took the opportunity to state more fully the proofs of these discoveries.

[5] Compare what is said in the Author's Preface respecting the complete edition of the Harris Papyrus published by the British Museum. The list of donations referred to will be found in the translation in *Records of the Past*, vol. vi. pp. 36, foll.—ED.

The translations of it, which several scholars have written with the document before them, are partly unintelligible, unless we have the original at hand, partly evidently incorrect, so that it is difficult to obtain a clear view of the several buildings and donations mentioned in it. The Ramessea are found in various parts of the country. Thebes possesses the lion's share, and next to it Heliopolis and Memphis. With regard to other places, new temples of Ramses III. are named in a summary, in their succession from south to north :—

A Ramesseum in Thinis (VIIIth nome) in honour of the Egyptian Mars, Anhur (called Onuris by the Greeks),

A Ramesseum in Abydus (VIIIth nome) for the god Osiris,

A Ramesseum in Coptos (Vth nome),

A Ramesseum in Apu (Panopolis, IXth nome),

Two Ramessea in Lycopolis (XIIIth nome),

Two Ramessea in Hermopolis (XVth nome),

A Ramesseum in the temple-town of Sutekh, in the city of Pi-Ramses Miamun (the Raamses of the Bible).

The reader desirous of further information will find in my 'Geographical Dictionary' a general list of the buildings and sanctuaries, which Ramses III. erected both in Upper and Lower Egypt. The great Harris papyrus, which has been made known in the meantime, enables us to supply the gaps which were perceptible in that list.

The temple of Amon at Medinet Abou, on Nebankh, the holy mountain of the dead, still remains the most beautiful and remarkable monument of this king. The abundant reliefs, which cover the interior and exterior walls, represent various detached episodes in his campaigns, even to an occasional lion-hunt, in a lifelike and artistic style. The appended inscriptions give an instructive explanation of the scenes. Other inscriptions, as the one on the wall which runs along the south side, give us an insight into the order of the feasts, as then observed, inclusive of the sacrifices,[6] and into the fixed holidays of the old Egyptian calendar, according to the latest arrangement. We find here a 'heavenly' calendar, expressly distinguished from the 'earthly' one. Among the general holidays were the 29th, 30th, 1st, 2nd, 4th, 6th, 8th, and 15th days of each month. The days are set forth in this order, according to the Egyptian assumption that the 29th day is that on which the conjunction of the sun and moon takes place, and on which the world was created.[7] So far as the several feast-days have been preserved, they give us a further insight into the festivals celebrated at Thebes in the 13th century B.C., as the reader will see from the following extract:—

    1   Thot. Rising of the Sothis-star (Sirius), a sacrifice for Amon.

---

[6] Science is indebted to Mr. Dümichen for the publication of these important lists, from which the same scholar has with great acumen fixed the size of several very important measures of corn used in ancient times.

[7] Compare Horapollo, i. 10.

17	Thot.	Eve of the Uaga feast.
18	,,	Uaga feast.
19	,,	Feast of Thut (Hermes).
22	,,	Feast of the great manifestation of Osiris.
17	Paophi.	Eve of the Amon-feast of Api.
19-23	,,	The first five days of the Amon-feast of Api.
12	Athyr.	Last day of the festival of Api.
17	,,	Special feast after the festival of Api.
1	Khoiak.	Feast of Hathor.
20	,,	Feast of sacrifice.
21	,,	Opening of the Tomb (of Osiris).
22	,,	Feast of the hoeing of the earth.
23	,,	Preparation of the sacrificial altar in the Tomb (of Osiris).
24	,,	Exhibition of [the corpse] of Sokar (Osiris) in the midst of the sacrifice.
25	,,	Feast of the (mourning) goddesses.
26	,,	Feast of Sokar (Osiris).
27	,,	Feast (of the father) of the palms.
28	,,	Feast of the procession of the obelisk.
30	,,	Feast of the setting up of the image of Did.
1	Tybi.	Feast of the coronation of Horus, which served also for that of king Ramses III.
6	,,	A new Amon-feast founded by Ramses III.
22	,,	Heri-feast.
29 (?)	,,	Day of the exhibition of the meadow.

The feasts which follow these are unfortunately obliterated. To the special feast-days must be added still further the 26th of Pakhons, in commemoration of the king's accession to the throne.

On the eastern side of Thebes, Ramses III. laid the foundation-stone of an oracle-giving temple of the god Khonsu, the son of Amon and of the goddess Mut. He likewise founded a new Ramesseum, which adjoined on the south the great forecourt of the temple of Amon, and which was dedicated to Amon of Ape. To this day it still stands tolerably well preserved in its parts, but it is a very ordinary piece of architecture, almost worthless from an artistic point of view. An inscription on its eastern outer side hands down to us the record of a royal ordinance, according to which Ramses III., in the 16th year of his reign, in the month Payni, appointed special sacrifices for the god. The altar dedicated for this purpose was an artistic work of silver.

Not only in Egypt proper, but in foreign countries also, temples were built in honour of the gods by the command of Ramses. According to a statement in the Harris papyrus, the king erected in the land of Zahi (the Philistia of later times), a Ramesseum to Amon in the city of Kanaan, which is already well known to us. A statue of the god was set up in its holy of holies in the name of the king. The obligation was laid on the tribes of the Ruthen to provide this temple with all necessaries.

That Ramses, in spite of his good fortune and his riches, did not enjoy his throne without cares and alarms, is proved by a harem conspiracy, which aimed at his overthrow. The highest officials and servants were mixed up in this plot. The threads of the conspiracy had their centre in the women's apartments, and extended even beyond the king's court. It was discovered. The king immediately summoned a court of justice, and himself named the judges who were to try and sentence the guilty. By great good fortune the judgments which were delivered have been handed down to us nearly complete. Science has to thank our deceased French friend, Devéria, for having been the first to explain and elucidate this remarkable document, which is now at Turin.[8] The names of the judges are contained in the following extract:—

PAGE 2. (1) 'And the commission was given to the treasurer Monthu-em-taui, the treasurer Paif-roui, (2) the fan-bearer Karo, the councillor Pi-besat, the councillor Kedenden, the councillor Baal-mahar, (3) the councillor Pi-aru-sunu, the councillor Thut-rekh-nofer, the royal interpreter Pen-rennu, the scribe Mai, (4) the scribe Pra-em-hib of the chancery, the colour-bearer Hor-a, of the garrison; to this effect:

(5) 'Regarding the speeches which people have uttered, and which are unknown, you shall institute an enquiry about them. (6) They shall be brought to a trial to see if they deserve death. Then they shall put themselves to death with their own hand.'[9]

Ramses III. warns the judges to conduct the affair conscientiously, and concludes with these words:—

PAGE 3. (1) 'If all that has happened was such that it was actually done by them, (2) let their doing be upon their own heads. (3) I am the guardian and protector for ever, and (4) bearer of the royal insignia of justice in presence of the god-king (5) Amon-ra, and in presence of the prince of eternity, Osiris.'

This is followed by a second and longer section, which enables us to understand very clearly the result of the trial:—

[8] This document, called by M. Devéria (*Journal Asiatique*, 1865) 'Le Papyrus Judiciaire de Turin,' is translated by Mr. Le Page Renouf in *Records of the Past*, vol. viii. pp. 53, foll. We add the numbers of the pages, lines, and sections of the papyrus from that translation.—ED.

[9] This judicial suicide, which is repeatedly mentioned in the document, furnishes an interesting parallel in those remote times to the form of execution under later despotisms, from the Roman Cæsars to the 'happy despatch' of Japan. (Comp. p. 109, note.)—ED.

PAGE 4. (1) 'These are the persons who were brought up on account of their great crimes before the judgment-seat, to be judged by the treasurer Monthu-em-taui, by the treasurer Paif-roui, by the fan-bearer Karo, by the councillor Pi-besat, by the scribe Mai of the chancery, and by the standard-bearer Hor-a, and who were judged and found guilty, and to whom punishment was awarded, that their offence might be expiated.

(2) 'The chief culprit Boka-kamon. He was house-steward. He was brought up because of actual participation in the doings of the wife Thi and the women of the harem. He had conspired with them, and had carried abroad their commission given by word of mouth to their mothers and sisters there, to stir up the people, and to assemble the malcontents, to commit a crime against their lord. They set him before the elders of the judgment-seat. They judged his offence, and found him guilty of having done so, and he was fully convicted of his crime. The judges awarded him his punishment.

(3) 'The chief culprit Mestu-su-ra. He was a councillor. He was brought up because of his actual participation in the doings of Boka-kamon, the house-steward. He had conspired with the women to stir up the malcontents, to commit a crime against their lord. They set him before the elders of the judgment-seat. They judged his offence. They found him guilty, and awarded him his punishment.

(4) 'The chief culprit Panauk. He was the royal secretary of the harem, for the service of the women's house. He was brought up on account of his actual participation in the conspiracy of Boka-kamon and Mestu-su-ra, to commit a crime against their lord. They set him before the elders of the judgment-seat. They judged his offence. They found him guilty, and awarded him his punishment.

(5) 'The chief culprit Pen-tuauu. He was the royal secretary of the harem, for the service of the women's house. He was brought up on account of his actual participation in the conspiracy of Boka-kamon and Mestu-su-ra and the other chief culprit, who was the overseer of the harem of the women in the women's house, to increase the number of the malcontents who had conspired to commit a crime against their lord. They set him before the elders of the judgment-seat. They judged his offence. They found him guilty, and awarded him his punishment.

(6) 'The chief culprit Pi-nif-emtu-amon. He was a land-surveyor, for the service of the women's house. He was brought up because he had listened to the speeches which the conspirators and the women of the women's house had indulged in, without giving information of them. He was set before the elders of the judgment-seat. They judged his offence, and found him guilty, and awarded him his punishment.

(7) 'The chief culprit Karpusa. He was a land-surveyor, for the service of the women's house. He was brought up on account of the talk which he had heard, but had kept silence. He was set before the elders of the judgment-seat, and they judged his offence, and found him guilty, and awarded him his punishment.

(8) 'The chief culprit Kha-m-apet. He was a land-surveyor, for the service of the women's house. He was brought up on account of the talk which he had heard, but had kept silence. He was set before the elders of the judgment-seat, and they judged his offence, and found him guilty, and awarded him his punishment.

(9) 'The chief culprit Kha-em-maanro. He was a land-surveyor, for the service of the women's house. He was brought up because of the talk which he had heard, but had kept silence. He was set before the elders of the judgment-seat, and they judged his offence, and found him guilty, and awarded him his punishment.

(10) 'The chief culprit Seti-em-pi-thut. He was a land-surveyor, for the service of the women's house. He was brought up on account of the talk which he had heard, but had kept silence. He was set before the elders of the judgment-seat, and they judged his offence, and found him guilty, and awarded him his punishment.

(11) 'The chief culprit Seti-em-pi amon. He was a land-surveyor, for the service of the women's house. He was brought up on account of the talk which he had heard, but had kept silence. He was set before the elders of the judgment-seat, and they judged his offence, and found him guilty, and awarded him his punishment.

(12) 'The chief culprit Ua-ro-ma. He was a councillor. He was brought up because he had been an ear-witness of the communications of the overseer of the house, and had held his tongue and kept silence, without giving any information thereof. He was set before the elders of the judgment-seat, and they found him guilty, and awarded him his punishment.

(13) 'The chief culprit Akh-hib-set. He was the accomplice of Boka-kamon. He was brought up because he had been an ear-

witness of the communications of Boka-kamon. He had been his confidant, without having reported it. He was set before the elders of the judgment-seat, and they found him guilty, and awarded him his punishment.

(14) 'The chief culprit Pi-lo-ka. He was a councillor, and scribe of the treasury. He was brought up on account of his actual participation with Boka-kamon. He had also heard his communications, without having made report of them. He was set before the elders of the judgment-seat, they found him guilty, and awarded him his punishment.

(15) 'The chief culprit, the Libyan Inini. He was a councillor. He was brought up because of his actual participation with Boka-kamon. He had listened to his communications without having made report of them. He was set before the elders of the judgment-seat, they found him guilty, and awarded him his punishment.

PAGE 5. (1) 'The wives of the people of the gate of the women's house, who had joined the conspirators, were brought before the elders of the judgment-seat. They found them guilty, and awarded them their punishment. Six women.

(2) 'The chief culprit Pi-keti, a son of Lema. He was treasurer. He was brought up on account of his actual participation with the chief accused, Pen-hiban. He had conspired with him to assemble the malcontents, to commit a crime against their lord. He was brought before the elders of the judgment-seat. They found him guilty, and awarded him his punishment.

(3) 'The chief culprit Ban-em-us. He was the captain of the foreign legion of the Kushi. He was brought up on account of a message, which his sister, who was in the service of the women's house, had sent to him, to stir up the people who were malcontent (saying), "Come, accomplish the crime against thy lord." He was set before Kedenden, Baal-mahar, Pi-aru-sunu, and Thut-rekh-nofer. They judged him, and found him guilty, and awarded him his punishment.

(4) 'Persons who were brought up on account of their crime, and on account of their actual participation with Boka-kamon (namely), Pi-as and Pen-ta-ur. They were set before the elders of the judgment-seat to be tried. They found them guilty, laid them down by their arms (i.e. by force) at the judgment-seat, and they died by their own hand [1] without their expiation being completed.

---

[1] Mr. Le Page Renouf observes :—'The expression *àu-f mut-nef t'esef* is a very remarkable one. The pronoun *t'esef* has a re-

(5) 'The chief accused Pi-as: he was a captain of the soldiers. The chief accused Mes-sui: he was a scribe of the treasury. The chief accused Kamon: he was an overseer. The chief accused I-ri: he was a priest of the goddess Sokhet. The chief accused Nebzefau: he was a councillor. The chief accused Shat-sotem: he was a scribe of the treasury. Making together, 6.

(6) 'These are the persons who were brought up, on account of their crime, to the judgment-seat, before Kedenden, Baal-mahar, Pi-aru-sunu, Thut-rekh-nofer, and Meri-usi-amon. They judged them for their crime, they found them guilty. They laid them down before the tribunal. They died by their own hand.

(7) 'Pen-ta-ur, so is called the second of this name. He was brought up because of his actual participation with Thi, his mother, when they hatched the conspiracy with the women of the women's house, and because of the crime which was to have been committed against their lord. He was set before the councillors to be judged. They found him guilty, they laid him down where he stood. He died by his own hand.

(8) 'The chief accused Han-uten-amon. He was a councillor. He was brought up because of the crime of the women of the women's house. He had been an ear-witness in the midst of them, without having given information. They set him before the councillors to judge him. They found him guilty. They laid him down where he stood. He died by his own hand.

(9) 'The chief accused Amen-khau. He was Adon for the service of the women's house. He was brought up because of the crime of the women of the women's house. He had been an ear-witness among them, without having given information. They set him before the councillors to be judged. They found him guilty. They laid him down where he stood. He died by his own hand.

(10) 'The chief accused Pi-ari. He was a royal scribe of the harem, for the service of the women's house. He was brought up because of the crime of the women of the women's house. He had been an ear-witness in the midst of them, without having given information of it. They set him before the councillors to be judged. They found him guilty. They laid him down where he stood. He died by his own hand.

---

flexive force, and very emphatically marks the agent of the deed or the efficient cause of the state expressed by the verb. As χ*eper t'esef* signifies αὐτογενής, *self-existent*, so *mut t'esef* has the sense of αὐτοθάνατος, *dying by one's own hand*.'—ED.

PAGE 6. (1) 'These are the persons who received their punishment, and had their noses and their ears cut off, because they had in fact neglected to give full evidence in their depositions. The women had arrived and had reached the place where these were. They kept a beer-house there, and they were in league with Pi-as. Their crime was thus expiated.

(2) 'The chief culprit Pi-bast. He was a councillor. His punishment was accomplished on him. He died by his own hand.

(3) 'The chief culprit Mai. He was scribe in the chancery.

(4) 'The chief culprit Tai-nakht-tha. He was commander of the garrison.

(5) 'The chief culprit Nanai. He was the overseer of the Sakht (?).

(6) 'Persons, about whom it was doubtful if they had conspired with them with thoroughly evil intentions.

(7) 'They laid down, without completing his expiation, the chief culprit Hor-a. He was the standard-bearer of the garrison.'

Here ends the Turin papyrus. The following extracts, which belong to the same trial, are found in two separate fragments of the Lee and Rollin papyrus.[2]

The translation of the first fragment is as follows :—

'. . . . to all the people of this place, in which I am staying, and to all inhabitants of the country. Thus then spake Penhi, who was superintendent of the herds of cattle, to him : " If I only possessed a writing, which would give me power and strength ! "

'Then he gave him a writing from the rolls of the books of Ramses III., the great god, his lord. Then there came upon him a divine magic, an enchantment for men. He reached (thereby ?) to the side | of the women's house, and into that other great and deep place. He formed human figures of wax, with the intention of having them carried in by the hand of the land-surveyor Adiroma ; | to alienate the mind of one of the girls, and to bewitch the

---

[2] The Lee papyrus (so named from its former owner Dr. Lee) and the Rollin papyrus (in the Bibliothèque Nationale at Paris) are two fragments of the same papyrus, and have been published by M. Chabas on the same plate, in the *Papyrus Magique de Harris*.—ED.

others. Some of the discourses were carried in, others were brought out. Now, however, he was brought to trial | on account of them, and there was found in them incitation to all kinds of wickedness, and all kinds of villany, which it was his intention to have done. It was true, that he had done all this in conjunction with | the other chief culprits, who, like him, were without a god or a goddess. They inflicted on him the great punishment of death, such as the holy writings pronounced against him.'

In a second fragment of the same papyrus the following words can be further made out:—

'[He had committed this offence and was judged] for it. They found in it the material for all kinds of wickedness and all kinds of villany which his heart had imagined to do. It was true, (namely) [all that he had done in conjunction with] the other chief culprits, who, like him, were without a god or a goddess. Such were the grievous crimes, worthy of death, and the grievous sins [in the country], which he had done. But now he was convicted on account of these grievous offences worthy of death, which he had committed. He died by his own hand. For the elders, who were before him, had given sentence that he should die by his own hand | [with the other chief culprits, who like him] were without the sun-god Ra, according as the holy writings declared what should be done to him.'

The contents of the Rollin papyrus, and likewise a fragment of a greater papyrus, are confined to the following official statement:—

'He had made some magical writings to ward off ill luck; he had made some gods of wax, and some human figures, to paralyze the limbs of a man; | and he had put these into the hand of Boka-kamon, though the sun-god Ra did not permit that he should accomplish this, either he or the superintendent of the house, or the other chief culprits, because he (the god) said, "Let them go forward with it, that they may furnish grounds for proceeding against them." Thus had he attempted to complete the shameful deeds which he had prepared, without the sun-god Ra having granted them actual success. He was brought to trial, and they found out the real facts, consisting in all kinds of crime and | all sorts of villany, which his heart had imagined to do. It was true that he had purposed to do all this in concert with all the chief culprits, who were like him. This was | a grievous crime, worthy of death, and grievous wickedness for the land, which he had committed. But they found out the grievous crime, worthy of death, which he had committed. He died by his own hand.'

The reader can now, from the preceding translations, form his own idea of the way in which the harem conspiracy endeavoured to compass the destruction of the king by magical influence. At the head of the women of the royal harem there was a lady, Thi, who is frequently named, and her son Pentaur, a second accused person of this name. We shall not err in supposing her to have been a wife of the king, and her son the son of Ramses III., who had plotted, during the lifetime of his own father, to place himself upon the throne. This wide-spread conspiracy, in which humble and distinguished persons took part, and above all the immediate officials of the king in the service of the harem, points to an intrigue at the court in opposition to the reigning king, which vividly reminds us of similar events in Eastern history. In spite of the parts that are missing of this great trial, what has been preserved will always form a remarkable contribution to the life of the Pharaohs and the dangers which threatened them in their immediate circle.

The wife of Ramses, or at least the one of whose name and origin the monuments inform us, bore, besides her Egyptian appellation, Ise, that is, Isis, the foreign name of Hema-rozath, or Hemalozatha. The name also of her father, Hebuanrozanath, has nothing of an Egyptian sound, so that we may suppose that the Pharaoh had followed the custom of the time, and had brought home a foreign princess (of Khita? or Assyria?) as his wife, and had placed her beside him on the throne. We are accurately informed from the monuments about the number and names of his sons. The list of them in the temple of victory of Medinet Abou is all the more precious, because it gives us likewise the opportunity of knowing beforehand and settling the names of the successors of the king. The following are the sons in their order:—

1. Prince Ramessu I., commander of the infantry, afterwards king Ramessu IV.
2. Prince Ramessu II., afterwards king Ramessu VI.
3. Prince Ramessu III., royal master of the horse, afterwards king Ramessu VII.
4. Prince Ramessu IV., Set-hi-khopeshef, royal master of the horse, afterwards king Ramessu VIII.
5. Prince Pra-hi-unamif, first captain of the chariots of war.
6. Prince Menthu-hi-khopeshef, chief marshal of the army.
7. Prince Ramessu V., Meritum, high-priest of the Sun in Heliopolis, afterwards king Meritum.
8. Prince Ramessu VI., Khamus, high-priest of Ptah-Sokar in Memphis.
9. Prince Ramessu VII., Amon-hi-khopeshef.
10. Prince Ramessu VIII., Miamun.

Of eight other princes and fourteen princesses we do not know the names. Their portraits have no explanatory inscriptions appended.

Among the contemporaries of the king we must mention, above all the rest, the Theban chief priest of Amon, Meribast.

After the example of his predecessors, Ramses III. had prepared during his lifetime his 'orbit of light,' that is, his future sepulchre in the valley of the royal tombs, according to the pattern of the age, in the form of a long tunnel in the rock, divided into rooms and halls. In its decoration it corresponds with the modest proportions of the other buildings of the king, being remarkable only for a range of side-chambers, in which, among other things, the possessions of the king, such as weapons, household furniture, and so forth, are represented in coloured pictures, just as they were once actually deposited in the rooms apportioned for them.

After the death of king Rhampsinitus, the eldest of his sons ascended the throne—

II. RAMESSU IV. MIAMUN III. HAQ MAA,

Ramses IV.

or, as he afterwards changed his name, according to the probable supposition of Lepsius,—

RAMESSU IV. MIAMUN III. MAMA. ABOUT B.C. 1166.

According to the inscriptions which cover the walls of the rock in the valleys of Hammamat, this Ramses took especial pleasure in the exploration of the desert mountain valleys on the Arabian side of Egypt. Under the pretext of making search there for stones suitable for the erection of monuments, the most distinguished Egyptians were sent away to these gloomy regions, and their mission was perpetuated by inscriptions on the rock. We will subjoin in a literal translation the historical contents of a rock-tablet of the third year of his reign, in order to give an idea of the number of officials and workmen who, in the twelfth century before our era, gave life to these wild valleys.

The memorial tablet begins with the date of the 27th Payni in the third year of the reign of king Ramessu. We will, as usual, pass over in silence the long list of official flatteries, of which two, unusually detailed, must have had an historical foundation. In one of them the praise of the Pharaoh is sung, for that he had 'laid waste the lands and plundered the inhabitants in their valleys,' which evidently refers to a war in some mountain regions. In the other it is vauntingly declared that

'Good times were in Egypt, as in those of the Sun-god Ra, in his kingdom, for this divine benefactor was like the god Thut, on account of the keeping of the laws.'

Without doubt our Ramses IV. must have occupied himself in establishing a state of order by means of wise ordinances; and this is the more likely, as it is evidently not without a purpose that the remark follows immediately—

'Crimes had increased, but the lies were put down, and the land was restored to a peaceful state in the time of his reign.'

After the closing words, in the usual official language,—

'He prepared joy for Egypt a hundred-thousandfold,'—

the especial purport of the memorial tablet begins to be set forth in the following terms:—

'His heart watched to seek out something good for his father (Hor of Coptos), the creator of his body. He caused to be opened for him (9) an entrance to the Holy Land, which was not known before, because the (existing) road to it was too distant for all the people, and their memory was not sufficient to discover it. Then the king considered in his mind, like his father Horus, the son of Isis, how he might lay down a road, to reach the place at his pleasure. (10) He made a circuit through this splendid mountain land, for the creation of monuments of granite for his father and for his ancestors, and for the gods and goddesses, who are the lords of Egypt. He set up a memorial-tablet on the summit of this mountain, inscribed with the full name of king Ramessu.

'(11) Then did the king give directions to the scribe of the holy sciences, Ramessu-akhtu-hib, and to the scribe of Pharaoh, Hora, and to the seer, User-ma-ra-nakhtu, of the temple of Khim-Hor, and of Isis in Coptos, to seek a suitable site for (12) a temple in the mountain of Bukhan. When they had gone (thither) [they found a fit place], which was very good. There were great quarries of granite.

'And the king issued a command, and gave directions to the chief priest of Amon, and the chief architect (13) Ramessu-nakhtu, to bring such (monuments) to Egypt.

'These are the distinguished councillors, who were in his company (namely):

The royal councillor User-ma-ra-Sekheper,
The royal councillor Nakhtu-amon,
And the Adon Kha-m-thir of the warriors,
The treasurer Kha-m-thir,
(14) The superintendent of the quarry, prince Amon-mas of the city (Thebes),
The superintendent of the quarry and overseer of the (holy) herds, Bok-en-khonsu, of the temple of User-ma-ra-Miamun,
The colonel of the war chariots, Nakhtu-amon of the court,
The scribe of the enlistment of the warriors, Suanar,
(15) The scribe of the Adon of the warriors, Ramessu-nakhtu,
20 scribes of the warriors,
20 superior officials of the court administration,
The colonel of the marshal's-men of the warriors, Kha-m-maa-anar,
20 marshal's-men of the warriors,
(16) 50 captains of the two-horse chariots,
50 superiors of the seers, superintendents of the (holy) animals, seers, scribes, and land surveyors,
5,000 people of the warriors,
(17) 200 foremen of the guild of the fishermen,
800 redskins (Erythræans, *Aper*) from the tribes of *'Ain* (between the Red Sea and the Nile),

2,000 house servants of the house of Pharaoh,
1 Adon as chief overseer (of these),
50 men of the police (*Mazai*),
The superintendent of the works of art, Nakhtu-amon,
3 architects for the workmen of the (18) quarries,
130 quarrymen and masons,
2 draftsmen,
4 sculptors ;
900 of the number had died in consequence of the long journey, making together 8,368 men.[3]

'(19) And the necessaries for them were carried on ten carts. Six pair of oxen drew each cart which was brought from Egypt to the mountains of Bukhan. (20) [There were also] many runners, who were laden with bread, flesh, and vegetables, for they had not placed them thereon (i.e. on the waggons); and there were also brought the expiatory offerings for the gods of heaven and of the earth from the capital city of Patoris (Thebes) in great purity.'

After some unintelligible and half-obliterated words, the conclusion of the inscription follows :—

'(21) And the priests made a proper offering, the oxen were slain, the calves were killed, the incense steamed heavenward, wine flowed as if in rivers, and there was no end of the mead, in that place. The singers raised their song. Then was made the holy offering to Khim, to Horus, to Isis, [to Amon, to Mut, to Khonsu], and to the divinities, the lords of these mountains. Their

---

[3] The exact total of all the persons of the expedition enumerated gives the number 8,365, instead of 8,368. The difference of three lies in some error of the copy which I possess. The original total, including those who died on the road, was 9,268. A loss of nearly 10 per cent. is enormous, and exemplifies the hardships which a sojourn in the inhospitable regions and rocky valleys of Hammamat inflicts upon the traveller, even to the present day. So much the more is the endurance and perseverance to be admired, with which, at the command of the Khedive, the officers of the Egyptian staff, for the most part Europeans and Americans, have now been engaged for several years in the task of most carefully improving these sterile mountain-valleys.

heart was joyful, they received the gifts, which may they requite with millions of 30-years' feasts of jubilee to their dear son, king Ramessu, the dispenser of life for ever!'

With the exception of some additions to the temple of Khonsu in Thebes, erected by his father, and some insignificant sculptures on the walls and columns of the great temple of Amon at Api, the memory of this king has not been preserved in any remarkable manner. With what object he sent a company so grandly equipped to the valley of monuments at Hammamat, we can hardly understand, since no traces have been preserved of important monuments bearing his name. Might this whole journey have been undertaken only with the object of driving away, or perhaps exterminating, a number of disaffected people? The immense number of 900 deaths at least favours this conjecture.

That his rule over Egypt was contested by a claimant to the throne, who was beyond the immediate family of Ramses III., is proved by the name of his successor—

III. RAMESSU V. AMUNHIKHOPESHEF I. MIAMUN IV.,

Ramses V.

whose sepulchral chamber, in the valley of Biban-el-Molouk, was appropriated by Ramses VI., herein a true son of Ramses III., after he had substituted his own names for those of his hated rival. What this Ramses V. thought of himself, is proved by the contents of his rock-tablet at Silsilis:—

'As a mountain of gold he enlightens the whole world, like the god of the circle of light. Men were enraptured at his coronation, and the gods were highly delighted on account of his proofs of love, for he rendered to them what was due, whereby they live, as a good son does for his father.—His ordinances caused contentment, his measures doubled his kingdom and his revenues. The Nile-god opened his mouth at his (the king's) name. There was in his whole realm plenty without measure. He adorned the houses of the gods with monuments, preparing them well for eternity. Like the Sun in heaven is his duration of life, equalling the duration of His life. His being is like that of Monthu. He has doubled the revenues of the gods for their sacrifices, which are well provided with all necessaries, to satisfy them by reason of good laws.—It was he who made the whole people what it is. Small and great rejoice, because they are subjected to his name. He is to them like the new moon, so to speak : people go to bed, and he is received as a benefactor ; they wake up, and he is born as a father.'

Poetic self-praises of this kind, without any historic background, merely cause disgust, since the empty forms of speech have not even the merit of beauty of language, or any richness of new thought. With the Ramessids of the Nineteenth Dynasty the true poetic inspiration appears to have vanished, during a troublous and disastrous period, and the dry official tone and the legal forms seem to have taken its place. Some productions of value in a higher style of language prove on a closer examination to be copies of the master-pieces of earlier times. The Thutmeses, Amenhoteps, and Ramses II. found imitators among the Pharaohs with little trouble, but new models have now and henceforward disappeared from Egyptian history.

Of the sons of Ramses III., who followed next in order, two seem to have reigned simultaneously. One of these was the seventh son,

(V.) RAMESSU MERITUM,

a son of the queen Muf-nofer-ari, whose cartouche, with the name Miamun Meritum, I accidentally discovered many years ago, during a visit to the ruins of Heliopolis, on one of the stones lying in the road. It led me to the conjecture, that Meritum reigned as viceroy in Lower Egypt in the name of his brother. The Theban monuments give us the names of this brother with perfect distinctness. He was called

IV. RA-NEB-MA MIAMUN RAMESSU VI.
AMEN-HI-KHOPESHEF II. NUTER HAQ-ON.

Ramses VI.

The inscriptions which mention him speak with a certain emphasis of his monuments in honour of the gods; but of these, those which have survived the ravages of time are reduced to a very small number. The most important edifice, and the most instructive on account of its representations and inscriptions, is his great and splendid tomb in the royal valley of Biban-el-Molouk. The tables of the hours, with the times of the risings of the stars, which formed the houses of the sun's course in the 36 or 37 weeks of the Egyptian year, will be for all times the most valuable contribution to astronomical science in the 12th century before our era. According to the researches of the French savant, Biot, whose labours in the department of astronomical calculation, in order to fix certain epochs of Egyptian history, are almost the only ones which have treated the subject with scientific accuracy, the drawing up of these tables of stars would fall in the reign of Ramessu VI., in the year 1240 B.C. Our learned fellow countryman, Professor Lepsius, has, however, from his own point of view, sought to prove that herein lay an error, and that, on the authority of the already cited table of hours in the grave of this king, the year 1194 B.C. is indicated as the only proper date. This last view does not differ very much from our calculation of 1166 B.C., deduced from the number of successive generations.

We cannot pass over in silence a record of this time, which has faithfully preserved the name of the king in a sepulchral chamber in Nubia. We refer to the following document, which we now for the first time present to the learned world in a literal translation:—

'Land (which is devoted to the maintenance of the holy service) of the statue of king Ramessu VI., which is dedicated to the city of 'Ama (consisting of the following districts) :

'I. The district to the north of Pi-ra (that is the temple of the sun), and of the town in the midst of the temple of Ra, the lord of this earth, and to the east and south of the fields of the land of the (statue) of Queen Nofer-tera, which is dedicated to the city of 'Ama. (The position of this district is as follows) ; (it is bounded)
    on the east by the great mountain,.
    on the north by the papyrus-field of Pharaoh,
    on the west is the river. Size, 3 x 100 cubits.

'II. The district at the commencement (*lesha-t*, 'head') of the land of Ma-iu, opposite to the field of the Adon of Wawa,
    on the south by the land of the statue of the king, which is under the administration of the chief priest Amen-em-api,
    on the east by the great mountain,
    on the north by the papyrus-field of Pharaoh, which is set apart as a field for the Adon of Wawa,
    on the west by the river. Size, 2 x 100 cubits.

'III. The district of the overseers of the temple of the goddess, east of the field just described :

on the east by the great mountain,
on the south by the field of the estate of the king's statue, which is under the administration of the Adon Meri of the land of Wawa, east of the great mountain,
on the north by the field of the keeper of the herds (?) Bih,
on the west by the river. Size, 4 × 100 cubits.

'IV. The district at the commencement of the land of Thuhen at the extreme west boundary of the basin of Thuhen, in the direction of the papyrus-field of Pharaoh, and behind the field that has been described:
east by the great mountain,
south by the papyrus-field of Pharaoh, which lies east of the great mountain,
north by the field of the land of Airos,
west by the river. Size, 6 × 100 cubits.
Total superficies of the fields, which belong to him (the statue), 15 × 100 cubits.

'V. With regard to the high-lying field (of) Nif-ti, the Adon Penni, the son of Heru-nofer, has written and set up his proprietorship of the land of Wawa as an estate, which he has chosen, to furnish him with (sustenance) for each ox, which is yearly slaughtered in his honour.

'The circuit of the superficies of the fields of the potters' earth, which are in the possession of the (former) Adon of Wawa, is not included in the roll.
Its west is at the gravelly land of the Adon Pen-ni,
its south is at the gravelly fields of the Adon Pen-ni,
on the north are the fields with potters' earth, which are the property of Pharaoh,
the east is at the gravelly fields of the Adon Pen-ni.
Size of the whole, 4 × 200, and 2 × 200 cubits.

'Any one who will not observe these demarcations, to him will Amon-Ra be an avenger, from one avenging to (another) avenging; Mut will take vengeance on his wife, Khonsu will take vengeance on his children, he shall hunger, he shall thirst, he shall be miserable, he shall vanish away.'

The foregoing inscription is found in a rock-tomb at Anibe, little visited by travellers, on the western bank of the Nile, opposite the village of Ibrim, about fifty kilomètres (31 miles) north of Ibsamboul. The owner of the tomb was an official of king Ramessu VI., of the name of Penni, who, in his office as Adon or governor of the land of Wawa, died and was buried in this lonely region. The directions he left behind him, particularly with regard to the number of estates, the produce of which was devoted to the maintenance of the service of a statue of the king, hardly require an explanation. What makes the inscription particularly valuable is the designation of lands in those parts, and the offices connected with them. He himself, as we have already remarked, was Adon of Wawa.[4] Another Adon is mentioned by the name of Meri. The sun-city of Pira is the ancient designation of the modern place called Derr, or Dirr. The city mentioned by the name of Ama, in which a Nubian Horus enjoyed an especial worship, is very often named in the inscriptions, and seems to have been the ancient appellation of Ibrim. At Pira (Derr), in all probability, was the seat of the administration of the whole country of Wawa. The districts of Ahi and the gold land of Akita[5] belonged to it, the revenues of which Penni had to collect and pay over to Pharaoh. For his especial diligence in the fulfilment of his service to the court he was most warmly commended by the 'King's son of Kush' of that time, whose name unfortunately is passed over in silence. On a royal visit, the king appears accompanied by the above-named Meri, who is also

---

[4] See Vol. I. p. 145.
[5] See Vol. II. p. 81.

called 'the superintendent of the temple,' to recommend his officials to the grace of Pharaoh. The statue of the royal lord, which had been set up, plays here an important part. His Majesty appears to have been much pleased with the services of his faithful servant, since he presented Penni with two silver vessels filled with precious ointments, as a reward of honour. Penni was certainly an artist, as is shown by the statue of Pharaoh, and by his rock-tomb adorned with rich sculptures in stone, but especially by his office, mentioned in the inscriptions, of 'master of the quarry,' besides that of a 'superintendent of the temple of· Horus, the lord of the town of 'Ama.'

These and similar statements are confirmed by the pictures and writings in his eternal dwelling, where he rests surrounded by his numerous relations. The several members of his family appear to have all held during their lifetime various offices in the Horus-city of 'Ama. I find among them a chief priest of Isis (H'at-ae), whose son was the Amenemapi named in the inscription; also two treasurers of the king in 'Ama, a captain of the city of 'Ama, a priest and a scribe, while the women are mostly named as female singers of Amon or of Horus the lord of the town of 'Ama.[6]

When all historical data for depicting the life and deeds of a king fail, the family information contained in the tomb of a contemporary becomes of importance, even if it teaches us nothing else than that in the times

[6] Respecting the pictures in the tomb of Ramses VI., representing the king's court and family, see Villiers Stuart, *Nile Gleanings*, p. 194.—ED.

of Ramessu VI. the Egyptian dominion south of the tropic was still maintained, and that under the 'King's son of Kush' there were several Adons, corresponding to the districts of Kush, to whom again were subordinated the H'a, or governors of the towns.

Passing over in silence the two insignificant successors and brothers of this king, who perhaps reigned simultaneously as Pharaohs, and of whom the monuments have merely handed down the names,

VI. RAMESSU VII., and
VII. RAMESSU VIII.,

Ramses VII.   Ramses VIII.

we now come to the last Ramessids of the Twentieth Dynasty.

Our attention is first claimed by Ramessu IX., who bore the full name of

VIII. NOFER-KA-RA SOTEP-EN-RA RAMESSU IX.
MIAMUN VI. KHAMUS. B.C. 1133.

Ramses IX.

It is not his deeds, about which the monuments tell us next to nothing, nor his buildings, which are extremely few in number (his pictures and inscriptions are placed on the already existing monuments of his predecessors), but his relations to the chief priests of Amon at Thebes at this time, that require us to pay particular attention to his memory.

The enquirer who examines the monuments of the Theban capital with a clear and discerning eye, and who knows how to read between the lines, cannot avoid being struck with the very evident fact that, from the time of Ramses III., the holy fathers, who bore the exalted dignity of a chief priest in the temple-city of Amon, are always coming more and more into the foreground of Egyptian history. Their influence with the kings assumes, step by step, a growing importance. As formerly it was the priests who expressed in the name of the gods their thanks to the kings for the temple-buildings in Thebes, so now it is the kings who begin to testify their gratitude to the chief priest of Amon for the care bestowed on the temple of Amon by the erection of new buildings, and by the improvement and maintenance of the older ones.

In this connection, a great value belongs to the representations and inscriptions on the eastern wall and the adjoining buildings, which connect the third and fourth pylon to the south of the temple of Amon at Ape. We there see the 'hereditary prince and chief priest of Amon-ra, the king of the gods, Amenhotep, in the place of his father, the chief priest of Amon-ra in Api, Ramessu-nakht;' in other words, the chief priest Amenhotep, who had just taken the place of his predecessor and father. Opposite to him stands king Ramessu IX., and the meaning of his presence in this place is made quite clear by the inscription annexed:—

'The king in person, he speaks to the princes and companions by his side: Give rich reward and much recompense in good gold and silver, and in a hundred-thousandfold of good things, to the high-priest of Amon-ra, the king of the gods, Amenhotep, on account of these many splendid buildings [which he has erected] at the temple of Amon-ra to the great name of the divine benefactor, the king Ramessu IX.'

The presentation of the reward took place in a

right worthy and official manner. The appended document, of which a literal translation is here for the first time published, not only gives us information of this fact, but at the same time preserves for us an excellent example of the court language of the period :—

'In the 10th year, the month Athyr, the 19th day, in the temple of Amon-ra, the king of the gods. The chief priest of Amon-ra, the king of the gods, Amenhotep, was conducted to the great forecourt of the temple of Amon. His (the king's) words uttered his reward, to honour him by good and choice discourses.

' These are the princes, who had come to reward him, namely : the treasurer of Pharaoh and the royal councillor, Amen-hotep; the royal councillor, Nes-Amon ; the secretary of Pharaoh and the royal councillor, Noferkara-em-piamon, who is the interpreter of Pharaoh.

' The discourses which were addressed to him related to the rewards for his services on this day in the great forecourt of Amon-ra, the king of the gods. They were of this import:

' Monthu was invoked as a witness :

' As witness is invoked the name of Amon-ra, the king of the gods, that of the god Hormakhu, of Ptah of Memphis, of Thot, the lord of the holy speech, of the gods of heaven, of the gods of the earth :

' As witness is invoked the name of Ramessu IX., the great king of Egypt, the son and friend of all the gods, for levying all services. Let the taxing and the usufruct of the labours of the inhabitants for the temple of Amon-ra, the king of the gods, be placed under thy administration. Let the full revenues be given over to thee, according to their number. Thou shalt collect the duties. Thou shalt undertake the interior administration (literally, side) of the treasuries, of the store-houses, and of the granaries of the temple of Amon-ra, the king of the gods ; so that the income of the heads and hands for the maintenance of Amon-ra, the king of the gods, may be applied to the service. [Thus does] Pharaoh, thy lord, [reward] the deeds of a good and distinguished servant of Pharaoh, his lord. He shall be strengthened to do the best for Amon-ra, the king of the gods, the great and glorious god, and to do the best for Pharaoh, his lord, who has seen and admired what thou hast done. This is for explanation of the commission to these (present) treasurers and the two councillors of Pharaoh concerning the gold, silver, [and all other gifts, which are given to thee as a reward].'

In fact, the representation belonging to this inscription shows that the words of the king were exactly fulfilled, for the two councillors of Pharaoh (*Ab-en-pir'ao*)[7] who are named adorn the meritorious priest of Amon with necklaces and other jewels.

What the high-priest did for the temple of his god is related to us at the place we have mentioned, in his own words:—

'Thus has the teacher of the king, the chief priest of Amon-ra, the king of the gods, Amenhotep, done, namely:

'I found this holy house of the chief priests of Amon of old time, which is in the temple of Amon-ra, the king of the gods, hastening to decay. What was done to it dates since the time of King Usurtasen I.[8] I took the building in hand, and restored it anew in good work, and in a work pleasant to look at. I strengthened its walls behind, around, and in front. I built it anew. I made its columns, which were bound together with great stones in skilful work. I inserted in the gates great folding doors of acacia wood, for closing them up. I built out on its great stone wall, which is seen at the . . . . I built my high new house for the chief priest of Amon, who dwells in the temple of Amon. I inserted the whole gate of [acacia wood]. The bolts in it are of bronze; the engraved pictures are of the finest gold and [silver]. I built a great forecourt of stone, which opens on the southern temple-lake, [to serve for] the purification in the temple of Amon. I chased [the whole with . . . .] of Seb. I set up its great blocks of carved stone in the connecting hall. The valves of the doors are of acacia wood. I [caused to be erected one ?] of great carved blocks of stone. The outlines of the carved work were drawn in red chalk. . . . The whole was inscribed with the full name of Pharaoh.—Also a new treasury was built on the ground within the great hall which

---

[7] See Vol. I. p. 307; Vol. II. p. 146.
[8] See Vol. I. p. 154.

bears the name : . . . . The columns are of stone, the doors of acacia wood, painted with . . . . [Also I built a chamber for] the king. It lies behind the store-chamber for the necessaries of the temple of Amon. [It is constructed] of stone, the doors and door-valves are of acacia wood. . . . . [I made and set up statues in] the great splendid forecourt for each chief priest of Amon-ra [the king of the gods. I laid out gardens behind] Asheru. They were planted with trees.'

We break off the translation here, because the great gaps in the following lines destroy all connection in the sense. Towards the end, the architect declares that he had done all this, 'to glorify my lord Amon-ra, the king of the gods, whose greatness, doctrine, and [power?] I acknowledge.' To this is appended the usual prayer for life, welfare, health, and a long enjoyment of existence for the king and—for himself.

Emphatically as Amenhotep, the chief priest of Amon, and also called repeatedly the 'great architect in the city of Amon,' speaks of 'his lord the Pharaoh,' the power of the latter was already broken. For with Amenhotep the chief priests began to play that double part which at last raised them to the royal throne. It is right, therefore, to pay particular attention beforehand to their names, since they are not only of importance for determining the chronology by the succession of their generations, but also in a purely historical relation they have the value of actual kings' names.

To the time of the same king, who occupied such a peculiar position in relation to his high-priest, belong the burglaries and thefts in the tombs of the earlier kings, about which a whole series of judicial documents on papyrus afford us express information. There existed in Thebes a regularly constituted thieves' society, formed for the secret opening and robbing of the tombs of the kings, in which even sacerdotal persons took a part. It required full and extensive enquiries to follow the track of the offenders. Among the persons entrusted in the name of the king with the conduct of this official enquiry, according to extant documents, there are some officials of Pharaoh whose acquaintance we have already made. They are the following:—the chief priest of Amon, Amenhotep; the governor of Thebes, Khamus; the governor of Thebes, Ranebma-Nakht; the royal councillor and scribe of Pharaoh, Nes-su-amon; the royal councillor and interpreter of Pharaoh, Noferkara-em-piamon; Pharaoh's councillor and secretary, Pi-notem; the leader of the Mazaiu (police), Menthu-khopeshef; and some other persons, whose names we will pass over. The tombs, which were broken open and partly plundered, contained the kings and queens of the XIth, XIIIth, XVIIth, and XVIIIth Dynasties, a list of whom we have already laid before our readers.[9]

According to the arrangement of Lepsius, the following are to be ranked as Pharaohs following Ramessu IX.:—

Ramses X. Ramses XII.

VIII. KHEPER-MA-RA SOTEP-EN-RA RAMESSU X. AMEN-HI-KHOPESHEF;

IX. SEKHA-EN-RA MIAMUN RAMESSU XI.;

X. USER-MA-RA SOTEP-EN-RA MIAMUN RAMESSU XII.

[9] See Vol. I. p. 283.

Their names are found only here and there on the monuments, most frequently in the small oracle-temple of Khonsu in Thebes, which their forefather Ramessu III. had founded, and which since that time had received the particular attention of the kings of the Twentieth Dynasty, as a sort of family temple. The god Khonsu, the young son of Amon and of the goddess Mut of Asheru, was worshipped in this temple in his particular character as Khonsu-em-us Nofer-hotep, that is, 'Khonsu of Thebes, the good and friendly,' and a special importance was attached to his oracles on all grave occasions. The kings and priests enquire of him, and he gives his answers as he pleases.

These introductory remarks appear to us necessary in order to understand the following inscription on a stone of the time of king Ramessu XII., which was formerly set up in the temple of Khonsu. We pass over as unimportant for our purpose the king's names and titles of honour, and begin with the properly historical introduction, which, commencing at the 4th line, runs as follows:—

'(4) When Pharaoh was in the river-land of Naharain, as his custom was every year, the kings of all the nations came with humility and friendship to the person of Pharaoh. From the extremest ends (of their countries) they brought the gifts of gold, silver, blue and (5) green stones; and all sorts of (sweet-smelling) woods of the holy land were upon their shoulders; and each one endeavoured to outdo his neighbour.

'Then the king of Bakhatana brought his tribute, and placed at the head of it his eldest daughter, to honour Pharaoh and to beg for his friendship. And the woman (6) was much more beautiful to please Pharaoh than all other things. Then was the king's name written upon her, as the king's wife, Noferu-Ra.

When the Pharaoh had come to Egypt, everything was done for her which a queen required to use.

'It happened in the year 15, in the month Payni, on the 22nd day. Then Pharaoh was in Thebes, the strong, the queen of cities, in order to thank (7) his father Amon-ra, the lord of Thebes, at his beautiful feast of Api of the south, the seat of his desire from the beginning. They came to announce to Pharaoh: A messenger of the king of Bakhatana has arrived with rich gifts for the queen. Then was he brought (8) before Pharaoh, together with his gifts. He spoke in honour of Pharaoh: "Greeting to thee, thou sun of the nations, let us live before thee!" Thus he spake, while he fell down before Pharaoh, and repeated the message to Pharaoh: "I am come to thee, the great lord, on account of Bint-resh, the youngest sister of the queen Noferu-ra. (9) She is suffering in her body. May thy Majesty send a learned expert to see her." Then spake Pharaoh: "Let them bring to me the learned men from the places of the holy sciences, and the knowers of the most intimate secrets." (10) They brought them to him forthwith. Then spake Pharaoh after a time: "Ye have been assembled here to hear these words. Now, then, bring to me a man of a clever mind, and a finger skilful in writing, out of your company." When the royal scribe, (11) Thut-emhib, had come before Pharaoh, Pharaoh bade him, that he should start for Bakhatana with the envoy, who was present. When the expert had reached the city of the land of Bakhatana, in which Bint-resh dwelt after the manner of one possessed with a spirit, then he found himself (12) unable to contend with him (the spirit).

'And the king again sent to Pharaoh, speaking thus: "Great lord and ruler! May thy Majesty order that the god may be sent [Khonsu, the oracular, of Thebes, to the youngest sister of the queen." (13) And the messenger remained with] Pharaoh till the 26th year. In the month Pakhons (of that year), at the time of the feast of Amon, Pharaoh abode in Thebes, and Pharaoh stood again before the god Khonsu of Thebes, the kind and friendly, while he spake thus: "O thou good lord! I present myself again before thee on account of the daughter of the king of Bakhatana." (14) Then went from thence the god Khonsu of Thebes, the kind and friendly, to Khonsu, the oracular, the great god, the driver away of evil. Then spake Pharaoh in presence of Khonsu of Thebes, the kind and friendly, "Thou good lord, shouldest thou not charge Khonsu (15), the oracular, the great god, the driver away of evil, that he may betake himself to Bakhatana?" To that there was a very gracious consent. Then spake Pharaoh, "Give him thy talisman to take with him. I will let his Holiness be drawn to Bakhatana, to release the daughter of the king of Bakhatana."[1] (16) Thereupon a very gracious consent of Khonsu of Thebes, the kind and friendly. Then he gave the talisman to Khonsu, the oracular, of Thebes, at four different times. And Pharaoh gave command, to cause Khonsu, the oracular, of Thebes, to embark on the great ship. Five barks and many (17) carriages and horses were on his right and on his left.

'That god reached the city of the land of Bakhatana after the space of a year and five months. Then the king of Bakhatana and his people and his princes went to meet Khonsu, the oracular. And he threw himself (18) prostrate, and spake thus: "Come to us, be friendly to us, according to the commands of the king of Upper and Lower Egypt, Miamun Ramessu." Then that god went to the place where Bint-resh dwelt. Then he caused the talisman to work upon the daughter of the king of Bakhatana. She became well (19) on the spot. Then spake that spirit, which possessed her, before Khonsu, the oracular, of Thebes: "Welcome as a friend, thou great god, driver away of evil. Thine is the city of Bakhatana. Thy servants are its inhabitants. I am thy servant. (20) I will return whence I came, to make thy heart satisfied about the object for which thou wast brought hither. May I request thy Holiness, that there may be a feast celebrated in my company and in the company of the king of Bakhatana?" Then this god assented graciously to his prophet, and he said: (21) "Let the king of Bakhatana prepare a great sacrifice for this spirit. When that has been done, then will Khonsu, the oracular, unite himself with the spirit." And the king of Bakhatana stood there, together with his people, and was very much afraid. Then (22) he prepared a great sacrifice for Khonsu, the oracular, of Thebes, and for this spirit. The king of Bakhatana celebrated a feast for them. Then the glorious spirit went thence, whither it pleased him, as Khonsu, the oracular, of Thebes, had commanded. (23) And the king of Bakhatana was delighted beyond all measure, together with

---

[1] This refers to the conveyance of the ark of the god on its carriage, which is represented in a picture.—ED.

all the men who dwelt in Bakhatana. Then he considered in his heart, and he spake to them thus: "Might it be so, that this god should remain in the city of the land of Bakhatana? I will not let him return to Egypt." Then (24) this god remained three years and nine months in Bakhatana. Then the king of Bakhatana rested on his bed, and he saw as if this god stepped out from his holy shrine, as in the form of a golden sparrow-hawk he took his flight heavenwards towards Egypt. (25) When he awoke he was lame. Then spake he to the prophet of Khonsu, the oracular, of Thebes: "This god he staid among us, and now he withdraws to Egypt. His carriage must return to Egypt." (26) Then the king of Bakhatana had the god drawn back to Egypt, and gave him very many presents of all sorts of good things, and they arrived safely at Thebes. Then went Khonsu, the oracular, of Thebes, (27) into the temple of Khonsu of Thebes, the kind and friendly, and he laid down the presents just as the king of Bakhatana had presented them to him, namely, all kinds of good things, before Khonsu of Thebes, the kind and friendly; he kept nothing of them for his house. But Khonsu, the oracular, of Thebes, (28) returned happily to his house in the 33rd year, in the month of Mekhir, on the 13th day, of king Miamun Ramessu. Such was what happened to him; to him, the dispenser of life to-day and for ever.'

Many reflections will naturally crowd upon the reader's mind on the perusal of this inscription, the first interpretation of which is due to the labours of two masters of our science, Dr. S. Birch and Monsieur E. de Rougé. Our own translation has, perhaps, the modest merit of having utilized the latest discoveries in old Egyptian philology for the elucidation of this stone. It is difficult to say where the land of Bakhatana should be sought. A journey of seventeen months from Thebes to the foreign city shows that it was very distant. The (doubtful?) stay of Ramessu XII. in the riverland of Naharain suggests a Syrian town. Its identification with Bagistan, as proposed by E. de Rougé, as well as my own with Ecbatana, must be given up, in face of the fact that, in those times of the decay of the rule of the Ramessids, such distant towns and countries could not have been subject to the empire of the Pharaohs. Probably the town referred to may be Bakhi or Bakh, which is mentioned in the lists of the victories of Ramessu III. and earlier kings as a conquered place.

With his successor—

XI. MEN-MA-RA SOTEP-EN-PTAH KHAMUS MIAMUN
RAMESSU XIII. NUTER HAQ-ON, B.C. 1100,

we seem to have arrived at the end of this Dynasty, although it is proved by the monuments that some Ramessids, as unimportant petty kings, put forward their claim to the throne of their fathers, even in the time of the Assyrian conqueror, Shashanq I. They did so truly with little success, for the chief priests of the god Amon had already placed the crown of the country on their own heads, and being the lords of Thebes they behaved as lords also of the whole country.

The temple of Khonsu at Thebes, which was likewise the family chapel of the last Ramessids, had been finished under Ramessu XIII., as far as the open forecourt with the small colonnade round it. The king prides himself on having erected these last buildings ' as a memorial to his father Khonsu ;' and ' the kind and friendly Khonsu of Thebes' promises him as a reward ' the kingdom of Tum.' In other parts of the first hall the king insists in a still more earnest manner on his own importance as a builder. Thus he caused these words to be engraved on a carved stone :—

'Splendid things has he made, many and wonderful monuments; all his schemes were carried out immediately like those of his father, the Memphian Ptah. He has embellished Thebes with great monuments. No other king has done the like.'

Poor king! While he gave life to the dead stones by these and other inscriptions in the temple of his house, for the honour of his name, to hand down his remembrance to posterity, the traitor was lurking behind his back, who gave the death-blow to him and to his race. This was the chief priest of Amon, Hirhor, who became the founder of the following dynasty.

I learn by a letter from my honoured friend, Mariette-Bey, that the discovery was made last year (1876), at Abydus, on the spot named Shune-el-zebib, of a memorial-stone of Ramses XIII., bearing the date of the 27th year, the month Mesori, the 8th day.

Also, in the collection of papyrus-rolls in the Turin Museum, as published by M. Pleyte, there exists what is possibly an *autograph* letter of the same king, with the date of the 17th year, the month Khoiakh, the 25th day. The contents of this MS. (omitting the formal introduction) will be best understood from the following translation :—

'A royal order is issued to the King's son of Kush, the royal scribe of the warriors, the superintendent of the granaries, the commander of Pharaoh's foreigners, Painehas, to the following effect :—The king's order will be brought to thee, making the communication, that Jani, the Major-domus and counsellor (Ab) of Pharaoh, has set out on his journey. His departure has been caused by commissions from Pharaoh, his lord, which he has started to execute in the land of the South. As soon as this letter of Pharaoh, thy lord, reaches thee, do thou act in the fullest accord with him, for he is to execute the commissions of Pharaoh, his lord, on account of which he has departed from hence.

'Thou art to look up the hand-barrows of the great goddess, to load them and put them on board the ship. Thou art to have them brought into his presence, where the statue is appointed to stand.

'Thou art to have the precious stones (here follows a list of unknown sorts of stones)—brought together to the same place where the statue stands, to deliver them into the hands of the artists. Let no delay be interposed in the execution of this commission, or else I should degrade thee. Behold! I expect thy best attention to this message. Such is the message which is made known to thee.'.

The conclusion of the letter is clear and explicit, evidently on the assumption that the viceroy of Ethiopia might prove a negligent servant.

LIST OF VALUES AND PRICES, ABOUT B.C. 1000.

Preliminary Note.[2]

1 *Ten* = 10 *Ket*.
1 *Ket* = 9·0959 grammes = 154 grains nearly (or ⅓ oz. Troy).
1 *Ten* = 90·959 ,, = 1537 grains (above ¼ lb. Troy).

Table of the Estimated Value of Ancient Egyptian uncoined Silver and Copper Money. Ratio of silver to copper, 1 : 80.

Egyptian weights		Weight in grammes	Silver (1 Mark = 1 Shilling)		Copper	
			Mark	Pfennige	Mark	Pfennige
⅓	Ket	3·0319	—	53⅓	—	⅔
½	,,	4·5479	—	80	—	1
⅔	,,	6·0638	1	6⅔	—	1⅓
1	,,	9·0959	1	60	—	2
2	,,	18·1918	3	20	—	4
3	,,	27·2877	4	80	—	6
4	,,	36·3836	6	40	—	8
5	,,	45·4795	8	—	—	10
6	,,	54·5754	9	60	—	12
7	,,	63·6713	11	20	—	14
8	,,	72·7672	12	80	—	16
9	,,	81·8631	14	40	—	18
1	Ten	90·959	16	—	—	20
2	,,	181·918	32	—	—	40
3	,,	272·877	48	—	—	60
4	,,	363·836	64	—	—	80
5	,,	454·795	80	—	1	—
6	,,	636·713	96	—	1	20
7	,,	727·672	112	—	1	40
8	,,	818·631	128	—	1	60

By the help of this Table the reader will find it easy to form a correct idea of the values and prices in the following List.

I have further to observe, that the *Ket of Silver* corresponds to the Greek *Didrachmon* or *Stater*, and the *Ket of Copper* to the *Chalcus* (= ⅛th of the Obolus). Accordingly the Copts translate the Greek didrachmon by *Kiti* or *Kite*.

---

[2] In the table of Egyptian Measures and Weights, given in the *Records of the Past* (vol. ii. p. 164), the *Kat* (Ket) is estimated at 140 grains, and the *Ten* at 1,400 grains. The *Ten* is roughly called a Pound, and the *Kat* or *Ket* an Ounce or Didrachm; but these terms by no means correspond to their actual values. The equivalents of the *measures of capacity* named in the following list are unknown.—ED.

LIST OF VALUES AND PRICES, ABOUT B.C. 1000.

1 Slave cost 3 Ten, 1 Ket, silver.
1 Ox   „   1 Ket, silver (=8 Ten, copper).
1 Goat cost 2 Ten, copper.
1 Pair of Fowls (Geese?) cost $\frac{1}{3}$ Ten, copper.
500 Fish, of a particular kind, cost 1 Ket, silver (=8 Ten, copper).
800 Fish, of another kind, cost 1 Ket, silver.
100 Fish, of a third kind, „ 1 „   „
1 Tena of Corn of Upper Egypt cost 5–7 Ten, copper.
1 Hotep of Wheat cost 2 Ten, copper.
1   „   „ Spelt   „ 2 „   „
5 Hin of Honey   „ 4 „   „
(Hence 1 Hin of Honey cost 8 Ket, copper.)
365 Hin of Honey cost $3\frac{2}{3}$ Ten, silver.
(Hence 1 Hin of Honey cost $\frac{1}{10}$ Ket, silver.)
11 Hin of Oil cost 17 Ten, copper.
50 Acres (Set) of arable land cost 5 Ten, silver.
1 Garden land cost 2 Ten, silver.
1 Knife cost 3 Ten, copper.
1 Razor „ 1 „   „
1 Metal Vessel, weighing 20 Ten, cost 40 Ten, copper.
1   Ditto   „   6 „   „ 18 „   „
1   Ditto   „   1 „   „   3 „   „
1 Apron of fine stuff cost 3 Ten, copper.

The month's wages of an ordinary workman amounted to 5 Ten of copper.

The above values are derived from inscriptions, and there can be no doubt as to the accuracy of their interpretation.

Hirhor.   Pinotem.

CHAPTER XVI.

THE TWENTY-FIRST DYNASTY.

THE PRIEST HIRHOR AND HIS SUCCESSORS.

1100—966 B.C.

'THE king of Upper and Lower Egypt, the chief priest of Amon, SI-AMON (SON OF AMON) HIRHOR:'—

Thus did the ambitious priest of Amon, the head of the Theban clergy, style himself officially, when he took possession of the throne of Egypt, or, to speak more correctly, of that of the Thebaid in particular. His lord, Ramessu XIII., had before his own fall honoured the first servant of the god Amon in a distinguished manner, inasmuch as he had entrusted him with the highest and most important offices of the government. Hirhor calls himself, in the representations of his person by the side of the king, an 'hereditary prince, the fan-bearer on the right of the king, King's son of Kush, chief architect of the king, chief general of the army in Upper and Lower Egypt, administrator of the granaries,' as Joseph was of old at the court of Pharaoh. Such high dignities, which in the course of time were held by one and the same person, either together or in succession, must have essentially facilitated his project, when once formed, to overthrow the sovereign. His position and inviolability as the chief priest of Amon secured to the proud Hirhor, on the other hand, no inconsiderable following among the most powerful of all the priestly societies in the whole country, which gave a steady support to his secret plans. As in Upper Egypt it was the inhabitants of the Theban nome and the priests of Amon who took part with the new king, so, on the other hand, in Lower Egypt he had won over a moderate but not to be despised number of the priestly societies of the holy fathers of the Ramses-city of Zoan-Tanis, who stood in close connection with the imperial city of Thebes owing to their common worship of Amon. The letters and documents of the Ramessids which have come down to us leave not the slightest doubt upon this point. And yet the plans of Hirhor were not destined to attain complete success. While Ramessu XIII. and his successors, according to all probability, ate the bread of banishment in the Great Oasis, they had raised up in silence an enemy to the priest-kings, whose power and importance might be brought in to aid their cause.

On the east, in the vast plains of Mesopotamia, the great empire of the Khita had been succeeded by a new race of rulers, known to us in history under the name of the Assyrian Empire. The Egyptian monuments of the time give to the successors of the Khita the short name which, with the assistance of the cuneiform inscriptions, we understand as *Mat*, and they designate the king of the Mat, that is 'the peoples,' as the 'great king of the Mat, the great king of kings.' Even though, in a style which is rather pompous than historically true, Hirhor conferred on himself the honorary title of conqueror of the Ruthen, to which in all probability he had no right, it may be assumed that the power of the Assyrians, these Mat, had reached a strength which must at any rate have restrained the priest-king, in the internal decay of the Egyptian empire, from thinking of conquests on the East.

The successors of the priest-king, whom the reader will find named in the Genealogical Table (IV.), were far from securing a firm position in the country. Their most determined enemies were the banished race of the Ramessids, who succeeded in forming alliances with Assyria. A great-grandson of that Ramessu XIII. who was overthrown by Hirhor, according to our reckoning Ramessu XVI., married an unnamed daughter of 'the great king of the Assyrians,' whose name is distinctly transmitted to us. The monuments call him PANRSHNS (Parrash-nes, Pallash-nes, Pallash-nisu). The name in its first part reminds us of the second portion of the Assyrian royal names, Ninip-Pallasar and Teglath-phalasar (about 1100 B.C.), as they have been read by interpreters of the Assyrian cuneiform inscriptions.

The consequences of such a connection of the banished but legitimate royal race of the Egyptians with the powerful dynasty of Nineveh quickly appeared. The Assyrians marched against Egypt.

At that time PINOTEM I., a grandson of Hirhor, ruled the land as king and high-priest. His residence was at Tanis, already familiar to us as the strong frontier fortress in the Delta towards the East. In the twenty-fifth year of his reign, disturbances had broken out in the Thebaid in favour of the banished Ramessids. Pinotem I., who had to await the attack of the great king of Assyria, Nimrod, and his army, remained in Tanis. His son, Men-kheper-ra, was sent with full powers to Thebes, to check the insurrection. After succeeding in doing this, though how far must remain uncertain, we find him named as the successor of his father in the high-priesthood of Amon. His first act was to recal the Egyptians banished to the Oasis, namely, the Ramessids and their adherents. This was apparently done with the consent of the god Amon, whose oracle had approved the proposal of Men-kheper-ra.

This fact is transmitted to us by an inscription, in which, in spite of many lacunæ, we can clearly understand the general connection of the whole. I now give for the first time the translation of this important document, after having had the opportunity of again comparing it with the original at Thebes:—

'(1) In the year 25, the month Epiphi, the 29th day, at the same time as the feast of the god Amon-ra, the king of the gods, at his [beautiful] monthly feast of Ape [of the south]. . . . . (2) Nes-hir-hor in their multitude. The Majesty of this noble god Amon [-ra, the king of the gods,] was . . . . (3) Thebes. He showed the way to the scribes, the land-surveyors, and people. . . . . (4) In the year 25, in the first month of the year . . . . Amon-ra, the lord of Thebes. . . . (5) . . . the high-priest of Amon-ra, the king of the gods, the general in chief of the army, Men-kheper-ra, the son of the king . . . Miamun Pinotem . . . (6) at his feet.

'Their heart was joyfully moved on account of his design. He had come to Patoris (to the south land) in victorious power, to restore order in the land and to chastise the opponents. He gave to them [the punishment they deserved, and established the old order of things, just as] (7) it had been in the times of the reign of the sun-god Ra. He entered the city (of Thebes) with a contented soul. The families of Thebes received him with songs of joy. Messengers had been sent before him. The Majesty of this noble god, the lord of the gods, Amon-ra, the lord of Thebes, was brought out in procession. He (8) rewarded (?) him very much. He placed him in the seat of his father as chief priest of Amon-ra, the king of the gods, and as general in chief of the army of Upper and Lower Egypt. He dedicated to him numerous and splendid wonderful works, such as had never been seen before.

'Now [had reached its end] (9) the month Mesori. On the 4th intercalary day, the day of the birthday feast of Isis, at the same time as the feast of Amon on the new year, the Majesty of this glorious god, the lord of the gods, Amon-ra, the king of the gods, was brought out in procession. He came to the great hall of the temple of Amon, and rested before the pylon of Amon. And (10) the general in chief of the army, Men-kheper-ra, went in to Amon-ra, the king of the gods. He worshipped him much with many prayers, and set before him an offering of all sorts of good things. Then the high-priest of Amon-ra, Men-kheper-ra, added the words : " O thou, my good lord ! There is a talk and it is repeated [by the people.]" (11) Then the god gave full assent to him. Then he again went to the god, and spake thus : " O thou, my good lord ! This talk of the people is a complaint, on account of thy anger against those who are in the Oasis, in the land which thou hast appointed for them." Then the god gave full assent (12) to him. Therefore this chief captain lifted up his hands praying, in order to worship his lord. As the moon changes with the sun, thus he spake : " Hail to thee ! thou creator of all [being, thou bringer forth] of all being which exists, father of the gods, creator of the goddesses, as they remain in the cities and in the villages, begetter (13) of men, bearer of women, who dispenses life to all men, for he is a skilful master of work . . . . . the life . . . . of the great god Ptah, (the fashioner) . . . . . [who creates provisions] in abundance, who brings forth sustenance for gods and men, sunshine by day, moonlight by night, who traverses the heaven in peace, (14) without rest, as the greatest among the spirits, powerful as the goddess Sokhet, resembling the sun . . . . [be again friendly disposed to the banished ones, against whom thy command went out]. Do thou recal it, to heal what is diseased; look [graciously upon] this people, who do not stand before thy countenance, for there are (15) a hundred thousand of them. Is any one able to appease thee, if thou at all turnest thyself away? [Hail to thee] thou shining beam! [Listen to] my words on this very day. Mayest thou [feel a pity for] the servants, whom thou hast banished (16) to the Oasis, that they may be brought back to Egypt." Then the great god gave full assent to him. Then went in the captain of the army again to the great god, speaking thus: "O thou, my good lord! Since [thou hast assented] to their return, let it be published abroad, that thou [art] friendly [disposed] to [the banished ones."] Then the great god gave full assent to him. Then went he in again (17) to the great god, and spake thus: "O thou, my good lord! Give forth a valid command in thy name, that no inhabitant of the land shall be banished to the far distance of the Oasis, that no one . . . . from this very day for ever." (18) Then the great god gave full assent to him. Then he spake again to him: "Speak that it may be done thus according to thy command, which shall [be written down] on a memorial stone [in writing], and set up in thy cities, to last and to remain for ever." Then the great god gave full assent to him.

Then spake again the chief priest (19) of Amon, Men-kheper-ra: "O thou, my good lord! Now am I contented (?) a hundred thousand times; this was my intention, that all families should hear it. All (their) words express contentment with me. I am thy servant in truth, [for I am thy likeness] (20) in youthful form for thy city. I was created as originator of all riches according to thy [word], when I was yet in my mother's womb. Thou didst fashion me in the egg. Thou didst bring me to the light to the great joy of thy people. Give me a beautiful duration of life (21) in the service of thy [being], and purity and protection from all thy plagues (?). Let my feet walk in thy ways, and make thy path straight for me. May my heart be friendly towards (thy?) house, to do [what thy commands enjoin]. (22) Give me consideration with the great god, in peace, that I may abide and live in thy

glorious house. In like manner may all reward be mine from
. . ." (23) Then did the high priest of Amon, Men-kheper-ra, go
in to the great god, and spake thus: "If any one of the people
should in thy presence contradict, saying that he has done great
things for the people, that the land may gain life,—then destroy
him, kill him." Then the great god gave full assent to him.'

The distracted state of the empire could not have been more clearly exhibited than in this inscription. Even if we reject 'the 100,000 banished ones,' of whom the high-priest speaks to the god, at all events the whole proceeding throws a sad light on the state of things then prevailing in Egypt. Persecutions and banishments form, in every age, a measure of the internal condition of an empire. That the recal of the exiles from the Oasis, proposed by the priest-king Men-kheper-ra to the god Amon, did not spring from any special goodness of heart, but was a politic measure, to quiet the agitation fermenting in the country, can hardly require further proof on our part.

While these events were taking place, which the inscription sets forth in such an ambiguous manner, it appears that Naromath (Nimrod), the great king of Assyria, who had been associated on the throne by his father Shashanq, had advanced into Egypt with an army, not only to render help and support to the Ramessids, but also with the intention of conquering the country, and turning it into an Assyrian dependency. Here in Egypt death surprised him. His mother, Mehet-en-usekh, was an Egyptian, in all probability a daughter of the 14th Ramessu. According to her desire, her son, 'the great king of kings,' was buried in Abydus, and the feasts of the dead were instituted in his honour, the cost of which was to be defrayed from the income of certain estates. At the same time men and women were appointed for the preservation of his tomb, herds of cattle were purchased, and all other things provided, which could serve for a worthy establishment in honour of the dead.

When Egypt had thus become virtually a province of the Assyrian empire, Shashanq, the son of the great king Naromath (Nimrod), of whom we have just spoken, was made king. Pisebkhan I., the brother of the chief priest Men-kheper-ra, was, according to the Assyrian practice, left as under-king in Tanis, while Shashanq fixed his royal seat in the town of Bubastus. Men-kheper-ra carried on his functions as chief priest of Amon in Thebes, where, as we have reason to suppose, Ramses XVI. was for some time, in name at least, recognized as king.

These measures were evidently taken during the presence of the great king of Assyria, Shashanq, in Egypt.[1] He visited Thebes, and did not fail, on his journey to the city of Amon, to pay a visit to the grave of his beloved son at Abydus. He was bitterly chagrined at its neglected state. The Egyptian officials, who probably had little inclination to honour the remains of an Assyrian great king, had plundered, as far as they could, both the living and lifeless temple-

[1] To guard against a possible confusion, we may remind the reader that the Shashanq here spoken of, king of *Assyria*, and *father* of Nimrod, is the *grandfather* of the Shashanq, *son* of Nimrod, who is mentioned in the preceding paragraph as having ultimately become Shashanq I., king of *Egypt*. (See the Genealogical Table IV.)—ED.

revenues which had been appointed for keeping up the grave. They were brought to an account by the great king Shashanq, and, with the approval of the Theban god Amon, they were all punished with death.

These circumstances have been handed down to us in an inscription of unusual magnitude on the front side of a granite block at Abydus. Even though the whole upper half of the stone is probably wanting, and must lie buried somewhere in Abydus, the under part is, however, well preserved, so far at least that the contents of this remarkable memorial tablet can be read without misunderstanding. It was with great trouble that I made a transcript from its weather-beaten surface, which will give my readers a general representation of the decrees of the Assyrian great king, whose names and titles, especially in what relates to the truly Eastern appellations of honour of the king of kings, are completely preserved. I give here the translation of the part which has been preserved, in the persuasion that my colleagues in these studies will welcome with pleasure the publication of this remarkable but hitherto unknown inscription :—

'[To Amon-ra spake the great king of Assyria, when] the great king, the king Shashanq, [had visited] his son, at his beautiful burial-place with his father Osiris, where his body had been laid on his bed of rest in the city of Nifur (Abydus), in sight of [the temple of Osiris]: "Thou hast freed him from attaining to an infirm old age, while he remained on earth. Thou hast granted him his rest. My feasts will consist in this, to receive the undivided victory." Very, very much did the great god give assent to him.

'Then spake his Majesty anew to the great god thus : "O thou good lord, put to death [the captains] of the army, the . . . . secretary, the land-surveyor, and all . . . ? whom [I] sent [with a

INSCRIPTION AT ABYDUS.

commission] to this estate, and who plundered [the property] of the altar of the Osirian great lord of Assyria, Na-ro-math (Nimrod), the son of Mehet-en-usekh, who is buried in Abydus, and all the people who have robbed his holy property, his people, his herds of cattle, his gardens, his offerings, and all that was dedicated for his honour. Act according to thy great spirit in its whole extent, to replace them again, and to replace the women and their children." The great god assented to this most graciously.

'Then his Majesty threw himself on the ground before him, and his Majesty spake thus: "Grant triumph to Shashanq, the great king of Assyria, the great king of kings, the glorious . . . . and all those who are with him, and all warriors, and all [his people] together."

'Then [spake to him] Amon-ra, the king of the gods : "I will do [according to thy wish]. Thou shalt receive (the blessing of) a great age and remain on earth, and thy heir shall sit on thy throne for ever."

'Then his Majesty had the statue, in the form of a walking man, of the Osirian great king of Assyria, the great king of kings, Na-ro-math, brought up the river to Abydus. There were in attendance on it a large body of soldiers in many ships, no man knows their number, together with the ambassadors of the great king of Assyria. And it was set down in the splendid royal chamber of the holy of holies of the right eye of the sun, to carry the offerings on the altar-table of Nifur. According to the directions of the holy anointing, the dedication was accomplished.

'The incense was burnt in the room of the star-chamber for three days. This was set up for the temple-ordinances in the form of a written record, according to the contents of the ordinances for the feasts of the gods. A memorial tablet was erected in the language of the land of Bab[el], containing the command [of the great lord] in his name. And it (the memorial tablet) was laid up in the holy of holies of the gods for ever and ever.

'[This is the catalogue] of that which was appointed for the altar of the Osirian great king of the Assyrians, Na-ro-math, the son of Mehet-en-usekh, who is buried at Abydus. There were allotted (to it) the people who had been [bought ?] out of [the countries ?] of the great king of Assyria, namely : Aïromapatut, of the people of the Phœnicians, and obedient at call : Khu-amon . . . . and . . . . a Phœnician (called) Bek-ptah. (The price of) their purchase makes in silver money 15 lbs. His Majesty had given for them in silver money 20 lbs., making together 35 lbs. This is the number of that which they cost. The 50 aruræ of land, which are situated in the region of the heights to the south of Abydus, which is called "permanent duration of the kingdom (*Heh-suteni*)," cost 5 lbs. of silver money. The (fields) which are situated by the side (?) of the canal which is at Abydus, an estate of 50 aruræ, for these there was paid 5 lbs. in silver money. This makes together an estate [of 100 aruræ] in these two places in the region of the heights to the south of Abydus, and in the region of the heights to the north of Abydus. For this estate of 100 aruræ there was also paid 10 lbs. in silver.

'[Catalogue of the servants for the estate]: His servant Pi-uër, his servant . . . . , his servant Ari-bek, his servant Bu-pi-amonkha, his servant Nai-shennu, his servant Pesh-en-Hor. Making a total of 6 servants, for whom there was paid, for each 3 lbs. and 1 ounce of silver money, making in all 1[8] pounds 6 ounces of silver money. [His boy (?) . . . . and his boy (?)] . . . . son of Hor-si-ise, for these was paid $4\frac{2}{3}$ ounces of silver money.

'The garden, which is situated in the district of the northern heights of Abydus, cost 2 lbs. of silver money; the gardener, Hormes. the son of Pen-mer, $x + \frac{2}{3}$ ounces of silver money, the water-carrier . . . . , the son of . . . . for $6\frac{2}{3}$ ounces of silver money.

'Catalogue of maid-servants: Nes-ta-tep, whose mother is *Tat-mut*; the maiden Tat-ise, the daughter of Nebt-hepet, whose mother is Ariamakh; the maiden Tat-amon, the daughter of Pinehas, [the maiden . . . . , the daughter of . . . .], each one for $5\frac{2}{3}$ ounces of silver money.

'The outlay for [the purchase of honey] is to amount to $3\frac{2}{3}$ lbs. of silver money, and is charged upon the treasury of Osiris, so that a hin-measure of honey shall be given by the treasury of Osiris [for the daily supply of honey of the Osirian] great king of Assyria, Na-ro-math, whose father is the great king of kings, [Shashanq, and whose mother is Mehet-en-usekh, for all eternity]. The treasury of Osiris is charged with the money for this, neither more nor less. [The outlay for the purchase] of balsam shall amount to $4\frac{2}{3}$ lbs. of silver money, and is charged on the treasury of Osiris, so that 4 ounces of balsam shall be delivered from the treasury of Osiris every day for the offering of the Osirian great king of the Assyrians, Na-ro-math, whose mother is Mehet-en-usekh, to all eternity. [For the provision] of the balsam the treasury of Osiris is thus charged with the money, neither more nor less. [The outlay for the purchase of] incense shall amount to $5\frac{2}{3}$ ounces of silver money, and is charged on the treasury of Osiris, so that a hin of $x + \frac{2}{3}$ ounces shall be delivered from the treasury of Osiris every day for the [keeping up] of the burning of incense for the Osirian great king of Assyria, Na-ro-math, whose mother is Mehet-en-usekh, to all times. For the procuring of the incense the treasury of Osiris is thus charged with the money, neither more nor less. [The outlay for the different persons of the spice-kitchen, and for the persons of the labours of the harvest, shall amount to for each] $x + 3$ ounces, and for each 1 ounce of silver money, and these are charged on the treasury of Osiris; so that there shall be delivered [. . . . the spice-cakes] each day from the treasury of Osiris, and [that there shall be delivered . . . .] from the treasury of Osiris, and that there shall be delivered . . . . from the treasury of Osiris for the altars of the Osirian great king of Assyria, Na-ro-math, whose mother is Mehet-en-usekh, to all eternity. For the support of the workmen of his spice-kitchen, the money for it also is charged on the treasury of Osiris. [Also for the] harvest workers in the upper fields, [the payments for these] are charged on the treasury of Osiris, to the amount of . . . . in silver money, neither more nor less. This is the sum total of the silver money for the people, which is charged on the treasury of Osiris, [so that all payments shall be made from it] which are to be borne by [the treasury of Osiris] for the altars of the Osirian great king of Assyria, the king of kings, Na-ro-math, the son of the great king of the Assyrians, Shashanq, whose mother is Mehet-en-usekh. It is assigned for the Osirian great king of the Assyrians, Na-ro-math, the son of Mehet-en-usekh, who [is buried] in Abydus, for the estate of 100 aruræ of land, for the 25 men and women, for the gardens, and it amounts in silver money to $100 + x$ lbs., x ounces . . . . . .'

My respected colleagues in science will, I think, readily admit, that in spite of its very ruinous and injured state, this inscription is one of the most remarkable, and, I will add, one of the most surprising, ever found on Egyptian soil. Who could have expected such direct evidence of the presence of an Assyrian great king in the Valley of the Nile, when the monuments had obstinately suppressed all information of the fact? We can only suppose that the Egyptians, after the departure of their Assyrian great kings, carefully destroyed all their monuments, and that the one we have quoted only escaped the same fate because it was used as a convenient block to work into some building in the cemetery of Abydus.

I will add to these remarks the mention of a new and not less remarkable fact. It relates to the statue of the great king Nimrod, about which mention is made in the inscription. By a strange accident of fate this also has been preserved. From the hieroglyphic inscription carved upon it, which has been thoroughly well preserved in the most important passages, I have recognized it in a sitting figure of red granite, which is exhibited in the middle of the chief hall of the Egyptian collection in Florence.

Who could ever have supposed that this headless statue represented the effigy of an Assyrian great king of about 1000 B.C.? But the surprises about this matter are not yet exhausted. I shall prove, as we go on, the presence of Assyrian satraps of the family of this same Nimrod, who have hitherto been set before our eyes in inscriptions, without the conjecture having occurred to any scholar, that Ser-'a-mat, 'the great prince of the peoples,' was an Assyrian official title.

As we have already remarked, a son of that great king Nimrod was raised to the Egyptian throne. He is that Shashanq, of whom, as the founder of the Twenty-second Dynasty, we have to speak in the next chapter.

At about the same time, by direction of this Shashanq, the affair of the inheritance of the princess Karamat (for thus, and not Mat-ke-ra or Ra-mat-ke, ought the name to be read) was regulated by express royal command, in the name of the Theban circle of gods. This lady was the offspring of the marriage of king Pisebkhan I. with a Theban (Ramessid?), and, according to a frequent Egyptian custom, she had been robbed of her patrimony situated in Upper Egypt. By her marriage with king Shashanq I. (for this Kar-am-at was his wife), her position was completely changed. The ordinance, which relates to the agreement for placing the princess in her full hereditary right, is engraved in large letters on the north wall of the third pylon on the south of the great temple of Amon in Karnak. The upper half of this wall is completely destroyed; and in this case also the first lines of the inscription, which contained the date and the name of the king, are unfortunately wanting.[2] We give the complete literal translation of this stone document, so important historically, and leave it to our readers themselves to draw all the conclusions which follow from it:—

'Thus spake Amon-ra, the king of the gods, the great god of the beginning of all being, and Mut and Khonsu, and the great gods:

'With regard to any object of any kind, which Karamat, the daughter of the king of Upper Egypt, Miamun Pisebkhan, has brought with her, of the hereditary possession which had descended to her in the southern district of the country, and with regard to each object of any kind whatever, which (1) (the people) of the land have presented to her, which they have at any time taken from the (royal) lady, we hereby restore it to her. Any object of any kind whatsoever [which] belongs [as an inheritance to the children], that [we hereby restore] to her children for all time. Thus speaks Amon-ra, the king of the gods, the great king of the beginning of all being, Mut, Khonsu, and the great gods: (2) "Every

[2] Among the copies taken by me at Thebes in 1851 is that of an inscription on stone, which begins with the names and titles of Shashanq I., and thus supplies these formulæ.

king, every chief priest of Amon, every general, every captain, and the people of every condition, whether male or female, who had great designs, and they who carried out their designs later, they shall restore the property of all kinds, which Karamat, the daughter of the king of Upper Egypt, Miamun Pisebkhan, brought with her as her inherited estate in the southern district (3) of the country, together with all possessions of all kinds, which the inhabitants of the country have given her, and what they have at any time taken from the lady, it shall be restored into her hand, we restore it into the hand of her son and of her grandson, and to her daughter and to her grand-daughter, the child of the child of her daughter. It shall be preserved to the latest times."

'Again [spake Amon-ra], the king of the gods, the great god of the beginning (4) of all being, and Mut, and Khonsu, and the great gods: "Slain shall be all people of every condition of the whole land, whether male or female, who shall claim any object of any kind whatsoever, which Karamat, the daughter of the king, and lord of the land, Miamun Pisebkhan, brought with her, as inherited estate of the south land, and any object of any kind whatsoever, which the inhabitants (5) of the land have given her, which they have at any time taken from the lady as property. They who shall keep back any object thereof one morning after (another) morning, upon them shall our great spirits fall heavily, we will not be a helper (?) to them. They shall be full, full of [snares?] on the part of the great god, of Mut, of Khonsu, and of the great gods."

'Then spake Amon-ra, the king of the gods, the great god [of the beginning of all being, and Mut, and Khonsu, and the great gods:] (6) "We will slay every inhabitant of every condition in the whole land, whether male or female, who shall claim any object of any sort whatsoever, which Karamat, the daughter of the king of Upper Egypt, and the lord of the land, Miamun Pisebkhan, brought with her, as inherited estate of the south land, and any object of any kind whatsoever, which the inhabitants of the country have presented to her, and which they have at any time taken away from the [lady as their possession. They who shall keep back any object thereof] (7) one morning after the (other) morning, to them shall our great spirits be heavy. We will not be any help to them, we will sink (their) noses into the earth, we will . . . . . "'

Shashanq I., or Shishak.   Usarkon I., or Sargon.   Takeloth I., or Tiglath.   Usarkon II.

CHAPTER XVII.

THE TWENTY-SECOND DYNASTY.

I. HAT-KHEPER-RA-SOTEP-EN-RA MIAMUN SHASHANQ I.

B.C. 966.

THE throne of Egypt was mounted, as has been said, by the son of an Assyrian sovereign, the great king Nimrod, who had met his death in Egypt and was buried at Abydus. This remarkable and hitherto unknown event—the foundation by the son of an actual king of Assyria of a kingdom in Egypt for himself and his family—is further confirmed by the chief names of his children and successors: for *Takeloth, Usarkon, Nemaroth*, represent in the Egyptian form and writing the names *Tiglath, Sargon*, and *Nimrod*, so well known in Assyria.

As we have remarked above, Shashanq[1] had set up his seat of royalty in Bubastus, and only seldom extended his visits to the upper country of Patoris. He lived on the best understanding with the Ramessids, and therein followed the traditions of his family, who had contracted marriages with the daughters of the Ramessids, as had these also on their part with the daughters of the great king of Assyria. We have

[1] Written by other Egyptologers Sheshonk.

already remarked elsewhere, that the children of Ramses XVI., the prince Zi-hor-auf-ankh and the princess Zi-an-nub-aus-ankh, had testified their friendly homage to king Shashanq I. by marriage presents.

SHASHANQ I.—the SHISHAK of the Bible, the SESONCHIS of Manetho—has become a conspicuous person in the history of Egypt, in connection with the records of the Jewish monarchy, through his expedition against the kingdom of Judah. It is well known how Jeroboam, the servant of king Solomon, rebelled against the king his master. After the prophet Ahijah had publicly designated him beforehand, as the man best qualified to be the future sovereign, Jeroboam was obliged to save himself from the anger and the snares of the king, and for this reason he fled to Egypt, to the court of Shashanq I.[2] Recalled after the death of Solomon, he returned to his home, to be elected king of Israel according to the word of the prophet, while the crown of Judah fell to Solomon's son, Rehoboam.[3] In the fifth year of this latter king's reign, and probably at the instigation of his former guest (Jeroboam), Shashanq made his expedition against the kingdom of Judah, which ended in the capture and pillaging of Jerusalem.[4]

This attack of the Egyptian king on the kingdom of Judah and the Levitical cities, which the Scripture relates fully and in all its details, has been also handed down to later ages in outline on a wall of the temple of Amon in the Theban Api. On the south external wall,

---

[2] 1 Kings xi. 26–40.   [3] 1 Kings xii.; 2 Chron. iii.
[4] 1 Kings xiv. 25–28; 2 Chron. xii.

SHASHANQ'S CONQUEST OF JUDAH.

behind the picture of the victories of king Ramessu II., to the east of the room called the Hall of the Bubastids,[5] the spectator beholds the colossal image of the Egyptian sovereign dealing the heavy blows of his victorious club upon the captive Jews. The names of the towns and districts, which Shashanq I. conquered in his expedition against Judah, are paraded in long rows, in their Egyptian forms of writing, and frequently with considerable repetitions, each name being enclosed in an embattled shield.

We subjoin a list of them, so far as the names and signs are preserved in a legible form:—

Ra-bi-tha (Rabbith)	Beith-'a-l-moth (Allemeth)
Ta-'an-kau (Taanach)	Ke-qa-li
She-n-mau (Shunem)	Shau-ke (Socho)
Beith-Shanlau (Beth-shean ?)	Beith-tapuh (Beth-tappuah)
Re-ha-bau (Rehob)	A-bi-lau (Abel)
Ha-pu-re-mau (Hapharaïm)	Beith-zab ..
A-dul-ma (Adullam)	Nu-p-a-l
She-ua-di ...	P .. d-shath
Ma-ha-ne-ma (Mahanaïm)	Pa-(shel)-keteth
Qe-be-'a-na (Gibeon)	A-do-maa (EDOM)
Beith-Huaron (Beth-horon)	Za-le-ma (Zalmonah ?)
Qa-de-moth (Kedemoth)	.... lela
A-ju-lon (Ajalon)	.... lzau
Ma-ke-thu (Megiddo)	.... apen
A-dir	Pi-'Amaq, 'the valley-plain' (Emek)
Judah-malek	
Ha-an-ma	'A-au-za-maa (Azmon)
Aa-le-na (Eglon ?)	A-na-la
Bi-le-ma (Bileam)	Pi-Ha-qa-laa, 'the stone of'
Zad-poth-el	Fe-thiu-shaa
A .. ha .. ma	A-ro-ha-lel (Aroër ?)

---
[5] See below, p. 219.

Pi-Ha-qa-laa, 'the stone of'	Pi-ha-ga-l
A-bi-ro-ma	Thel-uan
She-bi-leth	Ha-i-do-baa
Na-ga-bi-li	Sha-li-n-laa
She-bi-leth	Ha-i-do-baa
Ua-ro-kith	Di-ua-thi
Pi-Ha-qa-laa, 'the stone of'	Ha-qe-le-ma
Ne-'a-baith	'A-l-daa-(t)
'A-de-de-maa	Ri-bith
Za-pe-qe-qa	'A-l-daai
Ma . . . . a	Neb-tath
Ta	Jur-he-ma
Ga-naa-t, 'the garden'	Ari . . . m
Pi-Na-ga-bu, 'the Negeb (i.e. south) of'	A-d-raa
	Pi-bi-aa
'A-za-m . . . th	Ma-he-gaa
Ta-shed-na	. . ariuk
Pi-Ha-ga-le-(t), 'the stone of'	Freth-maa
She-nai-aa	A-bi-r
Ha-qa	Bal-ro-za
Pi-Na-ga-bu, 'the Negeb of'	Beith-'A-n-th (Beth-anoth)
Ua-hath-lu-ka	Sha-r (?)-ha-tau
A-sha-ha-tha-t	A-ro-ma-then (Ramah?)
Pi-Ha-ga-li, 'the stone of'	Ga-le-naa
Ha-ni-ni-au	A-ro-ma . . .
Pi-Ha-ga-lau, 'the stone of'	. . . . r-hath
A-le-qad	. . . . raa
A-do-mam-t	Ma . . .
Ha-ni-ni	A-li . . . .
A-do-rau	Jula . . . .

The speech, with which the divine Amon of Thebes accompanies his delivery of the conquered cities to his beloved son, Shashanq I., contains not the slightest indication from which we might construct a background of facts for the names of the conquered peoples, or for the historical events connected with them. The whole representation, in accordance with the general pattern of Egyptian temple-pictures, is a mere skeleton without flesh and blood, which, as usual, gives the enquirer more to guess at than to understand.

The single indication contained in the speech of the god Amon to the victorious king is confined to general appellations. The smitten peoples (Jews and Edomites) are named ' the '*Am* of a distant land ' and the '*Fenekh*' (Phœnicians).[6] The '*Am* would, in this case, answer exactly to the equivalent Hebrew '*Am*, which signifies 'people,' but especially the people of Israel and their tribes. As to the mention of the *Fenekh*, I have a presentiment that we shall one day discover the evidence of their most intimate relationship with the Jews.

In Karnak—that is, to use the language of the old Egyptians, in Ape—Shashanq I. built a sort of entrance hall, which leads from the south, close by the east wall of the sanctuary of Ramses III., into the great front court of the temple. Seeing that the family names of the line of Shashanq have been perpetuated here, from the builder of this modest hall down to several of his successors, we have a full right to regard the edifice as the memorial hall of the Bubastids. Respecting the building and the architect of this hall some instructive information is furnished by a very remarkable inscription in the quarries of Silsilis.

The record runs as follows :—

' In the year 21, in the month Payni, at that time his Majesty was in his capital city, the abode of the great presence of the god Hormakhu. And his Majesty gave command and issued an order to the priest of the god Amon, the privy councillor of the city of

---

[6] Compare above, Vol. I. p. 296.

Hormakhu, and the architect of the monuments of the lord of the land,—Hor-em-saf,—whose skill was great in all manner of work, to hew the best stone of Silsilis, in order to make many and great monuments for the temple of his glorious father, Amon-ra, the lord of Thebes.

'His Majesty issued the order to build a great temple-gate of wrought stones, in order to glorify the city (Thebes), to set up its doors several cubits in height, to build a festival-hall for his father Amon-ra, the king of the gods, and to enclose the house of the god with a thick wall.

'And Hor-em-saf, the priest of Amon-ra the king of the gods, the privy councillor of the city of Hormakhu, the architect over the house of king Shashanq I. at Thebes, had a prosperous journey back to the city of Patoris (Thebes), to the place where his Majesty resided; and his love was great towards his master, the lord of might, the lord of the land, for he spake thus:—

'"All thy words shall be accomplished, O my good lord! I will not sleep by night, I will not slumber by day. The building shall go on uninterruptedly, without rest or pause."

'And he was received graciously by the king, who gave him rich presents in silver and gold.'

What gives a special value to this inscription—which tends more to the praise of the architect than of the king—is the discovery, which I first made in the year 1859, of the position of this architect in the genealogy of his race, the last scion of which, by name Khnum-ab-ra—an architect like all his ancestors—has perpetuated his name in different places on the cliffs of the valley of Hammamat, in the 29th and 30th years of the Persian king Darius I. Hor-em-sefa, his fourteenth ancestor, falls *exactly* on the line of the pedigree, on which his master and contemporary, king Shashanq, is found.[7]

[7] This statement refers to the line of architects which we have added to the Genealogical Table of the Kings. (See the left column of Table IV., of the Royal Families of Dynasties XX.-XXVI.)

The quarries of Silsilis have elsewhere also furnished to this architect—who, like all the successors of his race, was devoted to the Assyrian rulers—the fit opportunity of immortalizing the memory of king Shashanq I. in a conspicuous manner. On a great memorial tablet the king is seen in company with his son Auputh. The goddess Mut, the Egyptian Istar, presents him, or both of them (the king and his son), to the three chief gods of Egypt—Amon of Thebes, Hormakhu-Tum of Heliopolis, Ptah of Memphis—as king and lord of the land, in solemn form, as beseems gods. In the inscription beneath, the king is eulogized under his official names (among them that of 'a great conqueror of all peoples'), and it is further said of him as follows :—

'This is the divine benefactor. The sun-god Ra has his form. He is the image of Hormakhu. Amon has placed him on his throne to make good what he had begun in taking possession of Egypt for the second time. This is king Shashanq. He caused a new quarry to be opened in order to begin a building, the work of king Shashanq I. Of such a nature is the service which he has done to his father, the Theban Amon-ra. May he grant him the thirty years' jubilee-feasts of Ra, and the years of the god Tum! May the king live for ever!'

After this promising introduction, the king himself comes forward as the speaker, and gives us the opportunity of listening, twenty-eight centuries later, to the substance of the words addressed by him to the god :—

'My gracious lord! Grant that my words may live for hundreds of thousands of years. It is a high privilege to work for Amon. Grant me, in recompense for what I have done, a lasting kingdom. I have caused a new quarry to be opened for him for the beginning of a work. It has been carried out by Auputh—the high-priest of Amon, the king of the gods, and the commander-in-chief of the most excellent soldiery, the head of the whole body of warriors of Patoris, the son of king Shashanq I.—for his lord Amon-ra, the king of the gods. May he grant life, welfare, health, a long term of life, power, and strength, an old age in prosperity! My gracious lord! Grant that my words may live for hundreds of thousands of years! It is a high privilege to work for Amon. Grant me power, in recompense for what I have done!'

The new person, who here comes into the foreground, is the king's eldest son, Auputh, who, however, died afterwards before his father. After the example of the priest-kings of the line of Hirhor, the prince and heir-apparent was already invested with the high function of chief priest of the Theban Amon. With this dignity was joined the high position of commander-in-chief of the whole military force in the South, that is, the land of Patoris. In a side-inscription, near the memorial tablet mentioned above, he has not omitted to recal himself once more to the special remembrance of future generations:—

'This was made by the chief priest of Amon-ra, the king of the gods, the commander-in-chief and general, Auputh, who stands at the head of the whole body of the great warriors of Patoris, the son of king Shashanq I.'

In the hall of the Bubastids at Karnak, also, the name of this high-priest of the god Amon appears beside the name of his father.

After the death of Shashanq, the throne was mounted by his second son—

II. SEKHEM KHEPER-RA MIAMUN-USARKON I. (SARGON). B.C. 933.

Except a passing mention of his name, the monuments tell us nothing about this son of Shashanq. Of his two wives, who are mentioned in the Egyptian monumental inscriptions, the one—by name Tashedkhunsu—bore him a son, Takelath (Tiglath), who was his successor in the kingdom. His right as the firstborn appears to have secured him this position.

The second son, Shashanq, born of his marriage with his second wife, the daughter of the Tanite king Hor-Pisebkhan II., and thus of royal race, was named high-priest of Amon, and was invested with the same rank which had been held by his uncle and predecessor Auputh, as commander-in-chief of the soldiery; but with this difference, that not only the military force of Patoris, but the whole Egyptian army, was placed under his command.

There seems to have been a contest between the brothers for the crown. The inheritance, which was assured to the first by his right as the firstborn, seemed to the second to belong rightfully to him, as son of a royal princess. Hence we may explain the phenomenon, that some monuments assign to him the royal cartouche, with the remarkable addition of 'Lord of Upper and Lower Egypt.' The claim, which was not admitted in his person, seems however to have been conceded to his descendants, the younger line of kings of the race of Shashanq.

Takelath (Tiglath) received, as king of Egypt, the name of

III. HAT-RA SOTEP-EN-AMON NUTER HAQ-US MIAMUN
SI-ISE THAKELATH I., B.C. 900,

also called in short Thakeluth and Thakelath.[8] The monuments pass over the history of his time with persistent silence.

His son by his wife Kapos, an Usarkon (Sargon), was his successor. His full name as king ran thus:

IV. USER-MA-RA SOTEP-EN-AMON MIAMUN SI-BAST
USARKON II. B.C. 866.

According to the monuments he had two wives. The first had the name, already well known to us, of Ka-ra-ma. She is the mother of his first-born son, Shashanq, who as crown prince was at once invested with the dignity of a chief priest of Ptah of Memphis. In this character he conducted the burial of the Apis-bull, which died in the 23rd year of the reign of Usarkon II.

His younger brother Naromath (Nimrod), a son of the second wife Mut-ut-ankhes, was next appointed overseer of the prophets and commander of the soldiery of Khinensu (Ahnas), that is, Heracleopolis Magna; but the office was also conferred on him of a governor of Patoris and a chief priest of Amon of Thebes. His descendants, down to the last Pi-son-Hor,[9] succeeded

---

[8] The author gives also the form Thakeloth in the Genealogical Table.—ED.

[9] See the Genealogical Table IV. of Dynasties XX.-XXVI.

their father in the hereditary office of priests of Khnum, in the city of Heracleopolis Magna. On the other hand, the descendants of prince Shashanq, the chief priest of Ptah of Memphis, inherited in like manner the high office of their father, and appear as officiating high-priests at the burial of several holy Apis-bulls.

With Usarkon II. the elder legitimate line of the kings died out, and a second branch within the same dynasty began, which embraces the descendants of Shashanq, the high-priest of Amon. After the death of Usarkon II., a grandson of Shashanq, of the same name, mounted the throne, and received as king the full name of

IV. SEKHEM-KHEPER-RA SOTEP-EN-AMON MIAMUN
SHASHANQ II. B.C. 833.

There is a universal silence of the monuments about his time and history.

After him reigned a Thakelath, in all probability his son, with the full name of

V. HAT-KHEPER-RA SOTEP-EN-RA MIAMUN SI-ISE
THAKELATH II. B.C. 800.

Take-
loth II.

He is the husband of the queen Mi-mut Keromama Sit-amen Mut-em-hat, a daughter of Nimrod, the high-priest of Amon. Their eldest son is expressly designated by the inscriptions as high-priest of the Theban Amon, and as commander-in-chief of the military force of the whole land; and he was at the same time a petty king. He is the Usarkon of whom so much is related on a long memorial tablet in the interior of the Hall of the Bubastids. This account begins with the date of the 9th of the month Thoth in the 12th regnal year of his father. Although the continuity of the record is broken in several places by greater or lesser gaps, yet the following sense comes out with full certainty from a careful examination of the still extant and legible portions of the great inscriptions.

In the year above named, the prince Usarkon went to Thebes in his character of high-priest of Amon, to enter on his office. His mission had also the agreeable purpose of subjecting the Theban temple and its territory to a careful examination, and of restoring the offerings to the god Amon and his festivals in a splendid manner, according to the good old custom. Thus began the unlucky 15th year of the king's reign. Grievous times were at hand; for as is expressly said in the inscription:—

'When now had arrived the 15th year, the month Mesori, the 25th day, under the reign of his father, the lordly Horus, the godlike prince of Thebes, *the heaven could not be distinguished, the moon was eclipsed* (literally *was horrible*), for a sign of the (coming) events in this land; as it also happened, for enemies (*literally*, the children of revolt) invaded with war the southern and northern districts (of Egypt).'

I have not the slightest doubt that the foregoing words have reference to the irruptions of the Ethiopians from the South and to the attack of the Assyrian power from the North. The Assyrian inscriptions will some day no longer withhold from us the answer to the question—which it was of the rulers of Assyria, of the family of Shalmaneser III., who made a hostile invasion of Egypt, and to whom the descendants of Shashanq I.—Takelath and his son Petise, both high-priests at Memphis—as Assyrian satraps, showed themselves, in remembrance of the old family connection, especially compliant.

The eclipse of the moon, which is mentioned in the discourse as a warning of the coming events, I still continue to maintain, notwithstanding all the objections of M. Chabas. So long as no better-founded objection is brought against it than such as have been hitherto urged, it must surely be accepted as a fact, that on the 25th of Mesori,[1] in the 15th year of the reign of king Thakelath II., a total eclipse of the moon took place in Egypt.

The rest of the inscription allows us to suppose the return, however temporary, of a period of rest for Egypt. The priest-king Usarkon used this respite to evince his complete devotion to Amon, the god of Thebes, and to his temple. The sacrifices were established in such a manner, that certain sums of money were put aside for the maintenance of the offerings, exactly as we have already seen in the case of the memorial tablet of Abydus.

Before we turn our attention to the kingdom of the Ethiopians, which had established itself in the south of Egypt and had begun its attacks upon Kemi, it seems proper first to look a little closer at the last descendants of the line of Shashanq, who had sunk to the position of petty kings in the divided realm.

[1] I have several times confirmed the statement of the day from the monument itself.

Their names and succession, with reference to their chronology, are given in the Genealogical Table.² We here take the opportunity that occurs to make the reader acquainted with their full names :—

Shashanq III.   Pimai.   Shashanq IV.

VI. USER-MA-RA SOTEP-EN-RA MIAMUN SI-BAST SHASHANQ III. B.C. 766.

VII. USER-MA-RA SOTEP-EN-AMON MIAMUN PIMAI. B.C. 733.

VIII. A-KHEPER-RA SHASHANQ IV. B.C. 700.

Their historical importance disappears in the conflict of the petty kings who rose up against one another, now on the side of the Assyrians, now on that of the Ethiopians. We owe our knowledge of them chiefly to the Apis-bulls, whose inscribed tombstones refer to the reigns of these kings with all the needful data of time.

The royal seat and locality of their petty kingdom, in the eighth century, can be pretty clearly seen from these Apis-tablets. If they no longer possessed the seat of government of their old house, Bubastus in Lower Egypt, the city of the goddess Bast—which had now become Assyrian—yet still the ancient and important capital of Memphis remained in their possession. It was here that the sacred Bull lived in the temple of Ptah-Sokar-Osiris; and hence it was that

² See Genealogical Table IV. of the Families of Dynasties XX.-XXVI.

the solemn translation of the deceased Apis was made, on a car fitted with thick heavy wheels of wood, to the Serapeum in the desert, between the Arabian villages of Abousir (the ancient Pi-usiri, 'the temple of Osiris') and Saqqarah (the name of which clearly calls to remembrance that of the god Sokar).

We subjoin a literal translation of the memorial stones, which the fortunate discoverer of the Serapeum, Mariette-Bey, brought to light during the year of our residence on the spot and under our own eye (1850), in so far as they relate to the above-named last kings of the Twenty-second Dynasty. Quite apart from their special importance for determining the length of each king's reign, the reader will probably find an interest in learning the contents of these inscriptions, which have also contributed to throw light on the darkest parts of the great picture of Egyptian history, and which for the first time exhibit a true image of the strange Bull-worship practised by the people of Memphis.

I. MEMORIAL STONE OF THE PRIEST AND SEER OF THE APIS-BULL, SENEBEF, SON OF SHED-NOFAR-TUM, AND OF HIS SON, THE MEMPHIAN PRIEST HOR-HEB.

'In the year [2], the month [Mekhir] on the [1st] day, under the reign of king Pimai, the friend of the Apis-god in the West. This is the day on which this (deceased) god was carried to the beautiful region of the West, and was laid at rest in the grave, at rest with the great god, with Osiris, with Anubis, and with the goddesses of the nether world, in the West. His introduction into the temple of Ptah beside his father, the Memphian god Ptah, had taken place in the year 29, in the month Paophi, in the time of king Shashanq III.'

II. MEMORIAL STONE OF THE HIGH-PRIEST OF MEMPHIS, PETISE.

In the year 2, the month Mekhir, on the 1st day, under the reign of king Pimai, the friend of the great god Apis in the West.—This is the day on which the god was carried to his rest, in the beautiful region of the West, and was laid in the grave, and on which he was deposited in his everlasting house and in his eternal abode. He was born in the year 28, in the times of the deceased king Shashanq III. His glory was sought for in all places of Pitomih (that is, Lower Egypt). He was found, after (some) months, in the city of Ha-shed-abot. They had searched through the lakes of Natho and all the islands of Pitomih. He had been solemnly introduced into the temple of Ptah, beside his father, the Memphian god Ptah of the south wall, by the high-priest in the temple of Ptah, the great [prince] of the Mashush (the Maxyes), Petise, the son of the high-priest [of Memphis and the great prince of the] Mashush, Thakelath, and of the princess of royal race, Thes-bast-pir, in the year 28,[3] in the month Paophi, on the 1st day. The full lifetime of this god amounted to 26 years.'

III. MEMORIAL STONE OF THE MEMPHIAN PRIEST, HOR-SI-ISE.

'In the year 2, the month Mekhir, the 1st day, under the reign of king Pimai, the friend of the great god Apis in the West, the god was carried to his rest in the beautiful region of the West. He had been solemnly introduced into the temple of Ptah beside his father, the Memphian god Ptah of the south wall, in the year . . . . . . under the reign of king Shashanq . . . [in the year] 5 [+x] after he had shown his   ?   , after they had sought for [his glory . . .]. The full lifetime of this god amounted to 26 years. (This tablet is dedicated) by the hereditary [prince] (here follows a string of titles in the priestly style) Hor-si-ise, the son of the high-priest [of Memphis and prince of the] Mashush, Pet-ise, and of the eldest of the wives . . . . [and by the . . .] Thakelath, whose mother Ta-ti-hor . . . . is.'[4]

---

[3] Observe the discrepancy between this and No. I. It seems from the calculation given below, that the 29 of No. I. is the right date.—ED.

[4] The order of words is here preserved to show that 'is' ends the inscription.—ED.

IV. Memorial Stone of the Satrap Pet-ise, and his Sons
Pef-tot-bast and Thakelath.

'In the 28th year of king Shashanq.'

Then follows a sculpture, in which three men are seen before the bull-headed god, 'Apis-Tum with horns on his head.' The first of them has on his head the fillet of an Assyrian satrap; the last is adorned with the youth-locks worn by royal and princely persons. Above and beside these persons are the following inscriptions :—

'May he grant health, life, prosperity, to the Assyrian satrap Pet-ise, the son of the Assyrian satrap Thakelath—his mother is Thes-bast-pir—the son of the first and greatest of the princely heirs of his Majesty Shashanq, the son of the king and lord of the land, Usarkon II.,—

'And to his venerator and friend, the high-priest of Ptah, Pef-tot-bast, the son of the satrap Pet-ise, whose mother is Ta-ari, a daughter of the satrap Thakelath,—

'And to his venerator and friend, the priest of Ptah, Thakelath, the son of the satrap Pet-ise and of (his wife) Herse.'

From these four inscriptions it follows, with irrefragable certainty, that, under the reign of Shashanq III., Petise and his son Peftotbast ascribe to themselves the title and the badges of *Satraps*. This was exactly the time when the Assyrians had laid their hands on Egypt, and it was only by their permission that Shashanq ruled as king over the lowlands of Lower Egypt.[5] The new Apis is sought for in all *Lower*

[5] It is perhaps superfluous to warn the reader against confusing the new Assyrian domination here referred to with the former Assyrian conquest of Egypt. The Assyrian line of Shashanq, after becoming real Egyptian kings, succumbed in their turn to the new Assyrian conquerors of the line of Shalmaneser, under whom they became satraps in Lower Egypt, alternating with their subjection to the rival power of the Ethiopians.—Ed.

Egypt. As to *Upper Egypt*,—where Usarkon, the king and high-priest of Amon, maintained the kingdom, until the time when the Ethiopian Pi-ankhi broke his power,—the inscription is completely silent.

On the memorial tablets of king Pimai the title *Sar'a en Mat* (' Satrap') disappears, and is replaced by another, *Sar'a en Mashush*, 'Prince of the Maxyes,' doubtless with reference to the Ethiopian conquerors, who had at this time taken possession of the land, as will be shown more particularly below.

With regard to the Apis himself, the following results are obtained from the four memorial tablets now cited :—He was born in the 28th year of the reign of king Shashanq III., at the city of Hashed-abot in Lower Egypt. Months passed by before he was discovered. On the 1st of Paophi, in the 29th regnal year of the king,[6] he was solemnly introduced into the temple of Ptah of Memphis. After a life of 26 years, he was buried in the Serapeum of Memphis on the 1st of Mekhir in the 2nd year of the reign of king Pimai. His death must therefore have happened 70 days earlier, that is, on the 20th of Athyr. Supposing him to have lived 26 years *complete*, as the inscription expressly testifies, his birth must have fallen on the 20th of Athyr in the 28th regnal year of king Shashanq III. In that case about ten months and a half would have elapsed until his introduction into Memphis on the 1st of Paophi in the 29th year of the reign of Shashanq III.

---

[6] The reader should carefully recal to memory our remark on the numbering of the regnal years of the Egyptian kings (Vol. I. p. 363).

THE TWENTY-THIRD DYNASTY, OF TANIS.

Under this title, the priest Manetho, in his Book of the Kings, sets down the reigns of the three kings:—

PETUBASTES, with 40 years;
OSORKHON, with 9 years;
PSAMUS, with 10 years.

Petubastes.

All three disappear again in the struggle waged against Egypt with varying success by Ethiopia from the South and Assyria from the North. Hence their names emerge but occasionally in the historical records of this time. In these, PETUBASTES appears with the full names, SE-HER-AB-RA PET-SI-BAST; OSORKHON as A-KHEPER-RA SOTEP-EN-AMON MIAMUN USARKAN; and the third, lastly, meets us as US(ER)RA SOTEP-EN-PTAH PSIMUT. Judging from the elements contained in these titles, Petubastes seems to have had his royal seat in Bubastus, Osorkhon in Thebes or Tanis, Psamus in Memphis. The last we shall have to recognize again under his Assyrian appellation of Is-pi-ma-tu, in the story of the conquest by the Assyrians, as a contemporary of king Tirhaqa, about 700 B.C.

And now we pass on to the Ethiopians.

[NOTE.—TWENTY-FOURTH DYNASTY.

The story of king BOCCHORIS, who stands alone in the *Twenty-fourth Dynasty* of Manetho, forms a part of the history of the Ethiopian sovereignty over Egypt (see below, p. 280).—ED.]

Bocchoris.

Piankhi. Sabaco. Shabatak. Tirhakah.

CHAPTER XVIII.

THE TWENTY-FIFTH DYNASTY.

THE ETHIOPIANS.

WE have already had occasion to become acquainted with and to estimate the position and character of Hirhor, the high-priest of the Theban Amon and founder of the Twenty-first Dynasty.[1] Urged on by haughty pride, Hirhor had realized his ambitious designs upon the crown of Egypt, had robbed his benefactor Ramessu XIII. of his throne, had banished his whole family and connections to the Great Oasis, and had placed himself, to the best of his power, in the forefront of Egyptian history. Retribution was not long delayed; and the avenger came from Assyria. The history of the Dynasty ended with the overthrow of the royal and priestly family, which suddenly vanishes from the stage, as soon as Shashanq I. obtained the throne, to find however in Ethiopia the satisfaction of their lust for a sceptre and a crown.

Towards the end of the eleventh century, Egypt had far too much to do in defending herself and her independence, to trouble herself further about the supremacy in the South, which she had formerly won

[1] See Chap. XVI. p. 200.

and till now had carefully guarded. The 'Viceroys of the South' and 'King's sons of Kush' are now struck out of the official list of court dignitaries, and the 'Kings of Kush' take their place. The whole South, from the boundary line at the city of Syene, recovers its freedom, and the tribes of Ethiopia begin to enjoy a state of independence. Meanwhile however, if the power of Egypt was no longer felt, Egyptian civilization and the Egyptian doctrine of the gods had survived. All that was wanting was a leader, to keep alive the ideas that had been once acquired.

Nothing could have appeared more opportune for the priests of Amon, who had now become unpopular, to make their profit out of the favourable opportunity of the moment, than this state of things in Nubia and Ethiopia, where the minds of an imperfectly developed people must needs, under skilful guidance, soon show themselves pliable and submissive to the dominant priestly caste. Mount Barkal, where Amenhotep III. had already raised for the great Amon of Thebes a sanctuary in the form of a strongly fortified temple-city,[2] was the site chosen by the newly arrived priests of Amon for the seat of their future royalty. The capital of this newly founded kingdom of Kush was the city of Nap or Napata, which is so often mentioned in the inscriptions of Ethiopian origin.

It is difficult to say which it was of the chief priests of Amon of the race of Hirhor, that first entered Napata and made preparations for the founda-

[2] See Vol. I. p. 486.

tion of that Ethiopian kingdom which became afterwards so dangerous to the Egyptians. The Ethiopian monuments, from which the royal shields have been carefully erased by a later Egyptian dynasty, give not the slightest information on this point. So much the more important is the circumstance, that several successors of this priest—among whom we have already met with the son and successor of Hirhor—bore the same name, namely, that of the priest-king Pi-ankhi, an Egyptian word, which signifies 'the living one.' Before we pass on to that Piankhi whose invasion of Egypt will form the most striking subject of this chapter, it seems convenient to premise, however briefly, some observations on the kingdom of Kush.

. As we have already stated, the sovereign enthroned at Napata, 'the City of the Holy Mountain,' called himself 'King of the land of Kush.' The Theban Amon-ra was reverenced as the supreme god of the country. The king's full name was formed exactly according to the old Egyptian pattern. The Egyptian language and writing, divisions of time, and everything else relating to manners and customs, were preserved. A distinguished position was assigned to the mother, daughters, and sisters of the king; each of whom bore the title of honour—'Queen of Kush.'

In the course of time, the power of the Ethiopians extended beyond the southern boundary of Egypt; till at last the whole of Patoris came into their possession, and the 'great city' of Ni-'a, that is, Thebes, became their capital in that region. While the Assyrians regarded Lower Egypt—the Muzur³ so often mentioned in the cuneiform inscriptions—as their permanent fief, the districts of Patoris were virtually an Ethiopian province. Middle Egypt formed a ' march,' contested on both sides between the two kingdoms, and at the same time a barrier which tended to hinder the outbreak of open hostilities between the one and the other.

Thus the old priestly race had succeeded in again acquiring full possession of Thebes, the city out of which the Assyrian Shashanq I. had chased them with contumely and shame. The loss of the city of Amon, through the occasional expeditions of the Assyrians southwards, was to them equivalent to suffering a conquest. That this in fact did sometimes happen, we shall presently see authentic evidence.

As in Lower Egypt the Assyrians were content with drawing a tribute from the petty kings and satraps, whom they confirmed in power, so in Patoris and Middle Egypt petty kings or vassals were set up by the Ethiopians, whose supremacy these princes had to recognize, and to pay their taxes. Ethiopian garrisons served to guard the Ethiopic-Egyptian territory, under the command of Ethiopian generals.

Thus had Egypt become a shuttlecock in the hands of the Assyrians and the Ethiopians, those princes of *Naph* or *Noph*, whom we find mentioned in Scripture.[4]

---

[3] This name, the Mazor of the hieroglyphic inscriptions, is probably the special name of the Tanitic nome.

[4] Isaiah xix. 13; Jer. ii. 16, xlvi. 14, 19; Ezek. xxx. 13, 16.

The great kingdom of Kemi was split up into little dependent states, which leant, now on Ethiopia, now on Assyria, as each foreign master gained preponderance for the time.

About the year 766 (estimating the chronology by the sequence of generations) the Assyrians still held Lower Egypt in their possession. Petty kings and Assyrian satraps obeyed the Great King. At this time a revolt broke out under an enterprising petty king of Saïs and Memphis, by name TAFNAKHTH, the Technactis or Tnephachthus of the classic writers. Profiting by the momentary weakness of the Assyrian Empire, he had prevailed on the other princes of Lower Egypt to join him, whether through persuasion or force. As soon as he was thus strengthened, he made an inroad with his whole force upon Middle Egypt, where the Egyptian vassals of Piankhi at once submitted to him. The tidings reached Piankhi, who forthwith sent orders to his generals to check the advance of Tafnakhth, and so to force the bold petty king to beat a retreat.

We leave our readers to construct for themselves a picture of the whole campaign from the long and remarkable description of it preserved for us on the memorial stone of Piankhi, discovered several years ago at Mount Barkal. This monument, a block of granite covered with writing on all sides, up to the very edges, was set up, on the spot where it now stands, by command of the Ethiopian king Pi-ankhi, in remembrance of his complete conquest of Middle and Lower Egypt. The subjoined translation of this record will set in the clearest light, far better than any description, the several stages of the Ethiopian expedition, and the peculiar position of the Egyptian petty kings and satraps.[5] Of these we give a list according to the account furnished by the stone :—

>King and Satrap TAFNAKHTH, Prince of Saïs and Memphis;
>King NIMROD, lord of Hermopolis Magna;
>King AUPOTH, of the nome of Clysma;
>Satrap SHASHANQ, of the city of Busiris;
>Satrap ZI-AMUN-AUF-ANKH, of the city of Mendes:
>His eldest son ANKH-HOR, commander of the city of Hermopolis, in Lower Egypt.
>The hereditary lord, BOK-EN-NISI;
>Satrap NES-NA-'AI (or NES-NA-KETI), of the nome of Xoïs;
>King USARKON, of the city of Bubastus;
>Prince PAF-TOT-BAST, of the city of Heracleopolis Magna;
>The hereditary lord, PET-ISE, of the city of Athribis;
>Satrap PI-THENEF, of Pi-saptu (the Arabian nome);
>Satrap PI-MA, of the (second) city (named) Busiris;
>Satrap NAKHT-HOR-NA-SHENNU, of Phagroriopolis;
>Satrap of Tanis (not named, being a native Assyrian);
>Satrap of Ostracine (not named, for the same reason);
>Prophet of Horus, PET-HOR-SAM-TAUI, of the city of Letopolis;
>Prince HE-RO-BI-SA, of the cities of Sa and Hesaui;
>Prince ZI-CHI-AU, of Khont-nofer (Onuphites?);
>Prince PI-BI-SA, of Babylon and Nilopolis (in the Heliopolitan nome).

[5] The translations of this important document, with which I am acquainted, one in English and another in German, are far from giving, even approximately, the right sense of all the clauses of this inscription, which has been of the greatest service to me in the preparation of my Hieroglyphical Dictionary. In the passages that are easy to understand the translator can claim no special merit. It is when he comes to the hard ones that the old proverb applies: 'Hic Rhodus, hic salta.' [The inscription has been translated into English by Canon Cook, first as a separate pamphlet—'The Inscription of Pianchi Mer-Amon, king of Egypt, in the 8th century B.C. Translated by F. C. Cook, M.A., Canon of Exeter, &c.' 1873—and again in *Records of the Past*, vol. ii. pp. 81, foll.—ED.]

We have also indicated, by the addition 'Vassal,' on the great Genealogical Table,[6] the princes subject to king Pi-ankhi, in order to show that the events, of which the inscription of the Ethiopian king gives us such precise information, must have taken place, as to their chronology, within the period of the one generation between B.C. 766 and B.C. 733.

Having premised these necessary remarks, we leave our readers to follow the translation of this record of victory.

'In the 21st year, in the month Thoth, under the reign of the king of Upper and Lower Egypt, Miamun Piankhi—may he live for ever!—My Royal Majesty issued the command that men should be informed of what I have done more than all my predecessors. I the king am a part of God, a living image of Tum. As soon as I came out of my mother's womb I was chosen to be ruler, before whom the great men were afraid, knowing that I [was to be a powerful lord].

'(2) His mother well knew that he was destined for a ruler in his mother's womb, he, the god-like benefactor, the friend of the gods, the son of Ra, who had formed him with his hands, Miamun Pi-ankhi.

'Messengers came to inform the king : " The lord of the West country (that is, the Western part of the Delta), the great prince in the holy city (Saïs), Tafnakhth, has established himself in the nome [name wanting], in the nome of Xoïs, in the city of Hap (Nilopolis), in the city [. . . .], (3) in the city of 'Ain, in the city of Pi-nub (Momemphis), and in the city of Memphis. He has taken possession of the whole West country, from the Mediterranean coast (of Buto) up to the boundary city (between Upper and Lower Egypt). He is advancing up the river with many warriors. The inhabitants of both parts of Egypt have joined themselves to him. The princes and lords of the cities are like dogs at his feet. The fortresses are not shut (against him) (4) of the nomes of the South. The cities of Mi-tum (Meidoum), Pi-sekhem-kheper-ra (Crocodilo-

---

[6] See Table IV., at the end of this Volume.

polis, the city of Usarkon I., at the entrance to the Fayoum), Pimaz (Oxyrhynchus), Thekanath, and all the (other) cities of the West, have opened their gates to him, through fear of him. He turns himself to the nomes of the East. They open their gates to him, namely, the following: Habennu (the Phœnix-city, Hipponon), Tai-uzai, and Aphroditopolis. He is preparing (5) to beleaguer the city of Heracleopolis Magna. He has surrounded it as with a ring. None who would go out can go out, none who would go in can go in, because of the uninterrupted assaults. He has girt it round on every side. All the princes who acknowledge his power, he lets them abide every one in his own district, as princes and kings of the cities. And they [do homage to him] (6) as to one who is distinguished through his wise mind; his heart is joyful."

'And the lords and the princes and the chiefs of the warriors, every one according to his city, sent continual messages to his Majesty (i.e. Piankhi) to this effect: "Art thou then silent, so as not to wish to have any knowledge of the South country and of the inland regions? Tafnakhth is winning them to himself, and finds no one that withstands him. Nimrod, the [lord of Hermopolis Magna] (7) and prince of Ha-uër (Megalopolis), has demolished the fortress of Nofrus, and has razed his city with his own hands, through fear that he (Tafnakhth) should take it from him, in order to cut it off after the manner of the other cities. Now he has departed, to throw himself at his feet, and he has renounced allegiance to his Majesty. He is leagued with him like any [of the other princes. The lord] (8) of the nome of Oxyrhynchus has offered him gifts according to his heart's desire, of everything that he could find."

'Then his Majesty sent orders to the princes and captains of the army, who were set over the land of Egypt, (namely) the captain Pi-ua-ro-ma, and the captain La-mis-ke-ni, and to all his Majesty's captains, who were set over the land of Egypt, that they should hasten to prevent the arming (of the rebels) for war, to invest [the city of Hermopolis], (9) to take captive its inhabitants, their cattle, and their vessels on the river, to let no labourer go out to the field, nor suffer any ploughman to plough, and to blockade all that were in the city of Hermopolis, and to fight against it without ceasing. And they did so.

'Then his Majesty sent his warriors to Egypt, enjoining upon them very very strictly: "Take [care, watch, do not pass] (10) the night in the enjoyment of play. Be on the alert against the attack (of the enemy), and be armed for the battle even afar off. If any (of the commanders) says, 'The army and the chariots are to turn to another city: why will ye delay to go against its army?'—ye shall fight as he has said. If any (of the enemy) attempts to fetch his defenders from another city, (11) turn about to meet them. If any of these princes should have brought with him, for his protection, warriors from Marmarica, or combatants from those faithful (to him), arm yourselves to fight against them. As an old hero says, 'It avails not to gather together the warriors and numerous chariots with the best horses out of the stable, but, (12) when going into the battle, to confess that Amon, the divine, is he who sends us.' When you have arrived at Thebes, in sight of (the temple of) Ape, go into the water, wash yourselves in the river, draw yourselves up at the chief canal, unstring your bows and lay aside your weapons before (13) the king (of the gods), as the Almighty. No strength shall the man have who despises him; he makes the weak strong, and however many there be of them (the strong), they must turn their back before the few, and be one (ever so weak), he copes with a thousand. Sprinkle yourselves with the water from his altars of sacrifice, fall down before him on your faces, and speak (14) to him thus: 'Show us the way to fight in the shadow of thy mighty arm. The peoples that go forth for thee shall beat down the enemy in many defeats.'"

'Then they threw themselves prostrate before his Majesty (saying): "Is it not thy name that makes our arm strong? Is it not thy wisdom that gives firmness to thy warriors? Thy bread is in our bodies during all our march, and thy mead (15) quenches our thirst. Does not thy power give us strength and manly courage at the thought of thee? An army is naught, whose commander is a coward. And who is like unto thee? Thou art the king whose hands create victory, a master in the work of war."

'When they had gone (16) down the river, they reached the city of Thebes, and did all that his Majesty had commanded. Proceeding down the stream upon the river, they met a number of vessels sailing up the stream with soldiers, sailors, and captains, of the best warriors of Upper Egypt, equipped with all munitions, (17) for the war against the army of his Majesty. Then they inflicted on them a great overthrow. No one knows the number of their prisoners, together with their ships, who were brought as living prisoners to the place where his Majesty resided. When they had advanced further to the city of Heracleopolis Magna, they arrayed themselves for the battle.

(18) 'The following is the list of the princes and kings of Lower Egypt:

The king NIMROD, and
The king AUPOTH:
The satrap SHASHANQ, of the city of Busiris; and
The satrap ZI-AMUN-AUF-ANKH of the city of Mendes; and
His eldest son, who was military commander of the city of Hermopolis Parva:
The warriors of the hereditary lord BOK-EN-NISI; and
His eldest son, the satrap (19) NES-NA-'AI of the nome of Xoïs:
The grand-master of the fan-bearers in Lower Egypt; and
The king USARKON, who resides in the city of Bubastus and in the city of Uu-n-r'a-nofer:

and all the princes and kings of the cities on the West side, on the East side, and on the islands between. They had gathered themselves together at the bidding of that one, and they sat thus at the feet of the great lord of the West country, the prince of the cities of Lower Egypt, the prophet of Neith, the Lady of Saïs, (20) and the high-priest of Ptah (of Memphis), TAFNAKHTH.

'When they had advanced further, they inflicted on them a great defeat, greater than ever, and captured their ships upon the river. When the survivors had fled, they landed on the West side, in the territory of the city of Pi-pek. When the earth had become light in the early morning (of the next day), the warriors of his Majesty advanced (21) against them, and army joined in battle with army. Then they slew much people of them, as well as their horses. No one knows the number of the slain. Those that were left alive fled to Lower Egypt, because of the tremendous overthrow, for it was more terrible than ever.

'*List of the people of them that were killed:* Men [. . . . .]

'(22) The king Nimrod (advanced) up the river to Upper Egypt, because the news had been brought to him that the city of Hermopolis Magna had fallen into the power of the enemy—meaning the warriors of his Majesty—who had captured its inhabitants and their cattle. Then he came before Hermopolis. But the army of his Majesty was on the river at the harbour (23) of the Hermopolitan nome. When they heard that the king (Nimrod) had surrounded them on all four sides, so that none could go either out or in, they sent a messenger to his Majesty Miamun Pi-ankhi, the dispenser of life, (to tell him) of the complete overthrow which had been prepared for them by all the forces of his Majesty (king Nimrod).

'Then was his Majesty furious against them, like a panther, (and said): "Then did they leave (24) a remnant of the army of Lower Egypt surviving, and suffer to escape from them whosoever would escape in order to give information, that he might advance, so that they should not suffer death, (but) make their escape? I swear, as truly as I love the god Ra, as truly as I hallow the god Amon, I will myself go down the river; I will frustrate (25) what that man has done; I will drive him back, even should the struggle last long; after performing the solemnity of the customary rites of the new year's feast. I will offer a sacrifice to my father Amon at his beautiful feast; he shall celebrate his procession on the beautiful day of the new year. I will go in peace to behold Amon on his beautiful feast of the Theban month (Paopi). I will cause his image to go forth (26) to Api of the south on his beautiful feast of the Theban month (Paopi), in the night of the feast which is established for Thebes, and which the Sun-god Ra first instituted for him. I will conduct him back to his temple, where he sits on his throne. But on the day of the god's return, on the second of the month Athyr, I will let the people of Lower Egypt feel the weight of my finger."[7]

'(27) Then the king's warriors remained in Egypt. They had heard of the wrath which his Majesty had conceived against them. Then they fought against the city of Pi-maz, in the Oxyrhynchite nome, and they took it like a flood of water. And they sent a message to his Majesty; but his heart was not appeased thereby.

'Then they fought against the very strong city of Ta-tehan (now Tehneh), and they found it filled (28) with soldiers, of the best warriors of Lower Egypt. Then they made the battering-ram play against it, which threw down its walls. They in-

---

[7] Literally, 'taste the taste of my finger.' Compare the boast of Rehoboam, 'My little finger shall be thicker than my father's loins' (1 Kings xii. 10).—ED.

flicted on them a great overthrow—no one knows the numbers—among them (the slain) was also the son of the satrap Tafnakhth. Then they sent a message to his Majesty; but his heart was not appeased thereby.

'(29) Then they fought against the city of Ha-bennu and broke it open, and the warriors of his Majesty entered. Then they sent a message to his Majesty; but his heart was not appeased thereby.

In the month Thoth, on the 9th day of the month, when his Majesty had gone down to Thebes, he celebrated the feast of Amon in the Theban month Paopi. When his Majesty had sailed (30) down the river to the city of Hermopolis Magna, he came forth out of the cabin of his ship, caused the horses to be harnessed, and mounted his war-chariots, the names of which were, "The fear of his Majesty reaches to the Asiatics," and "The hearts of all men fear him." When his Majesty had marched on, he threw himself upon the (31) haters of his warriors, full of wrath against them, like the panther, (saying) : " Are they not standing there ? Fight, I tell you ! This is loitering over my business ! The time is at length come once for all to make the land of Lower Egypt respect me." A mighty overthrow was inflicted upon them, frightful for the slaughter which they suffered.

' His tent was pitched on the south-west of Hermopolis Magna. The city remained cut off (32) continually. A rampart was thrown up, to overtop the high wall of the fortress. When the wooden structure (raised) against it was high enough, the archers shot in (their arrows), and the catapults (*lit.* slinging machines) threw stones, so as continually to kill the people. This lasted three days. Then those in Hermopolis had become stinking, and had lost their sweet savour.[8] (33) Then Hermopolis surrendered and supplicated the king of Lower Egypt, and ambassadors came

---

[8] We translate this literally after Dr. Brugsch, without venturing to decide whether (as we suppose) it is a figure, not uncommon, for the distress of the Hermopolites, or whether it means (more literally) that the stench of the corpses drove them to surrender. The parallel is striking with Isaiah iii. 24, 'instead of sweet smell there shall be stink' (compare Gen. xxxiv. 30 ; Exod. v. 21 ; 1 Sam. xxvii. 12; Isaiah xxxiv. 3 ; Joel ii. 20 ; Amos iv. 10).—ED.

out of it and presented themselves with all things good to behold
—gold, precious stones, garments of cotton—(before his Majesty),
who had put on the serpent-diadem, in order to inspire respect
for his presence. But several days passed before they dared to
supplicate his Uræus. Then (Nimrod) sent forth (34) his wife,
the queen and daughter of a king, Nes-thent-nes, to supplicate
the queens and the royal concubines and the king's daughters and
sisters. And she threw herself prostrate in the women's house
before the queens (saying): "Pray come to me, ye queens, king's
daughters, and king's sisters! Appease Horus, the ruler of the
palace. Exalted is his person, great his triumph. Cause (35) his
[anger to be appeased before] my [prayer]; else he will give [over
to death the king, my husband, but] (36) he is brought low."
When she had finished [her speech, her Majesty] (37) was moved
in her heart at the supplication of the queen . . . . . (38–50)
(*This part of the inscription is entirely erased*) . . . . . (51) before (?) thee. Who is leader? Who is leader? Who, when he is
led, who is led . . . . (52) to thee the boon of living. Is not the
swollen stream like an arrow? I am . . . .

'(53) The inhabitants of the South bowed down; the people
of the North said, "Let us be under thy shadow! If any one has
done wrong, let him [come] to [thee] (54) with his peace-offerings.
This is the helm which turns about (like a ship) its governor
towards him who belongs (henceforth) to the divine person. He
has seen the fire in . . . . (55) Worth naught is the great man,
who is admired for his father's sake. Thy fields are full of little
men."

'Then he (king Nimrod) threw himself prostrate before his
Majesty [speaking thus: "Thou art] (56) Horus, the lord of the
palace. Wilt thou not grant me to become one of the king's servants, and to pay tribute of my productions for the treasury [like
those who pay contributions] (57) of their productions? I will
furnish thee more than they do."

'Then he offered silver, gold, blue and green stones, iron, and
many jewels. (58) Then was the treasury filled with these gifts.
He led forward a horse with his right hand, in his left was a
sistrum, and the striking-plate was of gold and blue stones. Then
the king went forth out of (59) his palace, and betook himself to
the temple of Thut, the lord of the city of the eight (gods)
(Achnum, Hermopolis Magna). He sacrificed oxen, calves, and

birds, to his father Thut, the lord of the city of the eight (gods), and to the eight deities in the (60) temple of the eight deities. And the people of Hermopolis played a hymn, and they sang: " Beautiful is Horus, who abides in (61) his city, the son of the Sun, Pi-ankhi! Thou makest festival for us, as if thou wert the tutelar lord of the nome of Hermopolis."

'When the king had entered into (62) the house of king Nimrod, he visited all the chambers of the king, his treasury and his store-rooms. And he was content.

'Then came (63) to him the king's wives and the king's daughters, and they praised his Majesty after the manner of women, but his Majesty did not turn his countenance upon (64) them.

'When his Majesty visited the stables and the studs of foals, he observed that [they had] (65) let them starve. He said: " I swear, as surely as the youthful Sun-god Ra loves me, as surely as I breathe in life, it is a viler thing to my heart (66) to let the horses starve, than all the other faults that thou hast committed. That thou hast laid thy heart bare through this, evidence is furnished me of thy habitual views (?). (67) Hast thou forgotten that the shadow of God rests upon me? The proof thereof shall not be wanting to him on my part! (68) Would that another had done such a thing to me, an ignorant man, not a haughty one, as he is! I was born out of my mother's womb, and created out of the egg of a divine essence. I was begotten (69) by a god. By his name! I will not forget him in what he has commanded me to do." Then he ordered his (Nimrod's) possessions to be assigned to the treasury, (70) and his granaries to the property of the god Amon of Api.

'When the prince of Heracleopolis Magna, Paf-tot-bast, had come with his presents (71) to the great house of the god-like one (Pi-ankhi), with gold, silver, fine precious stones, horses from the best of his stable, then he threw himself prostrate before his Majesty, and spake thus: " Hail to thee, Horus, (72) mighty king! Bull that wardest off the bulls! The abyss has swallowed me up; I am sunk in darkness; give me light (73) for my countenance. I have not found a friend in the day of adversity, nor one that could stand in the day of battle save thee, O king! (74) Chase away the darkness from before my face. I will be a servant (to thee), together with my subjects of Heracleopolis Magna, who will pay tribute (75) to thy house; for thou art like the god Hormakhu, the prince of the planets. He is what thou art as king. He does not pass away, (76) thou dost not pass away, O king of Upper and Lower Egypt, Pi-ankhi, the ever-living."

'When his Majesty had sailed downwards to the point of the lake region (the Fayoum), to the place of the sluice (77) of the canal, he came to the city of Pi-sekhem-kheper-ra (the capital of Usarkon I.), whose walls were high and its citadel close shut, filled with the best troops of the land of Lower Egypt. Then he sent a summons to it, saying : " To live in dying is dreadful : (78) thy life shall be [rescued] from death, if (the gates) are at once opened. If you do not open to me, you are counted in the number of my fallen foes. It is an affront to a king, to shut him out before the gates. Your life will be good for the high court of justice, good will be this day, from him who loves death to him who hates life. (79) [Make your decision] in the face of the whole land."

'Then they sent an embassy to his Majesty, to address him thus : "The shadow of God rests upon thee, thou son of the goddess Nut. He lends thee his hand. What thy heart wishes, that forthwith happens. As the word is uttered from the mouth of God, so it comes to pass. Thou art born of God, to behold us in thy hand. Safe is the city which is thine, and the possessions in its houses."

'(80) Then they threw open all that was shut. Whoever would go in went in, and whoever would come out came out; his Majesty did as it pleased him. Then they came out with a son of the satrap Tafnakhth. When the warriors of his Majesty had entered, they did not kill one of the inhabitants. He found (81) [the people of the prince busy] with the officers of the court in putting seals on his property. But his treasuries were assigned to the (king's) treasury, and his granaries to the property of his father, the Theban Amon-ra.

'When his Majesty had sailed down the river, he reached the city of Mi-tum (Meidoum), the city of Sokar, the lord of enlightenment. It was shut and not to be entered, for their intention was to fight, and [they had] (82) gathered [many warriors, but] they were afraid of his power, and they (the people of the city) had shut their mouth. Then his Majesty sent them a message, to this effect : " Two ways lie before you ; it is for you to choose. Decide to open, then you shall live; to shut, then you are doomed to death. My Majesty does not pass by any shut-up city." Then they opened forthwith.

His Majesty entered. He offered (83) [a sacrifice to the] god Men-hi, the author of enlightenment. He assigned his treasury (to his own), and his granaries to the property of the god Amon of Api.

'When his Majesty had sailed down the river to the city of Thi-taui (on the borders of Upper and Lower Egypt), he found the fortress shut and the walls full of warriors of Lower Egypt. Then they opened the bolts and threw themselves prostrate, (84) [saying to] his Majesty : " Thy father hath given thee the charge of his inheritance. Thou art the world; thou art that which is in it; thou art the lord of all that is upon the earth." When his Majesty had set out, a great sacrifice was offered to the gods in this city, of oxen, calves, birds, and all things good and clean. Then his treasury was assigned to the treasury, and his granaries to the property (85) [of the god Amon of Api].

'When his Majesty had reached the city of Memphis, he sent it a summons to this effect : " Shut not; fight not; thou seat of the god Shou from the beginning of all things ! Whoever will go in, let him go in; and whoever will come out, let him come out. No traveller shall be molested. I wish to celebrate a sacrifice to the god Ptah, and to the gods of Memphis. I wish to do homage to the god Sokar in his crypt. I wish to behold the god Anbu-ris-ef. Then I will proceed down the river in peace. (86) [No harm shall befal the inhabitants] of Memphis; let them prosper and be in health; the children shall not weep. Look at each several district of the South country. No one was killed, except the impious who blasphemed the gods. None but felons were delivered up to execution."

'But they shut up their fortress, and sent out warriors to some of the warriors of his Majesty (disguised) as workmen, mastermasons, and sailors, (87) [who approached] the harbour of Memphis. For at the same time the prince of Saïs had arrived at the city of Memphis towards evening, having given directions to his warriors, his sailors, and all the captains of his warriors, 8,000 men. And he had very very urgently given them (the following) directions : " Memphis is full of warriors, of the best of Lower Egypt. There is in it wheat, durra, and all manner of corn of the granaries, in abundant [9] measure ; all sorts of implements (88) [of

---

[9] The literal sense of this word expresses in the original, 'in the measure of an inundation.'

war are prepared]. The citadel [is well fortified] ; the battlements are strong, where the work is planned with reference to the river which surrounds it on the East. At that part no assault is possible. The cattle-layers are full of oxen. The treasury is provided with all that is needful, of silver, gold, bronze, woven stuffs, balsam, honey, butter. I am advancing, I will give up their possessions to the under-kings of the South country. I am (again) opening their territories; I will be (89) [their deliverer. Only wait during] the days till my return."

'When he had mounted his horse, for he did not desire his war-chariot, and when he had gone down the river through fear of his Majesty, the earth grew light on (the next) morning very early. Then his Majesty came to the city of Memphis, and he landed on its north side, and he found the water reaching up to the walls. The vessels came to land (90) at the harbour of Memphis. Then his Majesty saw how strong the city was. The walls were high, quite newly built, the battlements were formed strongly, so that there was no means of assaulting it. Among the warriors of his Majesty every one spoke in conversation of all possible modes of attack, and every one said : " Come now ! Let us blockade (91) [the city." Whereupon the king said :] " The soldiers must not make too many words about the passage to it. We will raise up the earth up to its wall; we will fasten wood-works together ; we will set up masts; we will make a bridge of the yard-arms, we will reach by help of them to all its parts by means of the ladders and (92) [bridges] against its north side, so as to raise up the earth to its wall. So shall we find a way for our feet."

'Then was his Majesty furious against them, like a panther. He said : " I swear, as truly as I love the Sun-god Ra, as truly as I reverence my father Amon, I have found that all this happens according to the will of Amon. But this comes from the fact that the people say : (93) "[The king had an easy task] with the districts of the South. They opened to him even from afar." They do not regard Amon in their heart; they do not know that what he has ordained must happen, in order that his presence may show itself, and that his power may be manifest. I will come upon them like a flood of water. What he commands me (94) [that shall happen]."

'Then he ordered his ships and his warriors to advance, to fight against the harbour of Memphis. They brought to him all the vessels, all the barges, all the passenger-vessels and ships of burthen, as many as there were of them. The landing took place at the harbour of Memphis. The foremost landed at the houses [of the port. (95) The inhabitants of it, great and] small, wept because of all the army of his Majesty. Then came his Majesty in person, to lead on the ships, as many as there were Then his Majesty ordered his warriors : " Take heed in encircling the walls and entering the dwelling-houses from the river. Each of you, when he has set foot on the wall, let him not remain standing in his place. (96) [Go forwards], do not press the commanders back ; that would be miserable to bear. Our fortress is the South country ; let our landing-place be the North country ; we will establish ourselves in the city of Maki-taui (a quarter of Memphis)."

'Then was Memphis taken, like an inundation, and many people in it were killed or were brought alive as prisoners to the king. When (97) [the earth] grew light, on the second day, his Majesty sent people to the city, to guard the temples of God. For it was of great moment with him, on account of the supreme holiness of the gods, to offer libations of water to the chief gods of Memphis, and to purify Memphis with salt, balsam, and frankincense, and to set the priests in their place upon their feet. His Majesty went into the house (98) [of Ptah], purifying himself with the holy water in the star-chamber. He performed all that is prescribed for the king. He entered the house of the god, where a great sacrifice was prepared to his father Ptah of his south wall, of bulls, calves, birds, and of all good things.

'When his Majesty had entered his house, the inhabitants heard thereof in all the districts that lie round about Memphis, (namely), Heri the town, Peni- (99) na-'au'a'a, the tower of Bui, and the village of Biu. They opened their gates, and they fled all at once, without any one's knowing whither they were gone.

'Upon the arrival of Aupoth, and the satrap A-ka-neshu, and the hereditary lord Pet-ise, (100) and all the princes of Lower Egypt, with their presents, to behold the grace of his Majesty, the treasuries and the granaries of the city of Memphis were assigned to the possession of Amon, of Ptah, and of the company of divinities in the city of Ptah.

'When the earth grew light, at the dawn of the next morning, his Majesty proceeded eastward. A libation of holy water was poured out to the god Tum of Khar-kharan (Babylon), (101) and to the host of divinities in the temple of Pi-paut, a grotto, and to the gods there, of bulls, calves, and birds, in order that they might grant life, prosperity, and health, to the king of Upper and Lower Egypt, Pi-ankhi, the ever-living.

'His Majesty proceeded to On, over that hill of Babylon, along the road of the god Sep to Babylon. His Majesty entered the tent, which (was pitched) on the west side of the canal of Ao. He performed his purification by bathing in the middle (102) of the lake Kebhu, and he washed his face with the milk of the Nun (i.e. with the water of the rising Nile), where Ra is wont to wash his face. His Majesty went to the sand-hill in On, and offered a great sacrifice on the sand-hill in On, before the Sun-god Ra at his rising, of white cows, milk, balsam, and frankincense, of the best and (103) the most fragrant woods.

'Returning and on his way to the temple of the Sun, he was greeted most warmly by the overseer of the house of the god, and the leader of the prayers pronounced the formula "of the keeping away of evil spirits from the king." The arrangement of the house of stars was completed, the fillets were put on, he was purified with balsam and holy water, and the flowers were presented to him for the house of the obelisk (Ha-benben).[1] He took the flowers, ascended (104) the stairs to the great window, to look upon the Sun-god Ra in the house of the obelisk. Thus the king himself stood there. The prince was alone. He drew back the bolt and opened the doors, and beheld his father Ra in the exalted house of the obelisk, and the morning-bark of Ra and the evening-bark of Tum. The doors were (then) shut, the sealing-clay was laid (105) on, and the king himself impressed his seal. He commanded the priests (as follows): "I have satisfied myself of the secure closing; none other of all the kings shall enter any more." As he stood there, they threw themselves prostrate before his Majesty, while they spake thus: "May Horus, the friend of the city of On, endure and increase and never vanish away!" On his return, as he entered the temple of Tum, the statue of (106) his father, the god Tum, the creator, the king of On, was brought in (in procession).

'Then came the king Usarkon to behold the grace of his Majesty.

'When the earth grew light, at the dawn of the next morning,

---

[1] Comp. Vol. I. pp. 150, 151.

the king took the road to the harbour, and the foremost of his ships sailed to the harbour of the nome of Athribis. There a tent was pitched for his Majesty on the south of the place (called) Kahani on the east side of the (107) nome of Athribis.

'When the kings of Upper Egypt, and the princes of Lower Egypt, all the grand-masters of the whole body of fan-bearers, all the grand-masters of the whole body of the kings' grandsons, had arrived from the West country and from the East country and from the islands between, with the purpose of beholding the grace of his Majesty, the hereditary lord Pet-ise laid himself prostrate (108) before his Majesty, saying thus : " Come to the nome of Athribis ; look upon the god Khonti-khetthi of the cities ; honour the goddess Khui ; offer a sacrifice to Horus in his temple, of bulls, calves, and birds ; enter into my house, I lay open to thee my treasury, with the possessions inherited from my father. I give thee gold after the desire of thy heart, (109) green stones, heaped up before thy face, and numerous horses of the noblest breed out of the stalls, the best from the prince's stable.

'When his Majesty had gone into the temple of Horus Khont-Kheteth, a sacrifice was offered of bulls, calves, and birds to his father, Hor-Khont-Khethi, the lord of Kem-ur (Athribis). (Then) his Majesty went into the house of the hereditary lord Pet-ise, who made him a present of silver, gold, (110) blue and green stones, a great abundance of every sort, woven stuffs, cloths of byssus in great number, beds covered with linen, frankincense, oil in anointing-vials, stallions and mares, of the best of his stable. He took an oath of expurgation before God, in the presence of those kings of Upper Egypt and of the great princes of the land of (111) Lower Egypt—(for) every one of them (had said that) he had hidden away his horses and had concealed his riches, because they desired that he might die the death of his father—(and he spake thus) : " An abhorrence to me is this, that ye desire to crush a servant (of the king). Be well assured, that the sovereign is on my side. Your talk is an abhorrence to me, that I have hidden from his Majesty the whole inheritance (112) of the house of my father. The gold, the golden objects (set) with precious stones, in all manner of vessels and rings for the hands, the golden neckchains, the breast ornaments composed of precious stones, the talismans for every part of the body, the head-bands, the earrings, and all other royal array, all the vessels of gold and jewels for the king's ablutions,—all these (113) I here openly present. The stuffs of byssus and the woven cloths by thousands, are of the best from my house. I know now that thou art content with them. Go into the prince's stable, choose according to thy pleasure of all the horses whichever thou desirest." And his Majesty did so.

'And the kings and the princes said to his Majesty : " Let us go (each) to our city; we will open (114) our treasuries; we will select whatever thy heart loveth : we will bring to thee the best of our stable, the most excellent of our horses." Then his Majesty did so.

'This is the list of them : namely :

King USARKON of Bubastus and Uu-n-r'a nofer ;
King AUPOTH of the city of Thent-ram and Ta-'ain-ta ;
(115) Prince ZI-AMUN-AUF-ANKH of Mendes and Ta-'ap-r'a ;
His eldest son, a lord, captain of Hermopolis Parva, 'ANKH HOR ;
Prince (Satrap [2]) A-KA-NESH of Sebennytus, of Hebi (Iseum), and of Samhud (Diospolis Parva);
Prince and Satrap PI-THENEF, of Pi-saptu and in 'Ap-en-An-buhat ;
(116) Prince and Satrap PI-MA of Busiris ;
Prince and Satrap NES-NA-KETI of Xoïs ;
Prince and Satrap NAKHT-HOR-NA-SHENNU of Pi-garer (Phagroriopolis) ;
Prince and Satrap (unnamed) of Ta-ur (Tanis) ;
Prince and Satrap (unnamed) of Bekhen (Ostracine) ;
(117) Prophet of Horus, the lord of Letopolis, PET-HOR-SAM-TAUI ;
Prince HE-RO-BISA of the city of the goddess Sekhet, the lady of Sa, and of the city of Sekhet, the lady of Hesani ;
Prince ZI-KHI-AU of Khont-nofer (Onuphis ?) ;
Prince PI-BI-SA of Babylon and Nilopolis (in the Heliopolitan nome).

'They brought to him their presents of all good things; (118) of gold, silver, [blue and green stones], of [stuffs, beds] covered

---

[2] This title of his is taken from the additional inscription on the sculpture over the inscription of Pi-ankhi. He is there represented as lying on the ground, with the fillet of an Assyrian satrap on his head (just as Darius I. is distinguished in the temple of the Oasis of Hibe), and in the annexed inscription he is designated as 'Satrap A-ka-nesh.'

SUBMISSION OF TAFNAKHTH.

with linen, of frankincense, of (119) anointing-vials, of . . . .
trappings (?) well adapted for the horses, (120) of . . . . .

'After this (messengers) came to his Majesty saying : (121) ["The king and satrap Tafnakhth of] the city of [Saïs] has assembled his [warriors]. He has razed the walls (122) [of his city,] he has set fire to [his] treasury, [he has fled to the islands] in the midst of the river, he has strengthened the city of Mas-di (123) with his warriors. Whatever [he needs] is brought to him."

'Then his Majesty ordered his soldiers to go forth (124) and see what had happened, and his body-guards were entrusted to the hereditary lord Pet-ise. Then they came to report to (125) his Majesty as follows : " We have killed all the people that we found there." Then his Majesty gave rewards to (126) the hereditary lord Pet-ise. When the king and satrap Tafnakhth heard this, he sent (127) an ambassador to the place where his Majesty was staying, to supplicate his grace thus : " Be of friendly mind ! I have not beheld thy face in (128) the days of disgrace. I cannot stand before thy fire. My manhood is in thy power, for thou art the god Nub in the land of the South, (thou art) Monthu, (129) the powerful bull. If thou settest thy face towards anything, thou findest no servant (able) to resist thee, so that I betook myself to the islands of the great river. (130) I am full of anguish before thy presence on account of the sentence, that the flaming fire is preparing enmity for me. (131) Is not your Majesty's heart softened by all that you have done to me? If I have been a despiser of the truth, punish me not after the measure of my guilt. (132) Measured with the balance is the produce in ounces.[3] Thou hast dealt it to me threefold. The seed is sown for thee, which was (sown) for me. Is it then proper to cut down (133) the fruit-trees, instead of gathering them (i.e. the fruit) ? By thy name ! The fear of thee is in my body, and distress before thee in my bones. I sit not in (134) the festive hall (*lit.* the chamber of mead), nor do I take down the harp. I eat bread for hunger, and I drink

---

[3] There seems to be here a twofold meaning : first, an appeal to the general principle, that punishment ought not to exceed the measure of the crime ; and, secondly, a particular application of that principle to the sparing of the trees and fruits (which the Egyptians were wont to destroy in war), especially as they now belonged to the victorious king.—ED.

water for (135) thirst every day, since thou hast heard of my name. A shivering is in my bones, my head is shorn, my garments (136) are old, in order that I may appease the goddess Neith. Long is the race which has brought thee to me. Turn thy (face from) above on me who am below. Is it well to (137) torment my existence? Purify thy servant from his haughtiness. Come! receive my property for thy treasury: (138) gold and jewels, also the most excellent of the horses. They may pay for all. (139) Let a messenger straightway come to me. Let him chase away the anguish from my heart. My desire is to go up into a sanctuary before him: I will purify myself by an oath (140) before God."

'Then his Majesty sent the leader of the prayers, Pet-amon-nes-taui, and the general Pi-ur-ma. He (i.e. Tafnakhth) presented (141) them with silver and gold, with robes and jewels. He went up into a sanctuary. He prayed to God, he (142) purified himself by an oath before God, speaking thus: "I will not transgress the king's command, nor will I neglect (143) the words of his Majesty. I will not compass harm to any prince without thy knowledge. I will behave according to the words (144) of the king, and will not transgress what he has commanded." With this his Majesty was satisfied.

'Tidings were brought to (145) his Majesty: "The city of Crocodilopolis has opened its fortress and the city of Matennu has surrendered."

'(146) Thus no district was shut against his Majesty, of the nomes of the South and of the North. The West and the East and the islands in the midst had submitted through fear before him, and (147) brought their presents to the place where his Majesty resided, as subjects of the palace.

'When the earth grew light, in the morning, (148) very early, there came the two kings of the South and two kings of the North, with their royal serpent-diadems, to worship before the presence (149) of his Majesty. With them also the kings of Upper Egypt and the princes of Lower Egypt, who came to behold the grace of his Majesty. (150) Their legs were the legs of women. They did not enter the king's house, because they were unclean, (151) and besides they ate fish, which is an abomination to the king. But as for king Nimrod, he went (152) into the king's house, because he was clean and ate no fish. They stood there (153) upon their legs, every one at the entrance of the king's house.

'Then were the ships laden with silver, gold, bronze, (154) stuffs, and all the good things of Lower Egypt, and with all the products of Phœnicia and with all the woods of the Holy Land.

'When his Majesty sailed up (155) the river, his heart was glad. All its banks resounded with music. The inhabitants in the West and East took their drums (156) to make music at his Majesty's approach. To the notes of the music they sang, " O King, thou conqueror ! (157) Pi-ankhi ! O thou conquering king ! Thou hast come and thou hast smitten Lower Egypt. Thou madest the men (158) as women. The heart of thy mother rejoices, who bore (such) a son, for he who begat thee dwells in the valley (of the dead). Happiness to thee, the cow, (159) who hast borne the bull ! Thou shalt live for ever in after ages ! Thy victory shall endure, thou king and friend of Thebes ! "

Pi-ankhi does not seem to have enjoyed his success long. Whether it was that the power of the Assyrians again got the upper hand, or that Taf-nakhth or his sons rose up afresh, and, supported by the other petty kings of the lower country, threw off the Ethiopian sovereignty, at all events it is certain that the successor (and son ?) of king Pi-ankhi, by name Miamun Nut (whose third regnal year I have found on a Theban monument), was left in possession of Patoris only, with the capital Thebes, and had lost all hope of supremacy in Lower Egypt.

His campaign against the low country of Egypt is justified by a dream. The war which, in consequence thereof, he undertook against the kings and satraps in the North, seems to have had some temporary success, rather from special circumstances than through the bravery of his army. But he too dedicated to the fame of this passing victory a memorial stone, which was found several years ago on the site of the ruins of Napata at the foot of Mount Barkal.

The inscription engraved thereon, which we shall presently place before our readers in a faithful translation, is accompanied by a sculptured representation, which is not without importance in several ways. It consists of a double relief, on the right side of which the king testifies his devotion for the Theban Amon-ra. To the name of the king is appended an official royal shield, on which he is designated as Bi-ka-ra. Behind him is seen 'the king's sister and wife, the queen of Kemi (Egypt) Ge-ro-a-ro-pi.' She must have been married a second time to an Egyptian of high rank, named Usa-hor, and have borne a son, to whom the inscriptions assign the title of a 'royal grandson.' The monuments name him Pet-amon. I shall treat of his remarkable history in another place.

In the scene on the left hand, king Nut himself offers a breastplate with chains, as a talisman, to the Theban Amon 'of the holy mountain' (that is, Noph or Napata), who is here represented with a ram's head. He is accompanied by 'the king's sister, the queen of Ta-Khont (Nubia).' We have here before our eyes one of several examples in proof of the distinguished position which the women of the Ethiopian court must have occupied. While this sister of the king is designated as 'Queen of Nubia,' another, who was also a wife of Miamun Nut, is called 'Queen of Egypt.'

The inscription begins with titles of honour, than which a Pharaoh himself could not have wished for any higher. The oriental pomp of rhetoric without a background of facts is here conspicuous. Let us hear how the king is overwhelmed with flattery by the author of the inscription : [4]—

'On the day on which he was brought forth to light, he became as a god Tum for mankind. He is the lord of the two horns, a prince of the living, a great king, who has taken possession of the whole world. Of a victorious arm in the day of slaughter, of piercing look on the day [of battle], a slayer and lord of the strong, like the god Monthu, powerful like a raging lion, prudent as the god Hiser (i.e. Thut), beautiful as he sets forth upon the river as pursuer and achiever of his purpose, bringing back what he has won. He gained possession of this land without fighting: no one had the power to resist him.'

Of this same Nut the inscription further relates what follows :—

'(3) In the first year, which was that of his coronation as king, (4) his Majesty had a dream in the night. There were two serpents, the one on his right hand, the other on his left. When his Majesty woke, he did not find them. Then spake his Majesty [to the interpreters of dreams]: (5) "Why has such a thing happened to me?" Then they explained it to him, speaking as follows :—"The land of Upper Egypt is thine. Thou shalt take possession of the land of Lower Egypt. The double crown shall adorn thy head. The land is given to thee in its length and in its breadth. Amon, besides whom (6) there is no other god, will be with thee."

'His Majesty held a court, sitting on the throne of Horus, in this year. When his Majesty had come out from the place where he had been staying, as Horus came out of his marsh, then he went forth : in [his suite were] (7) a hundred thousand, who marched near him.

'His Majesty said : "So may the dream come true." For this was indeed a thing that coincided with his purpose ; and it would have fallen out ill, if he had desisted from it.

---

[4] Monsieur G. Maspero's translation of this 'Stélé of the Dream' has appeared in French in the *Revue Archéologique*, 1868, tome i. p. 329 ; and in English in *Records of the Past*, vol. iv. pp. 79, foll.—ED.

'When his Majesty had repaired to the city of Noph (Napata), no one was [with him] (8) when he entered it. After his Majesty had visited the temple of Amon of Noph, on the holy mountain, his heart was strengthened when he had seen the Theban god Amon-ra on the holy mountain. They presented him with garlands for the god. (9) Then his Majesty caused Amon to be brought out (in procession) from Noph. He prepared for him a rich sacrifice, for he offered to him what [was acceptable to] his heart: 36 bulls, 40 jars of mead, 100 asses.

'When his Majesty had sailed down the river to the land of Upper Egypt, he wished to behold the god (10) whose being is more hidden than that of all the gods (i.e. the god Amon).

'When he arrived at Elephantiné, his Majesty put in at Elephantiné. When he had come into the temple of Khnum-ra, the lord of the city of the new water (i.e. the inundation), (11) he caused the god to be brought out (in procession). A rich sacrifice was prepared for him. He offered bread and mead to the gods of the two sources. He propitiated the river in its hidden cave.

'When his Majesty had sailed down the river towards [the territory of the city of] Thebes, which belongs to Amon, then his Majesty landed (12) before Thebes. When his Majesty had entered the temple of the Theban Amon-ra, there came to him the chief priest and the ministers of the temple of Amon-ra, (13) the Theban god, and they brought him flowers for him whose being is hidden. And his Majesty's heart was glad, when he beheld this house of the god. He caused the Theban Amon-ra to be brought out (in procession), and a great feast was celebrated in all the land.

'(14) When his Majesty sailed down the river towards Lower Egypt, then the inhabitants on the right and on the left bank were jubilant, great was the rejoicing. They said: "Go onward in the peace of thy name, in the peace of thy name! Dispense life (15) through all the land; that the temples may be restored, which are hastening to ruin; that their statues of the gods may be set up after their manner; that the revenues may be given to the gods and the goddesses, and the offerings for the dead to the deceased; (16) that the priest may be established in his place; and that all may be fulfilled according to the holy learning" (i.e. of the ritual). Even those, whose intention it was to fight, were moved with joy.

'When his Majesty had come to Memphis, and (17) the rebels (*lit.* the sons of revolt) had made a sally, to fight against his Majesty, then his Majesty inflicted on them a great slaughter, without number. And his Majesty took Memphis, and entered into the temple of (18) Ptah of his south wall. He prepared a sacrifice to Ptah-Sokar, he adored Sokhet, whose love is so great. For the heart of his Majesty was joyful for what his father Amon of Noph had done for him.

'And he issued an ordinance, (19) to enlarge [the temple of Ptah], and that a new hall should be built for him. No such building was seen in the times of his predecessors. His Majesty caused it to be built of stones which were inlaid with gold. (20) Its panelling was made of acacia-wood, (21) which was impregnated with frankincense of the land of Pun. Its doors were of white brass,[5] and (22) their frames of iron. He built for him a second hall as an outbuilding behind, wherein to milk his milk (23) from a numerous herd of 116 goats. No one can count the number of young calves (24) with their mothers.

'When all this was done, his Majesty sailed downwards, to fight with the princes of (25) Lower Egypt, for they had retired within their walls in order [to avoid battle] near their towns. Before these his Majesty spent many days, but none of them came out (26) to fight with his Majesty.

'After his Majesty had sailed up to Memphis, he rested in his palace, and meditated a resolution (27) with himself, to send his warriors to seek them.

'[Before the army set out], tidings were brought to him, saying: "The great princes have come to (28) the place where his Majesty resides. [What does] our lord [decide]?" His Majesty said, "Are they come to fight? Or are they come to serve me? In that case they shall live from this hour." (29) Then spake

---

[5] We take this to mean pale yellow *brass* (the alloy of *copper* and *zinc*) in contradistinction to the darker *bronze* (the alloy of copper and tin). Though the ancients seem to have had but a very slight knowledge of the *metal* zinc, under the name of 'mock-silver' (ψευδάργυρος), they were certainly acquainted with the true *brass*, formed from *zinc ore* (calamine) with copper, the *orichalcum* of the Greeks and Romans. (See especially Strabo, xiii. p. 610.) M. Maspero translates the word in the text *electrum*, an alloy of gold and silver.—ED.

they to his Majesty, "They are come to serve the great lord, our governor." The king said : " My governor is that glorious god, the Theban Amon on the holy mountain. The great god is gracious to him who confesses his name; he watches (30) over him who loves him; he grants strength to him who does his will, and transgresses not his bidding. He who walks according to his commandments will not stagger, for he leads him and guides him. It is he that speaks to me in the night (31) of that which I shall see in the day."

'His Majesty said : " What they wish cannot be transacted at this hour." They spake before the king : " They are without, they stand near the king's house."

' When his Majesty had gone forth (32) out of his [palace], then he beheld these princes, who learned to know the god Ra on the horizon. He found them lying prostrate, in order to supplicate before his face. The king speaks : " Since that is the truth, which Amon decrees, (33) I will act according to the [command that he shall reveal to me]. Lo ! to know what will happen means this—what God ordains, that shall come to pass. I swear, as truly as the Sun-god Ra loves me, as truly as I hallow Amon in his house, I will [enquire of] this glorious god (34) of Noph on the holy mountain whether he stands against me. Whatever he shall say to me, to that let effect be given by all means and in every way. Good for naught is the saying : 'O that I had waited with my resolution till the next morning which shall arise ! ' (35) I am as a servant [mindful of his master's] interest, and every workman must know what tends to the interest of his Majesty. [Say not, Why] should I wait for the morning, which comes later ? Had I only thy power ! "

' Then they answered him and spake thus : " May this glorious god (36) be thy guide and leader ! May he give what is good into thy hand ! Turn thyself not away from that which shall come out of his mouth, O great king, our lord ! "

' When Pi-qe-ro-ro, the hereditary lord and prince of the city Pi-saptu, had stood up to speak as follows : (37) " Kill whom thou wilt; let live whom thou wilt; there shall be no reproach against our lord on account of that which is just ; "—then they responded to him all together, speaking thus : " Grant us the breath of life, for none can live without (38) it. We will serve him (i.e. Amon) as his dependents, just as thou hast said from the beginning, from the day when thou wast made king."

'Then was the heart of his Majesty glad, when he had heard these words. He entertained (39) them with food and drink and all good things.

'After many days had passed in this manner, and he had imparted to them all good things, notwithstanding their great number, then they said: "Shall we stay longer? Is such the will of the great lord, our governor?" Then spake (40) his Majesty, saying thus: "Why?" They speak before his Majesty: "We would return home to our cities; we would care for our inhabitants and our servants according to the need of the city." Then his Majesty let them depart thence (41) (each) to his city, and they remained in life.

'Then the inhabitants of the South sailed down the river, and those of the North up the river, to the place where his Majesty resided, and brought all the good things of Upper Egypt and all the riches (42) of Lower Egypt, to propitiate the heart of his Majesty.

'May the king of Upper and Lower Egypt, Bi-ka-ra, the son of the Sun, Miamun Nut—to him be health, prosperity, life!—sit enthroned upon the seat of Horus for ever!'

What gives an especial value to this inscription, is the mention of the prince of the city of Pi-saptu (the capital of the later nome of Arabia) Pi-qe-ro-ro, who here comes forward as spokesman in the name of the petty kings of the low country, and treats direct with the Ethiopian. For his name appears again in the celebrated Assyrian account of the campaign of king Assur-ban-habal, the son of Assur-ah-idin,[6] against the Ethiopian king Tarquu, the king Taharaqa of the monuments.

King Nut also (like Pi-ankhi) was not permitted to

---

[6] Asshur-bani-pal, the son of Esar-haddon, are the forms of the names more familiar to English readers. See the late lamented Mr. George Smith's *History of Assur-bani-pal*, and his translation of the *Annals of Assurbanipal* in *Records of the Past*, vols. i and ix.—ED.

enjoy long the double-serpent-crown of Lower Egypt. As in Egypt a perpetual struggle and dispute for the sceptre at last partitioned the country and played into the hands of foreign potentates, so likewise in Ethiopia a schism appears to have broken out in the reigning family, which could only be decided by arms. The statement, in the list of titles of king Nut—that 'he had gained possession of this land (Ethiopia) without fighting'—alludes clearly enough to some such circumstances. It even seems as if a division had been made from the original beginning of the empire, inasmuch as three different regions formed thenceforth the three chief parts of the divided Ethiopian state: namely, Patoris, with the capital Thebes; Takhont (Nubia, the land of Meluḫḫa of the cuneiform inscriptions), with the capital Kipkip; and Kush, with the old Ethiopian royal city of Napata.

It is only in this way that a satisfactory explanation can be found for the crowding of several Ethiopian royal names on one and the same line of the genealogy.[7]

With Taharaqa, king of Ethiopia (according to our view about 700 B.C.), begins the latest period of the history of the kingdom of the Pharaohs, in which the numbers obtain a more certain form, and the classical writers begin by degrees to contribute authentic data respecting the fortunes of the Egyptian kings, their contemporaries.

The Ethiopian king just mentioned bore the full names of—

[7] See the great Genealogical Table (IV.)

NOFER-TUM-KHU-RA TA-HA-RA-QA. B.C. 693–666.

The length of his reign extended to more than twenty-six years, as it is obtained with full exactness from the data of the life of an Apis-bull. To him belonged the South country, Patoris, with its capital, Thebes, in which several monuments, mostly in the form of dedicatory inscriptions, are memorials of the dominion and presence of this Ethiopian king. His name was well known in antiquity, from the Bible down to the classic writers. While Holy Scripture introduces him under the name of Thirhaqah (Tirhakah,[8] A.V.), his name appears in the Greek writers in the forms, Tearko, Etearchus, Tarakus, Tarkus. His renown as a great conqueror pervades the records of antiquity, although all other proof of this from the monuments is wanting. The Egyptian inscriptions know him simply as the lord of Kemi (i.e. Egypt), Tesher (i.e. the land of the Erythræans), and Kepkep (i.e. Nubia).

It is to the Assyrian cuneiform inscriptions that

[8] At 2 Kings xix. 9, and Isaiah xxxvii. 9, we read that while Sennacherib, in his great campaign against Judah (B.C. 700), was besieging Libnah, he received news that 'TIRHAKAH, *king of Ethiopia,*' had come out to fight against him. Shortly before this, as we learn from Sennacherib's own annals, he had signally defeated the united forces of the *kings of Egypt* and the *king of Ethiopia,* who had advanced to aid the rebel city of Migron (Ekron), at Altaku (Eltekeh : Joshua xix. 44 ; xxi. 23). It would seem, therefore, that the resistance of Hezekiah encouraged Tirhakah and his Egyptian allies to a new effort ; and it was on his advance to meet them, probably near Pelusium, that Sennacherib's army was miraculously destroyed. At this time, it is to be observed, Tirhakah was only *king of Ethiopia,* not yet of Egypt.—ED.

historical science owes the most important elucidation of the reign of this king in Egypt, and of his wars against the great kings of Assyria. The French scholar, Jules Oppert, was the first who, with his usual penetration, deciphered the fragments relating to these wars, and brought out the connection of their contents with the events in Egypt. From his work, entitled 'Mémoire sur les rapports de l'Égypte et de l'Assyrie dans l'antiquité éclaircis par l'étude des textes cunéiformes' (Paris, 1869), we have borrowed the important text which is here placed before the reader. We have here and there amended some Egyptian proper names, from the necessary corrections furnished by the latest researches in this field.[9]

[*Preliminary Note by the Editor.*]

[We must be content to refer the reader to M. Oppert's own account of the various inscriptions and fragments which his ingenuity has pieced together, to make up this most momentous record of the Assyrian king (son of Esarhaddon and grandson of Sennacherib), whom he calls Asur-ban-habal or Sardanapalus IV., the 'warrior Sardanapalus' of Layard. M. Oppert prints (1) the Assyrian cuneiform text, (2) the same in Italic letters, and (3) a Latin version, all in parallel lines and words. These texts are accompanied by a most valuable 'Memoir,' on cuneiform interpretation, the history of the Assyrian kingdom, and other matters.

In translating Dr. Brugsch's German version, we have compared it, word by word, with the Latin of

---

[9] The reader would do well to look at Haigh's remarks in the *Aegyptische Zeitschrift*, 1871, p. 112, and 1872, p. 125, and my own in the same journal, 1871, p. 29.

M. Oppert, which we have occasionally preferred. We have not thought it necessary to confuse the reader with brackets indicating lacunæ in the text of the principal inscriptions, as these are for the most part supplied, not from conjecture, but by the help of the other copies. The Assyrian custom of repeating the same inscription on tablets of terra-cotta—thus, in fact, multiplying copies of their clay books (such as were found by thousands in the library of this very king Assur-bani-pal at Nineveh)—has here proved of the greatest service to historical science. The Roman numerals indicate the several chief inscriptions. The . . . . . denote Assyrian words or phrases that are either illegible, or, though legible, have baffled the interpreter.—ED.]

RECORD OF ASSURBANIPAL.

I. 'In my first expedition I went against Muzur (Egypt) and Meluḫḫa (Meroë). Tarquu, the king[1] of Muzur and Ku-u-si (Ethiopia), whom Asur-ah-idin (Assarhaddon), the father who begat me,[2] had subdued, returned out of his land. Trusting in his strength (*lit.* hands) he despised the commandments of Asur and Istar, the great gods, my lords. His heart was hardened, and he sinned of his own will (*lit.* of himself). The kings, satraps, and generals, whom Assarhaddon, my father, had set over the kingdom of Egypt, were driven out by him.

II. 'They betook themselves to Ninua (Nineveh). Against such deeds my heart was moved and my bile (*lit.* liver) was stirred up. I numbered my army and my whole forces, with which the great gods had filled my hands, to bring help to the kings, satraps, generals, and servants, who were expecting my presence (*lit.* face). I set forth speedily and came to the city Karbanit (Canopus).

---

[1] The Assyrian word which we translate 'king' throughout the inscription is *sar*, which Brugsch keeps.—ED.

[2] On the frequent recurrence of this phrase, we translate it simply 'father' or 'parent.'—ED.

When Tarquu, the king of Egypt and Ethiopia, in the city of Memphis, heard of the arrival of my expedition, he prepared for battle his munitions of war, and counted the host of his warriors.'

III. 'Tarquu, king of Egypt and Ethiopia, despised the gods. He put in motion his strength to take possession of Egypt. He disregarded the commandments of the great god Asur, my lord. He trusted in his own strength, and did not observe his own treaties, which my father who begat me had made (with him). He came from Ethiopia and entered Memphis, and took that city for himself. Upon the Assyrians (*lit.* men of Assur), who were servants in Egypt expecting my presence, whom Assarhaddon, my father, had set over the kingdom in it (Egypt), he ordered his army to inflict death, imprisonment, and plunder.

'A messenger came in haste to Nineveh and . . . . On account of such deeds my heart was moved and my bile was stirred. I was incensed, and I ordered, by an imperative decree, the Tartan (general), the satraps, with the men of their hands [3] (?), and my chief guards, to start on an expedition to the help . . . . . of the kings, satraps, and servants. I ordered an expedition to be made to Egypt . . . . (they) went down quickly, and came to Karbanit. Tarqa,[4] (the king of) Kuusi, when he had heard in the city of Memphis of the approach of my army, numbered his host to make war and battle, and drew up his army opposite to my army.

'With invocations to Asur, Sin (the Moon-god), the great gods, my lords, I ordered the onslaught of my forces. In a fierce battle they put them to flight, and conquered with arms the men who served him (*lit.* of his service). Fear and terror seized him, and he turned back. He escaped from Memphis, the city of his kingdom, the place of his honour, and he fled away in ships to save his life (*lit.* soul). He left his tent standing and withdrew himself alone and came to Ni (the 'great city,' i.e. Thebes), and gave orders to his men of battle to embark [5] on all the ships and barks (?) that were with him, and he commanded the man set over the barks (?) . . . . .

'I gathered together the commander of the satraps of the

[3] That is, 'under their command,' but the sense is not quite certain.

[4] So Oppert gives the name here, *Tarka*. We keep Dr. Brugsch's *q*.—ED.

[5] So Brugsch. Oppert gives 'naves rates (?) quæquæ cum se (erant) viros pugnæ suæ *prehendi* jussit.'—ED.

cities beyond the river, the servants faithful before me, them and their garrisons, their ships, the kings of Egypt, the servants faithful before me, and their garrisons and their ships, in order to drive out Tarquu from Egypt and Ethiopia. There were more of them than before.[6] I sent them against Thebes, the city of the empire of Tarquu, the king of Ethiopia. They went a journey of a month and ten days. Tarquu, when he heard of the approach of my army, left Thebes, the city of his empire, and went up the river. My soldiers made a slaughter in that city.

'Nikuu (Necho), Sarludari,[7] Paakruru, whom my father had made satraps, sinned against the commandments of Asur and the great gods, my lords, and did not keep to their treaties (with him). They despised the glory of my father, and hardened their hearts to enmity; they devised a plan of rebellion, and sinned wilfully (*lit.* of themselves) against their flesh, speaking thus: "Tarquu will not go back from his designs upon Egypt; he is afraid, and do ye all watch over your safety (?)"[8] They sent their envoys to Tarquu, king of Ethiopia, to make peace and friendship (speaking) thus: "Let peace be made in our league, and let us be friendly to each other. On this side (i.e. on our part) we pledge our faith; from no other quarter shall there be a breach in our alliance, O our Lord.[9] They tried to entice [1] into their league the whole army of Asur, the guards of my dominion; they prepared what their revenge desired. . . . . .

'My judges heard of their designs, and derided their cunning. They intercepted their envoys with the letters, and perceived the work of their treason. They bound those kings hand and foot 'in fetters. The justice of Asur, king of the gods, reached them, be-

---

[6] Oppert translates this clause: 'Insuper præsidia mea anteriora auxi.'—ED.   [7] Salukakri (Oppert).

[8] This sentence is of doubtful interpretation. Oppert renders it: 'Tearco e media Ægypto non retrovadet, reformidatur et vos . . . . . . (the gap represents the words *asabani mi i-nu*, which he leaves untranslated).—ED.

[9] 'Hinc fidem obligamus, nunquam peccabitur in fœdere nostro aliorsum, domine' (Oppert). The meaning of the contrast —*hinc* and *aliorsum*—is not quite clear. Is it—'We will keep it on our own part, and not let others (the Assyrians) make us break it'?—ED.

[1] Brugsch. Oppert has simply 'illexerunt.'—ED.

cause they had sinned against the commandments of the great gods. At their hands they found what my will had devised for them. Memphis, Saïs, Mendes, Tanis [2]—all the cities which they had enticed to themselves and which had formed intrigues in the desire of revenge,—I subdued with arms, male and female, small and great; they did not leave in them one, ... they brought into my presence. Thus (I spake) : " I am Asur-ban-habal. . . . performing glorious deeds . . . . . they delivered up in the city Karbelmate ('of the great mother,' i.e. Saïs)." [3]

IV. 'About 20 kings, satraps, commanders of the cities, who in Egypt had obeyed my father before me—all those kings I gave over to the hand of Nabu-sezibanni, who waited in my presence (Some lines are wanting) . . . . . of Asur, of Istar, of the gods my lords . . . . . I made a great slaughter of his army . . . . . over his army Nabu . . . . .

'Nikuu (Necho) was seized with great terror of my Majesty. He left his gods in the city of Memphis, and fled, to save his life, to the middle city, Ni (Thebes). I took that city, and placed my army in it.

' Ni-ku-u,[4] king of Memphis and Saïs,
Sar-lu-da-ri, king of Tanis,
Pi-sa-an-hu-ru (Pi-son-hor), king of Na-athu-u (Na-athu, Natho),
Pa-ak-ru-ru (Pa-qror), king of Pi-sa-ptu (Pisapt, in the Arabian nome),
Pu-uk-ku-na-an-ni'-pi (Bok-en-nifi), king of Ha-at-hi-ri-bi (Ha-ta-hir-ab, Athribis),
Na-ah-ki-e, king of Hi-ni-in-si (Khinensu, Heracleopolis),
Pu-tu-bas-ti (Pef-tut-bast), king of Za'nu (Za'n, Zoan-Tanis),
U-na-mu-nu, king of Na-at-hu-u (Natho),
Har-si-e-su (Hor-si-ise), king of Zab-an-nuti (Thebnuti, Sebennytus),
Pu-u-iu-ma (Pimai), king of Bi-in-di (Bindid, Mendes),
Shu-shi-in-qu (Shashanq, Sesonchis), king of Pu-si-ru (Pi-usiri, Busiris),

---

[2] The Assyrian names are *Mempi, Sai, Bindidi, Sa'nu.*

[3] M. Oppert (p. 72) quotes the suggestion of M. Lenormant, that the Assyrian expression *bel-mate* is the exact translation of the Egyptian royal title ' Lord of the two regions.'—ED.

[4] The reader will notice that these names are an introductory part of the sentence that follows the list. The Egyptian forms of the names are placed in ( ) after the Assyrian forms, with the classical equivalents, when they can be recognized.— ED.

Tap-na-akh-ti (Taf-nakhth, Tnephachthus), king of Pu-nu . . . (Pinub, Momemphis?),
Bu-uk-ku-na-an-ni'-pi (Bok-en-nifi), king of Aḥnir (On ?),⁵
Ipti-ḥar-si-e-su (Pet-ḥor-si-ise), king of Pi-za-at-ti-ḥu-ru-un-pi (Pi . . . Ḥor-en-pi),
Na-aḥ-ti-ḥu-ru-an-shi-ni (Nakbt-Ḥor-na-shennu), king of Pi-sap-ti-nu-ti),
Bu-kur-ni-ni-ip (Bok-en-ran-ef, Bocchoris), king of Pa-aḥ-nu-ti,
Si-ḥa-a (Zichiau, Tachos), king of Si-ya-a-tu (Siaut, Lycopolis),
La-mi-in-tu (Na-li-moth, Li-ma-noth=Nimrod), king of Ḥi-mu-ni (Khmu-ni, Hermopolis Magna),
Is-pi-ma-tu (Psi-mut), king of Ta-i-ni (Tini, Thinis),
Ma-an-ti-mi-au-ḥi-e (Monthu-em-ḥ'a), king of Ni (Ni'a, Thebes);—

these (are the) kings, commanders, satraps, who in Egypt had obeyed my father, (but) who on account of the arms of Tarquu had forgotten their allegiance. I brought them back to their state of obedience. I recovered (or, restored) Egypt and Ethiopia, which my father had conquered, I strengthened the garrisons more than in former days; I surrounded them with ditches. With a great treasure and splendid booty I returned safe to Nineveh.

'Afterwards those kings, whom I had subdued, sinned against me and broke the commandments of the great gods . . . . . . They revolted, and their heart was hardened in wickedness; they plotted the artifices of rebellion; they sinned wilfully, (saying): "Tarquu will not go back from his designs upon Egypt;⁶ he is afraid. Do ye all watch over your own safety." They sent envoys to Tarquu, king of Ethiopia, to make peace and friendship, saying: "Let there be peace in our alliance, and let us be friendly to one another. On our part we pledge our faith, and we give as security the land . . . . . the city. . . . . . Never shall there be a desertion in our alliance to any other party, O our lord." The army of Assyria, the support of my dominion, they tried to seduce to their league; they prepared for their desired revenge.

'My judges heard of their purpose. They intercepted their envoys and their letters, and perceived the works of their treason. They seized these kings, and bound them hand and foot in iron

---

⁵ So Brugsch, but the line is very imperfect. Oppert gives only . . . na-an-du (?) sar Aḥ . . . .—ED.

⁶ So Brugsch. Oppert has 'Tearco ex media Ægypto non retrovadet.'—ED.

fetters and iron chains. The vengeance of Asur, king of the gods, reached them, and, because they had sinned against the commandments of the great gods, they experienced at their hands what my will had devised for them. [The city of Memphis],[7] the city of Saïs, Mendes, Tanis, and all the cities which they had led away with them [I took by storm],[7] (putting to death) both great and small.'

According to Oppert's view, here followed the account of the conquest of Egypt, the return of Tirhakah, his death, and the first exploits of his successor, Urdamaneh, who succeeded in reconquering Kemi, while he advanced as far as Lower Egypt. Thebes was still his capital. Sardanapalus marches against Egypt the second time, and defeats the army of Urdamaneh.

[*Note by the Editor.*]

[M. Oppert's comments, to which Dr. Brugsch refers, are too interesting not to be laid more fully before our readers. After the document III. (for he gives Brugsch's No. IV. before this) he proceeds (p. 72):—

'The thirteen lines which follow relate the first campaign of Sardanapalus to the end. This part is, in general, too much mutilated to enable us to give the text; but we find that Tirhakah comes to Thebes, and conquers it again. Necho, now a prisoner in Assyria, obtains his pardon from Sardanapalus, and returns to Egypt; the Ninevite king giving him presents with the view of detaching him from the Ethiopian. Necho makes his entry into Saïs, and changes its name to Kar-Bel-mate (see the Note on p. 270). But an Asiatic governor watches over the Egyptian. Meanwhile a son of Necho, who also receives an Assyrian name, Nabu-sezibani, is raised to the kingdom over the city of Mahariba, which is likewise honoured with an Assyrian name, Limir-patisi-Asur, i.e. "which the lieutenant of Asur governs." The name of Nabusezibani is found in Jeremiah xxxix. 13, נבושזבן "Nebo, deliver me!"

'This inscription gives the complete sequence of the historical events. It alone gives an account of the first capture of Thebes by

---

[7] The phrases in brackets are supplied from the identical narrative in document III.—ED.

the Assyrians. This event, which the prism doubtless set forth with fuller details, was the result of the Ethiopian intrigues after the death of Assar-haddon. Tirhakah, in violation of the treaty, had killed, imprisoned, and spoiled the Assyrians who were left in Egypt. Sardanapalus marches against him, and joins in battle with him near the city of Karbanit. The Ethiopian, who had established his residence at Memphis, retreats on Thebes, whither the Assyrians pursue him. The Assyrians, after a forty days' march, reach Thebes and massacre its inhabitants.

'This part of the first campaign was contained in the lost portion of the prism. After the retreat of Tirhakah, Sardanapalus defeats Necho, and then follow the events forming the narrative which is preserved.

'The great document (No. II. above) tells us nothing about the sequel of this campaign. Then the document *a* (No. III.) continues the war of Sardanapalus against Urdamaneh, which we shall relate presently. Scarcely is Egypt pacified, when Tirhakah dies, and his step-son (his wife's son) Urdamaneh succeeds him. This king invades Egypt, and forces the Ninevite king to try the fortune of war a second time. Urdamaneh had penetrated as far as Memphis, whither Sardanapalus marches to attack him. Here is the sequel of the inscription, after a chasm of about 30 lines:—

'" In . . . of my expedition I directed . . . my march. Urdamaneh heard of the advance of my expedition "—and so forth, as in the text, No. IV.'

We would also refer the reader to M. Oppert's reconstruction of the whole narrative about Tirhakah and Urdamaneh from the inscriptions (pp. 80, *seq.*) —ED.]

RECORD OF ASSURBANIPAL CONTINUED.

V. 'Urdamaneh heard of the advance of my expedition. He [lost?] Me-luh-hi (Meroë) and Egypt, abandoned Memphis, and fled to Thebes to save his life. The kings, commanders, and satraps, whom I had established in Egypt, came to me and kissed my feet. I directed my march in pursuit of (*lit.* after) Urdamaneh. I came to Thebes, the city of his dominion. He saw the strength of my army, and left Thebes (and) fled to the city of Kipkip. Of that whole city, with thanksgiving to (*lit.* in adoration of) Asur and Istar, my hands took the complete possession. Silver, gold, metals, stones, all the treasures of its palace whatsoever, dyed garments of berom and linen, great horses (elephants? Oppert), men and women, great and small, works of zaḥali (basalt?) and marble, their kelal and manzas, the gates of their palace, their . . . I tore away and carried to Assyria. I made spoil of [the animals of the land] without number, and [carried them forth] in the midst out of Thebes. . . . of my weapons . . . I caused a catalogue to be made [of the spoil]. I returned in safety to Nineveh, the city of my dominion.'[8]

The first lines of another document,[9] which stand in immediate connection with the inscription No. III., present unfortunately great gaps through obliteration. According to Oppert's acute researches, they contained the enumeration of the tributes and the booty, which the king of Assyria had carried away out of Egypt, as well as the account of the end of the campaign. Sardanapalus increased the tribute imposed by his father, and set up Necho's son, Nabu-sezibanni,[1] as governor of the western districts of Mahariba (?) and Limirpatesi-Assur. Then the death of Tirhakah is touched upon, and the king continues his record as follows :[2]—

VI. 'The fear of the terror of Asur my lord carried off Tarquu, king of Ethiopia, and his destined night came. Urda-

---

[8] The narratives of the double capture of Thebes by Assurbanipal are of singular interest for the light they throw on the striking allusion to its fate in Nahum iii. 8–10, which had no known historical counterpart till the discovery of these records.—ED.

[9] The β of Oppert, p. 87.   [1] See above, p. 272.

[2] M. Oppert (p. 77) remarks on the perplexity caused by the use, in this document, of the 3rd person plural, instead of the 1st singular, as seeming to imply that the Assyrian king did not himself go to Thebes. We supply from Oppert's text the first sentence, which Dr. Brugsch omits.—ED.

maneh, the son of his wife,³ sat upon the throne, and ruled the land. He brought Ni (Thebes) under his power, and collected his strength. He led out his forces to make war and battle against my army, and he marched forth (*lit.* directed his step). With the invocation of Asur, Sin, and the great gods, my lords, (my warriors) routed him in a great and victorious battle, and broke his pride. Urdamaneh fled alone, and entered Thebes, the city of his kingdom.

'In a march of a month and ten days through intricate roads (my warriors) pursued him up to Thebes. They attacked that city and razed it to its foundations, like a thunderbolt. Gold, silver, the treasure of the land, metals, precious stones, stuffs of berom and linen, great horses, men male and female, . . . huge apes, the race of their mountains—without number (even for skilful counters),—they took out of the midst of the city, and treated as spoil.' They brought it entire to Nineveh, the city of my dominion, and they kissed my feet.'

We have here set before us a remarkable portion of the history of Egypt, in this case not according to an Egyptian version, but in the contemporaneous description of her enemy. The conclusions, which we are justified in drawing from the contents of the cuneiform inscriptions, furnish us with the following data, as firm foundations for the reconstruction of the historical events of this time.

In the year 680 B.C. (according to Oppert's calculations), Sennacherib, king of Assyria, died, and Assarhaddon (Esarhaddon) succeeded in his stead. Towards the end of his reign (about 670 B.C.), Assarhaddon attacked Egypt. defeated the reigning king of

---

³ In this passage, on one of the cylinders, Urdamaneh is called 'the son of Sabaku,' from which it may be inferred that Tirhakah, after displacing Sabaco, married that king's wife (see Birch's *Ancient History from the Monuments: Egypt*, p. 169). This discovery affords another illustration of the disturbed and complicated relations between the Ethiopian kings of this period (comp. pp. 264, 277).—ED.

Ethiopia and Egypt, Taharaqa (Tarkuu), and set up petty kings (*sar*) and satraps in the land, from the northern sea-board to the city of Thebes. The complete list of these we have already laid before our readers. We have now to add that the king, on his return out of Egypt, had an immense memorial tablet constructed on the surface of the rock at the mouth of the Nahr-el-Kelb, in the neighbourhood of Beirout, near that of his father, as a monument of his victory over Tarquu. Henceforth Assarhaddon styles himself 'King of Muzur (Lower Egypt), of Paturusi (the Egyptian Patoris, Upper Egypt), and of Miluhhi (Nubia).'

Scarcely had this king died (668 B.C.), when Tarquu broke the treaties and seized the city of Memphis, while at the same time he made a league with several of the under-kings, who had been acknowledged or set up by Assarhaddon, for driving the Assyrians out of Egypt. At the head of the petty kings, as arch-conspirators, stood Nikuu of Memphis and Saïs, Sar-lu-da-ri of Zi'nu, and Pa-ak-ru-ru of Pi-saptu.

The Assyrian satraps and the other adherents of the king, those who had been set up by Assarhaddon, were driven out, and fled to Nineveh, to ask protection and the punishment of king Tarquu. Sardanapalus V.,[4] the son of Assarhaddon, who had been meanwhile crowned as king, was not slow in acting upon his sense of indignation, and marched against Egypt with a great army. The further de-

[4] Assurbanipal, Sardanapalus VI. according to Oppert.—ED.

tails are placed before us with all needful clearness in the duplicate records of the cuneiform inscriptions.

In these events a conspicuous part was played by the king Nikuu, or Neku (Nechao, Necho, Neco), of Saïs and Memphis, the son of that Tafnakhth who had opposed so long and obstinate a resistance to the Ethiopian king Pi-ankhi. Carried in fetters to Nineveh, he succeeded in obtaining pardon from Sardanapalus and his renewed establishment as petty king of Saïs and Memphis. Of his violent end, according to the Greek accounts,[5] the inscriptions give us no information.

A thick veil covers the ensuing times, in which the Ethiopians occupy the foreground of Egyptian history. Taharaqa, Pi-ankhi (with his oft-named wife, Ameniritis), Shabak and Shabatak—all appear as contemporary, and are frequently introduced in connection with each other. Their family relationships are set forth with all exactness on the large Genealogical Table.[6] If we might give credit to the lists of Manetho, they would seem to have reigned in succession[7] over Patoris, whose capital, Thebes, retains manifold evidences of their presence; but we are unable to find anything in the monuments to confirm this succession.

[5] Herodotus (ii. 152) says that Neco (Νέκων), the father of Psammitichus, was put to death by Sabaco, the Ethiopian.—ED.
[6] Table IV. Compare above, p. 275.
[7] They stand in Manetho as follows:—
Shabak (Sabacon) . . . . . 12 years.
Shabatak (Sebichus) . . . . . 12 „
Taharaqa (Taracus) . . . . . 26 „

Upon a sitting statue of king Shabatak in stone, unfortunately much broken, among the ruins on the site of Memphis, a brief inscription calls the Pharaoh thus represented Miptah Shabatak. But the latter name has already in ancient times been rendered half illegible by chisel-strokes, evidently made for the express purpose of obliterating the name of a usurper of the throne.

At Thebes, the memorials of king Taharaqa and of an Egyptian under-king have lasted the longest. He had given liberal tokens of his regard for the sanctuary of Apis by buildings and presents, and it is no wonder, therefore, that the walls of the temple sound his praise in varied strains.

On the other hand, an entire stone wall in the temple of Mut at Thebes preserves the list of the benefits received from a contemporary of the king. He had the festivals of the gods celebrated after the ancient usage; he provided the needful sacrifices; set up statues of the gods (even after the Assyrian model) and built the sacred barks; renewed the parts that had fallen into ruin, even to the enclosing wall; and caused the sacred pool and the canals to be lined with stone walls from the bottom. He also served Taharaqa as his faithful counsellor and helper.

This man was the eminent Egyptian Month-em-ha, a son of Nes-ptah, priest of Amon, and his wife Nes-khonsu. Month-em-ha was fourth prophet, and finally second prophet of the Theban Amon, and, like his father, a governor of Ni' (Thebes). At the same time he is mentioned in the inscriptions as the ' chief of the governors of Patoris.' There must have been some special reason for his high distinction in the Thebaïd, since he himself relates how ' [he] had smitten the enemy in the nomes of Patoris.' I recognize in him (as I have said) a faithful ally and friend of Taharaqa, who invested him with the government of the country named above.[8] He is the person whom the above-quoted Assyrian text introduces in the list of the petty kings, as Ma-an-ti-mi-an-hi-e, Sar of Ni' (Thebes),—a tolerably faithful transcription of the Egyptian name, Month-em-ha. Thus in this respect also the Assyrian narrative appears to have received a striking corroboration.

In the son of Taharaqa's wife, Urdamaneh, as the Assyrian text calls him, is certainly preserved the name of the king, Rud-amon, who is referred to on the Egyptian monuments. For the chronological position of this king I refer to the large Genealogical Table,[9] where I have inserted him as the second king of this name, inasmuch as his grandfather, Rudamon I., is described as the father-in-law of Pef-tot-bast, the ' satrap' and afterwards ' vassal' of Pi-ankhi, and hence he belongs to a considerably earlier generation.

---

[8] On this whole subject the reader should compare the hieroglyphic inscriptions and the pictures in Mariette's *Karnak* (Pl. 42-44). On a round enamelled plate, which was found in the temple of Mut (Pl. 47, 6), he bears the titles of 'hereditary lord, commander, prince of Patoris, president of the prophets, second prophet of Amon of Ape, fourth prophet of Amon, Month-em-ha.'

[9] Table IV. Comp. above, p. 275.

I have hitherto passed over the name of the king, who is introduced in the lists of Manetho as the sole Pharaoh of the Twenty-fourth Dynasty, of Saïs. I refer to king BOCCHORIS, whom Sabaco took prisoner and burnt alive, as is stated in the extracts from Manetho. Hence the two appear as contemporaries. Mariette has recognized in this king the UAH-KA-RA BEK-EN-RAN-EF, whose Apis-sarcophagus (of the 6th year of the king) was placed in the same chamber of the Serapeum, in which the deceased Apis of the 37th year of king Shashanq IV. was deposited. Here then we have brought to light a new connection in time between Bocchoris and Shashanq IV.

This same Bek-en-ran-ef appears again in the Assyrian list of the Egyptian petty kings, under the name of Bu-kur-ni-ni-ip, as sar of Pa-ah-nu-ti. The name of the city is not to be confused with the Assyrian transcription of Saïs, the city from which Bocchoris had his origin; but it must have denoted some other place in Egypt.

At all events, Bek-en-ran-ef belonged to the number of the petty kings who had formed a connection with the younger contemporaries of Taharaqa. It is difficult to lay hold of the clue in this complication of persons of royal race belonging to the Egyptian and Ethiopian families. Our Genealogical Table[1] marks the first attempt to exhibit the chief members of these houses in their family relationships.

[1] Table IV.

At length Psamethik I.,—the great-grandson of that Taf-nakhth who was the opponent of the Ethiopian Pi-ankhi,—comes to the forefront of the history, as the deliverer of his country from the condition of the Dodecarchy—the name which the Greeks chose to describe that period. His marriage with the Ethiopian heiress, Shep-en-apet—the great-granddaughter of the above-named Pi-ankhi, a daughter of king Pi-ankhi, and his beautiful queen Ameniritis— restored peace and order to the distracted relations of the royal succession. Regarded in this light, the founder of the Twenty-sixth Dynasty appears practically as the reconciler of all rival claims. The daughter of the renowned queen of Kush and Patoris, in giving her hand to the petty king of Saïs, brought Patoris as a wedding-gift to her husband; and thus Egypt was again united into a great kingdom.

The splendid alabaster statue of the queen-mother Ameniritis, which was found at Karnak and now adorns the rooms of the Egyptian Museum at Boulaq, is, from this point of view, a most important and suggestive memorial of that age. Sweet peace seems to hover about her features; even the flower in her hand suggests her high mission as reconciler of the long feud.

At her feet is the following inscription, which her contemporaries dedicated to her; though the bitter hatred of ingrained animosity prevailed so far as to erase the names of her brother and her father—as being Ethiopians—from the enclosure of their royal shields :—

'This is an offering for the Theban Amon-ra, of Ape, to the god Monthu-ra, the lord of Thebes.

'May he grant everything that is good and pure, by which the divine (nature) lives, all that the heaven bestows and the earth brings forth, to the princess, the most pleasant, the most gracious, the kindest and most amiable queen of Upper and Lower Egypt, the sister of the king [Sabaco] the ever-living, the daughter of the deceased king [Kashta], the wife of the divine one,[2]—AMENIRITIS. May she live!'

On the back of her statue she is introduced as speaking. Among other things, she says:—

'I was the wife of the divine one, a benefactress to her city (Thebes), a bounteous giver for her land. I gave food to the hungry, drink to the thirsty, clothes to the naked.'

The reader will allow me here to append the discussion of a question, which is not without importance for determining the descent of the kings of this period, although it involves considerations purely etymological. I am here repeating the opinions I expressed in a separate essay, several years ago. No one can fail to observe, that the majority of Ethiopian royal names, of men as well as women, terminate in the letters k or q, and towards the end they show a strikingly frequent recurrence of the elements, *ata* and *ta*. I need only cite the names Shaba-k, Shabata-k, Tahara-q (or Tahara-q-a), Kash-ta, Kanta-ki (Candace), and I may here likewise add the names Psam-eti-k and Ne-ku.

A similar peculiarity is shown in the existing lan-

[2] This epithet is to be referred either to her husband, king Pi-ankhi, or, as is more probable, to the god Amon, as whose high-priestesses the queens of Patoris used to bear the title: 'Wife of the god Amon.'

guage of the Nubian Barabra, which is still spoken at
this day, in three dialects, by the inhabitants of the
Nubian Nile-valley, from Edfou to Jebel Deqa. In
this language the article appears as a suffix, without
distinction of gender, in the forms k, ka, ki, gi, ga, qa,
q, as, for example, in the following names of places:
Pi-la-q (Philæ, in old Egyptian also Pila-q,[3] Kishi-ga
(near Qirsh), Da-ke, Ala-qa, Maharra-qa, Korus-qo,
Tosh-ke, Am-qe, Esh-qe, Am-qa, Son-qi, Fer-qe,
Moqra-qe, Sedeïn-qa, and so forth. In this language
the Genitive stands before the Nominative, the two
being frequently connected by an interposed n, as in
the names of places compounded with arti, 'island,'
as: Banga-n-arti, 'locust-island,' Taba-n-arti, Uru-n-
arti, 'king's-island' (whence its Arabic name, Jeziret-
el-melik), Nilu-arti, Mar-arti, 'durra-island,' Kom-n-
arti, 'camel-island.' The well-known word Senaar,
denoting the insular region between the Blue and
White Nile, south of Khartoum, is compounded of
Essi-n-arti, 'river island.'

The very frequent termination *kol, kal, kul*, &c.,
serves to denote a mountain or rock; whence such
names of places as Ambou-kol, 'hill of the dome-palm,'
in Arabic Abou-dom, 'father of the dome-palm,'
Kedin-kal, Kodo-kol, Kuru-kol, Ko-n-keli, 'lions'-
mount,' Mara-kol, 'durra-mount.' The well-known

[3] From the Ethiopic Pila-q the Greeks formed the well-known
name Philai (Philæ), by dropping the final article, as if they knew
that this formed no essential part of the word. Just the same
course was taken by the Hebrews, who changed the name of the
Ethiop-Egyptian king Shaba-k ('male-cat-the') to the simple form
Sewe (Shab, 'male-cat').

Mount Bar-kal certainly owes its name to an older form Berna-kal, 'Mount of Meroë,' unless we should give the preference to Buru-kol, 'virgins'-mount.' The southernmost of all the Kols is the Arash-kol in Kordofan, on the west bank of the White Nile.

The word *ato*, or, strengthened with the article, *ato-ki*, signifies 'the son;' whence, for example, Kash-gi-n-ato-gi, 'the-son-of-the-horse,'[4] that is, 'the foal.' The Barabra are very fond of personal names taken from animals conspicuous for their appearance or strength. Timsach, 'crocodile,' and Nimr, 'panther,' are to this day current among that people as names of honour. It seems to have been just the same in ancient times; for the greater number of the Ethiopian royal names can be completely explained by help of the existing language of the Barabra. Thus Shab-k (Sabaco) answers to the present Sab-ki, 'the male cat,' a designation which is the more striking, as, at the epoch of king Sabaco, not a few persons among the Egyptians, including even kings, called themselves Pi-ma or Pi-mai, 'the male cat.' King Shabata-k, the son of Sabaco, is in the Barabra language Sab-ato-ki, 'the male cat's son,' just as a Barabran word Kash-ato, 'horse's-son,' lies at the base of the name Kash-ta. In like manner the Græco-Ethiopic proper name Ammonat is explained as Amon-ato, 'Amon's-son,' and finally the Cushite name of Nimrod (so familiar to us) is equivalent to Nimr-ato, 'panther's-son.'

[4] But the inverse order of the English would correspond to the Ethiopic, thus: 'horse-the-son-of-the.'—ED.

I regret that space does not allow me to follow out here the further conclusions, which I have deduced from a comparison of the little known language of the Barabra with the Ethiopian proper names. But at all events I was anxious not to omit calling the reader's attention to the almost unknown treasures of a language, the importance of which for historical investigation should by no means be undervalued. I will only add the concluding remark, that within the Barabra language there are preserved no small number of old-Egyptian, nay even of Greek words, which attest an early connection and a long intercourse with the Egyptian people. Thus ur, uru, means 'king' (Egypt. ur), whence uru-n-arti, 'king's island;' nabi, 'gold' (Eg. nub); kafa, 'arm' (Eg. kabu); ashiran, 'bean' (Eg. arushana); uel, 'dog' (Eg. uher, uhel); hada (Eg. hoite), 'hyena;' minne (Eg. mini, minnu), 'dove;' al (Eg. ial), 'mirror;' siwuit (Eg. sifet), 'sword;' nibit (Eg. nibiti), 'mat;' kirage (Grk. kyriaké), 'Sunday;' korgos (Grk. krokios), 'yellow;' and many others.

The name of Psamethik also belonged to the Ethiopic language. I will elsewhere give the full proof that its signification was 'son of the Sun.' With him, in fact, a new sunlight breaks forth for Egypt, even though it were only that of the evening sun, illuminating with its brightness the setting of the great monarchy on the Nile.

CHAPTER XIX.

FROM THE TWENTY-SIXTH TO THE THIRTY-FIRST DYNASTY.

SUCCESSION OF THE KINGS, WITH THE DATES OF THEIR ACCESSION.

DYNASTY XXVI., OF SAÏS.

	B.C.
Psamethik I. (Psametichus, Psammitichus)	666
Neku (Nechao, Neco)	612
Psamethik II. (Psametichus)	596
Uah-ab-ra (Apries or Uaphris)	591
Aahmes (Amasis)	572
Psamethik III. (Psametichus)	528

DYNASTY XXVII. PERSIANS.

Cambyses (Kanbuza)	527
Darius I. (Nthariush)	521
Xerxes I. (Khskhiarsh)	486
(Khabbash, Egyptian anti-king)	
Artaxerxes (Artashesesh)	465
Xerxes II.	425
Sogdianus	—
Darius II.	424

Dynasty XXVIII., of Saïs.

. . . . (Amyrtæus).

Dynasty XXIX., of Mendes.

	B.C.
Naif-an-rot I. (Nephorites)	399
Hagar (Akoris)	393
[Psa-mut] (Psamuthis)	380
[Naif-an-rot II.] (Nephorites)	379

Dynasty XXX., of Sebennytus.

Nakht-hor-hib (Nectarebes)	378
Zi-ho (Teos, Tachos)	360
Nakht-neb-ef (Nectanebus)	358

Dynasty XXXI. Persians.

Ochus	340
Arses	338
Darius III.	336
Conquest of Egypt by Alexander the Great	332

We are standing beside the open grave of the Egyptian kingdom.[1] The array of kings, whose names are enrolled in these last dynasties—some of them native and some foreigners—appear as the bearers of the old decaying corpse, whose last light of life flickered up once more in the Dynasty of Saïs, only to go out soon and for ever. The monuments become more and more silent, from generation to generation, and from reign to reign. The ancient seats of splendour, Memphis and Thebes, have fallen

---
[1] See Note at the end of Chapter XX.

into ruin, or at all events are depopulated and deserted. The strong bulwark of the 'white citadel' of Memphis alone serves as a refuge for the persecuted native kings and their warriors in times of need. The Persian satraps dwell in the old royal halls of the city. The whole people has grown feeble with age, disordered to the marrow, and exhausted by the lengthened struggle of the petty kings and the satraps of the mighty power of Assyria.

The Persians, who after a short interval took up the part played by the Assyrians, gave Egypt her final deathblow. Although, by his sage and well-calculated measures, the distinguished king Psamethik I. succeeded in gaining the throne, as sole sovereign, for himself and his descendants; and though the monuments, from the extant ruins of Saïs to the weather-worn rocks of Elephantiné, show the scattered traces of the rule of the Pharaohs of the Twenty-sixth Dynasty; nevertheless the old splendour was gone—no Ptah, no Hormakhu, no Amon, any longer attests his help, or his thanks to the lord of the land for his great deeds.

The city of Sai (Saïs), in whose temples the great Mother of the Gods, Neit, was invoked and hallowed, standing near the sea, easily accessible for the Greek and Persian 'foreigners,' formed the last revered divine sanctuary under the Pharaohs, and the new capital of the kingdom, whence the kings issued their edicts to the land.

When Alexander the Great entered Egypt as a conqueror and deliverer, Saïs in its turn became deserted and forlorn. The new capital of Alexandria —which is called 'the fortress of the king of Upper and Lower Egypt, Alexander, on the shore of the great sea of the Ionians : it was before called Ra-kot (Racotis),'[2]—succeeded to the inheritance of Thebes, Memphis, and Saïs, assuredly not for the welfare of the Egyptians. All that they lost, all they were doomed to lose, turned to the profit of the young and energetic world in the North. Alexandria was one of the capitals of the world, with all the privileges and disadvantages pertaining to such a rank. The city itself grew with incredible speed; her foundations were laid from the destroyed temples and monuments of Saïs, which found a new destination in the construction of the royal palaces, temples, fountains, canals, and other public works. Thus was the young Grecian capital of the world built on the ruined greatness of ancient Egypt.

Strong as is the impression of pity made by the sight of this miserable end to the mighty empire of the Pharaohs, yet the temples and edifices built 'to last hundreds of thousands of years' could offer no resistance to the perishableness of all things earthly; for it was not in their everlasting stones, but on the enduring loyalty of their people, that the Pharaohs should have established their imperishable monument. The harassed and exhausted people, persecuted with war and oppression, a plaything for the

---

[2] Compare my Essay, 'A Decree of the Satrap Ptolemæus, the son of Lagus,' in the *Aegypt. Zeitschrift*, 1871, p. 2. For a further account of the text referred to, see below, p. 315.

caprices and ambition of their princes, easily broke their faith, when they no longer received their reward in the fidelity and affection of their rulers. Degraded into the mere means to a selfish end, it was the same to them whom they served, whether Assyrian, Persian, or Greek. No foreign prince could prove worse to them than Pharaoh and his court.

From this epoch the monuments are conspicuously silent. There are only isolated inscriptions, containing no more records of the victories of each age, but continual songs of woe, which we must read between the lines. They form the dying swan-song of the mighty empire on the Nile.

It is no longer the everlasting stone or monument that makes known to us the unenviable fortune of the land; but the inquisitive Greek, who travels through the Nile-valley under the protection of the Persians or the kings of his own race and gathers his information from ignorant interpreters, becomes henceforth the source of our knowledge.

The reader will find the history of Egypt, according to the classical accounts, from the year 666 B.C. to the times of the Greeks and Romans, in every handbook of Ancient History. But from this we refrain, as inconsistent with our purpose of depicting Egypt only according to the monuments.[3] What these teach us, in some conspicuous examples, of the last days of the kingdom of the Pharaohs, will form the conclusion of our work.

[3] For those readers, who may feel—as we ourselves have felt—a certain incompleteness in the mere fragments of monumental records which seem to want the background of continuous history for the real understanding of their value, we have added the brief summary at the end of Chapter XX.—ED.

BEAUTY OF THE MONUMENTS.

Psamethik I.   Neku.   Psamethik II.   Uahabra (Apries).   Anhmes (Amasis).   Psamethik III.

§ I. THE TWENTY-SIXTH DYNASTY.

The monuments of this time, belonging to the seventh and sixth centuries B.C.,[4] are distinguished by a peculiar beauty—one might almost use the word elegance—in which we cannot fail to recognize foreign, that is, Greek influence. An extreme neatness of manipulation in the drawings and lines, in imitation of the best epochs of art in earlier times, serves for the instant recognition of the work of this age, the fineness of which often reminds us of the performances of a seal-engraver. The work, executed in the hardest stone with a finish equal to metal-casting, bears the character of a gentle and almost feminine delicacy, which has impressed upon the imitations of living creatures the stamp of an incredible refinement both of conception and execution. The little statues, holding a shrine, of the Saïte dignitary Pi-tebhu, son of Psamethik-Seneb, and the monument (of which we shall have more to say) of Uza-hor-en-pi-ris in the Vatican at Rome;[5] the stone sarcophagi of the Saïte dignitaries, Auf-ao, surnamed Noferabra-Minit (among whose offices we find that of 'chief overseer of the Ionian peoples'), of Nahkt-hor-hib, called Nofer-hor-monkh, and of

---

[4] Most of these monuments were obtained from excavations at Saïs, and are in the Museums of Italy.

[5] Compare p. 304.

Psamethik, in the same city;—the famous cow of the celestial Hathor, and the statues of Osiris and Isis, the offerings of a certain Psamethik, in whose grave in the cemetery of Memphis these images of serpentine were found, which now form the admired masterpieces of the collection at Boulaq;—the splendid pair of lions of king Nahkt-neb-ef, which he dedicated to the Egyptian Hermes of Hermopolis Parva (now in the Vatican);—the numberless statuettes in bronze of the goddess Neit of Saïs:—these, and a hundred similar works of sculpture, furnish instructive examples of the refinement and delicacy of the monuments which came from the hands of the artists of the age now in question.

The return to the good old times, from which the intelligent artist took the models of his works, is proved by monuments, not few in number, upon which the representations, both of lifeless objects and of living creatures, standing out in relief upon a flat surface,[6] call to remembrance the masterpieces of the old kingdom. In fact, even to the newly created dignities and titles, the return to ancient times had become the general watchword. The stone door-posts, which were found in a house of the age of the kings named Psamethik in the mounds of *débris* at Mit-Rahineh (now at Boulaq), the offering of a certain Psamethik-nofersem, reveal the old Memphian style of art mirrored in its modern reflection after the lapse of 4,000 years.

[6] The special character of the work referred to is that called *intaglio rilevato*, in which the outline of the figure is cut deep into the stone, and the surface rises towards the central parts in curves adapted to the proportions of the figure. An exquisite specimen of this age is seen in a piece of a frieze in the British Museum.—ED.

While this effort to return to antiquity on the artistic side called forth distinctive aims in the province of æsthetics, which has hence been designated by the name of the Egyptian renaissance, so to another side of the national life—that of the old Egyptian theology and the esoteric traditions of the priestly schools—a new contribution appears to have been made, modelled closely after the Græco-Asiatic pattern, which was far from harmonizing with the old wisdom taught in the temples. Beside the great established gods of the old-Egyptian theology, there now come forward upon the monuments monstrous forms, the creations of a widely-roving fancy, which peopled the whole world, heaven, earth, and the subaqueous and subterranean depths, with demons and genii, of whom the older age and its pure doctrine had scarcely an idea.

Exorcisms of the demons in all manner of forms, from wild beasts with their ravening teeth to the scorpion with his venomous sting, formed henceforth a special science, which was destined to supersede the old and half-lost traditional lore of past ages. The demon-song of 'The old man who regained his youth, the hoary one who became young,' the exorcisms of Thot and the powers of witchcraft in league with him, are the favourite themes which cover the polished surfaces of the monuments of this remarkable time of transition. A priest Ankh-Psamethik, a son of the lady Thent-nub, finds an ancient writing in the temple of the Mnevis-bull of Heliopolis, in the time of king Nakht-hor-hib, and forthwith a whole stone is adorned with indescribably fine inscriptions and the most elegant figures—a unique work of art, which now forms the most remarkable ornament of Prince Metternich's collections at Königswerth in Bohemia.

The above-named founder of the Thirtieth Dynasty seems to have found particular delight in this new world, full of overstrained creations. All the walls of the sanctuary in the temple of Amon, founded by Darius I. in the Great Oasis of El Khargeh (the ancient Hibis), are covered with such demoniacal representations, the explanation of which is little aided by the annexed inscriptions. Their origin goes back to the same king, Nakht-hor-hib. The last Egyptian king, Nakht-neb-ef, earned the cheap reputation of an exorcist. He was a famous magician, who left Egypt and fled into Ethiopia, laden with rich treasures—never to return!

A flood of light has been thrown on the chronological relations—to the very day as well as year—of the several reigns of the Twenty-sixth Dynasty, since the discovery of memorial stones (*stêlæ*) of the Apis-bulls in the Serapeum at Memphis; and they have rendered even greater service by their data of time than by their occasional revelations of the part taken by the kings of that age in the honours paid to the bulls, both living and deceased. We subjoin the translations of the most important of these memorial inscriptions, in order to place our readers in a position to form their own judgment on the significance of these inscriptions for the purposes referred to.

TABLET I.

'Year 20, month Mesori, day 20, under the reign of king Psamethik I., the Majesty of the living Apis departed to heaven. This god was carried in peace (to his burial) to the beautiful land of the West, in the year 21, month Paophi, day 25; having been born in the 26th year of the king of Upper Egypt, Taharaqa; and after having been inaugurated at Memphis in the month Pharmuthi, on day 9. (The total) makes 21 years.' [7]

TABLET II.

After the full name of king Psamethik I., we read :—

'In the year 52, under the reign of this god, information was brought to his Majesty: "The temple of thy father Osiris-Apis, with what is therein, is in no choice condition. Look at the holy corpses (the bulls), in what a state they are! Decay has usurped its place in their chambers." Then his Majesty gave orders to make a renovation in his temple. It was made more beautiful than it had been before.

'His Majesty caused all that is due to a god to be performed for him (the deceased bull) on the day of his burial. All the dignitaries took the oversight of what had to be overseen. The holy corpse was embalmed with spices, and the cere-cloths were of byssus, the fabric becoming for all the gods. His chambers were pannelled with ket-wood, sycomore-wood, acacia-wood, and the best sorts of wood. Their carvings were the likenesses of men in a chamber of state. A courtier of the king was appointed specially for the office of imposing a contribution for the work on the inner country and the lower country of Egypt.'

As Mariette has already proved conclusively, Psamethik I. was the founder of a new gallery and

[7] Besides its determination of the lifetime of the Apis in question, this record is of special importance for the length of the reign of king Taharaqa. The reading—'made in the year 21,' which has not the least grammatical foundation—is absolutely contradicted by other inscriptions containing similar data. (See what is said below, under the reign of Cambyses, p. 299.)

new sepulchral chambers (with pannelled woodwork, as the inscription informs us), in the subterranean necropolis of the holy Apis-bulls. This was done, according to the above inscription, in the 52nd year of his reign, on the occasion of the burial of a bull who died at that time.

TABLET III.

'Year 16, month Khoiakh, day 16, under the reign of king Neku, the ever-living, the friend of Apis-Osiris. This is the day of the burial of this god, and of the arrival of this god in peace into the nether world. His interment was accomplished at his burial-place in his holy house in the Libyan Desert near Memphis, after they had fulfilled for him all that is customary in the chambers of purification, as has been done from early times.

'He was born in the year 53, in the month Mekhir, on the 19th day, under the reign of king Psamethik I. He was brought into the temple of Ptah (of Memphis) in the year 54, in the month Athyr, on the 12th day. His union with life took place [in the year 16,] month Paophi, day 6. The whole duration of his life amounted to 16 years, 7 months, 17 days.

'His Majesty king Neku II. supplied all the costs and everything else in splendour and glory for this sublime god. He built his subterranean tomb of fine white limestone in well-wrought workmanship. The like of it was never done before.'

TABLET IV.

'Year 12, month Payni, day 21, under the reign of the king Uah-ab-ra,[8] the friend of Apis-Osiris, the god was carried in peace to the good region of the West. His interment was accomplished in the West of the Libyan Desert near Memphis, after they had fulfilled for him all that is customary in the chambers of purification. The like was never done since the early times.

'This god departed to heaven in the year 12, month Pharmuthi, day 12. He was born in the year 16, month Paophi, day 7,

---

[8] The Pharaoh-Hophra of the Bible, and the Apries of Herodotus.

under the reign of king Neku II., the ever-living. His introduction into the temple of Ptah took place in the year 1, month Epiphi, day 9, under the reign of king Psamethik II. The full life-time of this god was 17 years, 6 months, 5 days.

'The god-like benefactor Uah-ab-ra supplied all the costs and everything else in splendour and glory for this sublime god. Thus has he done for him, who bestows life and prosperity for ever.'

Tablet V.[9]

'Year 23, month Pakhons, day 15, under the reign of king Khnum-ab-r'a (Amasis), who bestows life for ever, the god was carried in peace to the good region of the West. His interment in the nether-world was accomplished, in the place which his Majesty had prepared—never had the like been done since early times—after they had fulfilled for him all that is customary, in the chambers of purification; for his Majesty bore in mind what Horus had done for his father Osiris. He had a great sarcophagus of rose granite made for him, because his Majesty approved the custom, that all the kings in every age had caused it (the sarcophagus of each Apis-bull) to be made out of costly stone. He caused curtains of woven stuffs to be made as coverings for the south side and the north side (of the sarcophagus). He had his talismans put therein, and all his ornaments of gold and costly precious stones. They were prepared more splendidly than ever before, for his Majesty had loved the living Apis better than all (the other) kings.

'The holiness of this god went to heaven in the year 23, month Phamenoth, day 6. His birth took place in the year 5, month Thot, day 7; his inauguration at Memphis in the month Payni, day 8. The full lifetime of this god amounted to 18 years, 6 months. 'This is what was done for him by Aahmes Si-Neit, who bestows pure life for ever.'

The granite sarcophagus of this bull still stands to this day *in situ* in the Serapeum. On the cover are inscribed the words :—

---

[9] From Dr. Brugsch's *Additions and Corrections*. The text of the History gives only a summary of the dates derived from the inscription.—ED.

'The king Amasis. He has caused this to be made for his memorial of the living Apis, (namely) this huge sarcophagus of red granite, for his Majesty approved the custom, that all the kings in all ages had had such made of costly stones. This did he, the bestower of life for ever.'

While we are on the subject of the Apis-bulls and their gravestones, this is the best place to remark that under the Persian Empire also, as well as afterwards under the Lagidæ, the deceased Apis-bulls were solemnly buried at the cost of the kings in the Serapeum of Memphis. Besides the embalming and the funeral pomp, the kings were put to great expense for the restoration of the subterranean tombs, which were hewn out of the rock, each already during the lifetime of the Apis for which it was destined. Besides, the construction of the sepulchral vault required some time. On a memorial tablet inscribed with demotic characters, of the time of Ptolemy II., I find the following data as to the time occupied in the work:—

	Working Time		Holidays
	Months	Days	
From the year 32, 21st Payni, to the year 33, 1st Paophi, excavating the chamber	3	15	17
From the year 33, 4th Paophi, to [the year 33, 9th Pharmuthi], finishing the same	6	5	33
In the year 37, 8th Mesori, transport of sarcophagus; time	1	5	7
In the year 38, 17th Athyr, the completion of the whole edifice; time. .	2	9	12

In the reign of Cambyses there occurred the

death of one Apis, and the birth of another. This latter was born in the 5th year of the king, on the 28th day of the month Tybi; he died in the 4th year of Darius I., on the 3rd day of the month Pakhons; and seventy days later he was buried according to the prescribed usages. The whole length of his life amounted to seven years, three months, five days. His predecessor was the very Apis whom, according to the accounts of the Greek writers, Cambyses is said to have slain with the sword, immediately after his return from his disastrous expedition against Ethiopia;—a story on which little reliance can be placed. According to an inscription, first found by me in Egypt, but unfortunately much mutilated, this Apis was buried in the Serapeum 'in the 4th year' of the king's reign, 'in the month Epiphi' (the day not being specified). On the same stone we see Cambyses represented, under his regal name of Sam-taui[1] Mastu-ra, *in a kneeling posture, distinctly as a worshipper of the Apis-bull.* Underneath is a long inscription, of which I could only make out the first two lines:—

'Year 4, month Epiphi, under the reign [of king Cambyses] the bestower of life for ever, [this] god was carried to his burial [in peace to the Libyan Desert near Memphis, to be interred] in his place, which his Majesty had already caused to be prepared for him . . .'

---

[1] This regal name, which means 'uniter of the two worlds,' had already been borne by Thutmes III. By the irony of fate, the proud title of the great Pharaoh who conquered Western Asia —the Egyptian Alexander—was transferred, after a thousand years, to the Persian conqueror of Egypt.—Ed.

Now since, according to the express testimony of the monuments, Cambyses reigned over Egypt, not three or four years, but six full years, and therefore must have conquered Egypt, not in the year 525 B.C., the date generally received, but in the year 527 B.C.,[2] —it follows, of undeniable necessity, that the Apis in question died and was buried in the year 526[3] B.C., and that too, as we read, *under the auspices of the Great King Cambyses himself*;—in other words, that the Greek story of the slaughter of the Apis by the mad Persian king is a mere fiction, invented for the purpose of setting in a striking light the wickedness and oppression of the foreign tyrant. How strongly probability contradicts the popular assumption of a slaughter of the Apis by Cambyses, is confirmed also by the following considerations. Under Amasis,[4] the Apis died in the 23rd year of the king's reign, on the sixth day of the month Phamenoth, that is to say, about the year 550. His successor, as usual, was not long waited for. Supposing this to be the same that Cambyses caused to be buried in the year 526 B.C., the bull had reached an age of about 24 to 25 years, which is in perfect accord with the average lifetime of the sacred bulls, derived from other examples.

A special inscription on a monument of the time of king Darius I.[5] informs us, that this sovereign also

[2] See further below, p. 315.
[3] This year 526 B.C. was the 4th year of the reign of Cambyses over Persia, and the 2nd year of his reign over Egypt.
[4] See above, the inscription No. V., p. 297.
[5] No. 2296 of Mariette's List.

was pleased to show marked honour to the Apis-bulls. The literal translation of the inscription runs thus :—

'In the year 31 under the Majesty of the king and lord of the land, Nthariush—may he live for ever !—behold a living Apis appeared | in the city of Memphis. This (his future) sepulchre was opened, and his chamber was built for an endless duration of years.'

This record also agrees most precisely with the age of his predecessor, who in his turn had been born not long after the burial of the bull before him (in the 4th year of Darius I., p. 299), and must have died shortly before the appearance of the one now in question, and therefore in the 31st or 30th year of Darius; whence again we deduce for him a lifetime of 24 or 25 years.

The monuments enable us to pursue still further the traces of the Apis-bulls that appeared later.

As king Darius I. still enjoyed about five years more of life, after the manifestation of the Apis in his 31st year, so, if we continue to assume a lifetime of 25 years, the new bull must have died about the 20th regnal year of Xerxes I., and therefore about 466 B.C. Now, in place of this Xerxes, we find mention of a king Khabbash, whom the monuments designate as the *Egyptian rival king* to Xerxes. (See p. 315.) This rival must have succeeded in establishing himself at Memphis, where he provided a solemn burial for the Apis which was just deceased. But unexpected events occurred to frustrate his intention. The proof of this is furnished by the place in the subterranean galleries, where have stood, from ancient times down to the present day, the lid and base of the stone sarcophagus, with the dedicatory inscription of king Khabbash. The sarcophagus itself stands in the *northern* gallery leading to the Apis-tombs, and almost bars the approach, while the lid lies on the ground in the *southern* gallery. The two were never brought together to enclose the deceased bull. The lid itself bears the following inscription :—

'Year 2, month Athyr, under the Majesty of king Kabbash, the friend of Apis-Osiris, of Horus " of Kakem " (a name for the locality of the Apis tombs).'

The latest authentic inscription, proving the death of an Apis under the Pharaohs, is a memorial-stone of the 3rd year of king Nakht-neb-ef, in which the bull died, that is, about 356 B.C. With this we conclude our review of the Apis tablets, and turn to other inscriptions, which belong to the times of the Persian kings.

§ II. THE PERSIANS IN EGYPT.

Cambyses.   Darius.   Xerxes. Artaxerxes.

We can hardly award to the Egyptian nobles, who lived in the neighbourhood of the royal court at Saïs, the praise of especial loyalty to their masters. As soon as the Persians made good their footing in Egypt and honoured Saïs especially by their visits, there were found many descendants of the former royal houses, who did not think it beneath their dignity to prove themselves submissive to the Great King of Persia, and to enter his service.

Among these there was, in particular, a Suten-rekh (i.e. 'King's-grandson'), named Uza-hor-en-pi-ris, a son of Paf-tot-nit (the high-priest of the goddess Nit) and his wife Tum-iri-tis, probably a daughter of king Apries (Uah-ab-ra). To this nobleman the command of the royal fleet had been entrusted under the kings Amasis and Psamethik III. When Cambyses conquered Egypt, Uza-hor-en-pi-ris passed at once into the service of the Persian king. On the famous shrine-bearing statue of this eminent nobleman, in the Vatican at Rome,[6] he himself relates

---

[6] Already mentioned as a work of art, p. 291. The late Viscount E. de Rougé was the first who contributed to science some fragments of the above inscription (*Revue Archéologique*, 1851). Our translation—which has profited by the latest advances in the science of deciphering the old Egyptian writings—contains for the first time the whole inscription in its entire sequence. [The tenth volume of *Records of the Past* contains a new translation of this inscription, or rather series of ten inscriptions, on the statue

quite unaffectedly the history of his life, from which we have derived the foregoing account of his family.

I. 'When the great lord of all nations, Kambathet (Cambyses), came to Egypt,—at that time the people of all lands were with him,—he ruled this land as king in its whole extent. They settled in it, inasmuch as he was a great king of Egypt and the great lord of all lands. He committed to me the office of a president of the physicians, and kept me beside him as friend and temple-master. His official name was assigned to him as "King-Mastu-ra." I made known to him the greatness of the city of Saïs, as the city of Neith, the great mother, who gave birth to the sun-god Ra—he was the first-born, no (other) being was yet born:—moreover (I informed him) also of the high consequence of the habitation of Neith—it is such as a heaven—in all its quarters:—moreover also of the high importance of the chambers of Neith, which are the abodes of Neith and of all the gods in them; as well as the high consequence of the temple Hakheb, in which the great king and lord of the heaven resides;—moreover also of the high importance of the south-chamber, of the north-chamber, of the chamber of the morning-sun Ra, and of the chamber of the evening-sun Tum. These are the mysterious abodes of all the gods.

II. 'And I made my complaint to king Kambathet concerning all the foreigners, who had taken up their quarters in the temple of Neith, that they might be driven out, that so the temple of Neith might be established in its full splendour, as was the case formerly. Then the king gave command to drive out all foreigners, who had taken up their quarters in the temple of Neith, and to pull down all their huts and all their chattels in this temple, and they themselves were forced to remove out of the precincts of this temple. The king gave command to purify this temple of Neith, and to restore to it all its inhabitants, and to acknowledge the people as

---

called 'the Pastophorus of the Vatican,' by Mr. Le Page Renouf, who reads the name of the Egyptian officer *Ut'a-Hor-resenet*. Mr. Renouf acknowledges his obligation to the above translation (in the German) of Dr. Brugsch, whose example he follows in suppressing the name and titles which begin each inscription, and for which there is often no equivalent in our modern languages. We have followed Mr. Renouf in prefixing a distinctive number to each of the separate inscriptions.—ED.]

DYN. XXVII.   INSCRIPTION OF UZA-HOR-EN-PI-RIS.   305

servants of the temple. He gave command to replace the sacred property of Neith, the great mother, and of all the gods in Saïs, as it had been formerly. He gave command to re-establish the order of all their festivals and of all their processions, as they were formerly. All this did the king, because I had made him acquainted with the high consequence of Saïs, for it is the city of all the gods. May they remain on their thrones in her for ever!

III. 'When king Kambathet came to Saïs, he entered the temple of Neith in person. He testified in every good way his reverence for the great exalted holy goddess, Neith, the great mother, and for the great gods in Saïs, as all the pious kings had done. He did this, because I had made him acquainted with the high importance of the holy goddess, for she is the mother of the Sun-god Ra himself.

IV. 'The king bestowed all that was good upon the temple of Neith. He caused the libations to be offered to the Everlasting One in the house of Neith, as all the kings of former times had done. He did this because I had informed him of all the good that should be done for this temple.

V. 'I established the property of Neith, the great mother, as the king had ordered, for the duration of eternity. I caused the monuments of Neith, the lady of Saïs, to be set up in every proper way, as an able servant of his master ought to do. I was a good man before his face. I protected the people under the very heavy misfortune which had befallen the whole land, such as this country had never experienced before. I was a shield to the weak against the powerful; I protected him who honoured me, and he found it best for him. I did all good for them, when the time had come to do it.

VI. 'I entrusted to them the prophetic offices; I gave them the best land, as the king had commanded, to endure for ever. I made a present of proper burial to such as (died) without a coffin; I nourished all their children and built up again all their houses; I did for them all that is good, as a father does for his son, then when the calamity fell upon this nome, at the time when the grievous calamity befel the whole land.

VII. 'Now king Ntariuth (Darius)—may he live for ever!—commanded me to go to Egypt, while he was in the land of Elam,—for he also was the great lord of all lands and a great king of Egypt,—in order that I might reinstate the number of the sacred

VOL. II.   X

scribes of the temples, and might revive whatever had fallen into ruin. The foreigners escorted me from land to land, and brought me safe to Egypt, according to the command of the lord of the land. I did according to what he had commanded. I chose of the sons of the inhabitants from all their (schools?)—to the great sorrow of those who were childless—and I placed them under expert masters, skilful in all kinds of learning, that they might perform all their works. And the king ordered that all favour should be shown them, because of the pleasure with which they performed all their works. I supplied all those who distinguished themselves with whatever they needed for the scribe's profession, according to their progress. The king did all this because he knew that such a work was the best means of awakening to new life all that was falling into ruin, in order to uphold the name of all the gods, their temples, their revenues, and the ordinance of their feasts for ever.

VIII. 'I was honoured by each of my masters, so long as I sojourned on the earth. Therefore they gave me decorations of gold, and showed me all favour.

IX. 'O ye gods who are in Saïs! Remember all the good that has been done by the president of the physicians, Uza-hor-en-pi-ris. In all that ye are willing to requite him for all his benefits, establish for him a great name in this land for ever.

X. 'O Osiris! thou Eternal one! The president of the physicians Uza-hor-en-pi-ris throws his arms around thee, to guard thy image. Do for him all good according to what he has done, (as) the protector of thy shrine for ever.'[7]

We refrain from any further comment on the foregoing text, the historical value of which, as the contemporary record of an eye-witness, and in part the author, of the events which he relates, can hardly be overrated. In this account, king

---

[7] The last words, addressed to Osiris, the Eternal, have relation to the particular form of the statue. The chief physician of Saïs is represented as standing upright, with his hands embracing a shrine, in the interior of which is seen the mummy of Osiris. It should not be forgotten that the Persian kings were glad to employ the Egyptian physicians, whose skill gained them high renown in the ancient world.

Cambyses appears in a totally different light from that in which school-learning places him. He takes care for the gods and their temples, and has himself crowned in Saïs after the old Egyptian manner. Darius I., whom the Egyptian Uza-hor-en-pi-ris had accompanied to Elam (Elymaïs), took particular pleasure in rescuing the Egyptian temple-learning from its threatened extinction. He provided for the training of the energetic and gifted youth in the schools of the priests, to be the future maintainers and teachers of the lost wisdom of the Egyptians.

The best proof of the lively interest, which Darius himself took in the foundation of new sanctuaries, is furnished by the temple built in the Great Oasis of El-Khargeh, at the place called by the ancients Hibis (the Hib or Hibe of the hieroglyphs). This sanctuary, which I had the opportunity of visiting in the February of 1875, in company with the hereditary Grand-duke Augustus of Oldenburg, is in a pretty good state of preservation. The names of king Darius, in the Egyptian form of Nthariush, cover the sides of the various halls and chambers, as well as the outer walls of the temple. But the variation in the official coronation names leads to the inference, that Darius II. (with the name Mi-amun-ra), took part, as well as his ancestor Darius I. (with the shield Settu-ra, i.e. Sesostris), in the building of the temple, and in its internal and external ornamentation.[8]

[8] The inscription of Darius at the temple of El-Khargeh has been translated by Dr. Birch in the *Transactions of the Society of Biblical Archæology*, vol. v. pp. 293, foll. (with the original text), and in *Records of the Past*, vol. viii. pp. 135, foll.—ED.

The temple of Hibis was dedicated to the Theban Amon, under his special surname of Us-khopesh ('the strong-armed'). The record of the works executed by Darius II., on the northern outer wall, runs as follows:—

'He did this in remembrance of his father, the great god Amon-ra, the lord of Hibe, with the Strong Arm, and his associated gods, inasmuch as he built this new house of good white stone in the form of a Mesket.[9] Its doors were formed of the Libyan acacia-wood, which is called Pir-shennu, and covered with Asiatic bronze in well-wrought lasting work. His (the god's) monument was renewed according to its original plan. May the gods preserve him among living men for hundreds of thousands of thirty years' jubilee-feasts on the throne [of Horus], to-day and for ever and eternally!'

As we have already shown, the building and decoration of the temple was continued to the times of king Nakht-hor-hib (378–360 B.C.) No later names of kings appear there.[1]

The buildings erected here and elsewhere by king Darius were entrusted to an Egyptian architect, whose pedigree—up to his forefathers of the times of the Third Dynasty—we have been so fortunate as to suc-

---

[9] See above, p. 102.

[1] For further information about the temple and its inscriptions, I would refer to my work on the *Oasis of El-Khargeh and its Temple-ruins*, which is now [1877] in the press. [The work referred to has been since published, under the title of '*Reise nach dem grossen Oase el Khargeh in der libyschen Wüste*. Von Heinrich Brugsch-Bey.' Besides a full archæological account of the Great Oasis, down to Roman and Christian times, and translations of two very interesting inscriptions, containing hymns of the time of Darius II., the work abounds in new information on the secret writing, the mysteries of Osiris, and other matters concerning the geography, language, and mythology of ancient Egypt.—ED.]

(*Table to p.* 310.)

THE PEDIGREE OF THE ARCHITECTS.

IMHOTEP:	Architect of S. and N. Egypt; chief burgomaster; a high functionary of king Z'a-sar; (lived in the time of the Third Dynasty).
R'A-HOTEP:	Prophet of Amon-ra, king of the gods; secret-seer of Heliopolis: Architect of Upper and Lower Egypt; chief burgomaster.
BOK-EN-KHUNSU:	Chief burgomaster.
UZA-KHUNSU:	Architect; chief burgomaster.
NOFER-MENNU:	Architect; chief burgomaster.
MI (or Ai?)	Architect; chief burgomaster.
SI-UER-NENEN-HIB:	Architect.
PEPI:	Architect; chief burgomaster.
AMON-HIR-PI-MESH'A:	2nd, 3rd, and 4th prophet and high-priest of Amon, king of the gods; chief burgomaster.
HOR-EM-SAF:	Architect; chief burgomaster.
MERMER:	Architect; commander.
HOR-EM-SAF:	Architect; commander.
ZA-HIB:	Architect; commander.
NAS-SHUNU:	Architect; commander.
ZA-HIB:	Architect; commander.
NAS-SHUNU:	Architect; commander.
ZA-HIB:	Architect; commander.
NAS-SHUNU:	Architect; commander.
ZA-N-HIBU:	Architect of Upper and Lower Egypt; chief burgomaster.
NAS-SHUNU:	Architect.
UAH-AB-R'A RAN-UËR:	Architect.
'ANKH-PSAMTHIK:	Architect of Upper and Lower Egypt.
A'AHMES-SI-NIT: (*m.* SIT-NOFER-TUM)	Architect of Upper and Lower Egypt.
KHNUM-AB-R'A:	Chief minister of works for the whole country; architect of Upper and Lower Egypt, in the 27th to 30th years of king Darius I. (about 490 B.C.)

ceed in establishing, by the help of a dedicatory inscription in the valleys of Hammamat. We repeat the pedigree here, with the correction of some transcriptions of the proper names from a new copy of the inscription (p. 309).

Some lesser inscriptions of this same architect Khnum-ab-r'a—who has left us such valuable materials for determining the sequence of the generations —inform us that he held his office during the years 27 to 30 of king Darius I. The inscription of the 30th year runs thus :—

'On the 15th day of the month Pharmuthi, in the 30th year of the king of Upper and Lower Egypt and lord of the land, Nthariush (Darius I.), the ever-living, the friend of all the gods, (this was written by order of) the master of works in the whole land, the architect of Upper and Lower Egypt, Khnum-ab-r'a, son of the architect of Upper and Lower Egypt, A'ahmes-Si-nit.'

We have already shown[2] that his ancestor, the first Hor-em-saf, stands exactly on the genealogical line of Shashanq I., whose inscription in the quarries at Silsilis mentions an architect Hor-em-saf.

It is well known that Darius I. conceived the bold plan of connecting the Red Sea with the Nile by a canal. The remains of a statue of the king, as well as several memorial stones covered with triplicate cuneiform inscriptions and with Egyptian hieroglyphics, which have been found near the line of the canal (North of Suez), place the fact beyond all doubt. Science has to thank the acuteness of the celebrated cuneiform decipherer, Jules Oppert,[3] for

---

[2] See above, p. 220.
[3] *Mémoire sur les rapports de l'Egypte et de l'Assyrie*,

having made the contents of these tablets accessible to all by his translations. We subjoin the translation, after Oppert, of the best preserved and clearest of the inscriptions :—

'A great god is Auramazda, who created this heaven, who created this earth, who created man, who gave to man a will, who established Darius as king, who committed to king Darius so great, so [glorious] an empire.

'I am Darius, king of kings, king of lands of many tongues, king of this great earth, far and near, the son of Hystaspes, the Achæmenid.

'Says Darius the king: "I am a Persian; with (the power of) Persia I conquered Egypt (Mudrâya). I ordered this canal to be dug, from the river called Pirâva (the Nile), which flows in Egypt, to the sea which comes out of Persia.[4] This canal was afterwards dug there, as I had commanded, and I said: 'Go, and destroy half of the canal from Bira [5] to the coast.' For such was my will."'

According to Strabo's statement, cited by Oppert,[6] Darius left off constructing the canal, because some had assured him that Egypt lay below the level of the Red Sea, and so the danger was threatened of seeing the whole land laid under water.

pp. 125, f. As before, we have collated Dr. Brugsch's translation with M. Oppert's Latin and French versions.—ED.

[4] This seems to apply to the Erythræan Sea, in the wide sense in which the name is used by Herodotus, including what is now called the Arabian Sea, with the Persian Gulf and Red Sea, the latter having also the special name of the Arabian Gulf.—ED.

[5] May we perhaps understand by Bira the Egyptian Pi-ra 'the [city of] the Sun,' namely, Heliopolis?

[6] Strabo, xvii. p. 804. Oppert's own words will be found interesting :—' We can read through the laconism of this inscription, which, allowing for the position in which the king places himself, nevertheless establishes a failure. Darius wished to unite the Nile and the sea by a fresh-water canal; to resume and finish the work

As we have thus far mentioned the Egyptian officers who, under the Persians, rendered their service to the Great King, so, on the other hand, we must not pass over in silence the Persian courtiers who, as we learn from the Egyptian monuments, were settled in the Nile-valley as officers of the king.

Though we possess no records, in the Egyptian language, attesting the presence of the satrap Aryandes, who, as we learn from the ancient writers, governed Egypt in the names of kings Cambyses and Darius I., yet other persons of Persian extraction are named, some acquaintance with whom is important in a twofold relation.

The city of Coptos,—at the western terminus of the great caravan route, which led through the desert valleys of Hammamat from the Red Sea (near the modern Qosseir) to the Nile—was for a long course of years the residence of two eminent Persians, who were invested with the office of an Erpa (governor) under the great kings just named. They were two brothers, named Ataiuhi (also written Athiuhi), and Aliurta, sons of a certain Arthames and his Persian wife Qanzu. Both are designated as Seres (i.e. eunuchs) of Parse (Persia). Posted at Coptos—in which city the god of the mountaineers, Khim (the Egyptian Pan), was held in the highest honour—the two brothers had

which had been attributed first to Sesostris, and which Neco, the son of Psammetichus, had in vain tried to accomplish. But neither was Darius able to bring the work to a successful issue.' Then follows the reference to Strabo, who knew the fallacy of the opinion which, however, was current even to our own times : he says of Darius, ὁ ξὴ ψευδεῖ πεισθεὶς ἀφῆκε τὸ ἔργον περὶ συντέλειαν ἤδη.—ED.

frequent occasion to visit the valleys of Hammamat on the king's business, in order to have stones quarried for the materials of the royal Persian buildings. Through their long residence in the country they seem to have adopted Egyptian manners and customs, and so, like all earlier visitors of the times of the Pharaohs, they did not disdain to perpetuate their names on hieroglyphic memorial-tablets in that valley. The representations of the god Khim of Coptos are accompanied by hieroglyphic writing, in which the names of the 'eunuchs of Persia' are preceded, whenever they occur, by chronological data. In stating these, however, they departed from the old Egyptian rule, inasmuch as, instead of the current regnal year of the sovereigns in question, they chose to exhibit the full sum of the years of their reigns, and also the full sum of their own years of service under one or more kings, with the addition of *ar en*, 'has made,' i.e. lived during, (so many years); just as in the case of the name of Taharaqa on the Apis-stelæ.[7] Some examples of these inscriptions will illustrate this mode of dating :—

FIRST INSCRIPTION.

'The sum of the 6 years of the lord of the land Kanbuza (Cambyses), the sum of the 36 years of the sovereign Nthariush (Darius I.), and the sum of the 12 years of the sovereign Khshiarsh (Xerxes I.), has the eunuch of Persia (*seres en Parse*) Ataiuhi lived, remaining in the presence of the god Khim, the chief of the city.'

SECOND INSCRIPTION.

'The sum of the 36 years of the godlike benefactor and sovereign, the son of the Sun and wearer of the crown, Nthariush

---

[7] See above, p. 295.

(Darius I.)—may he live to-day and evermore!—and | the sum of the 13 years of his son, the sovereign, the son of the Sun and wearer of the crown, Khshiarsh (Xerxes I.)—may he live to-day and evermore!—has lived the eunuch of Persia and governor of the city of Coptos, Athiuhi.'

Third Inscription.

'The 5 years of the king of Upper and Lower Egypt, the sovereign, Arta-khshesesh (Artaxerxes), and | the 16 years of the god-like benefactor Arta-khshesesh (Artaxerxes) | has lived the eunuch of Persia Aliurta, the son of Arthames and the child of his wife Qanzu, remaining before the face of the [god Khim of Coptos].'

A comparison of all these rock-inscriptions gives the following determination of the regnal years of the kings, in their relation to the years of service of the two Persians.

Athiui lived—
(1) 6 full years under the reign of Kanbuza (Cambyses);
(2) 36 ,, ,, ,, ,, ,, Nthariush (Darius I.);
(3) 2 ,, ,,
(4) 6 ,, ,,
(5) 10 ,, ,, under the reign of Khshiarsh (Xerxes I.).
(6) 12 ,, ,,
(7) 16 ,, ,,

Aliurta lived—
(1) 5 ,, ,, under the reign of Arta-khshesesh
(2) 16 ,, ,, (Artaxerxes).

That the phrase 'he lived' referred, not to the whole lifetime of the person from his birth, but to his actual years of service spent in Egypt, is proved by the dates given in the two inscriptions of Aliurta, who expressed the five years, besides the sixteen years, in order to put before the reader's eyes his service under Artaxerxes. And we draw this further conclusion, that, if Cambyses reigned six years as king of Egypt, the conquest of Egypt must be placed, not in the year 525, but in 527, as we have shown before.

King Xerxes I.—or, as he is named in the Egyptian inscriptions, Khshiarsh or Khsherish—did not enjoy the best reputation among the Egyptians, who had learnt to esteem his predecessor, Darius I., as a benignant and well-disposed ruler. After Xerxes had by force of arms crushed the insurrection made by the Egyptians to throw off the Persian yoke, the foreign rule pressed more severely than ever on the land, over which Achæmenes, the king's brother, was placed as satrap.

The defeats which the Persians soon after suffered from Greek valour roused anew the desire of the Egyptians for liberty, and an anti-king Khabbash, with the coronation name of Senen-Tanen Sotep-en-ptah, boldly made head against the Persian sovereign. The memorial inscription of the satrap Ptolemy, already cited,[8] recals the memory of the anti-king in the following terms:—

'The sea-board, which bears the name of Patanut (in Greek, Phthenotes), had been assigned by the king Khabbash to the gods

---

[8] See above, p. 289, note. The tenth volume of *Records of the Past* (pp. 67, foll.) contains an English translation, by Mr. Drach, of Dr. Brugsch's German translation of the whole inscription in the *Zeitschrift für Aegypt. Sprach.* Jan. 1871. The title of 'satrap,' used by the future founder of the dynasty of the Ptolemies, refers to his nominal subjection to Alexander Ægus, the son of Alexander the Great and Roxana (B.C. 323–311), in whose 7th year the inscription is dated. See also Dr. Birch's Paper on the Tablet in the *Transactions of the Society of Biblical Archæology*, vol. i. p. 20.—ED.

of the city of Buto, when his Majesty had gone to Buto to examine the sea-board, which lies in their whole domain, with the purpose of penetrating into the interior of the marsh-land of Natho, to inspect that arm of the Nile, which flows into the sea, in order that the Asiatic fleet might be kept at a distance from Egypt.

'This lake-district, called Patanut, belonged to the deities of Buto from early times. But the hereditary foe Xerxes had alienated it. He kept none of it for the gods of the city of Buto.

'Thus the hereditary foe Xerxes had shown an evil example against the city of Buto. But the great king, our lord, the god Horus, the son of Isis and the son of Osiris, the prince of the princes, the king of the kings of Upper and Lower Egypt, the avenger of his father, the lord of Buto, the beginning of the gods and he who came after, after whom no (god) was king, he drove out the hereditary enemy Xerxes out of his palace together with his eldest son, and so he made himself famous in Saïs, the city of the goddess Neith, on that day by the side of the Mother of the Gods.'

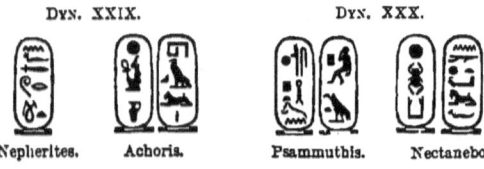

Dyn. XXIX. Dyn. XXX.

Nepherites. Achoris. Psammuthis. Nectanebo.

§ III. THE LAST PHARAOHS.

Once more, after the retreat of the Persians, a ray of hope for freedom dawned upon the Egyptians.[9] During a period of about sixty years, two dynasties (the Twenty-ninth and Thirtieth) established themselves, at Mendes and Sebennytus, on the ruins of the past ages, to venture on the last effort to reconquer their lost independence. The monuments, on which the names of the kings of these dynasties can only be discovered

[9] See the NOTE inserted after Chapter XX.—ED.

with difficulty, are silent about their deeds. The hour of Egypt's death had struck. No god had the power to grant the land the respite of a longer existence.

As the most remarkable monument of their times, we may point to a sarcophagus of dark granite, which belonged to a descendant of the last kings of the Thirtieth Dynasty.[1] The inscriptions upon it have accurately preserved for us its owner's pedigree, as a valuable memorial of the former greatness of ancient Egypt. We subjoin it, according to the indications of the hieroglyphs, in the following translation:—

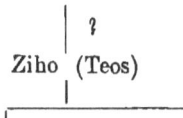

KING NAKHT-HOR-IB.
|
?
Ziho (Teos)
|

Nes-bi-n-didi, = Mertuhap *   KING NAKHT-NEB-EF
a military   (*the last Pharaoh*).
commander,   Thakebes * = Petamon, hereditary prince and
nomarch of   military commander.
Sebennytus.   NAKHT-NEB-EF,
nomarch of the district of Buto, Sebennytus and Tanis,
commander-in-chief of the king.

* *The names thus marked are those of women.*

Nakhtnebef, 'the chief captain of his Majesty,' the grandson of the last Pharaoh, Nakhtnebef, had his last resting-place in that Berlin sarcophagus of stone. But who was 'his Majesty,' to whom he gave his service as commander? The question can only be answered approximately. As grandson of king Nakhtnebef, who reigned over the land from 358–340 B.C.,

[1] Now in the Royal Museum at Berlin. [Another sarcophagus, which vies with this in beauty, is that of king Nakht-Hor-ib, in the British Museum.—ED.]

the end of his life falls about sixty years after his grandfather's death, and therefore about 280 B.C., that is, about fifty years after the conquest of Egypt by Alexander the Great. He could not therefore have served either him or his immediate successors, Philip Arrhidæus and Alexander II., as commander. We must rather reckon Ptolemy I. Soter, or Ptolemy II. Philadelphus, as his contemporary. From these calculations we should be already carried over into the history of Egypt under the Ptolemies.

TOMB AT SAQQARAH, INSCRIBED WITH THE NAME OF PSAMMETICHUS.

Alexander.   Philip Arrhidæus.   Ptolemy Soter.

CHAPTER XX.

FALL OF THE KINGDOM OF THE PHARAOHS.

As through a thin transparent mist, we cast a glance at the close of our historical subject—the climax and fall of the Pharaohs—with the perusal of the following inscription of an eminent priest, a contemporary of the Persian great king, Darius III., and of the hero Alexander of Macedon. His own words are engraved on a memorial stone, which is now preserved in the collection of Greek and Roman antiquities at Naples. The translation will form a fit conclusion to our History of Egypt according to the Monuments.

'(1) The hereditary prince, the noble, one of the friends; the seer of Horus, the lord of Hibonu (Hipponon); the seer of the gods of the nome of Hibonu; the seer of the god Samtaui, of the city of (2) A-hehu: the chief seer of the goddess and the president of the priests of Sokhet in the whole land—SAMTAUI-TAF-NAKHT—the son of the temple-master and (3) seer of the god Amon-ra, the lord of the city Pi-sha, Nes-samtaui-auf-'ankh, and the child of his wife 'Ankhet: he speaks as follows:—

'O thou lord of the gods, Khnum, thou king of Upper and Lower Egypt, (4) thou prince of the land, at whose rising the world is enlightened, whose right eye is the sun's disk, whose left eye is the moon, whose spirit (5) is the beam of light, and out of whose nostrils comes the North wind, to give life to all.

'I was thy servant, who did according to thy will, and whose heart was replenished by thee. (6) I have not let any city be higher than thy city, I have not failed to impart of thy spirit to all the children of men among hundreds of thousands, which (spirit) is the most wonderful in all houses, (7) day by day. Thou hast for this recompensed me good a hundred-thousandfold. Thus wast thou diffused everywhere, and (wast made) a leader for the king's house. The heart of the divine benefactor was moved to clemency (8) at my speech. I was exalted to be the first among hundreds of thousands. *When thou turnedst thy back upon the land of Egypt, thou didst incline thyself in thy heart to the master of Asia.* His (9) twice five friends loved me. He conferred on me the office of president of the priests of the goddess Sokhet on the seat of my mother's brother, the president of the goddess Sokhet (10) in Upper and Lower Egypt, Ser-honb. *Thou didst protect me in the battle of the Ionians* (i.e. the army of Alexander) *when thou didst rout the Asiatic* (Darius III.).

'(11) They slew a hundred thousand at my side, (but) none lifted up his hand against me. When what befel had befallen, there was peace (12) afterwards. Thy Holiness spake to me: "Proceed to Khinensu (Heracleopolis Magna); I will be with thee; I will be thy guide among the foreign people."

'(13) I was alone, I sailed up the great stream; I was not afraid, for I thought of thee. Since I did not transgress thy commandment, I reached the city of Khinensu (14) without having a hair of my head rumpled. And as was the beginning, only by the one appointment of thy decree, so also was the end, for thou gavest me a long life in peace of heart.

'(15) O all ye priests, who serve this glorious god Khnum, the king of both worlds, the (god) Hormakhu, the lord of the universe, the good spirit in the city of Khinensu, (16) the (god) Tum in the city of Tanis, the king of the rams, the primordial male power, the Majesty of the ram, the male, the begetter, the last king of the kings of the land;—(17) the son, who loved the king of Upper and Lower Egypt, has departed to the heavenly kingdom, to see what is there: (to see) the god Khnum, the king of Upper and Lower Egypt, the god Tum in his shrine, Khnum, (18) the great god in his hall, the king Unnofer.

'May your name remain for ever upon the earth, reaping the reward of honour from Khnum, the king of both worlds! And sing ye praise and laud to the kingly gods of Khinensu, and praise ye the image of the godlike, who was reverenced in his nome, SAM-TAUI-TAF-NAKHT: so shall all that is best be your portion, and another will praise your name in turn in years to come.'

SUPPLEMENTARY NOTE BY THE EDITOR.

HISTORY OF EGYPT FROM PSAMMETICHUS TO PTOLEMY.

Dr. Brugsch's plan, of excluding all historical information from any other sources than the monuments, necessarily gives an air of incompleteness to this concluding period, for the *authentic* evidence of contemporary writers is as abundant as the notices on the monuments are scanty. It may therefore be an acceptable service to readers who are not already familiar with the subject, if we fill up what our Author has designedly omitted, by a brief consecutive outline of the history of Egypt's revival under the New Monarchy, and her final conquest by the Persians, down to the time when these were expelled by Alexander the Great and the long Greek Dynasty of the Ptolemies was established in Egypt. The outline now given may be filled up by the reader from Mr. Sharpe's excellent *History of Egypt*; Dr. Birch's summary, entitled *Egypt from the Earliest Times to* B.C. 300 (Christian Knowledge Society); the present Editor's *Student's Ancient History of the East*; and especially the full and learned work of Dr. Alfred Wiedemann, *Geschichte Aegyptens von Psammetich I. bis auf Alexander den Grossen* (Leipzig, 1880).

§ I. EGYPT'S RECOVERED INDEPENDENCE UNDER THE TWENTY-SIXTH DYNASTY OF SAÏS (B.C. 666-527).—Though Herodotus, who is our chief authority for this period, did not write till a hundred years after its close, and though his story is not free from some admixture of fable, yet the generally authentic character of the history is marked by the line which he so emphatically draws at this point of his work :—'In what follows I have the authority, not of the Egyptians only, but also of others who agree with them.'[1] It is at this epoch also, as we have seen Dr. Brugsch stating more than once, that the *certain chronology of Egypt begins*; and the dates derived from the Greek authors and the parallel parts of Scripture history are confirmed, with some corrections, from the invaluable data of the Apis tombstones. (See pp. 294, foll.)

---

[1] Herod. ii. 147.

1. The cessation of invasions, from the Ethiopians on the one side and the Assyrians on the other, left the petty kings of Lower Egypt free to settle the question of supremacy among themselves. After a struggle, the details of which are involved in fable, but chiefly (it seems) by the aid of Greek mercenaries, the united crown was secured by PSAMETHIK, with the regal name RA-UAH-AB, whom the Greeks call Psammetichus or Psammitichus, son of that Neku (Necho), who figures in the annals of Assurbanipal as king of Memphis and Saïs (see Chap. XVIII. pp. 269, 270), and who had been put to death by Sabaco (Herod. ii. 152; see p. 277). By his marriage with the Ethiopian princess, Shep-en-apet, Psammetichus legitimated his sovereignty over Upper Egypt (see p. 281); and the reunited kingdom enjoyed very high prosperity under his reign of fifty-four years (B.C. 666–612). He first established commercial intercourse with the Greeks, and allowed their merchants to settle in Egypt. He enlisted a force of Greek mercenaries, but the favour he showed them alienated the Egyptian and Libyan soldiers, who, to the number of 200,000, deserted in a body and marched away to Ethiopia. Though this disaster is, naturally enough, not attested by Egyptian monumental records, it is confirmed by a Greek inscription at Ibsamboul, carved by the mercenaries on their return from the fruitless pursuit of the deserters. He formed a fleet by the aid of the Phœnicians; and in the decay of Assyria, he attempted to recover the Egyptian empire in Western Asia, but the scheme was checked by the resistance of Ashdod, which he only took after a siege of twenty-nine years.

2. But the possession of this *strong* place (such is the meaning of the name Ashdod) opened the old Asiatic road to his son NEKU or NECHAO II., with the regal name RA-OUAH-EM-AB (the Pharaoh-Necho of Scripture) (B.C. 612–596), at the very crisis of the fall of the Assyrian monarchy. The opposition of the king of Judah was crushed, and Josiah himself slain, at the battle of Megiddo;[2] and the border of the Egyptian Empire was once more fixed for a moment at the Euphrates, where Carchemish again received an Egyptian garrison (B C. 610). But the tide of dominion was quickly rolled back by the new power of Babylon. Nebuchadnezzar crushed the Egyptian army at Carchemish, marched upon Jerusalem, and received the submission of Jehoiakim, whom Necho

---

[2] See *Student's Old Test. History*, p. 499.

had placed on the throne of Judah, thus annihilating at one blow the newly recovered power of Egypt in Western Asia (B.C. 605). In the words of the prophet Jeremiah, 'Pharaoh, king of Egypt, had passed the time appointed,' and his own land was doomed to an invasion by Nebuchadnezzar, as disastrous as that by the Assyrians under Assur-bani-pal.[3] The danger was averted for the moment, as Nebuchadnezzar, suddenly recalled to Babylon to secure his succession on the death of his father Nabopolassar (B.C. 604), made peace with Necho, who was left at liberty to carry on his plans for the improvement of Egypt and the consolidation of his military and naval force. He maintained fleets both at the mouths of the Nile and on the Red Sea; and the latter is said to have accomplished the circumnavigation of Africa—a feat in which Herodotus disbelieved for reasons which really furnish evidence in its favour; but modern opinion seems hopelessly divided on the question of its real performance.[4]

A more certain enterprise is the attempt of Necho to reconstruct the canal, which had been made by Seti I. and Ramses II., from the Nile to the Red Sea. The tradition ascribing this work to the great Sesostris, on the united testimony of Aristotle, Strabo, and Pliny, is confirmed by the fragments of stones bearing the name of Ramses II. along its line. Unlike the great modern canal of M. de Lesseps, which goes nearly in a straight line north and south from the Mediterranean to the Red Sea, the ancient *freshwater* canal left the Pelusiac arm of the Nile a little above Bubastus, and went by a circuitous course, first eastward to Lake Timsah, whence it turned south almost parallel to the modern canal, along the west side of the Great Bitter Lake to the head of the Gulf of Suez. The failure of Necho, after spending the lives of 120,000 Egyptians on the work, was veiled under the alleged command of an oracle to desist. The subsequent attempt and failure of Darius I. has been noticed in the text (pp. 310-11).

3. Under Necho's son, PSAMETHIK II., with the regal name RA-NOFER-HET, the PSAMMIS of Herodotus and PSAMMUTHIS of Manetho, who reigned only five or six years (B.C. 596-591), war was renewed with the Ethiopian kingdom of Napata, and the king died just after his return from an expedition against that country.

4. His son, UAHABRA, with the regal name RA-HAA-AB, the

---

[3] Jeremiah xlvi.
[4] See the *Student's Ancient History of the East*, pp. 148, 149.

PHARAOH-HOPHRA of Scripture (Οὐαφρῆ, LXX.), whom Manetho calls VAPHRES, and Herodotus APRIES (B.C. 591-572), resumed the ambitious projects of Necho in Western Asia; and for a short time he succeeded so well that, Herodotus tells us, Apries believed there was not a god who could cast him down from his eminence, so firmly did he think he had established himself in his kingdom.[5] The historian himself esteemed Apries as, with the exception of his great-grandfather Psammetichus, the most prosperous of all the kings that ever ruled over Egypt [6] (meaning, of course, in the more recent times within historic knowledge). He marched an army to attack Sidon, and fought a battle with the king of Tyre at sea. The ruins of an Egyptian temple of this age at Gebel in Phœnicia seem to prove that the country was restored for some time to the subjection in which it had been held by the great kings of the Eighteenth and Nineteenth Dynasties.[7] In pursuance of the attempt to recover the supremacy of Egypt in Western Asia, Pharaoh-Hophra made a league with Zedekiah, to support that vassal king of Judah in rebelling against Nebuchadnezzar;[8] and by advancing with an army, which took Gaza, he forced Nebuchadnezzar to raise the siege of Jerusalem and march against him.[9] According to Josephus, the Egyptians were defeated in battle, but the contemporary prophets, Jeremiah and Ezekiel, seem rather to imply that they retreated without venturing to make a stand.[1] Pharaoh-Hophra gave the Jews no further help, but only a refuge in Egypt for the remnant that escaped from the destruction of Jerusalem [2] (B.C. 586).

He had, however, done enough to provoke the vengeance of Nebuchadnezzar against Egypt denounced by Jeremiah in his prophecy made twenty years before, and now repeated both by him and Ezekiel.[3] Here again, as in the famous prophecy of Nahum about the Assyrian invasions,[4] the inspired voice of prophecy reflects, in images as vivid as any historic narrative, events which

---

[5] Herod. ii. 169.   [6] Ibid. 161.
[7] Renan, *Mission de Phénicie*, and De Rougé, *Sur les débris égyptiens trouvés en Phénicie par M. Renan*, cited by Maspero, *Histoire Ancienne de l'Orient*, p. 505.
[8] Ezek. xvii. 15.   [9] Jer. xlvii. 1-7.
[1] Jer. xxxvii. 5-8; Ezek. xvii. 17.   [2] Jer. xliii. 5-7.
[3] Jer. xlvi.; Ezek. xxix., xxx., xxxi.   [4] See p. 274.

have escaped the notice of history, or have been only partly preserved by it, till modern research recovers them in the contemporary and official records buried for nearly twenty-five centuries. Writing when Pharaoh-Hophra was in the height of pride, and preparing to march to the aid of Judah, both the prophets declare that the land and spoil and people of Egypt, with Amon in Thebes and all their gods, should be given into the hand of Nebuchadnezzar; that Pharaoh himself should be given into the hand of his enemies who sought his life; and that Egypt, after being desolated 'from Migdol to Syene and the border of Ethiopia,' was to be restored as 'the basest of the kingdoms'—that is, as a subject and tributary state, nevermore to 'exalt itself to rule over the nations.' Awaiting the light, which is now being gained step by step from the cuneiform annals of Nebuchadnezzar, we have to be content with the statement preserved by Josephus [5] from the Babylonian historian Berosus, that Nebuchadnezzar led an army into Egypt to punish Vaphres (Hophra) for the aid he had given to Zedekiah, that he *conquered* the land, put Vaphres himself to death, and set up a new king as his own vassal.

This shameful catastrophe was probably glozed over by the Egyptian priests of Saïs in the story which they told Herodotus of the fall of Apries.[6] His ambition led him to attempt the conquest of the Greek colony of Cyrene, against which he sent a vast army of *Egyptians*—an indication that the desertion of the military caste under Psammetichus had been repaired, probably from their descendants left behind in Egypt. Marching forth in their old native pride, and despising their unknown enemy, the Egyptian warriors suffered a severe defeat from the Greeks. Already doubtless predisposed to jealousy by the favour shown to the king's Greek mercenaries, they cried out that they were betrayed and sent purposely to destruction. 'They believed that he had wished a great number of them to be slain, in order that he might reign the more securely over the rest of the Egyptians.' Marching back in open mutiny, in which they were joined by the friends of the slain,

---

[5] Joseph. *Antiq.* x. 9, § 7; *c. Apion.* i. 19. The evident confusion in the two passages suggests *two* invasions of Egypt, which is the more probable, as we have presently to adduce the *original* evidence of another invasion some years later.

[6] Herod. ii. 161, f.; iv. 159.

they were met by an envoy of the king, who bore the famous name of the founder of the Eighteenth Dynasty, Aahmes, in Greek Amasis. As he was haranguing the mutineers, a soldier, coming behind him, placed a crown upon his head, and the army saluted him as king. He led them against Apries, who, abandoned by the Egyptians, led out his 30,000 mercenaries to an unequal battle at Momemphis, where he was utterly defeated and brought back a prisoner to the palace at Saïs. After a time, Amasis was forced to give him up to his Egyptian enemies—'into the hands of all that hated him,' as Jeremiah had foretold, and Herodotus relates : 'Then the Egyptians took him and strangled him, but, having done so, they buried him in the sepulchre of his fathers.'[7]

Each of these two accounts may contain parts of the true story. At the time of the destruction of Jerusalem, Nebuchadnezzar had still on his hands the long siege of Tyre, which, according to the more probable view of the disputed chronology, occupied him for some years longer, during which he had to postpone his revenge on Egypt. The enterprise of Apries against Cyrene may have been undertaken during the latter part of this interval of respite; and the civil war, which ensued upon its disastrous issue, may have been ended by the intervention of Nebuchadnezzar. Or, it seems far from improbable that Amasis may have purchased the confirmation of his usurped crown by giving up his defeated rival—not to the Egyptians, as the priests of Saïs said, but to the offended king of Babylon.

5. At all events it seems certain that the prosperity of the long reign of AMASIS (B.C. 572-528) was secured *at first* by his submission to the suzerainty of Nebuchadnezzar, and the connection was drawn closer by the marriage of the Egyptian princess, who bore the same name as the famous queen of the Sixth Dynasty Nitocris (Neitaker)—a name denoting the royal race of Saïs, the special city of Neit.[8] Like former winners of the crown in olden times, Amasis, who was born in a low condition at Siouph, in the Saïte nome, legitimated his power by a marriage with Ankhs-en-Ranofrehet, the daughter of Psamethik II., and he assumed the additional name of Si-nit ('son of Neit.') His full regal style is

---

[7] Herod. ii. 169.

[8] Further light is needed on the date of Nitocris, and her precise relationship to the royal families both of Egypt and of Babylon.

Khnum-ab-r'a Aahmes Si-Neit.[9] But unlike those kings who had submitted to all the burthensome state and priestly rules that fettered Pharaoh, Amasis clung to the free habits of his old life with his comrades, but not at all to the neglect of his regal duties. From early dawn to the busy hours of the forenoon he transacted all affairs that were brought before him, and he spent the rest of the day in drinking and jesting with his guests. The remonstrances of his friends, who would have had the Egyptians see him always in royal dignity on his throne, were met by the proverb of not keeping the bow always bent. This behaviour was suited to the new times, and so was the full encouragement he gave to foreign commerce. He allowed the Greeks a permanent settlement at Naucratis, on the Canopic branch of the Nile; and he granted sites for temples to those who only wished to trade upon the coast. The example of Greek art in these buildings, with their sculptures, must have contributed to that new character of refinement in the Egyptian works of this age, on which Dr. Brugsch has laid so much stress (Chap. XIX. pp. 291-2). Amasis showed his sympathy with the Hellenic world by contributing to the rebuilding of the temple at Delphi, when it was burnt in B.C. 548, and by dedicating statues in various Greek temples; while he adorned his own land with admirable works of art.[1] Herodotus reports the saying, 'that the reign of Amasis was the most prosperous time that Egypt ever saw; the river was more bountiful to the land, and the land brought forth more abundantly for the service of man than had ever been known before; and the number of inhabited cities was not less than twenty thousand.'[2]

It was only natural that so able, active, and prosperous a ruler should have aimed at recovering independence, and the opportunity was offered by the rapid decline of Babylon under the successors of Nebuchadnezzar, and the ensuing contest of Crœsus and Cyrus for supremacy. But even during the reign of the great king of Babylon Amasis seems to have made an attempt to shake off the yoke, and thereby to have brought on Egypt another invasion. We learn this from one of those new discoveries which

---

[9] See the inscriptions, pp. 298, 310.

[1] For an account of these, see the *Student's Ancient History of the East*, pp. 153, 154.

[2] Herod. ii. 177.

are rapidly restoring to our knowledge the long-lost original history of the East. Mr. Theophilus G. Pinches, of the British Museum, has deciphered the cuneiform inscriptions on a fragment of a tablet, containing the records of one year of Nebuchadnezzar's reign, namely the 37th = B.C. 572.[3] One side of the tablet, after the usual invocation and thanks to some deity, relates that *somebody* revolted, trusting to his army, and that *some one* went down to *Mitsir* to make battle. This *some one* was doubtless a general of Nebuchadnezzar, and by *Mitsir* we can only understand the *Mizraim* of Scripture, the *Muzur* of the Assyrian records. As to the *somebody* who revolted, we are left in no doubt by the other side of the fragment, which (says Mr. Pinches) 'begins by stating that *the king of Mitsir* collected his [troops], and from the words that follow it seems as if the king of Mitsir had *bribed the people of the sea-coast* (evidently the Mediterranean) to help him; but the mutilated state of the record makes the translation of the passage very doubtful. Soldiers, horses, and chariots (?) are then mentioned, and the next line states that some persons agreed to help him, and that the person helped trusted to them. After this the ends of a few lines only appear, and then the record breaks off altogether.' The supposition, which seems established by the words and date of the record, that it refers to a revolt of Amasis, 'is strengthened by the fact that the words *king of Mitsir* are, in one place, preceded by the syllable *śu*, which may be completed *A-ma-a-śu*, the probable Babylonian form of the name *Amasis*.'

The 'bribing the people of the sea-coast' is in striking agreement with what Herodotus tells us of the foreign policy of Amasis. He followed the example of Necho in keeping up his navy, and used it to conquer Cyprus, which was a dependency of Phœnicia. He maintained relations with the Greeks of Asia Minor, and his alliance with Polycrates, tyrant of Samos, has become for ever famous by one of the most romantic stories of ancient history.[4] The doom which Polycrates foresaw for the too prosperous man, whose sacrifice of his choicest treasure was refused by the gods, was at last brought upon him by his alliance with Crœsus, king of Lydia, and Nabonidus, king of Babylon, in the effort to resist the

---

[3] *Proceedings of the Society of Biblical Archæology*, Dec. 3, 1878.

[4] Herod. iii. 39–43; Schiller, *Der Ring des Polykrates*, beautifully translated by Lord Lytton, *Schiller's Ballads*.

conquering power of Persia. He seems, indeed, to have made his peace with Cyrus, but Cambyses had no sooner succeeded to the throne than he found a pretext for attacking Egypt. His vast preparations were completed in the third year of his reign (B.C. 527);[5] but Amasis died at the very beginning of the invasion, leaving the inheritance of a lost kingdom to his son PSAMETHIK III., the PSAMMENITUS of Herodotus.

6. In a battle at Pelusium the Egyptian soldiers and Greek mercenaries were overwhelmed after a desperate resistance to the Persian hosts. The king was taken prisoner, and was at first treated with respect, but, being suspected of conspiring against Cambyses, he was put to death within six months of his accession (B.C. 527). It is needless to relate here the details of the conquest, and the stories, doubtless greatly exaggerated, of the outrages perpetrated by Cambyses.[6]

§ II. EGYPT UNDER THE PERSIAN KINGS, Dynasty XXVII. (B.C. 527-414 ?).[7]

1. Notwithstanding the tales just referred to, CAMBYSES (B.C. 527-522), (in Egyptian KAMBATHET or KANBUZA, with the regal name SAM-TAUI MASTU-RA), set the example, which was followed by the succeeding Persian kings, of assuming the style and titles of true Pharaohs, respecting Egyptian institutions, worshipping the gods of the country, honouring the priests, and maintaining and enlarging the temples. The government was usually committed to Persian viceroys, the first of whom, Aryandes, was installed by Cambyses when he left Egypt in B.C. 522. He died in Syria on his way home, probably by his own hand, through despair on receiving the news of the successful usurpation of the Magian Pseudo-Smerdis.[8]

2. DARIUS I., son of Hystaspes, in Egyptian NTHARIUSH (B.C. 521-486), with the regal name *Settu-ra* (a near equivalent to

---

[5] The true date—long disputed between B.C. 527 and B.C. 525—is now established by Dr. Brugsch from the Apis tablets. (See pp. 299–301.)

[6] See the *Student's Ancient History of the East*, chap. xxvi. §§ 4-9. On his alleged slaughter of the Apis, see above, p. 299.

[7] The lower date is rendered uncertain by the confused accounts about Amyrtæus and the recovery of Egyptian independence.

[8] *Ibid.* p. 511. The usurper has no place in the list of Manetho.

Sesostris), used his best efforts to conciliate his Egyptian subjects. We have already seen the measures he took to foster education according to native ideas, and to bring forward the youth in the public service (p. 307); his building of the new and splendid temple to Amon in the Great Oasis (*ibid.*); and his attempt to reopen the canal between the Nile and the Gulf of Suez (pp. 310, 311). The last was an enterprise of great importance, not for Egypt only, but for the whole empire, which now extended as far as India; and so was the king's restoration of the old caravan route through the rocky desert of Hammamat from Coptos to the Red Sea.

The invaluable records of the Apis tablets not only show the honour paid in the king's name to the religion of his Egyptian subjects,[9] but supply a test for the accounts handed down by the Greek writers. Thus we are told[1] that, when the tyranny of Aryandes provoked disaffection, Darius put the satrap to death, and committed the government to an Egyptian of the royal house of Saïs, who bore the popular name of Amasis. But the rebellion had already broken out, and Darius hastened to Egypt in person. It happened that an Apis had died a few days before his arrival at Memphis. Darius mourned for the god, and promised a hundred talents to any one who should discover his successor. His piety so won the hearts of the rebels that they submitted without a blow.

Now to test this story by the tablets of the Serapeum. We have the epitaph of an Apis bull, who died in the 4th year of the reign of Darius (B.C. 518).[2] This then might be the date of the visit, but for two strong objections: first, no revolt of Egypt is mentioned in the great Behistun inscription, which records the annals of Darius, and especially the insurrections he had to put down, during his first six years, to B.C. 516: secondly, the conquest of Cyrenaica was effected by the satrap Aryandes after the Scythian expedition of Darius, that is, after 506. Now another Greek story places a personal visit of Darius to Egypt in a curious relation to his invasion of Scythia.

---

[9] See p. 301. It is fair to observe that the name of Darius appears on the tablet only, as fixing the *date*; but it supplies another proof of the free exercise of the old sacred rites under the Persian dominion.

[1] Polyæn. *Strateg.* vii. 11, § 7.

[2] See p. 300.

In his account of Sesostris, Herodotus[3] tells us incidentally that Darius the Persian wished to set up his own statue beside the great image of Sesostris in front of the temple of Hephæstus (Ptah) at Memphis—that famous colossus of Ramses II. which now lies in the ditch at Mit-Rahineh. But the priest of Ptah withstood the king's purpose, telling him that he had not done such deeds as those of Sesostris the Egyptian; for besides the other conquests equal to his own, Sesostris had also conquered the Scythians, whom Darius had not been able to subdue; and the king yielded to the objection. Diodorus repeats the story, with the variation that the priest said 'not yet,' and that Darius, instead of being angry with the priest, replied that he hoped in no way to fall short of the deeds of Sesostris, if he reigned as long.[4] By the different turn given to the story it seems clearly implied that Diodorus places the visit *before*, while the older and more trustworthy historian fixes it *after*, the unsuccessful invasion of Scythia by Darius.

Now we have another tablet recording the manifestation of an Apis in the 31st year of Darius, so that the death of his predecessor would fall in that or the preceding year (B.C. 492).[5] A visit of the king to Egypt during the full tide of his preparations against Greece seems improbable; but a stronger objection arises from the absence of any mention of an insurrection at this time. But we do know that in the 35th year of Darius, the last but one of his reign (B.C. 487), the Egyptians—encouraged probably by the weakness of the Persian Empire from the battle of Marathon and the disputed succession—broke out into a revolt which compelled Darius to postpone his second attempt against Greece, and he died near the end of the following year.[6] We learn from the monuments that the Egyptians set up a native anti-king, KHABBASH,

---

[3] Herod. ii. 110. The story has a special interest and verisimilitude from the fact, now revealed by the monuments, that Darius assumed the regal name of *Settura* (Sesostris), after that of Ramses II. (*Sestura*). [4] Diod. i. 58.

[5] See p. 301; where Dr. Brugsch regards it as certain that the Apis just deceased was the successor of the one that died in the fourth year of Darius, so that there would be no time between B.C. 518 and B.C. 492 for the death of an Apis coinciding with a visit of Darius to Egypt.

[6] Herod. vii. 4.

who held his ground for some time in the marshes about the lake of Buto against 'the hereditary foe Xerxes.'[7]

3. XERXES I., on the Egyptian monuments KSHIARSH or KHSHERISH (B.C. 486-465), engaged the more zealously in the reconquest of Egypt, as he was at first disinclined to renew the expedition against Greece.[8] With his overwhelming force he subdued the revolt in person in his second year, and entrusted the government to his brother Achæmenes. Herodotus says that he made all Egypt much more enslaved than it had been under Darius ;[9] and the native monuments, as yet known, contain none of those tributes of respect to Xerxes which we have seen rendered to Darius, and even to Cambyses.[1] We are not told what became of Khabbash, but the inscription of the satrap Ptolemy[2] seems to imply that he gained some further success against Xerxes, and the sequel proves that native princes still maintained the smouldering fire of national independence.

4. The opportunity arrived for Egypt in the fifth year of ARTAXERXES I. LONGIMANUS (B.C. 465-425), the ARTA-KHSHESESH of the monuments, when the Libyan king Inaros,[3] of Marea, drew the princes of the Delta into a revolt, which was supported by an Athenian fleet of 200 ships. The arrival of this force in the Nile was followed by a great victory over the Persians at Papremis, where Inaros killed the satrap Achæmenes with his own hand.[4] A few days later, the Athenian squadron destroyed the greater part of a Phœnician fleet sent to aid the Persian army, and the allies sailed up the river to Memphis. The ancient capital was soon taken, except its old fortress called the White Wall, where the remnant of the Persians held out, and gave Artaxerxes time to send a new army to their aid. This great force, led by Megabyzus, retook Memphis, and shut up the defeated allies in the island of Prosopitis, where they were blockaded for eighteen months. At length Megabyzus diverted an arm of the Nile, and stranded the ships, which were destroyed by the Athenians themselves. Most of the Greeks fell in battle, and the survivors escaped to Cyrene. Inaros, betrayed by his own followers, was carried prisoner to Persia and there crucified ; but his ally, Amyr-

---

[7] See pp. 302, 315, 316.   [8] Herod. vii. 5.
[9] *Ibid.* 7.   [1] See p. 304.   [2] Pp. 315-16.
[3] The name is Inarōs ('Ινάρως), not Inarus ("Ιναρος).
[4] Thucyd. i. 104 ; Ctesias, *Persica*, §§ 30, *seq.*

tæus, prince of Saïs, escaped to the old asylum of Egyptian independence in the marshes (B.C. 455). The native resistance was encouraged by the attempts which the Athenians made to create a diversion in Egypt during their contest with Persia; but no events of importance are recorded under the reigns of

5, 6, 7. XERXES II. (B.C. 425-4), the usurper SOGDIANUS (B.C. 424), and DARIUS II. NOTHUS (B.C. 424–405), except the evidence furnished by the works of the last-named king at the temple in the Great Oasis, that respect was still paid by the Persian kings to the religion of Egypt.[5] The Egyptian style and title of Darius II. was MIAMUN-RA NTHARIUSH. To the latter part of this period belongs the somewhat intricate question of the first successful steps towards shaking off the Persian yoke. The following seems the most probable account.

§ III. THE TWENTY-EIGHTH DYNASTY OF SAÏS.—'AMYRTES or AMYRTÆUS, six years'—is the entry in the list of Manetho, as preserved in the *Chronicon* of Eusebius. It has been generally assumed that this Amyrtæus is the same who took part in the revolt of Inaros, though the interval is no less than forty years! But an incidental notice in Herodotus sets the matter in another light. In speaking of the first good intentions of Cambyses towards Psammenitus, to whom he would probably have committed the government of Egypt had he not distrusted him, Herodotus goes on to say : 'For the Persians are wont to honour the sons of kings; and even if kings revolt from them, nevertheless they give back the government to their sons;' and, among many other examples, he cites the cases of Thannyras, the son of the Libyan Inaros, and of *Pausiris*, the son of *Amyrtæus*, who received the governments which had been held by their fathers; and this, though none had done more harm to the Persians than Inaros and Amyrtæus.[6] This seems certainly to imply that, in agreement with the constant policy of maintaining the hereditary princes of nomes, the Persians had recognised Pausiris, the son of Amyrtæus (whether in place of his father or after his death), not assuredly as governor of Egypt, but in his father's principality of Saïs. The submission implied in such recognition would depend on the power of the Persians to enforce it; and when the opportunity for successful rebellion came, it was seized by a second Amyrtæus,

---

[5] See p. 307. [6] Herod. iii. 15.

whom we suppose to have been the son of Pausiris and the grandson of Amyrtæus, the ally of Inaros.[7]

As to the chronology, the *Chronicon* makes the six years of Amyrtæus parallel with the 13th–18th of Darius II. (B.C. 412–407); but the synchronisms in the Tables of Eusebius represent merely an artificial system of chronology, which is not of itself a decisive authority. As the Twenty-eighth Dynasty of Amyrtæus does not interrupt, but follows, that of the Persians, concluding with Darius II., it seems more reasonable to suppose that his successful revolt took place at or about the end of the reign of Darius, and that the Twenty-ninth Dynasty was continuous with the Twenty-eighth, taking up the successful struggle immediately after the death of Amyrtæus.[8] The struggle for the succession between Artaxerxes II. Mnemon and his brother Cyrus would give the opportunity so long watched for.[9]

§ IV. THE LAST NATIVE PHARAOHS (B.C. 399-340).—The distracted state of the Persian Empire not only allowed Egypt to secure full independence for about sixty years, but she even assumed the offensive against her late oppressors, in alliance with

---

[7] The distinction between the two Amyrtæi may be illustrated by the case of the two Nechos, the father and son of Psammetichus, whose place in Egyptian history was not made clear till the discovery of the annals of Assurbanipal.

[8] This is the view of M. Maspero, who places the six years of Amyrtæus between B.C. 405 and B.C. 399 (*Histoire Ancienne de l'Orient*, pp. 361, 362). In the articles AMYRTÆUS and DARIUS in the *Dict. of Greek and Roman Biography*, when the native Egyptian history was very little known, the present writer assumed only one Amyrtæus, and made Pausiris his successor after the six years of his reign over Egypt. Had this been the case, Pausiris would assuredly have appeared in the Twenty-eighth Dynasty as his father's successor. Besides, the six years' reign of Amyrtæus falls, in any case, later than the completion of the history of Herodotus. The whole matter still awaits light from the monuments. A cartouche read by some as that of Amyrtæus seems to be more than doubtful.

[9] It must be observed that the long reign of ARTAXERXES II. (B.C. 405-359), and nearly all that of OCHUS (359-340), have no place among the Dynasties of Manetho.

the Greeks. Whether by a failure in the house of Saïs, or from whatever cause, the sovereignty passed first to the princes of Mendes, and twenty years later to those of Sebennytus.

A. THE TWENTY-NINTH DYNASTY, OF MENDES, B.C. 399–378.[1]

1. NAIFAUROT I., with the regal name BANRA MI-NUTERU, the NEPHERITES I. of Manetho (B.C. 399–393), became king just at the time when Sparta had declared war against Persia, and Agesilaus was preparing to invade her territory. The gradual growth of the native Egyptian power for some time before this seems proved by the fleet of 100 ships, laden with corn, arms, and munitions of war, which Nepherites sent to the aid of the Lacedæmonians. But it was met at Rhodes and dispersed by the Athenian fleet under Conon, and the Egyptian army, which had advanced to the Syrian frontier, assumed a defensive attitude on the retreat of Agesilaus from Asia Minor. Artaxerxes, however, was obliged to reconquer the states of Asia Minor, which had revolted on the occasion offered by the expedition of Cyrus, before he could attack Egypt; and meanwhile the Greeks of Cyprus asserted their independence under Evagoras, the 'tyrant' of Cyprus, who sought to strengthen himself by alliances with Athens, the Carians, and Egypt (B.C. 391).

2. The offer was embraced by the new king HAGAR or HAKORI (with the regal name RA-KNUM MAT STEPEN-KHNUM), the ACHORIS (Ἀχωρίς) of Manetho (B.C. 393–380). His naval power was strengthened by the defection of the commander of the Persian fleet; but we are not told what part the Egyptians had in the successes which for some time attended the arms of Evagoras. But when the peace of Antalcidas relieved Persia from her Greek foes (B.C. 387), and Evagoras was defeated and shut up in Cyprus, Egypt was again placed on the defensive. The long siege of Salamis (B.C. 386–380) gave Achoris time to complete his preparations, and to engage in his service an army of Greek mercenaries under Greek generals.

3, 4. The short reigns of PSAMUT (PSAMMUTHIS, Man.; B.C. 380) and NAIFAUROT (NEPHERITES II.), may perhaps indicate a dispute for the succession; but we have no information of the cause of its transference to the princes of Sebennytus.

---

[1] We here follow the chronology of Brugsch, with which Maspero generally agrees, varying but slightly from the dates in the *Chronicon* of Eusebius.

B. THE THIRTIETH DYNASTY, OF SEBENNYTUS (B.C. 378-340).

1. NAKHT-HOR-IB, with the regal name RASNOTSEMHET STEPEN-ANHUR ISI-ANHUR SE ISI, the NECTANEBO I.[2] of Manetho (B.C. 378-360), had time to complete the preparations for defence, while Artaxerxes was engaged in an expedition against the Cadusii on the Caspian shore, and while his generals were restoring order in Asia Minor. Meanwhile, however, a great army was raised for the invasion of Egypt under the famous Persian general Pharnabazus, through whose influence the Athenians not only recalled their citizen Chabrias with his mercenaries from Egypt (B.C. 377), but sent Iphicrates with 20,000 mercenaries to reinforce Pharnabazus. But the divided command proved the ruin of the enterprise. After a year or two wasted in preparation, the invading force sailed from Aco (Acre), disembarked at the Mendesian mouth of the Nile, and defeated the Egyptians stationed to guard that frontier. But the refusal of Pharnabazus to advance on Memphis, as Iphicrates advised, gave the Egyptians time to resume the offensive. The inundation came on; the Persians were utterly defeated near Mendes; Pharnabazus re-embarked the remnant of his army, and Iphicrates, fearing to be made a scapegoat, fled to Athens (B.C. 375).[3] The failure of this attack secured peace to Egypt for a quarter of a century, and the disorders and rebellions of the western provinces during the later years of Artaxerxes encouraged her to assume the offensive.

This interval of peace and prosperity was marked by a last revival of Egyptian art. The name of Nectanebo is found on temples and monuments which he erected or restored through the whole land, from the Delta to Syene. Pliny, who calls him Nechthebis, mentions an obelisk eighty cubits high, prepared by this king, and afterwards erected by Ptolemy Philadelphus at Alexandria.[4] A Greek papyrus, in the Anastasi collection at

---

[2] Also called Nectanebes, -bis, -bus; Νεκτανέβως, Νεκτανέβης, Νεκτάνεβις, Νεκτάνεβος. But in this name there is evidently a confusion of *Nakhthorib* with *Nakhtnebef*, the next king but one after him.

[3] Diod. xv. 41-43; Nepos, *Vit. Iphicratis*, 2.

[4] Plin. *H. N.* xxxvi. 14. Its being *without inscriptions* is another sign of that unfinished state, which is not uncommon with the obelisks and monoliths of the later dynasties. Pliny adds, what might be said of many similar works, that 'it cost far more

Paris, relates how Nectanebo was censured by the god Mars (Anhur), in a dream, for leaving his temple at Sebennytus [5] unrepaired, and how he made ample amends for his unintentional neglect by restoring the edifice with great splendour.[6]

2. When ZIHO, the TEOS (Τέως) of Manetho, and Tachos (Ταχώς) of other Greek and Latin writers (B.C. 364–361),[7] succeeded to the throne, the suppression of the revolts in Asia Minor left Artaxerxes II. at liberty for the reconquest of Egypt. Fearing a new attack from the whole power of Persia, Tachos gathered an army of 80,000 Egyptians and 10,000 Greek mercenaries, and a fleet of 200 ships. He placed his fleet under the Athenian general Chabrias, and applied to Sparta for Agesilaus to take command of all his forces. It is said that Tachos, disappointed at seeing in the Spartan king a little old man of homely habits, treated him with scorn and disrespect, and set him over the mercenaries only, reserving the supreme command to himself. In opposition to the advice of Agesilaus, Tachos led his fleet and army in person into Phœnicia, leaving the government of Egypt to his brother, whose son Nectanebo accompanied the king, and was sent by him with his Egyptian forces to reduce the cities of Syria.[8] Nectanebo seized the opportunity to stir up a mutiny among the native troops, while his father raised a rebellion in Egypt. Agesilaus, whom the king had bitterly offended, went over to Nectanebo with the Greek mercenaries, and Tachos,

---

trouble in its carriage and elevation than had been originally expended in quarrying it;' and he gives an account of the process.

[5] Anhur was the tutelar god of Sebennytus and its nome (the 12th of Lower Egypt: see p. 348), and his name enters twice into the regal title of Nectanebo.

[7] Wilkinson, *Ancient Egyptians*, vol. i. pp. 139, 140; 2nd edition by Dr. Birch.

[8] We follow here the dates given by Maspero and the writers on Greek history, in preference to those given in Dr. Brugsch's lists of the kings (Appendix A.), inasmuch as the authorities place Tachos in the reign of Artaxerxes Mnemon, not of Ochus; and besides, the later date is inconsistent with the death of Agesilaus in B.C. 360. We do not, however, alter our author's dates in his Table.

[9] We choose what seems the most probable account amidst a considerable conflict of the authorities.

finding himself abandoned, took refuge in Sidon, and afterwards fled to Artaxerxes, by whom he was received kindly, and died at his court.[9]

3. NAKHTNEBEF, with the regal name RA-KHEPER-KA, the NECTANEBO II. of Manetho and the classic writers (B.C. 361–340), had first to defend his usurped crown against a rival prince of Mendes.[1] Though the latter had much the larger force—some say 100,000 men, but composed of townsmen and artificers—the military skill of Agesilaus won the victory for Nectanebo. The Spartan king left Egypt with an immense reward from the king (no less, it is said, than 220 talents), and died on his way home (B.C. 360). Chabrias also and his mercenaries were recalled by the Athenians, and the defence of Egypt's independence was left to a king whose taste inclined him rather to foster her arts and science. The monuments of Nectanebo throughout all the land exhibit the perfection of the later style of Egyptian art; and it was said that, had he shown the same skill as a general that he displayed as a builder and a magician,[2] the triumph of Egypt was certain. But he had at last, like Psammetichus III. nearly two centuries before, an enemy too strong for him. The cruel but energetic Ochus (who assumed the name of Artaxerxes III.), coming to the throne of Persia in B.C. 359, at once bent all efforts to reconquer Egypt. At first, however, fortune seemed to favour the national cause. The generals of Ochus were again and again defeated through the skill of the Greek commanders in the service of Nectanebo, Diophantus the Athenian, and the Spartan Lamia. These disasters excited Phœnicia and Cyprus to revolt, and Nectanebo sent 4,000 mercenaries to aid the Phœnicians under the Rhodian refugee Mentor, who, with his brother Memnon, had already played a conspicuous part against the Persians. Ochus

---

[9] Xenoph. *Ages.*; Plut. *Ages.*; Paus. iii. 10; Polyæn. iii. 1; Ælian, *V. H.* v. 1; Nepos, *Ages.* and *Chabrias*: the account of Diodorus, xv. 92, 93, is in some respects less probable.

[1] This is doubtless meant by 'a certain Mendesian' (Μενδήσιος) which some of the authorities seem to take for a proper name. We seem to have here another sign of that contest of supremacy between Mendes and Sebennytus, which may have caused the transition from the Twenty-ninth to the Thirtieth Dynasty.

[2] For the magical arts of Nectanebo, see above, p. 293, and the Pseudo-Callisthenes, i. 1–14.

meanwhile had taken the field in person with a great force, intent on the subjugation both of Phœnicia and Egypt. Mentor, probably foreseeing on which side the victory must remain, went over to Ochus with his mercenaries, and, after the reduction of Phœnicia, accompanied the king's march against Egypt. The vast preparations for defence were neutralized by the incompetence of Nectanebo, who insisted on keeping the chief command in his own hands. The Persian king appeared before Pelusium with an army of 300,000 Asiatics and 40,000 Greeks; and, instead of making the most of the natural difficulties presented by the marshes and canals, Nectanebo, on the first repulse of a portion of his force, shut himself up in Memphis, and thence fled with his treasures to Ethiopia. Other stories are told of his escape, with an evident view to gloze over the last shameful disaster, which ended 'the long majestic line' of Egypt's Pharaohs; but, from a sepulchral figure lately found, he seems to have been buried at Memphis.[3] The date of this reconquest of Egypt by Persia is given variously by chronologers as B.C. 353, 345, and 340.

§ V. THE THIRTY-FIRST DYNASTY OF PERSIANS (B.C. 340-332) held their recovered possession only for eight years.

1. OCHUS (B.C. 340-338) died two years after his restoration to the double crown, poisoned by the eunuch Bagoas. His youngest son

2. ARSES (B.C. 338-336) was set up and murdered within three years by the same minister, who placed on the throne his friend

3. DARIUS III. CODOMANNUS (B.C. 336-332),[4] only to succumb in the contest with the Macedonian conqueror, who was welcomed in Egypt as a deliverer. (See Chap. XX. p. 319.)

§ VI. THE THIRTY-SECOND DYNASTY OF MACEDONIANS (B.C. 332-311).

1. ALEXANDER THE GREAT (B.C. 332-323).
2. PHILIP ARRHIDÆUS (B.C. 323-317).
3. ALEXANDER ÆGUS (B.C. 323-311).

These names are given to complete the outline down to the

---

[3] Mariette-Bey, *Monuments divers*, 1872, pl. 32.

[4] The year B.C. 332 is that of the end of the Persian Dynasty in *Egypt* by Alexander's conquest of the country. The death of Darius and the end of the Persian Empire took place in the next year, B.C. 331.

Ptolemaic epoch; but the deeds of Alexander in and for Egypt are left to be read in the records of his life. Arrhidæus, the bastard son of Philip the Great, and the only remaining scion of the royal house of Macedon, being at Babylon when Alexander died, was elected his successor by the name of Philip. A few months later Roxana, the Bactrian wife of Alexander, gave birth to a son, who was named Alexander Ægus, and was recognized as the associate of Philip in the empire. Of these merely titular possessors of the thrones for which the generals of Alexander were contending, Philip fell a victim to the hatred of his father's widow, Olympias, in B.C. 317, and Alexander Ægus was murdered by Cassander in B.C. 311. Their royal cartouches are found on the Egyptian monuments, and that their titular sovereignty was recognized in that country is proved, at least in the case of Alexander Ægus, by the inscription distinctly dated in his seventh year, in which Ptolemy, the son of Lagus, the real possessor of the land, designates himself as satrap.[5]

But, in fact, the rule over Egypt was all this time in the hands of Ptolemy, who chose it in the division of Alexander's dominions after his death, and hastened at once to take possession. It was not till B.C. 306 that, after the example set by Antigonus, he assumed the title of king, by the name of PTOLEMÆUS I. SOTER; but, this step once taken, his regnal years were dated from the real beginning of his rule, in B.C. 323.

§ VII. THE THIRTY-THIRD DYNASTY OF THE (GREEK) PTOLEMIES (B.C. 323–30) lasted just 300 years, till, after Octavian's victory over Antony and Cleopatra, and the suicide of that last heiress of the line, Egypt was reduced to a Roman province. The Roman Cæsars are sometimes reckoned as a Thirty-fourth Dynasty; but it must be remembered that that title is only properly applied to the *Thirty Dynasties* of Manetho.

The History of the Ptolemies in Egypt is to form the Second Division of Dr. Brugsch's great work.

---

[5] This inscription has been cited in the text, pp. 289, 315.

APPENDIX.

A.

LIST OF THE KINGS, WITH THEIR EPOCHS,

who ruled in Egypt, from the first Pharaoh, Mena, to the end of the XXXIst Dynasty.

Their names and order, down to the Pharaoh Ramses II. (about B.C. 1350), are founded on the List of Kings in the Table of Abydus (Nos. 1–77).

The numbers added, to mark their Epochs, refer to the succession of generations assumed in our work; but these, from the year 666 onwards, are superseded by the regnal years actually proved.

IST DYNASTY: OF THINIS.   B.C.
1. Mena 4400
2. Tota 4366
3. Atoth 4333
4. Ata 4300
5. Sapti 4266
6. Mirbapen 4233
7. (Semempses) . . . 4200
8. Qebeh 4166

IIND DYNASTY: OF THINIS.
9. Buzau 4133
10. Kakau 4100
11. Bainnuter 4066
12. Utnas 4033
13. Senta 4000

IIIRD DYNASTY: OF MEMPHIS.   B.C.
14. Zazai 3966
15. Nebka 3933
16. Toser[sa] 3900
17. Tota 3866
18. Setes 3833
19. Noferkara 3800
20. Senofcru 3766

IVTH DYNASTY: OF MEMPHIS.
21. Khufu 3733
22. Ratatf 3700
23. Khafra 3666
24. Menkara 3633
25. Shepseskaf 3600

VTH DYNASTY: OF ELEPHANTINÉ.
26. Uskaf 3566
27. Sahura 3533
28. Keka 3500
29. Noferfra 3466
30. Ranuser 3433
31. Menkauhor 3400
32. Tatkara 3366
33. Unas 3333

VITH DYNASTY: OF MEMPHIS.
34. Uskara 3300
35. Teta 3266
36. Merira Pepi 3233
37. Merenra 3200
38. Noferkara 3166
39. Merenra Zafcmsaf . . 3133

VIITH–XITH DYNASTIES.

	B.C.
40. Nuterkara	3100
41. Menkara	3066
42. Noferkara	3033
43. Noferkara Nebi	3000
44. Tatkara Shema	2966
45. Noferkara Khontu	2933
46. Merenhor	2900
47. Senoferka	2866
48. Ranka	2833
49. Noferkara Terel	2800
50. Noferkahor	2766
51. Noferkara Pepiseneb	2733
52. Noferkara Annu	2700
53. . . . kaura	2666
54. Noferkaura	2633
55. Noferkauhor	2600
56. Noferarkara	2566
57. Nebkherra Mentuhotep	2533
58. Sankhkara	2500

XIITH DYNASTY: OF THEBES.

59. Amenemhat I.	2466
60. Usurtasen I.	2433
61. Amenemhat II.	2400
62. Usurtasen II.	2366
63. Usurtasen III.	2333
64. Amenemhat III.	2300
65. Amenemhat IV.	2266

A gap, which comprises more than 500 years, and during which the time of the Hyksos-kings falls. In all five dynasties (XIII.–XVII.) — 2233 to 1733 (circ.)

XVIIITH DYNASTY: OF THEBES.

B.C.

66. Aahmes 1700
67. Amenhotep I. . . . 1666
68. Thutmes I. 1633
69. Thutmes II. . . . ⎫
70. Thutmes III. . . . ⎬ 1600
                       ⎭
71. Amenhotep II. . . . 1566
72. Thutmes IV. 1533
73. Amenhotep III. . . . 1500
74. Horemhib 1466
(One generation of heretic kings) . 1433

XIXTH DYNASTY: OF THEBES.

75. Ramessu I. 1400
76. Mineptah I. Seti I. . . 1366
77. Miamun I. Ramessu II. . . 1333
    Mineptah II. Hotephima . . 1300
    Seti II. Mineptah III. . . 1266
    Setnakht Merer Miamun II. . 1233

XXTH DYNASTY: OF THEBES.

Ramessu III. Haq-On . . 1200
Ramessu IV. . . . ⎫
Ramessu VI. . . . ⎪
Meritum . . . . ⎬ 1166
Ramessu VII. . . . ⎪
Ramessu VIII. . . . ⎭
Ramessu IX–XII. . . . 1133

XXIST DYNASTY: OF THEBES AND TANIS.

Hirhor 1100
Piankhi 1066
Pinotem I. 1033
Pisebkhan I. . . . 1000

XXIInd Dynasty: of Bubastus.

	B.C.
Shashanq I.	966
Usarkon I.	933
Takeloth I.	900
Usarkon II.	866
Shashanq II.	833
Takeloth II.	800

XXIIIrd Dynasty: of Tanis and Thebes.

Usarkon	766

XXIVth Dynasty: of Saïs and Memphis.

Bokenranef	733

XXVth Dynasty: the Ethiopians.

Shabak	} 700
Shabatak	
Taharaqa	693

XXVIth Dynasty: of Saïs.

Psamethik I.	666
Neku	612
Psamethik II.	596
Uahabra	591
Aahmes	572
Psamethik III.	528

XXVIIth Dynasty: the Persians.

Cambyses	527
Darius I.	521
Xerxes I.	486
Artaxerxes	465
Xerxes II.	425
Sogdianus	—
Darius II.	424

XXVIIITH DYNASTY.   B.C.
(Amyrtæus).

XXIXTH DYNASTY: OF MENDES.
Naifaurot I. 399
Hagar 393
Psamut 380
Naifaurot II. 379

XXXTH DYNASTY: OF SEBENNYTUS.
Nakhthorib 378
Ziho 360
Nakhtnebef 358

XXXIST DYNASTY: THE PERSIANS.
Ochus 340
Arses 338
Darius III. 336
Conquest of Egypt by
  Alexander the Great . . . 332

B.

KEMI (EGYPT) AND ITS NOMES:
ACCORDING TO THE LISTS OF THE MONUMENTS.

I. PATORIS (the South Country, Upper Egypt).
1st Nome. *Capital*: AB (Elephantiné).
  Deities: Khnum and Sopet (Sothis).
2nd Nome. *Capital*: TEB (Apollinopolis Magna).
  Deities: Hor (Apollo) of Hut, and Hathor (Aphrodité).
3rd Nome. *Capital*: NEKHEB (Eileithyiapolis).
  Deity: The goddess Nekheb.
4th Nome. *Capital*: NI or NI-AMON (Diospolis Magna).
  Deities: Amon-ra (Zeus) and the goddess Mut.
5th Nome. *Capital*: QOBTI (Coptos). *Deity*: Khim (Pan).
6th Nome. *Capital*: TANTERER (Tentyra).
  Deities: Hathor and Hor-samta.
7th Nome. *Capital*: HA (Arab. Hou, Diospolis Parva).
  Deities: Nebtha (Nephthys) and Noferhotep.
8th Nome. *Capital*: ABDU (Abydus).
  Deity: Anhur (Mars).
9th Nome. *Capital*: APU (Panopolis). *Deity*: Khim (Pan).
10th Nome. *Capital*: TEBU (Aphroditopolis).
  Deity: Hor-mati.
11th Nome. *Capital*: SHAS-HOTEP (Hypselé). *Deity*: Khnum.
12th Nome. *Capital*: NI-ENT-BAK (Antæopolis).
  Deities: Hor and Mati (Isis).
13th Nome. *Capital*: SIAUT (Lycopolis).
  Deities: Ap-maten (Anubis) 'of the South,' and Ha.
14th Nome. *Capital*: QORS, QOS (Cusæ).
  Deity: Mat (Themis).
15th Nome. *Capital*: KHIMUNU (Hermopolis).
  Deity: Thut (Hermes).

16th Nome. *Capital*: HIBONU (Hipponon). *God*: Hor.
17th Nome. *Capital*: QA SA (Cynônpolis).
 God: Anup (Anubis).
18th Nome. *Capital*: HA-SUTEN (Alabastrônpolis).
 God: Anup.
19th Nome. *Capital*: PI-MAZA (Oxyrhynchus).
 God: Set (Typhon).
20th Nome. *Capital*: KHINENSU (Heracleopolis Magna).
 God: Khnum called Her-shaf.
21st Nome. *Capital*: SMEN-HOR (Ptolemais?). *God*: Khnum.
22nd Nome. *Capital*: TEP-AH (Aphroditopolis).
 Deity: Hathor.

II. PATOMHIT (the North Country, Lower Egypt).

1st Nome. *Capital*: MEN-NOFER (Memphis).
 Deities: Ptah (Hephæstus) and Sokhet.
2nd Nome. *Capital*: SOKHEM (Letopolis). *God*: Hor(-uër).
3rd Nome. *Capital*: NI-ENT-HAPI (Apis).
 Goddess: Senti (Hathor-Nub).
4th Nome. *Capital*: ZOQ'A (Canopus).
 Deities: Amon-ra and Neit (Athena).
5th Nome. *Capital*: SA (Saïs). *Goddess*: Neit.
6th Nome. *Capital*: KHESUU (Xoïs). *God*: Amon-ra.
7th Nome. *Capital*: SONTI-NOFER (Metelis).
 Deities: He, 'Lord of the West,' and Isis.
8th Nome. *Capital*: THUKOT (Sethroë).
 Deities: Tum (Helios) and Hathor.
9th Nome. *Capital*: PI-USIR (Busiris). *God*: Osiris.
10th Nome. *Capital*: HA-TA-HIR-AB (Athribis).
 Deities: Hor-khont-khethi, and the goddess Khut.
11th Nome. *Capital*: QA-HEBES (Cabasus). *Deity*: Isis.
12th Nome. *Capital*: THEB-NUTER (Sebennytus).
 God: Anhur (Mars).
13th Nome. *Capital*: ANU (On, Heliopolis).
 Deities: Hormakhu (Helios) and the goddess Iusas.

14th Nome. *Capital*: Zo'an (Tanis).
            Deities: Hor and the goddess Khont-Abot.
15th Nome. *Capital*: Pi-thut (Hermopolis).
            Deities: Thut and the goddess Nohem-aui.
16th Nome. *Capital*: Pi-bi-neb-dad (Mendes).
            Deities: Bi-neb-dad (Mendes) and the goddess Ha-mehit.
17th Nome. *Capital*: Pi-khun-en-amon (Diospolis).
            Deities: Amon-ra and the goddess Mut.
18th Nome. *Capital*: Pi-bast (Bubastus). *Goddess*: Bast.
19th Nome. *Capital*: Pi-uto (Buto). *Goddess*: Uto (Isis).
20th Nome. *Capital*: Qosem (Phacussa).
            God: Sapt, 'the Lord of the East.'

With regard to the geographical position of the respective Nomes, as they are determined, with a very few exceptions, in the order and arrangement denoted above, on the monuments alike of older and later times, I refer to the Maps appended to this work. These will also enable the reader to identify a number of cities and places in the old empire of the Pharaohs, which have been passed over in the above list of the Nomes and their capitals.

C.

TRANSCRIPTION OF THE ANCIENT EGYPTIAN NAMES.

Those of my readers who may wish to undertake the task of comparing the numerous Egyptian names occurring in the foregoing work with the corresponding names in non-Egyptian sources of history, will perhaps thank me for placing before them a list of the characters of the Old Egyptian alphabet, representing their proper value and our mode of transcribing them. I must add the remark, that, for the sake of simplicity in printing, I have as much as possible avoided the method of expressing the particular force of the letters by those dots and marks, which now-a-days form part of the scientific apparatus of orthographical transcription. Even the professed scholar and student will find this no disadvantage, when he understands that I cite all names according to the values assigned in the following list.

[The English reader will find some variations in our text from Dr. Brugsch's mode of representing the characters. These are added to the list in brackets ( ). The only cases requiring special notice are :—(1) The German *sch* is replaced by our simpler notation of the sound, *sh*. (2) The hard *ch* (χ) is changed to *kh*, a notation more usual with English Egyptologers, and avoiding the confusion with our common *ch*, a confusion, it is true, which *ought not* to be made, were GREEK retained in its proper place as *the most essential part of a liberal education.*—ED.]

OLD EGYPTIAN ALPHABET.

Scientific Characters.	In this Work.
$\dot{a}$	a (broad)
$\bar{a}$ (Heb. ע, Arab. ع)	' (above the line)
a (Vocal)	a and e (continental sound)
i	i (ditto)
u	u pure [1]
b	b
p	p
f	f
m	m
n	n
r	r
l	l
h (Heb. ה)	h
$\d{h}$ (Arab. ح)	h
χ (Heb. ח, Arab. خ)	ch (kh)
s	s
$\check{s}$ (Heb. ש, Arab. ش)	sch (Eng. sh)
q (Heb. ק, Arab. ق, the Greek koppa)	q (with sound of k, not of qu)
k (the Greek kappa)	k
$\d{k}$ (Heb. ג, Arab. ج)	g
t	t
θ	th
(Heb. ד)	d
t' (French z)	z

[1] As a convenient distinction, and in accordance with custom, we use the pure u in ancient names, as *Usurtasen*, but the *ou* for the same sound in modern names, as *Abou, Assouan*, &c.—ED.

As an example of a text transcribed according to the scientific method, I have chosen the following inscription on one of the two memorial stones spoken of in Vol. I. p. 182. The contents relate to the fixing of the southern boundary of Egypt at Wady-Halfah by the command of king Usurtasen III., who here speaks in his own person, in order to declare in pithy language to future ages his opinion of the importance of a conqueror. No one can fail to observe the contrast which the language and tone of this time (the twenty-fourth century B.C.) form to the style of later periods.

King Usurtasen III. speaks thus :—

[1] *renpit*   *XVI*   *ȧbot*   *III*   *pirt*   *ȧrt*   *ḥon-f*
'Year | 16 | month | 3 | winter | made | his Majesty (I)

taš   *ris*   *er*   *Ḥeh*   [2] *ȧu-ȧr-nȧ*
the boundary | of the south | at | (the land of) Heh. | I made

taš-ȧ   *χont-ȧ*   *ȧtef-ȧ*   *ȧu-erṭu-nȧ*   [3] *ḥau*
my boundary | my going up (was) | that of my fathers ; | I gave (added) | some more

ḥir   *si*   *utut*   *nȧ*   *nenok*   *suten*   *t'etu*   *ȧru*
to | it. | It was a resolve | to me | who became | king | to utter | the doing

kaat   [4] *ȧb-ȧ*   *pu*   *χepert*   *em*   *ṭot-ȧ*
wish | of my heart | was | what should come to pass | by | my hand.

aṭu   *er*   *θetet*   *seχemu*   *er*   [5] *mār.*   *tem*
A conqueror | to | take | let him avoid | the | covering. | Let not

seter   *t'etet*   *em*   *ȧb-fi*   *χemet*   *tuau*   *āḥā*
rest | the speech | in | his heart. | The (man) destitute of | fame | stands there

ḥir   [6] *sef*   *tem*   *sefen*   *en*   *χeri*   *peḥ*
in | being gentle | without | the gentleness | of the | enemy | reaches

su   *peḥu*   *peḥut-f*   *keru*   *kert*   [7] *ušebu*
him. | Has any one attained | his goal | let be silent | silence | let answer

teṭet	*mā*	*χepert*	*ȧm si*		*ter*	*entet ȧr*
the speech	as	it happened	accordingly;		therefore	that, if

ḳer	*em*	*χet*	*peḥ*	*si*	*seχem*
silence	is in	consequence	of him who has attained	it,	to strengthen

[8] *ȧb*	*pu*	*en*	*χeri*	*kent*	*pu*	*at*
the heart,	that means	of the	enemy.	Strength	means	attacking.

χest	*pu*	*ḥem*	*χet*	*ḥem*	*pu*	[9] *māaru*
Weakness	means	turning	back.	Cowardice	means	being taken

ḥir	*taś-j*	*ter*	*entet*	*sem*	*neḥes er*
upon	his borders.	Therefore	that	heard	the negro about

χer	*en*	*ro-ȧ*	*nen*	[10] *uśeb-f*	*tutu*	*ḥem*
what fell	from	my mouth,	not	gave he reply.	Made	turn back

fi	*aṭet*	*er*	*f*	*tutu-f*	*sa-f*	*ḥem* *χet*
him	the assailer	against	him,	he gave	his back	turning backwards,

ua-f	*er*	*aṭ*	[11] *nen*	*roθ*	*ȧs*	*ent*
he remained far	from the	assailer.	Not	men	so,	who

śefet	*set*	*ḥuru*	*pu*	*set'u ȧb*
manly	are.	To fail	that means	of strength and of courage.

[12] *ȧu-maa-en*	*set*	*ḥon*	*nen*	*em ȧmes*
Has beheld		them	the Majesty (I).	Not is it as imagination.

ḥak-nȧ	*ḥimt-sen*	*nen-nȧ*	[13] *χer-sen*	*pir*
I took	their women.	I drove away	their inhabitants	coming out

er χnumt-sen	*ḥu*	*ka-sen*	*uḥa*	*pir-sen*
to their wells	Were slain	their bulls,	destroyed	their corn,

[14] *ertu*	*seśet*	*ȧm*	*ānχ*	*nȧ*	*ȧtef-ȧ t'et-ȧ*
was set	fire	thereto.	An oath	to me	by my father, I speak

em māt	*nen*	*χen*	*ȧm*	[15] *en*	*ābā pir*
in truth.	No	room	therein	for	contradiction of that which comes out

em	*ro-ȧ*	*ȧr*	*ḳert*	*sa-ȧ*	*nib serutet-fi*
of	my mouth.	He is	however	my son	every one who keeps

354 TRANSCRIPTION OF TEXTS. APP. C.

taš [16] *pen år en hon sa-å pu*
boundary | this | made | by | the Majesty (me). | My son | is he called.

mast-f en hon tut sa-å net'nuti
He is born | of the | Majesty (me). | A likeness | my son | to the protector

åtef [17] *serut taš en utet*
of (his) father, | to the keeper | of the boundary | of him | who begat

su år kertu feχet su tem tef χer
him. | If | however | he lays bare | it, | so that not | he | should fight

[18] *hir fi nen sa-å ås nen mes-tef ås*
upon | it, | not | my son | then, | not | is he born | then

nå esθ kert ertu en hon årt tut
of me. | Behold! | however | causes | the Majesty (I) | to make | a likeness

[19] *en hon hir taš pen år en*
of the | Majesty (myself) | upon | boundary | this | made | by

hon nen mertu rut-θan hir fi en
Majesty (me). | Not | is it wished | ye worship | upon | it | in the

mertu χer-θan hir fi.
to be desired | ye fight | upon | it.

The translation, recast into a consecutive form, will run as follows:—

'In the 16th year, in the 3rd month of the winter season, I fixed the southern boundary at the land of Heh. I fixed my boundary by advancing upwards like my predecessors. I extended it. It was my firm resolve—I who became king—to declare how I would act, and what should be done by my hand according to the desire of my heart. A conqueror should avoid concealment: his speech should not rest in his heart. He who has no desire of fame waits still and is full of gentleness, without finding gentleness from his enemy. When any one has achieved his purpose, then let him refrain from silence, let him give an account how all has been done. For if silence follows him who has attained success, that is as much as to strengthen the courage of his adversary. To be strong means going forward to his goal; to be weak means turning backwards; to be cowardly means letting himself be taken upon his border. Therefore, because the negro people had heard what went forth out of my mouth, they made no reply. He who made an attack upon them put them to flight. They turned their back and fled away. They kept far from him who attacked them. They were therefore not men of manly spirit; and that means to be wanting in strength and courage. I beheld them, not only in imagination. I took their women, I led away their inhabitants, who had gone out to their fountains. Their bulls were slaughtered, their corn was destroyed, and fire was set to it. I swear by my father that I speak the truth. There is no ground for contradicting the utterance of my mouth.

'Every one of my sons, who maintains this boundary which I have fixed, he shall be called my son, who was born of me. My son is like the protector of his father (i.e. Horus), like the preserver of the boundary of his father (i.e. Osiris). But if he abandons it, so that he does not fight upon it, he is not my son, he is not then born of me.

'I have caused my own image to be set up on this boundary which I have fixed, not that ye may (only) worship it (the image) upon it (the boundary), but that ye may fight upon it.'

I have printed the above translation word for word, in order to furnish a proof, from this example, to one of my learned French critics, that inscriptions of the *older time* are indeed no child's play, and that their value for historical research depends wholly and solely on the *correct* explanation of the text. A fair-minded reader will not be willing to take up the reproach, which my French critic has made against me, that I have not made so much use of certain important inscriptions for the earlier history of Egypt, as they may probably have deserved. The deciphering of inscriptions has no real significance, until the translator is sure of his subject in its fullest compass. When the opposite course is taken, they bring more damage than profit, for they confuse the facts, and they deter the outer circle of students from availing themselves of even the most certain translations for their researches. I shall bear the blame of my French critic with the greatest composure until he himself shall have furnished the proof, that the most ancient texts are capable of being translated with fuller certainty than the examples hitherto given by him lead us to expect with any special confidence in the future.[2]

[2] In translating the last paragraph, we have not thought that the name of the critic referred to, or certain remarks on the translation of the same inscription by another French scholar, would be of interest to the English reader. In fact, Dr. Brugsch, in his pamphlet of 'Additions and Corrections,' directs the omission of the last paragraph; but the *principles* expressed in it with regard to our present understanding of the older inscriptions, seemed to us too important to be omitted. We may be permitted, finally, to remind the reader that the whole science of hieroglyphic interpretation is still only in its infancy; and perhaps the greatest lesson to be learned from its wonderful revelations is that of *patient expectation* for what yet remains to be discovered.—ED.

THE EXODUS

AND THE

EGYPTIAN MONUMENTS

A DISCOURSE DELIVERED ON THE OCCASION
OF THE INTERNATIONAL CONGRESS OF
ORIENTALISTS IN LONDON

September 17th, 1874

BY

HENRY BRUGSCH-BEY

DELEGATE OF HIS HIGHNESS ISMAËL I., KHEDIVE OF EGYPT

TRANSLATED FROM THE FRENCH ORIGINAL
1875

NOTE.—*The Map which accompanies the Original Pamphlet, and on which the Route of the Israelites is marked, is the same as the Map of Lower Egypt appended to this volume*

DEDICATED

TO

HIS HIGHNESS ISMAËL THE FIRST

KHEDIVE OF EGYPT

BY HIS VERY HUMBLE, VERY OBEDIENT,

AND VERY GRATEFUL SERVANT

HENRY BRUGSCH-BEY

ADVERTISEMENT.

THE publication of this Discourse, which should have appeared a year ago, has been delayed by the absence of the Author, while in official charge of an expedition into the interior of the Libyan Desert, of Egypt, and of Nubia. On returning from this journey, he was able to take advantage of his stay in the eastern part of Lower Egypt, to examine the sites, and to verify the topographical and geographical views, which form the subject of this Memoir.

The Author is happy to be able to state, that his new researches have contributed to prove, even to the smallest details, the conclusions which the papyri and the monuments compelled him to form with regard to the topographical direction of the Exodus, and to the stations where the Hebrews halted, as related in Holy Scripture.

In a special Memoir, which will form a complete chapter of my periodical publication, 'The Bible and the Monuments' (*Bibel und Denkmäler*), announced several months since, the reader will find a collection of all the materials drawn from the monuments, which have enabled me to re-establish the route of the Jews after their departure from Egypt, and which prove incontestably that the labours of Messrs. Unruh and Schleiden[1] on the same subject were based on views as near the truth as was then possible.

Notwithstanding the very hostile and sometimes not very Christian attacks, which these new views have had to sustain on the part of several orthodox scholars, the Author of this Discourse ventures to affirm that the number of monumental indications is every day accumulating, and continually furnishing new proofs in favour of our discovery. Any one must certainly be blind, who refuses to see the flood of light which the papyri and other Egyptian monuments are throwing upon the venerable records of Holy Scripture; and, above all, there must needs be a wilful mistaking of the first laws of criticism by those who wish to discover contradictions, which really exist only in the imagination of opponents.

Note.

In our Translation, we follow Dr. Brugsch's orthography of the proper names, which, in this Memoir, he has adapted to the French language in which it was written, as, for the chief example, in the use of *ou* for the pure *u* used in his German text.

We have not thought it necessary to encumber the pages with Notes referring to all the points already touched on in the History, and here collected into one focus of light thrown on the subject in hand.—Ed.

---

[1] See p. 366 of the following Discourse.

PREFACE.

The following pages contain the printed report of the Discourse, which the delegate of His Highness Ismaël I., Khedive of Egypt, had the honour to deliver on the evening of September 17, 1874, at the International Congress of Orientalists in London.

Although the necessarily restricted limits of time, and the consideration due to an indulgent audience, did not permit him to develop all the details of a question, the solution of which has occupied him through a long course of years, the lively marks of satisfaction with which his hearers were pleased to honour him, and which were echoed by journals held in the highest esteem, impose on him the duty of presenting to the public the contents of this Discourse under the form of a Memoir drawn up on the outlines of his subject.

The more that his researches and investigations on the Exodus, founded on the study of the monuments, appear to present to the Author results which are entirely opposed to the views hitherto adopted with regard to this part of the history of the Hebrews, so much the more does he feel almost compelled to publish the materials which have supplied him with a foundation, and which have imperatively led him to present the departure of the Jews from Egypt in its true light.

Those who are afraid of meeting in these new hypotheses attacks upon the statements of Holy Scripture—from which may God preserve me—or the suggestion of doubts relative to the sacred history, may feel completely reassured. Far from lessening the authority and the weight of the Books on which our religion is founded, the results at which the Author of this Memoir has arrived—thanks to the authentic indications of the monuments—will serve, on the contrary, as testimonies to establish the supreme veracity of the Sacred Scriptures, and to prove the antiquity of their origin and of their sources.

The Author cannot conclude without fulfilling a sacred duty by thanking his august Master, in the name of science, for the numerous efforts which he has generously devoted to the development of historical studies and to the service of the monuments of his country. Having found in the person of our excellent and learned friend and colleague, Mariette-Bey, one as devoted as he was qualified by skill and experience to carry out his enlightened ideas, His Highness the Khedive of Egypt has perfectly understood and accomplished the high mission which Divine Providence has reserved for him, that of being the regenerator of Egypt, ancient as well as modern.[1]

H. B.

[1] This is left as it was written; but 'much has happened since then.'—ED.

THE DISCOURSE.

HIS HIGHNESS the Khedive of Egypt, Ismaël Pasha, has granted me the honour of representing his country at the International Congress of Orientalists in London. On this occasion, the enlightened prince, who has rendered so many services to the science I profess, has ordered me to express, in his name, to the illustrious members of the Congress, his most lively sympathy and his sincere admiration for the invaluable labours with which they have enriched science, in bringing back to life by their researches the remotest past of those happy countries of the East, which were the cradle of humanity and the centres of primitive civilization.

If His Highness has deigned to fix his choice on me as his delegate to London, I owe this distinction less to my humble deserts than to the special character of my latest researches on the subject of the history of the Hebrews in Egypt.

Knowing the lively interest with which the English world follows those discoveries, above all others, which have a bearing upon the venerable records of Holy Scripture, His Highness has charged me to lay before this honourable Congress the most conspicuous results of my studies, founded on the interpretation of the monuments of Egypt.

In thus bringing before you a page of the history of the Hebrews in Egypt, I would flatter myself with the hope that I may be able to reward your attention, and thereby justify the high confidence with which His Highness has been pleased to honour me.

I am to speak of the Exodus of the Hebrews. But, before entering on my subject, I will take leave to make one observation. I wish to state that my discussion is based, on the one hand, upon the texts of Holy Scripture, in which I have not to change a single iota; on the other hand, upon the Egyptian monumental inscriptions, explained according to the laws of a sound criticism, free from all bias of a fanciful character.

If for almost twenty centuries, as I shall have occasion to prove, the translators and the interpreters of Holy Scripture have wrongly understood and rendered the geographical notions contained in that part of the Biblical text which describes the sojourn of the Hebrews in Egypt, the error, most certainly, is not due to the sacred narrative, but to those who, unacquainted with the history and geography of the remote times which were contemporary with the events in the history of the Hebrews in Egypt, have laboured to reconstruct, at any cost, the Exodus of the Hebrews after the scale of their scanty knowledge, not to say, of their most complete ignorance.

According to Holy Scripture, Moses, after having obtained from the Pharaoh of his age permission to lead into the Desert the children of Israel, worn out with their hard servitude in building the two cities of Pitom and Ramses,[1] started with his people from the city of Ramses,[2] and arrived successively at the stations of Succoth[3] and Etham.[4] At this last encampment he turned,[5] taking the direction towards Migdol and the sea—observe that there is not here a word about the 'Sea of sea-weed'[6] (the Red Sea)— opposite to the 'entry of Khiroth,'[7] over against Baalzephon. Then the Hebrews passed by way of the 'Sea of sea-weed' (translated by the interpreters 'the Red Sea');[8] they remained three days in the Desert without finding water;[9] they arrived at Marah, where the water was bitter;[1] and at length they encamped at Elim, a station with springs of sweet water and a little grove of date-palms.[2]

The different opinions and different results, in tracing the direction of the march of the Hebrews,

---

[1] Exod. i. 11. Observe that Rameses has already been mentioned *by anticipation*, to mark the locality in which the children of Israel were settled when they came into Egypt :—Gen. xlvii. 11 : 'And Joseph placed his father and his brethren, and gave them a possession in the land of Egypt, in the best of the land, in the land of Rameses, as Pharaoh had commanded.'—ED.

[2] Exod. xii. 37.   [3] *Ibid.* and xiii. 20.
[4] *Ibid.* xiii. 20.   [5] *Ibid.* xiv. 2.
[6] 'Mer des Algues,' the translation of the Hebrew ים־סוף 'the sea of *souph*,' which the LXX. always render by ἡ ἐρυθρὰ θάλασσα (as also in the N. T., Acts vii. 36, Heb. xi. 29), except in Judges ix. 16, where they preserve the Hebrew name in the form Σίφ. —ED.
[7] Pi-hahiroth, Exod. xiv. 2.   [8] Exod. xiii. 18, xv. 22.
[9] *Ibid.* xv. 22. As to the name Shur, see below, p. 390.
[1] *Ibid.* xv. 23.   [2] *Ibid.* xv. 27.

are just as many as the scholars who have attempted to reconstruct the route of the Hebrews from the data of Holy Scripture. But all these scholars, except only two (see p. 360), have agreed unanimously that the passage through the Red Sea must be regarded as the most fixed point in their system.

I dare not weary your patience by enumerating all the routes reconstructed by these scholars, who had certainly the best intentions, and who lacked only one thing—but that very essential—the necessary knowledge of facts in the geography of ancient Egypt. Their general practice, in order to rediscover the itinerary of the Hebrews, was to resort to the Greek and Roman geographers, who lived more than a thousand years after Moses, and to mark the stations of the Hebrews by the Greek or Latin names belonging to the geography of Egypt under the rule of the Ptolemies or the Cæsars.

If a happy chance had preserved that Manual of the Geography of Egypt which, according to the texts engraved on the walls of the temple of Edfou, was deposited in the Library of that vast sanctuary of the god Horus, and which bore the title of 'The Book of the Towns situated in Egypt, with a Description of all that relates to them,' we should have been relieved from all trouble in rediscovering the localities referred to in Holy Scripture. We should only have had to consult this book, to know of what we might be sure with regard to these Biblical names. Unfortunately, this work has perished together with so many other papyri, and science has once more to regret the loss of so important a record of Egyptian antiquity. But even this loss is not irreparable! The monuments and the papyri, especially those of the dynasty of the Ramessids, contain thousands of texts and notices of a purely geographical kind, making frequent allusion to topographical positions; besides which, a very considerable number of inscriptions, engraved on the walls of the temples, contain tables more or less extensive, which give us the most exact knowledge of the political divisions of Egypt, and the most complete lists of the departments of that country, accompanied by a host of the most curious details.

Let me lay before you the scattered leaves of the lost book of which I have just spoken. Our purpose is to collect them carefully, to put them together in their relation to each other, to try to fill up the gaps, and finally to make out the list of them.

After having been engaged on this work for twenty years, I have succeeded, at the beginning of this year, in reuniting the *membra disjecta* of the great *Corpus Geographiæ* of Egypt, which is composed, according to the Index of my collections, of a number exceeding 3,600 geographical names. In the work of applying the laws of a sound and calm criticism to these rich materials, without allowing myself to be enticed by an accidental resemblance of form in the foreign proper names, when compared with the Egyptian names, I have undertaken to traverse Egypt through all its quarters, in order to obtain a knowledge of the ancient ground in its modern condition, and to satisfy myself, from my own eyesight, of the changes which the surface of the soil has undergone in different parts of the country during the course of the past centuries.

Having in this manner accomplished a labour which had the only drawback of being sometimes beyond my strength, but which has never worn out my patience, I have the honour of presenting its results, in the form of a summary, to this honourable Congress, as a tribute of respect and esteem due to the illustrious scholars here assembled. While, for my own part, I experience deep satisfaction at having in some sort reached the goal which I proposed to myself twenty years ago, it would prove, on the other hand, my highest recompense, to learn from your judgment that I have recovered a great part of the lost book of the Geography of Ancient Egypt. The application of the geographical results settled and laid down in this summary, which will form the special subject of the present meeting, will furnish you with a fair test of the importance of these results and of their value to historical science.

Will you permit me to begin my exposition by a remark concerning the general topography of the country which we are about to traverse, in order to discover and follow the traces of the Hebrews during their sojourn in Egypt? All the scholars, who have given attention to this subject, are agreed that this country lay on the Eastern side of Lower Egypt, to the east of the ancient Pelusiac branch, which has disappeared from the map of modern Egypt, but the direction of which is clearly indicated by the position of the ruins of several great cities which stood on its banks in ancient times. Beginning from the South of the country in question, the city of Anu, the same which Holy Scripture designates by the name of On, identifies for us the position of the Heliopolite nome of the classic authors.

Next, the mounds of Tel-Bast, near the modern village of Zagazig, enable us to fix the ancient site of the city of Pi-bast, a name which Holy Scripture has rendered by the very exact transcription of Pibeseth,[3] while the Greeks called it Bubastus. It was the chief city of the ancient Bubastite nome.

Pursuing our course towards the North, the vast mounds, near a modern town called Qous by the Copts and Faqous by the Arabs, remove all doubt as to the site of the ancient city of Phacoussa, Phacoussæ, or Phacoussan, which, according to the Greek accounts, was regarded as the chief city of the Arabian nome. It is the same place, to which the monumental lists have given the appellation of Gosem, a name easily recognized in that of 'Guesem of Arabia,' used by the Septuagint Version as the geographical translation of the famous Land of Goshen.[4]

Directly to the North, between the Arabian nome, with its capital Gosem, and the Mediterranean Sea, the monumental lists make known to us a district, the Egyptian name of which, 'the point of the North,'

---
[3] Ezek. xxx. 17.
[4] Gen. xlv. 10; xlvi. 34; xlvii. 4, 6, 27; Ex. viii. 22; ix. 26.

indicates at once its northerly position. The Greek writers call it the Nomos Sethroïtes, a word which seems to be derived from the appellation Set-ro-hatu, 'the region of the river-mouths,' which the ancient Egyptians applied to this part of their country. While classical antiquity uses the name of Heracleopolis Parva to designate its chief town, the monumental lists cite the same place under the name of 'Pitom,' with the addition, 'in the country of Sukot.' Here we at once see two names of great importance, which occur in Holy Scripture under the same forms, the Pithom and the Succoth of the Hebrews.[5]

Without dwelling, for the moment, on this curious discovery, I pass on to the last district of this region, situated in the neighbourhood of the preceding one, between the Pelusiac and Tanitic branches of the Nile. The Egyptian monuments designate it by a compound name, which signifies 'the beginning of the Eastern country,' in complete agreement with its topographical position. Its chief town is named, sometimes Zoān, sometimes Pi-rāmses, 'the city of Ramses.' Here again we have before us two names, which Holy Scripture has preserved perfectly in the two names, Zoan and Rāmses, of one and the same Egyptian city.

As the new geographical definitions which I have now set forth tend necessarily to a certain conclusion, I do not for a moment hesitate to declare that I willingly take upon myself the whole responsibility, as much for the accuracy of the philological part of

[5] See reff. above. Respecting the name of Sukot, or Tukot, the reader is referred to the Note at Vol. I. p. 233.—ED.

my statement, as for the precision of the geographical sites which I have brought to your knowledge.

After these remarks, I return to Pitom and Ramses. When you have entered, at Port Saïd, from the Mediterranean into the maritime Canal of Suez, your vessel crosses the middle of a great plain, from one end to the other, before stopping on the south at the station called by the engineers of the canal El-Kantara. But during this transit you must give up all hope of being cheered by the view of those verdant and smiling meadows, those forests of date-palms and mulberry-trees, which give to the interior of Lower Egypt—covered with numerous villages and intersected with thousands of canals—the picturesque character of a real garden of God. This vast plain stretches out from the two sides of the maritime canal, without affording your eye, as it ranges over the wide space to the farthest bounds of the horizon, the least point to rest upon. It is a sea of sand, with an infinite number of islets covered with reeds and thorny plants, garnished with a sort of white efflorescence, which leads us to recognize the presence of salt water. In spite of the blue sky, the angel of death has spread his wings over this vast sad solitude, where the least sign of life seems an event. You but rarely meet with the tents of some poor Bedouins, who have wandered into this desert to seek food for their lean cattle.

But the scene changes from the time when the Nile, in the two months of January and February, has begun to cover the lands of Lower Egypt with its waters. The vast plains of sand disappear beneath the surface of immense lakes. The reeds and rushes, which form large thickets, shoot up wonderfully, and millions of water-birds, ranged along the banks of the lagoons or collected in flocks on the islets of the marsh, are busy fishing, disputing with man the rich prey of the waters. Then come the barks manned by the fishermen of Lake Menzaleh, who, during the two or three winter months, ply their calling vigorously, in order afterwards to sell the 'fassikh' (salted fish) to the inhabitants of the Delta and of Upper Egypt.

Such is the general character of this region, which I have traversed three times, at different seasons of the year, in order to become acquainted with the peculiarities of its surface; and such are the impressions which I have brought away from my repeated visits. These are the plains, now half desert, half lagoons and marshes, that correspond to the territory of the ancient district of the Sethroite nome, 'the point of the East' according to the monuments, the capital of which was called Pi-tom, the city of Pithom of the Bible.

In ancient times this district comprised both banks of the Pelusiac arm of the Nile, and extended on the western side as far as the eastern bank of the Tanitic arm. Marshes and lagoons, with a rich vegetation consisting of rushes and reeds, of the lotus and, above all, the papyrus plant, are met with towards the sea-shore: these are the places called by an Egyptian word, Athu, or by the foreign word

Souph, that is, 'the papyrus marshes' of the Egyptian texts. There were also pools and lakes, called by the Semitic name of Birkata, which reached to the neighbourhood of Pitom. The district was traversed in all directions by canals, two of which were near the city of Pelusium; each bearing a special name which recals the use of a Semitic language spoken by the inhabitants of the district in question. The city of Pithom, identical with that of Heracleopolis Parva, the capital of the Sethroite nome in the age of the Greeks and Romans, was situated halfway on the great road from Pelusium to Tanis; and this indication, given on the authority of the itineraries, furnishes the sole means of fixing its position towards the frontier of the conterminous district of Tanis.

The Egyptian texts give us evident and incontestable proofs that the whole of this region, which formed the district of the Sethroite nome, was denoted by the name of Suku or Sukot. The foreign source of this designation is indicated by the monuments, and is proved by its relations with the Hebrew words *sok*, *sukkah*, in the plural *sukkoth*, which bear the primary sense of 'tent.' There is nothing surprising in such an appellation, analogies to which are found in the names Scenæ Mandrorum, Scenæ Veteranorum, Scenæ extra Gerasa, given by the ancients to three places situated in Egypt. In these names, then, the principal word, Scenæ, 'tents,' has the same signification as the Semitic-Egyptian word Sukot, which recals to us the name of Succoth, given in Holy Scripture to the first station of the Hebrews when they had left the city of

Ramses. This name of 'tents' takes its origin from the encampments of the Bedouin Arabs, who, with the permission of the Pharaohs, had taken up their abode in the vast plains of the country of Sukot, and who, from the most remote periods of Egyptian history, had there preserved the manners, the customs, and the religious beliefs peculiar to their race, and had diffused the use of Semitic words, which were at length adopted officially by the Egyptian authorities and scribes.[6]

Thus it is that the greatest number of the proper names, used on the monuments and in the papyri to denote the towns, villages, and canals of the district of Sukot and of the adjacent nome of Tanis, are explained only by means of the vocabulary of the Semitic languages. Very often the existing Egyptian names are changed in such a manner that the Semitic name contains the exact translation of the sense of the Egyptian name. In this case the Semites have used the same method that the Greeks and Romans employed, namely, to render the proper names of the geography of Egypt by translation into the corresponding words of their own language. In this process they went so far as to substitute the names of the divinities of classical mythology for those of the gods and divinities of the Egyptian pantheon. Hence it is that the classic authors give us names of cities such as Andrôn-polis (the 'city of men'), Gynæcôn-polis (the 'city of women'), Leontôn-polis (the 'city of lions'), Crocodilôn-polis, Lycôn-polis, Elephantiné, that is, the cities of crocodiles, of wolves, of the elephant or

[6] Comp. the 'History,' Vol. II. pp. 105, *f*.

ivory, &c., which exhibit actual translations of the corresponding Egyptian names. And it is thus, also, that the same authors speak of cities called Dios-polis, Hermo-polis, Helio-polis, Aphrodito-polis—that is to say, the cities of the gods Zeus, Hermes, Helios (the Sun), and of the goddess Aphrodité—in order to render into Greek the Egyptian names No-Amon, ' the city of Amon,' Pi-thut, ' the city of Thut,' Pi-tom, ' the city of the sun-god Tom,' Pi-Hathor, ' the city of the goddess Hathor.' The Hebrews did just the same: and thus there was, at the entrance of the road leading to Palestine, near the lake Sirbonis, a small fortification, to which, as early as the time of the Nineteenth Dynasty, the Egyptians gave the name of Anbu, that is, ' the wall,' or ' fence,' a name which the Greeks translated according to their custom, calling it Gerrhon (τὸ Γέρρον), or in the plural Gerrha (τὰ Γέρρα).[7] The Hebrews likewise rendered the meaning of the Egyptian name by a translation, designating the military post on the Egyptian frontier by the name of Shur, which in their language signifies exactly the same as the word Anbu in Egyptian and the word Gerrhon in Greek, namely, ' the wall.' This Shur is the very place which is mentioned in Holy Scripture, not only as a frontier post between Egypt and Palestine, but also as the place whose name was given to the northern part of the desert on that side of Egypt.

Just in the same way, the Hebrew word Souph,—

[7] There was a Chaldæan town of the same name on the Euphrates, and another in Arabia; and a district Γέρρυς or Γέρροι on the Borysthenes, in European Sarmatia; all in positions where we should expect to find frontier fortresses.—ED.

whose meaning of 'weeds, reeds, rushes, papyrus-plant' is certified by the dictionaries of the Hebrew language, and which was used to denote a town situated on the Egyptian frontier; at the opposite end of the great Pharaonic road which led towards the south of the Dead Sea, and also gave its name to the Yam Souph, 'the Sea of Reeds'—this word, I say, contains simply the translation of the Egyptian Athu, which signifies the same as the Hebrew Souph, that is, 'reeds, weeds' or 'the papyrus plant,' and was applied as a general term to denote all the marshes and lagoons of Lower Egypt, which are characterized by their rich vegetation, consisting of papyrus and of rushes. The Egyptians, on their part, knew so well the meaning of the Hebrew word, that they frequently adopted the foreign name of Souph, instead of the word Athu in their own tongue, to denote not only the name of the City of Reeds, but also the Sea of Reeds, the Yam Souph, which we shall meet with further on.

After this remark of a philological character, which appeared to me indispensable for the understanding of my subject, I return to the city of Pitom, the chief place of the region of Sukot, about which the monuments furnish us with some very curious pieces of information. I will begin with the divinity worshipped at Pitom and in the district of Sukot. Although the lists of the nomes, as well as the Egyptian texts, expressly designate the sun-god Tom—the same who had splendid temples at On or Heliopolis—as the tutelar deity of Sukot, they nevertheless add, that the god Tom represents solely the Egyptian type corresponding to the divinity of Pitom who is called by the name of ānkh, and surnamed 'the great god.' The word ānkh, which is of Egyptian origin, signifies 'life' or 'He who lives,' 'the Living One.' This is the only case, in the Egyptian texts, of the occurrence of such a name for a god as seems to exclude the notion of idolatry. And in fact, if we take into consideration the presence of families of the Semitic race, who have resided in Egypt at all periods of her history—including the nation of the Hebrews —we cannot refuse to recognize in this divine name the trace of an old religious notion, which has been preserved even in the monumental records of the Egyptians. I will not venture to decide the question, whether the god 'He who lives' of the Egyptian text is identical with the Jehovah of the Hebrews; but, at all events, everything tends to this belief, when we remember that the name of Jehovah contains the same meaning as the Egyptian word ānkh, 'He who lives.' According to the monuments, this god, in whose honour a great feast was celebrated on the 13th day of the second month of summer, was served, not by priests, like the other divinities of the Egyptian pantheon, but by two young girls, sisters, who bore the sacred title of Ur-ti, that is, 'the two queens.' A serpent, to whom the Egyptian texts give the epithet of 'the magnificent, splendid,' was regarded as the living symbol of the god of Pitom. It bore the name of Kereh, that is, 'the smooth' (compare κερϱε, 'calvus,' גלה, 'smooth, bald'). And this serpent, again, transports us into the camp of the children of Israel in the wilderness ; it recals to us the brazen serpent of Moses, to which the Hebrews offered the perfumes of incense until the time when king Hezekiah decreed the abolition of this ancient serpent-worship.[8]

The relations of the Hebrews with Pitom and Sukot do not, however, end here.

According to the indications of the monuments, the town of Pitom, the chief place of the district of Sukot, had an appellation which it owed to the presence and existence of its god ānkh, 'He who lives' or 'the Living One,' and which, in the terms of the Egyptian language, was pronounced p-àa-ānkh, ' the habitation or the dwelling-place of the god ānkh.' In conformity with this name, the district of Sukot was otherwise called p-u-nt-pàa-ānkh, 'the district of the dwelling-place of the Living One.' Add to this monumental name the Egyptian word za, the well-known designation of the governor of a city or a district, and you will have the title Za-p-u-nt-p-aà-ānkh, 'the governor of the district of the dwelling-place of the Living One,' which a Greek of the time of the Ptolemies would have rendered by the translation, 'the nomarch of the Sethroite nome.'

And now turn to Holy Scripture : it will inform you that the Pharaoh of Joseph honoured his vizier with the long title of Zaphnatpāneakh, which, letter for letter, answers exactly to the long Egyptian word, the analysis of which I have just laid before you.[9]

[8] Numbers xxi. 9 ; 2 Kings xviii. 4.
[9] Comp. Vol. I. p. 307, where the hieroglyphs of this title are

More than this, according to the narrative in Holy Scripture, when Joseph made himself known to his astonished brethren, he said to them,[1] 'I am Joseph your brother; it is not you that sent me into Egypt, it is God. It is God who established me as privy councillor to Pharaoh, and as lord over all his house.' The first title, in Hebrew, is written Ab-le-Pharaoh, in which the translators, from the LXX. downwards, have recognized the Hebrew word, Ab, 'father;' but we learn from the Egyptian texts that, far from being Hebrew, the title of Ab-en-pirão designates the first minister or officer, who was attached exclusively to the Pharaonic household. Several of the precious historical papyri of the time of the Nineteenth Dynasty, now in the British Museum, the texts of which consist of simple letters and communications written by scribes and officers of the court, relate to these Ab-en-pirão, these superior officers of the Pharaoh, whose high rank is clearly indicated by the respectful style of these scribes of inferior rank.

All these observations, the number of which I could easily extend by other examples, will serve to demonstrate, in general, the presence of a foreign race on the soil of Sukot, and, especially, to give incontestable proofs of the close relations between the

given. We preserve Dr. Brugsch's slight variations in the orthography.—ED.

[1] Gen. xlv. 4, 8. We follow Dr. Brugsch's translation, which the reader can, of course, compare with the Authorized Version. Respecting the offices of *Ab* and *Adon*, see Vol. I. pp. 253, 307, 311-12, 517 (the elevation of Horemhib, so like that of Joseph); Vol. II. pp. 146, 188.—ED.

Egyptians and the Hebrews. By what we may call the international use of words belonging to their languages, the Egyptian texts furnish us with direct proofs which certify the existence of foreign peoples in the district of Pitom.

The Egyptian texts, with the famous papyrus of the British Museum at their head, tell us continually of the Hiru-pitu, or Egyptian officers who were charged with the oversight of these foreign populations residing in the region of Sukot. These same texts make known to us the Adon (a word entirely Semitic in its origin) or superior chiefs of Sukot, magistrates who served as intermediaries in the relations of the Egyptian authorities with these populations. This service, which was not always of a peaceable character, was supported by a body of police (the Mazaiou), whose commander (the Ser) was chosen from among the great personages of the Pharaonic court. The Egyptian garrisons of two fortresses constructed on the frontiers of the nome of Sukot watched the entrance and departure of all foreigners into and out of that territory. The first, called Khetam (that is, the fortress) of Sukot, was situated near the town of Pelusium. It guarded the entrance into the district of Sukot from the side of Arabia. The other, called by a Semitic name Segor or Segol, that is, 'the barrier,' of Sukot, prevented foreigners from passing the frontier on the southern side and setting foot on the territory of the district adjacent to Tanis-Ramses. Thus the two forts were placed at the two ends of the great road which

traversed the plain of Sukot in the midst of its lakes,
marshes, and canals. The description, which a Roman
author (Pliny, see p. 398) has left us of the nature of
the roads of this country, may serve to prove that,
as early as the beginning of our era, the great road
of the district of Sukot was somewhat like the track
of the present day, by which only the Bedouins
of the country and their families are able to travel.
As might be easily imagined beforehand, the marshy
condition of Sukot scarcely permitted the foundation
of towns in the interior of the district. Hence the
Egyptian texts, in agreement with the notices of the
classic writers, speak only of towns and forts *on the
frontier*. Allow me to direct your attention especially
to a fortress situated at the east of the nome of Sukot,
on the border of the Arabian desert, in the neighbourhood of a freshwater lake, and called by its
Semitic name, which was adopted by the Egyptians,
Migdol, that is, 'the tower,' and by its purely Egyptian name, Samout. The site of this place is fixed
by the position of Tel-es-Semout, a modern name
given to some heaps of ruins, which at once recals
the ancient appellation of Samout. As early as the age
of the Eighteenth Dynasty, about 200 years before the
time of Moses, this place was regarded as the most
northern point of Egypt, just as on the southern
border the city of Elephantiné or Souan (the Assouan
of our time) was considered the most southern point
of the country. When king Amenophis IV. summoned all the workmen of the country, from the city
of Elephantiné to Samout (Migdol), the Egyptian

text, which has preserved this information for us, says precisely the same as does the prophet Ezekiel, in predicting to the Egyptians of his time the devastation of their country 'from Migdol as far as Seve (Assouan) on the frontier of the land of Kush.'[2] When I observe that this Migdol is the only place of that name which I have met with in the Egyptian geographical texts, among more than three thousand geographical proper names, the probability at once follows, that the Migdol of the prophet Ezekiel is not different from the Migdol of the Exodus.

It is time to leave the district of Sukot, and to follow by way of Pitom the ancient road which led to Zoān-Tanis, the capital of the frontier district, a distance of 22 Roman miles, according to the ancient itineraries. A sandy plain, as vast as it is dreary, called at this day San in remembrance of the ancient name of Zoān, and covered with gigantic ruins of columns, pillars, sphinxes, stêlæ, and stones of buildings—all these fragments being cut in the hardest material from the granite of Syene,—shows you the position of that city of Tanis, to which the Egyptian texts and the classic authors are agreed in giving the epithet of ' a great and splendid city of Egypt.' According to the geographical inscriptions, the Egyptians gave to this plain, of which Tanis was the centre, the name of Sokhot Zoān, ' the plain of Zoān,' the origin of which name is traced back as far as the

[2] Ezek. xxix. 10; xxx. 6. In our Authorized Version, as so frequently happens, the *right* translation is given in the *margin*, 'from Migdol to Syene,' the text being wrong, and in fact nonsense : 'from the tower of Syene to the border of Ethiopia ' is like saying ' from Berwick to the frontier of Scotland.'—ED.

age of Ramses II. The author of the 78th Psalm makes use in two verses (12 and 43) of precisely the same phrase in reminding the Hebrews of his time of the miracles which God wrought before their ancestors ' the children of Israel, in Egypt, *in the plain of Zoan.*' This remarkable agreement is not accidental, for the knowledge of the Hebrews concerning all that related to Tanis is proved by the note of an annalist, likewise reported in Holy Scripture, that the city of Hebron was built seven years before the foundation of Zoan.³

If the name of Zoan—which the Egyptians, as well as the Hebrews, gave to this great city, and which means ' a station where beasts of burthen are laden before starting on a journey '—is of a purely Semitic origin, two other names, which are likewise given to the same place and are inscribed on the monuments discovered at San, reveal their derivation from the Egyptian language. These are the names of Zor and Pi-râmses. The first, Zor—sometimes Zoru in the plural—has the meaning of the ' strong ' place, or places, which agrees with the nature of the country lying towards the East and defended by a great number of fortifications, of which Tanis was one of the strongest.⁴

The second appellation, Pi-râmses, ' the city of

---

³ Numbers xiii. 22. Respecting the probable connection in the origin of the cities, which seems to be implied in this mention of them together, see the *Student's Ancient History of the East*, p. 115.—ED.

⁴ The Egyptian name of *Mazor*, applied to this country, shows us the origin of the Hebrew word *Mazor*, which is given in Holy Scripture to the same region.

Ramses,' dates from the time of the second king of that name, the founder of all those edifices whose gigantic ruins still astonish the traveller of our day. This is the new city, built close to the ancient Zor, and so often mentioned in the papyri of the British Museum,[5] at which Ramses II. erected sanctuaries and temples in honour of a circle of divinities, called ' the gods of Ramses.' The king caused himself also to be honoured with a religious worship, and the texts of the later age make mention of the ' god-king Ramses, surnamed the very valiant.' I cannot omit to quote the name of the high-priests who presided over the different services of religion in the sanctuaries of Zor-Ramses. According to the Egyptian texts these priests bore the name of Khar-tot, that is, ' the warrior.' The origin of this appellation, which seems strange for persons so peaceful, is satisfactorily explained by the Egyptian myths concerning the divinities of the city of Ramses. But the interest attached to this title arises not so much from these religious legends as from the fact, that Holy Scripture designates by the same name the priests whom Pharaoh summoned to imitate the miracles wrought by Moses. The interpreters of Holy Scripture are agreed that the name of Khartumim, given in the Bible to the Egyptian magicians, in spite of its Hebrew complexion, is evidently derived from an Egyptian word. And here we have the word Khartot, which supplies us not only with the means of discovering the real meaning of Khartumim, but also with a new proof that the

[5] See especially the contemporary description at Vol. II. pp. 100-102.—En.

scene of the interviews between Pharaoh and Moses is laid in the city of Zoan-Ramses.

The Egyptian records, especially the papyri, abound in dates relating to the building of the new city and sanctuaries of Ramses, and to the labours in stone and in bricks with which the workmen were overburthened, to make them complete their task quickly. These Egyptian documents furnish details so precise and specific on this sort of work, that it is impossible not to recognize in them the most evident connection with the 'hard bondage' and 'rigorous service' of the Hebrews on the occasion of building certain edifices at Pitom and Ramses.[6] Any one must be blind who refuses to see the light which is beginning to shine into the darkness of thirty centuries, and which enables us to transfer to their true places the events which the good Fathers of the Church —excellent Christians, indeed, but ill acquainted with antiquity—would have confounded till the end of time, had not the monuments of the Khedive and the treasures of the British Museum come in good time to our help.

To alter the position of the city of Ramses, in defiance of the evidences of the Egyptian documents, would involve the introduction of irreparable confusion into the geographical order of the nomes and cities of Egypt.

This city of Zoan-Ramses, from which, about the year 1600 before our era, and in the 22nd year of his glorious reign, the great conqueror, Thutmes III.,

[6] Exod. i. 11, 14.

set out at the head of his army to attack the land of Canaan:—This city, into which, in the 5th year of his reign, Ramses II. made his triumphal entry, after having won his victories over the people of the Khetians, and in which, sixteen years later, the same Pharaoh concluded the treaty of peace and alliance with the chief of that people:—This city, whose great plains served as the field for the cavalry and troops of the kings to practise their warlike manœuvres:—This city, whose harbour was filled with Egyptian and Phœnician vessels, which carried on the commerce between Egypt and Syria:—This city, which the Egyptian texts designate expressly as the end of the proper Egyptian territory and the beginning of that of the foreigner;—This city, of which an Egyptian poet has left us the beautiful description contained in a papyrus of the British Museum:—This same city where the Ramessids loved to reside, in order to receive foreign embassies and to give orders to the functionaries of their court:—This is the very city where the children of Israel experienced the rigours of a long and oppressive slavery, where Moses wrought his miracles in the presence of the Pharaoh of his age; and it was from this same city that the Hebrews set out, to quit the fertile land of Egypt.

We will now follow them, stage by stage.

Travellers by land, who were leaving Ramses to pursue their journey towards the East, had two roads that they might follow. One of these led, in a north-easterly direction, from Ramses to Pelusium; passing half-way through the city of Pitom, situated at an equal distance from Ramses and from Pelusium. This is that bad road, described by Pliny, across the lagoons, the marshes, and a whole system of canals, of the region of Sukot. According to what the monuments tell us, this road was not very much frequented. It was used by travellers without baggage, while the Pharaohs, accompanied by their horses, chariots, and troops, preferred the great Pharaonic road, the Sikkeh-es-soultanieh of the Orientals.

This last contained four stations, each separated from the next by a day's march. These were Ramses, 'the barrier' of Sukot, Khetam, and Migdol. We already know the names and position of these stations, with the exception of the third, called Khetam. This word Khetam, which the Hebrews have rendered by Etham, has the general sense of 'fortress,' as I have proved before. To distinguish it from other Khetams which existed in Egypt, and especially from the Khetam of the province of Sukot, situated near Pelusium, the Egyptian texts very often add to the word the explanatory remark, 'which is situated in the province of Zor,' that is, of Tanis-Ramses.

There is not the least doubt as to the position of this important place, of which we even possess a drawing displayed on a monument of Sethos I. at Karnak. According to this drawing, the strong place of Khetam was situated on both banks of a river (the Pelusiac arm of the Nile), and the two opposite parts of the fortress were joined by a great bridge, a Qanthareh (or Kantara), as it is called in Arabic. At a little distance from these two fortresses, and behind them, is found the inhabited town, called in Egyptian Tabenet. While this name at once recals the name of Daphnæ (Δάφναι), given by the Greek historian Herodotus[7] to an Egyptian fortress, the following observations will result in furnishing proofs of the greatest certainty for the identification now proposed. Herodotus speaks, in the first place, of Daphnæ in the plural, in agreement with the existence of the two fortresses according to the Egyptian drawing. He gives them the surname of 'the Pelusian' on account of the position of the fortresses in question, on the two opposite banks of the Pelusiac branch. Herodotus says expressly, that at his day (as in former times) there was in this Pelusian Daphnæ a garrison which guarded the entrance into Egypt on the side of Arabia and Syria. The ruins of these two forts, standing over against one another, still exist in our day; and the name of Tel-Defenneh, which they bear, at once recals the Egyptian name of Tabenet and the name of Daphnæ mentioned by Herodotus. The remembrance of the bridge, the Qanthareh, which joined the two forts of Khetam-Daphnæ, has been likewise preserved to our time, for the name of Guisr-el-Qanthareh, 'the dyke of the bridge,' which is now applied to a place situated a little distance east of Khetam, must be regarded as the last reminiscence

[7] Herod. ii. 30 : where all the three frontier fortresses and their objects are mentioned, viz. on the S., the N.E., and the N.W.:
ἐπὶ Ψαμμιτίχου βασιλέος φυλακαὶ κατέστασαν ἔν τε Ἐλεφαντίνῃ πόλι πρὸς Αἰθιόπων καὶ ἐν Δάφνῃσι τῇσι Πηλουσίῃσι ἄλλη δὲ πρὸς Ἀραβίων καὶ Σύρων, καὶ ἐν Μαρέῃ πρὸς Λιβύης ἄλλη.

of the only passage which, in ancient times, allowed a traveller to enter Egypt dryshod from the East.

Having thus re-discovered, by means of their ancient names and their modern positions, the four geographical points which Holy Scripture calls Ramses, Succoth, Etham, and Migdol, situated at a day's distance from one another, I am quite ready to answer the question, whether the Egyptian texts prove to us the existence of a road which led from Ramses to Migdol, through these intermediate stations of Succoth and Etham. Once more the answer is in the highest degree affirmative.

A happy chance—rather let us say, Divine Providence—has preserved, in one of the papyri of the British Museum, the most precious memorial of the epoch contemporary with the sojourn of the Israelites in Egypt. This is a simple letter, written more than thirty centuries before our time by the hand of an Egyptian scribe, to report his journey from the royal palace at Ramses, which was occasioned by the flight of two domestics.[8]

Thus (he says) 'I set out from the hall of the royal palace on the 9th day of the 3rd month of summer towards evening, in pursuit of the two domestics. Then I arrived at the barrier of Sukot on the 10th day of the same month. I was informed that they (that is, the two fugitives) had decided to go by the southern route. On the 12th day I arrived at Khetam. There I received news that the grooms who came from the country [the lagoons of Suf, said] that the fugitives had got beyond the region of the Wall to the north of the Migdol of king Seti Mineptah.'

If you will substitute, in this precious letter, for the mention of the two domestics the name of Moses

[8] Comp. the *History*, Vol. II. p. 138.

and the Hebrews, and put in place of the scribe who pursued the two fugitives the Pharaoh in person following the traces of the children of Israel, you will have the exact description of the march of the Hebrews related in Egyptian terms.

Exactly as the Hebrews, according to the biblical narrative, started on the 15th day of the 1st month from the city of Ramses,[9] so our scribe, on the 9th day of the 11th month of the Egyptian year, quits the palace of Ramses to go in pursuit of the two fugitives.

Exactly as the Hebrews arrive at Succoth on the day following their departure,[1] so the Egyptian enters Sukot the day after he set out from Ramses.

Exactly as the Hebrews stop at Etham on the third day from their leaving Ramses,[2] so the Egyptian scribe, on the third day of his journey, arrives at Khetam, where the desert begins.

Exactly as the two fugitives, pursued by the scribe, who dares no longer continue his route in the desert, had taken the northerly direction towards Migdol and the part called in Egyptian 'the Wall,' in Greek 'Gerrhon,' in the Bible 'Shur,'—all names of the same meaning,—so the Hebrews 'turned,' as Holy Scripture says,[3] to enter on the flats of the lake Sirbonis.

To add a single word to these topographical comparisons would only lessen their value. Truth is simple; it needs no long demonstrations.

According to the indications of the monuments, in agreement with what the classical accounts tell us, the

---

[9] Exod. xii. 37; Numb. xxxiii. 3.
[1] Exod. *ibid.*; Numb. xxxiii. 5.
[2] Exod. xiii. 20; Numb. xxxiii. 6.
[3] Exod. xiv. 2; Numb. xxxiii. 7.

Egyptian road led from Migdol towards the Mediterranean Sea, as far as the Wall of Gerrhon (the Shur of the Bible), situated at the (western) extremity of the lake Sirbonis. This latter, which was well known to the ancients, had again long fallen out of remembrance, and even in the last century a French traveller in Egypt naïvely observed that 'to speak of the lake Sirbon is speaking Greek to the Arabs.'[4] Divided from the Mediterranean by a long tongue of land which, in ancient times, formed the only road from Egypt to Palestine, this lake, or rather this lagoon, covered with a luxuriant vegetation of reeds and papyrus, but in our days almost entirely dried up, concealed unexpected dangers owing to the nature of its shores and the presence of those deadly abysses of which a classic author has left us the following description :[5]

'On the eastern side, Egypt is protected in part by the Nile, in part by the desert and marshy plains known under the name of Gulfs (or Pits, $\tau\grave{a}$ $\beta\acute{a}\rho a\theta\rho a$). For between Cœle-Syria and Egypt there is a lake, of very narrow width, but of a wonderful depth, and extending in length about 200 stadia (20 geog. miles), which is called Sirbonis ; and it exposes the traveller approaching it unawares to unforeseen dangers. For its basin being very narrow, like a riband, and surrounded on all sides by great banks of sand, when south winds blow for some time, a quantity of sand is drifted over it. This sand hides the sheet of water from the sight, and confuses the appearance of the lake

[4] Le Mascrier, *Description de l'Egypte*, 1735, p. 104.

[5] Diodorus, i. 30. We give a literal translation in place of Dr. Brugsch's free version.—ED.

with the dry land, so that they are indistinguishable. From which cause many *have been swallowed up with their whole armies* through unacquaintance with the nature of the spot and through having mistaken the road.[6] For as the traveller advances gradually the sand gives way under his feet and, as if of malignant purpose, deceives those who have ventured on it, till at length, suspecting what is about to happen, *they try to help themselves when there is no longer any means of getting away safe.*[7] For a man drawn in by the swamp can neither swim, the movements of his body being hampered by the mud, nor can he get out, there being no solid support to raise himself on. The water and sand being so mixed that the nature of both is changed, the place can neither be forded nor crossed in boats. Thus those who are caught in these places are

[6] In this description and a subsequent passage (see p. 396) Diodorus is generally thought to have exaggerated the fate which befel a part of the Persian army of Artaxerxes Ochus in B.C. 350; but the views of Dr. Brugsch would give a far more striking significance to the passage and to Milton's image founded on it (*Paradise Lost*, ii. 592-4):

'A gulf profound as that Serbonian bog
Betwixt Damiata and Mount Casius old,
Where armies whole have sunk.'

As to the different *manner* of the catastrophe, the description of Diodorus throws a new light on the narrative in Exodus. Pharaoh thought he had caught the Israelites 'entangled' between the sea, the desert, and the lake (Exod. xiv. 2); but when they were led safely through by the guiding pillar of fire, which was turned into darkness for their pursuers, it was the Egyptians that became entangled on the treacherous surface, through which 'their chariots dragged heavily' (verse 25) before the whelming wave borne in from the Mediterranean completed their destruction.—ED.

[7] Comp. Exod. xiv. 25: 'So that the Egyptians said, *Let us flee from the face of Israel.*'—ED.

drawn to the bottom of the abyss, having no resource to help themselves, as the banks of sand sink with them. Such is the nature of these plains, with which the name of gulfs (or pits, $βάραθρα$) agrees perfectly.'

Thus the Hebrews, on approaching this tongue of land in a north-easterly direction, found themselves in face of the Gulfs, or, in the language of the Egyptian texts, in face of the Khirot (this is the ancient word which applies exactly to the gulfs of weedy lakes) near the site of Gerrhon. We can now perfectly understand the biblical term Pi-hahiroth,[8] a word which literally signifies 'the entrance to the gulfs,' in agreement with the geographical situation. This indication is finally fixed with precision by another place, named Baal-zephon, for[9] 'The Lord spake unto Moses, saying, Speak to the children of Israel, that they turn and encamp before Pi-hahiroth, between Migdol and the sea, opposite to (lit. in face of) Baal-zephon; ye shall encamp opposite to it, by the sea.'

The name of Baal-zephon, which (as the eminent Egyptologist Mr. Goodwin has discovered) is met with in one of the papyri of the British Museum under its Egyptian orthography, Baali-Zapouna, denotes a divinity whose attribute is not difficult to recognize. According to the extremely curious indications furnished by the Egyptian texts on this point, the god Baal-zephon, the 'Lord of the North,' represented under his Semitic name the Egyptian god Amon, the

---

[8] Exod. xiv. 2. Mr. Greville Chester (see below, p. 400) observes that the curve of the sea-coast between the two headlands is such that the former could be spoken of as opposite the latter.

[9] *Ibid.*

great bird-catcher who frequents the lagoons, the lord of the northern districts, and especially of the marshes, to whom the inscriptions expressly give the title of Lord of the Khirot, that is 'gulfs' of the lagoons of papyrus. The Greeks, after their manner, compared him with one of their corresponding divine types, and thus it was that the god Amon of the lagoons was represented, from the time of the visits made to this region by the Greeks, under the new form of a 'Zeus Kasios (Casius).' The geographical epithet of Casius, given to this Zeus, is explained by the Semitic-Egyptian name of the region where his temple was built.[1] This is Hazi or Hazion, that is, 'the land of the asylum,' a name which perfectly suits the position of a sanctuary situated at the most advanced point of the Egyptian frontier towards the East.

It was on this narrow tongue of land, bounded on the one side by the Mediterranean Sea, on the other by the lagoons of weeds, between the entrance to the Khiroth, or the gulfs, on the West, and the sanctuary of Baal-zephon on the East, that the great catastrophe took place. I may repeat what I have already said upon this subject in another place.

After the Hebrews, marching on foot, had cleared the flats which extend between the Mediterranean Sea

---

[1] Professor Sayce, in his interesting letter on 'Brugsch-Bey's Theory of the Exodus' (*Academy*, April 10, 1880), confirms this identification from the Assyrian records:—'Tiglath-Pileser II., describing his campaign in Syria in B.C. 738, speaks of *another Baalzephon*, which the geographical indications of the inscription show must be *the Syrian Mount Casius* of classical geography (now Jebel-el-Akra) near Seleucia. *Here also was a noted temple of Baal*, like that on the Mount Casius of Egypt.'—ED.

and the lake Sirbonis, a great wave took by surprise the Egyptian cavalry and the captains of the war-chariots, who pursued the Hebrews. Hampered in their movements by their frightened horses and their disordered chariots, these captains and cavaliers suffered what, in the course of history, has occasionally befallen not only simple travellers, but whole armies. True, the miracle then ceases to be a miracle; but, let us avow it with full sincerity, the Providence of God still maintains its place and authority.[2]

When, in the first century of our era, the geographer Strabo, a thoughtful man and a good observer, was travelling in Egypt, he made the following entry in his journal:—

'At the time when I was staying at Alexandria, the sea rose so high about Pelusium and Mount Casius that it inundated the land, and made the mountain an island, so that the road, which leads past it to Phœnicia, became practicable for vessels.'[3]

---

[2] Dr. Brugsch has here made a perfectly gratuitous concession, and fallen into the common error of confounding a miracle with a special providence. The essence of the miracle consists in the attestation of the Divine presence with His messenger by the time and circumstances of an act, which may nevertheless be in itself an application of what we call the laws of nature to a particular case. It shows the Creator, whose word established the laws of nature—('He spake and it was done: He commanded and it stood fast')—repeating the word, through His prophet or minister, by which those laws are applied to a special purpose and occasion. Thus here the wind and sea-waves are the natural instruments: their use, at the will of God and the signal given by Moses, constitutes the miracle, without which all becomes unmeaning.—ED.

[3] Strabo, i. p. 58. The phrase 'practicable for vessels' plainly suggests that vessels could pass from the Mediterranean into the lake either across, or (as seems more likely from the nature of the

Another event of the same kind is related by an ancient historian. Diodorus, speaking of a campaign of the Persian king Artaxerxes Ochus against Egypt, mentions a catastrophe which befel his army in the same place :[4]—

'When the king of Persia (he says) had gathered all his forces, he led them against Egypt. But coming upon the great lake, about which are the places called the Gulfs, he lost a part of his army, because he was unaware of the nature of that region.'

Without intending to make the least allusion to the passage of the Hebrews, these authors inform us incidentally of historical facts, which are in perfect agreement with all that the sacred books tell us of the passage of the Hebrews across the sea.

Far from diminishing the value of the sacred records on the subject of the departure of the Hebrews out of Egypt, the Egyptian monuments, on the faith of which we are compelled to change our ideas respecting the passage of the Red Sea—traditions cherished from our infancy—the Egyptian monuments, I say, contribute rather to furnish the most striking proofs of the veracity of the biblical narratives, and thus to reassure weak and sceptical minds of the authenticity and the supreme authority of the sacred books.

If, during the course of eighteen centuries, the interpreters have misunderstood and mistranslated

ground) through a new gap in the causeway of sand, such as was broken through it in 1878, as described by Mr. Greville Chester. It is clear from Diodorus that, in his and Strabo's time, the Sirbonis was a lake of considerable depth; but Pliny describes it as an inconsiderable marsh (*H.N.* v. 13, s. 14).—ED.

[4] Diodorus, xvi. 46.

the geographical notions contained in Holy Scripture, the error is certainly not due to the sacred history, but to those who, without knowledge of the history and geography of ancient times, have attempted the task of reconstructing the Exodus of the Hebrews, at any cost, on the level of their own imperfect comprehension.

Permit me still one last word on the sequel of the march of the Hebrews, after their passage across the gulfs. The sacred books tell us:[5] 'Then Moses led the Israelites from the Sea of Reeds, and they went out into the desert of Shur, and, having gone three days in the desert, they found no water. From thence they came to Marah, but they could not drink of the waters of Marah, because they were bitter. Wherefore the place was called Marah (bitter). Then they came to Elim, where were twelve wells of water and seventy palm-trees; and they encamped there by the waters.'[6]

All these indications agree—as might have been expected beforehand—with our new views on the route of the Israelites. After reaching the Egyptian fortress near the sanctuary of the god Baal-zephon, which stood on one of the heights of Mount Casius, the Hebrews found in front of them the road which led from Egypt to the land of the Philistines. According to the command of God, forbidding them to follow this route,[7] they turned southwards, and thus came to the desert of Shur. This desert of 'the Wall'—so called from a place named in Egyptian 'the Wall'

[5] Exod. xv. 22, 23; Numb. xxxiii. 8.
[6] Exod. xv. 27; Numb. xxxiii. 9.   [7] *Ib.* xiii. 17.

and in Greek 'Gerrhon,' a word which likewise signifies 'the Wall,' as I have shown above—lay to the east of the two districts of Pitom and Ramses.[8] There was in this desert a road, but little frequented, towards the Gulf of Suez (as we now call it), a road which the Roman writer has characterized as 'rugged with hills and wanting in water-springs.'[9]

The bitter waters, at the place called Marah, are recognized in the Bitter Lakes of the Isthmus of Suez. Elim is the place which the Egyptian monuments designate by the name of Aa-lim or Tent-lim, that is 'the town of fish,' situate near the Gulf of Suez in a northerly direction.

When the Jews arrived at Elim, the words of Holy Scripture—'But God caused the people to make a circuit by the way of the wilderness, towards the Sea of Weeds,'—were definitively accomplished.[1]

To follow the Hebrews, stage by stage, till their arrival at Mount Sinai, is not our present task nor within the scope of this Conference. I will only say that the Egyptian monuments contain all the materials necessary for the recovery of their route, and for the identification of the Hebrew names of the different stations with their corresponding names in Egyptian.[2]

[8] This 'Desert of Shur' is, in Numbers xxxiii. 8, the 'desert of Etham,' which the people enter at once from their passage through the sea; and Etham is described as 'in the edge of the desert' (ver. 6).—ED.

[9] Plin. *H.N.* vi. 33 : 'asperum montibus et inops aquarum.'

[1] Exod. xiii. 18.

[2] See the mention, in the prefixed 'Advertisement,' of the Memoir on this subject in Dr. Brugsch's *Bibel und Denkmäler*.—ED.

NOTE BY THE EDITOR.

IT is not within the Editor's province to discuss the question treated in the foregoing Discourse. But the criticisms called forth by its publication in the first edition of this work suggest the desirableness of one or two remarks in further elucidation of Dr. Brugsch's views.

It may now be taken as established beyond question, not only that the Israelites lived in Lower Egypt, as a distinct Semitic tribe under appointed governors, but, further, that their abode was not in the neighbourhood of Memphis or of Heliopolis—whence their starting-point on the Exodus has generally been assumed— but in the lower part of the Delta, where the eastern border of Egypt proper lay along the Tanitic arm of the Nile.

The discoveries of Mariette and the arguments of Brugsch leave no reasonable doubt that the primeval city of Zoan, the Tanis of classical geography, whose name survives in *Sân*—was that same 'city of Ramses,' on the new buildings of which the Israelites were forced to labour, the 'Pi-Ramses' which was the favourite residence and delight of the early Pharaohs of the Nineteenth Dynasty, and especially of Ramses II. and his son Mineptah II ; though there are some who still pursue the fruitless labour of identifying this or that insignificant mound with the splendid city which must have left far other traces.[3] In fact the case is somewhat like the identification of Troy by Schliemann's researches at Hissarlik ;—there are *no other ruins*, save those of Tanis, adequate to represent the great and beautiful royal city of Ramses. To confirm this identification, there is a second and indubitable mark of the point whence the Exodus began : the miracles and deliverance were wrought in the land of Egypt, *in the field of Zoan* ' (Psalm lxxviii. 12, 43).

The starting-point thus fixed determines the *initial* direction of the march of the Israelites along the great eastern road leading out of Egypt towards Syria,—in the *general direction* (to say no more at present) of the route ascribed to them by Brugsch. The problem of their exact route, and especially of the spot where the great catastrophe took place, can only be solved by the study of the Scripture narrative in the light of *investigation of the ground*

---

[3] On the claim of Tel-el-Maskhoutah, see Vol. II., pp. 424-5.

by *competent enquirers*; for *both* conditions are essential, and few, if any, have hitherto united them in a degree at all comparable to Dr. Brugsch himself.

Quite recently, however, in February of the present year (1880), a personal examination of the whole route traced by Dr. Brugsch, from the ruins of Zoan-Ramses-Tanis to the tongue of land dividing Lake Sirbonis from the Mediterranean, has been made by Mr. Greville Chester, at the instance and with the aid of the Palestine Exploration Fund, whose 'Quarterly Statement' for July contains a most interesting account of Mr. Chester's adventurous journey. The discussion of the paper would be far beyond the limits of this Note, and we can only indicate its main results. Passing over some questions of detail, Mr. Chester agrees with Dr. Brugsch's identification of the stations along the route up to the most critical terminal points of Pi-hahiroth (now Gelse Hemdeyeh), at the entrance on the spit, and Baal-zephon at Mount Casius (now El-Gelse); and his own experience furnished almost a repetition of the circumstances of the passage of the Israelites on a small scale. He had encamped (like the Israelites) at sunset, on the tongue of sand between Pi-hahiroth and Baal-zephon. 'A light *northerly* breeze was blowing, and the Mediterranean broke with a loud noise upon the beach'—over which, Mr. Chester tells us, it is sometimes driven into the lake. 'About two o'clock in the morning I was awakened by a noise, and found that *the wind had changed and a furious S.E. by E. wind* was blowing across the lake. . . . Going out I found to my surprise that "the sea had seen that and fled." There was now a dead calm, and *the sea had retired no less than 26 paces further back from the point it had reached the previous night*.' Such is the comment of the winds and waves themselves upon the text—'And Jehovah caused the sea to go back by *a strong east wind* all that night' (Exod. xiv. 21); and Mr. Chester bears equally emphatic testimony to the effect of a violent *North wind* in causing '*the sea* to return to his strength' (ver. 27), sweeping over the tongue of land into the lake :—

'THE SEA:'—such is the phrase over and over again in the actual narrative (Exod. xiv. ; comp. Numb. xxxiii. 8), *without one mention* of the 'Red Sea,' or rather Yam Souph. *The Sea* is used in SS. *specifically* for the Mediterranean. The passages in which the *Yam Souph* is mentioned cannot be discussed within the limits of this Note.

ADDITIONS AND NOTES.

Communicated by Dr. Brugsch for the Second English Edition.

VOLUME I.

1. *Page* 10, *after first paragraph.*

Though I have expressed the opinion that the Egyptians migrated into Egypt from a primeval home in Asia, yet this idea is opposed by another view, according to which, by a method founded on historical data, the origin of the Egyptian people would have to be sought in the Nigritian (negro) Barabra. These are supposed to have ascended into the Nile-valley from the South, to have cultivated it and created one of the few centres of civilization in the ancient world, without thereby renouncing the peculiarities of African customs, and to have framed a kind of fetish worship, the foundation of which was laid in the observation of the periodical phenomena of the Nile. Their mingling with Syro-Arabian nomad races, who penetrated into Egypt from the East, and probably also with Libyan immigrants from the West, is supposed to have given origin to the mixed race of the ancient Egyptians, in which African blood largely predominated.[1] Lepsius has lately shown the reasons against this view[2] with remarkable clearness and great acuteness, and has proved, in the most convincing manner, the Asiatic home of the Egyptians, in agreement with the Biblical accounts in the list of nations.[3] Of the sons of Ham, Cush migrated from the East into the southern parts of Arabia and the opposite coasts of Africa[4] (the Somali countries), where their abodes are marked by the Egypto-Semitic name of *Pun*, which in my opinion signifies the East country, since in Hebrew the name Paneh (in proper names, penu, peni) indicates

[1] Rob. Hartmann, *Die Völker Africa's*, Leipzig, 1879, pp. 3, &c.
[2] See the Introduction to his *Nubian Grammar* (*Nubische Grammatik*. Berlin, 1880).
[3] Genesis x.   [4] Genesis x. 7.

the eastern side.[5] From hence one body (*Schwarm*), led by Nimrod, went to the region of the Euphrates, and ruled first in the land of Shinar in the towns of Babel, Erech, Accad, and Calneh.[6] The Babylonian tradition also fully recognized the arrival of these Cushite emigrants from the coasts of the Erythræan Sea, and had treated thereof in its own myths. A second branch passed over the Red Sea, and, conquering and driving out the native negro races, took possession of the country situated on the south of Egypt, between the coasts of the Red Sea and the eastern bank of the Upper Nile. The city of Meroë formed the centre of the kingdom founded there.

A third body of the Cushites went to the north of Egypt, and founded, on the east of the Delta, the kingdom of the so-called Hyksos, whom tradition designated sometimes as Phœnicians, sometimes as Arabians, and in both cases quite rightly. Lepsius has proved by excellent reasons the Cushite origin of the Hyksos-statues from Sán (Tanis) now in the museum of Boulaq, and has made more than merely probable the immigration of the Cushites into the region of the Delta, under the guidance of their *Hiq-shasu*, i.e. *Hyksos*—'Kings of the wandering people,' as I translate the word, not 'Kings of the Shepherds,' according to the usual interpretation.

The last authenticated migration of the Arabian Cushites, or *Pun*, took its direction to the Phœnician coasts, where their name *Phoinikes* (and still more the Latin form of *Pœni, Punici*) indicates their ancient native designation.[7] As the country which they occupied on the eastern coast of the Mediterranean Sea bore in the Egyptian inscriptions the name of *Kefa, Keft,* or *Keftha*, this designation also is very significant as to the migration of the Cushite races to Ethiopia, Babylonia, Egypt, and Phœnicia. For, according to classical traditions, the ancient name for Ethiopia was Cepheïs or Cephenia; the Ethiopians were called Cephenians; and a king of Ethiopia (father of Andromeda) is named Cepheus.[8] According to the ancient legend, as Lepsius shows, the Ethiopian

[5] Comp. Genesis xvi. 12; xxiii. 19; xxv. 18; 1 Kings xvii. 3, 5.
[6] Genesis x. 8-10.
[7] Herodotus (vii. 89) tells us that 'the Phœnicians, according to their own tradition, dwelt of old on the Red Sea, but passing over thence they inhabit the parts of Syria beside the sea; and this region, with that extending to Egypt, is called Palestine.'—ED.
[8] The names written with C, according to custom, have in the German, as in Greek, a K.

ADDITIONS AND NOTES. 403

king Cepheus resided in Iöpé (Joppa) on the coast of Palestine, where the myth of Andromeda had its special local source. Her mother, Cassiopeia, the wife of Cepheus, is called also wife of Phœnix, and daughter (*i.e.* '*native*') of Arabia. The Phœnicians themselves are called Cephenians, Cepheïds, and Cephids. According to Hellanicus the Chaldeans of Babylon bore the original designation of Cephenians. The Cepheian tower in Babylon was shown, and Cepheus is called a son of Belus.

To return to Egypt, the same name *Keft* appears to me to form the foundation of the designation *Caphtor*, which is mentioned in Holy Scripture as an island and as the fatherland of the Philistines.[9] Without being able to specify exactly its position on the Egyptian coast, I cannot pass over in silence the fact that the monuments, as early as the times of the Twelfth Dynasty, mention a country *Keftha-Hor*, that is 'Keftha of Horus,' for which local divinity a special priesthood was founded. In one of the tombs of the kings the same country appears under the name *Keft-Herau*, and is placed in connection with the *Utur*, or the great sea.

If from these observations, the bearing of which is of the highest importance for our knowledge of the migrations of the Cushites—the Phœnicians in the primeval times of all human history—the chief settlements of the Cushites in Arabia, Ethiopia, Phœnicia, and Egypt are determined once for all, then also with regard to the migration of the Egyptians to the valley of the Nile, the proof of their arrival from the East, and immediately from Arabia, may be inferred with some probability. As every nation, in which historical recollection fails, takes refuge in mythological legends, so the Egyptians also, in their myths preserved on the monuments, have not neglected to inform posterity of their opinions about their origin in mythological stories. The Land of the God, that is, Southern Arabia,[1] and the land of *Pun* or *Punt*, play a chief part in these fables. The principal and highest divinities, the god of light, Ra (also in his Theban form as Amon), and the cosmic goddess Hathor, are always, in the inscriptions of both the older and later monuments, placed in connection with this primitive cradle, and their arrival thence in Egypt is frequently and plainly referred to. A special local form of the god of light, the Horus of Apollinopolis Magna, appears in the heaven under his

[9] Deut. ii. 23 ; Jer. xlvii. 4 ; Amos ix. 7. [The word 'island' perhaps indicates only a maritime district.—ED.]

[1] Comp. Lepsius, *op. cit.* p. civ.

name Hud as at once the morning and the evening star, and his rising and setting are referred, not to Egypt, but to the primeval home of the Egyptians, the land of Pun. The red colour of the skin, which belongs to the Egyptians in the coloured representations of the monuments, is shared by them with the Ethiopian, Arabian, and Babylonian Cushites, and thus their relationship to this migratory people is indicated. The frequent mention on the monuments of the 'Land of the God' (*i.e.* of *Ra*, the god of light) and of Pun, together with the regions belonging to it,[2] showed to the Egyptians ancient representations about the land of their origin, the significance of which is the more to be valued, since the texts frequently strike the key of a yearning home-sickness, and glorify the East, the cradle of light and of their own childhood, as a land of perfect happiness.

Put (Phut) and Canaan are mentioned in Holy Scripture after Cush and Mizraim as sons of Ham.[3] No doubt can exist as to their ethnographical signification. According to the express words of the list of the nine nations found at Edfou, the name Puti denoted (in the compound *to-n-na-puti*, 'the land of the Puti') the people, called elsewhere by the more common name of *Thehennu*, *i.e.* the Marmaridæ dwelling to the west of the Delta. The ancient name of this people has also been clearly preserved in the Coptic language, since Ni-Phaiat (in the plural form) served as the general expression for the Libyan inhabitants of the districts situated to the west of the Delta. I may of course refrain from any further explanation of the meaning of Canaan in an ethnographic sense.

2. *Page* 149.

To the time of the double reign of the kings Amenemhat I. and Usurtasen I. belongs the death and burial of a faithful subject and warrior, named MENTHU-NESU, whose monument is preserved in the Louvre (under C 1). A very remarkable passage is found at the close of the inscriptions which cover this stone, and runs thus:—

'The words which this stone contains are an account of that which was done by my hand. This took place in truth, and no

[2] See Champollion, *Notices Descriptives*, ed. Maspero, p. 658. The most frequently mentioned are Uten (the Biblical Vedan), Men, Menti, Masen Fekhir, the position of which in Arabia is confirmed by the names of races preserved by Ptolemy, the Udeni, Minæi, Manitæ, Masonitæ, and Mocritæ.

[3] Genesis x. 6.

lie and no contradiction is contained therein. The *Menthu* and the *Her-sh'a* were destroyed, and the palaces of the Hethites (*Khetau*, Hittites) were overthrown.'

The mention of the last-named people at this time is extremely remarkable, for it appears to prove that at this time the Hethites were settled close to Egypt. In fact in the time of Abraham the Hethites were settled in the neighbourhood of Hebron, on the range of hills in the midst of the Amorites. (Gen. xxiii.)

3. *Page* 184, *end of first paragraph.*

On a monument preserved in the Museum at Geneva,[4] which was dedicated to the memory of a certain AMENI, a distinguished court official of this time, the following passage occurs, towards the conclusion of the dedicatory inscription :—

'I had come to Abydus in the suite of the Chief Treasurer I-THER-NOFIRT, to restore a statue of Osiris of the nether world, lord of Abydus, when king Usurtasen III., the ever-living, went by water to smite the miserable land of *Kash* (Cush) in the year 19.' This date affords us the certainty that the king mentioned undertook several campaigns against the Ethiopian Cushites.

4. *Page* 186, *sub fin.*

We may name as the most northern monument of Usurtasen III. his statue discovered in Tanis.[5]

5. *Page* 222, *sub fin.*

On the site of the ruins of Tanis is still to be seen the colossal statue of the fifth Sebekhotep, carved out of syenite, with short inscriptions which describe the king as 'friend of Ptah.'[6]

6. *Page* 342, *last line.*

The stélé mentioned on page 378 belongs to the time of this THUTMES I. I do not know how it happened that both Mariette (*Notices*, p. 345) and myself referred the origin of this monument to the third king of that name.[7]

7. *Page* 395.

The tomb of the Captain Amenemhib was not first discovered by Professor Ebers, but was already known before his time. Cham-

[4] Comp. *Mélanges d'Archéologie égypt. et assyr.* 1875, p. 217, &c.
[5] Comp. J. de Rougé, *Inscr. Hiérogl.* pl. 72. [6] Cf. *op. cit.* pl. 76.
[7] Comp. Wiedemann, *Geschichte der achtzehnten ägyptischen Dynastie*, p. 24, note 5.

pollion[8] also mentions the sepulchral chapel of an Amenemhib, the doors of which are adorned with the names of the kings Thutmes III. and Amenhotep II. In the inscriptions of this chapel the faithful servant of both the Pharaohs is called 'the hereditary lord, &c., whom the divine benefactor rewarded, who was the servant of the king from his cradle.' A certain Beki, who is named as his mother, is more exactly described as the 'great nurse of the lord of the country.'

8. *Pages* 412-415.

The verses of this poem of a court poet inspired by the deeds of his king, beginning 'I make them behold,' are repeated in an inscription which is found on the outside of the northern circuit walls of the temple of Karnak; only with the difference, that in the latter case they refer to the person and deeds of king Seti I.[9] Such plagiarisms in making use of older inscriptions are by no means rare on the monuments, even in the province of real historical records. They show how little scruple the ancient Egyptian felt at literary theft, if it only served *ad majorem Pharaonis gloriam*.

9. *Page* 452, *init.*

Among the contemporaries of the king we may here mention, on account of his prominent position, a former governor of Thebes, by name REKHMARA, in whose sepulchral chapel[1] there are some very remarkable inscriptions and representations, referring to the tributes rendered by the conquered nations, with the levying of which the person thus named was entrusted. The matter is thus spoken of in the inscriptions: 'This is the collection of the tributes of the countries of the South (Ethiopia) and of the land of *Punt* (Arabia), of the tributes of the land of *Ruthennu* (Syria), and of the land of *Kefa* (Phœnicia), and [of the tributes] of all nations, which king Thutmes III.—may he live for ever!—brought home [on] his victorious campaigns, by the hereditary lord *Rekhmara*.'

10. *Page* 467, *end.*

During the reign of this Thutmes IV. occurred the 'death of the royal scribe ZA-ANNI,' who had rendered important services to this Pharaoh and his two predecessors on the throne, by raising troops.[2] In the inscriptions of his sepulchral chapel at Thebes, he himself relates as follows about his own activity:—

[8] *Notices Descriptives*, p. 505, Tombeau No. 12.
[9] Comp. Champollion, *Notices Descriptives*, ii. p. 96.
[1] Cf. *op. cit.* p. 504.   [2] Cf. *op. cit.* p. 381, &c.

'I served king Thutmes III., and I was an eye-witness of the victories which he won over all peoples. He brought the kings of the land of Zahi as living captives to the land of Egypt. He conquered all their towns, and destroyed all their tribes. No land was able to make resistance to him. It was I also that recorded in writing the victories which he achieved over all peoples, even as they were accomplished. And I served king Amenhotep II., and his Majesty held me worthy of his affection. And I served king Thutmes IV., the dispenser of life now and for ever. I enlisted for him numerous warriors.'

Other monuments, which are now exhibited in the Museum of Turin, have also preserved the memory of this person, whose wife and sister is mentioned by the name of Mutari, and whose son and heir was the scribe H'atithi. Za-anni must have been, so to speak, the general staff-officer of his time, for his special activity in the levying of troops is intimated in the following inscription, which is over a representation referring to the matter :—[3]

'The warriors were enrolled in the presence of the king, all the classes of young men were separated according to their ages, and everyone was instructed in what concerned his duty in the assembled army by the scribe of the warriors, Za-anni.'

11. *Page* 490, *end.*

That Amenhotep III. had a Solomon-like desire for (Asiatic) women appears to me to be shown by a very remarkable inscription, which covers a great scarabæus (a kind of memorial-medal according to our modern ideas), which was acquired quite lately, through a lucky chance, by a lady-traveller in Egypt (Mme. Kaufmann). I here give a literal translation of the text, omitting the wearisome titles :—

'In the 10th year of the reign of king Amenhotep III. and his chief wife, queen Thi, whose father was called Juâ, and her mother Thuâ, a remarkable present was brought to his Majesty, (namely) Kirgipa, the daughter of Satarona, king of Naharana (Mesopotamia), and the choicest women of her women's house, in number 317 female persons.'

It is needless for me to draw attention to the value of this short text, which affords us the opportunity of learning the names of two contemporaries of Asiatic origin. The Bible also tells us of a king of Mesopotamia, Chushan-Rishathaim, who oppressed the children of Israel in the time of the Judges.[4]

[3] *Op. cit.* p. 830. [4] Judges iii. 8.

Another inscription on a stone scarabæus (in the collection in the Vatican) is dated the 11th year, the 1st day of the month Athyr of the reign of the same king and his wife Thi. In this it is mentioned that the king had formed a lake for his great wife in her city of Z'aru (the name recals the Hebrew Zoar) of the North country, the length of which was 3,600 cubits, and the breadth 600 cubits. It is added that the king in person celebrated on the lake the great festival of the inundation on the 16th of Athyr, and was conveyed in the ship Aten-nofru.

In conclusion, we may mention among the contemporaries of Amenhotep III. the chief priest of Amon, BEKEN-KHONSU, probably an ancestor of the chief priest and chief architect of the same name, who lived and died under Ramses II. His statue is in the possession of the Museum at Berlin. The inscriptions on it call his father 'a chief of the young men of the city of Amon (Diospolis), Amenemapet.' We may further mention, as having died during his reign, the scribe of the young men, and master of the horse, Horemhib, who had accompanied the king, for the last time, on a campaign into the interior of Africa, after having already rendered faithful service to the kings Amenhotep II. and Thutmes IV.[5]

12. *Page* 514, *line* 2.

Read: 'His tomb is preserved to the present day. The sarcophagus of rose granite was already broken to pieces intentionally in ancient times. A piece of it is in the Berlin Museum.'[6]

13. *Page* 514, *end*.

A memorial stêlé, with a long inscription, and the date '4th year, month Khoiahk, 1st day' of king Ai (whose names are half erased, as if men wished to obliterate the remembrance of a usurper), has preserved to us the name of one of his adherents, a certain Nakht Khim, priest of the god Khim in Panopolis, Khemmis.

14. *Page* 518, *line* 6.

Read: 'And *he* beheld the holiness of this god. And Hor the lord of Alabastrônpolis was accompanied by his son,' &c.

15. *Page* 520, *line* 14.

Read: 'He visited the localities of the gods, which were situated in the cities,' &c.

[5] Comp. Champollion, *Notices Descriptives*, p. 835.
[6] See Lepsius, *Katalog*, 1871, p. 43, under No. 201.

ADDITIONS AND NOTES. 409

16. *Page* 521, *line* 4.

This is especially proved by the relief on the stone plinth, which serves as a seat, and on the back of which the above-mentioned inscription is found. The artist has tried to present vividly before our eyes out of the dark granite the forms of king Horus and his wife Notem-mut in a sitting posture. The queen, specially entitled as 'worshipper of Isis, the mother of the god,' in fond love has placed her right arm round the body of her royal husband. On the left side of the throne she appears in the form of a recumbent sphinx, strangely conceived. The female head is decorated with a singular head-dress, with strange ornaments; out of the lion's body with *five* breasts springs an erect pair of wings, which, in form and execution, remind us of Assyrian models. On the opposite side of the throne are seen fettered enemies (Asiatics and Negroes), as conquered representatives of the Northern and Southern worlds.

VOLUME II.

17. *Page* 9, *third paragraph*.

To 'the second year of his reign' *add* ' the 20th of Mekhir.'

18. *Ibid., last line but one*.

For ' Hor-Khem ' *read* ' Khem-Amun.'

19. *Page* 34, *sub fin*.

Among the contemporaries of the king, PAUËR, the former governor of Thebes—son of the chief priest of Amon, Neb-mesir (surnamed Tera), and of the priestess of Amon, Merit-ra—appears to us worthy of mention on account of his high position. Besides Seti I., Ramses II. is also named as a royal contemporary of our Pauër. In his tomb at Thebes (No. 32 according to Champollion's enumeration) two renowned artists of his time are also mentioned, the painter *Amen-uah-su*, and the sculptor ('from the life') *Hi* (or *Hui*), both of whom doubtless exerted their utmost skill in adorning his tomb.

20. *Page* 37, *note*.

Add: 'The same date, in connection with the name of the festival, is found a second time in an inscription on the sepulchral chapel of the chief priest of Amon, NEB-UNON-F, who was thus a contemporary of Ramses II. The following is a literal translation :—

"In the year 1, the month Athyr, when his Majesty had descended the river from the capital of the South, and testified his homage to his father the Theban Amon-ra, the deities Mut and Khonsu of Thebes, (surnamed) Nofer-hotep, and the co-divinities of Thebes, at his (*i.e.* Amon's) splendid festival of Apet, his journey from thence was happily accomplished."'

21. *Page 46, end.*

Read thus: 'Gauzanitis, the Gosan (Goshen) of the Holy Scriptures.'

22. *Pages 56–59.*

We are now able to make the following corrections in the translation of the Heroic Poem, from the original text, published by J. de Rougé, which E. de Rougé copied at Luqsor.

Page 56, line 7. 'His heart is firm, *his strength like that* of the god of war,' &c.

Line 11. 'He seizes the bow, and no one *is equal* to him.'

Lines 15–16. 'No one knows the thousands of men who *fell down*, nor the hundreds of thousands *that sank down* at sight of him.'

Lines 20, foll. 'Wise counsel and most perfect resolution are found even at his first answer. He is a protector of his people, like a mountain of iron.'

Line 33. 'To bow themselves *through fear* before the king.'

Page 57, line 10. 'The people of *Khita* had arrived in full number, and that of *Naharain*, in like manner that of Arathu,'&c.[7]

Page 58, last two lines. 'I did not withhold my hand from goodness, so that anything else should be done but as thy wish required.'

Page 59, line 8 from bottom. 'In their breast *from terror*, their limbs,' &c.

23. *Page 76, last paragraph of the treaty.*

Read thus: 'That which is found in the middle of this silver

---

[7] The author has set forth the views of the school of Egyptologists who recognize the peoples enumerated as allies of the Khita in the nations of Asia Minor and the islands—the Dardanians, Mysians, Mæonians (old Lydians), Carians, Lycians, &c.—in his highly important *Appendix IX.* to Dr. Schliemann's *Ilios*, on *Troy and Egypt.*—ED.

tablet, and on the front side of it, represents the image of the god Sutekh, embracing the image of the great king of the land of Khita, and surrounded by an inscription as follows :—" This is the image of the god Sutekh, king of heaven, protector of this agreement,"' &c.[8]

24. *Page 92, line 3.*

The full title of Ameneman runs thus :—' The hereditary lord, the first prince in Memphis, the conductor of the festival of M'a-t, the architect in Heliopolis, the overseer of all the offices in Upper and Lower Egypt, the chief architect of the king, the chief commander of the troops of the lord of the country, the major domus in the house of Thutmes III.' (*i.e.* the house or temple built of old by Thutmes III.).[9]

25. *Page 93, before last paragraph.*

The great stêlé with inscriptions of the time of Ramses II., which was discovered in the neighbourhood of the place now called Maskhoutah (in the Wady-Toumeilât, near the railway station of Ramses), appears to me worthy of mention, both on account of the place where it was found, and for the sake of its contents. In it the god Hormakhu of On speaks to this Pharaoh in the following words :—

' I will reward thee for that which thou hast done, my son, who lovest me ; for I have known that thou lovest me. I, thy father, give thee time and eternity, to be king of the nations. Thy length of life shall equal my length of life on my throne on earth. Thy years shall equal the years of the god Tum. Thou shalt shine radiantly on both my zones of light (in the East and West), and thou shalt illuminate the two worlds. Thou shalt be a protector to Egypt, and wide shall be thy borders. Thou shalt conquer the countries of *Khal* (Phœnicia), of *Kush* (Ethiopia), of the *Thehennu*, (the Marmaridæ), and of the *Shasu* (Arabs), and the islands and coasts in the midst of the great sea, by the triumph of thine arm. Thou shalt bring their inhabitants to Egypt, king Ramses Miamun !'

In a second inscription the god says, among other things :—

' Thou shalt protect Egypt with thine arms, thou shalt subjugate all peoples, and they shall become warriors in thy service.'

The place where this remarkable stone was found, in the de-

[8] Comp. *Mélanges d'Archéologie ég. et assyr.*, 1875, p. 284, &c.
[9] Comp. Lepsius, *Denkmäler*, iii. 29 *e*.

pression to the west of Lake Timsah, through which, according to the Greek tradition, Ramses II. was the first to construct a fresh-water canal, confirms at least the existence of ancient Egyptian buildings and places of worship in this part of Egypt at the time of that king. But yet this does not furnish any proof that Ramses II. founded there a city of the name of Ramses, in the building of which the Jews had to perform compulsory labour.[1]

26. *Page 97, before last paragraph.*

Ramses caused the rock-temple to be erected after his wars and victories in the land of the Khita. The inscriptions of Ibsamboul bear witness that the king did not fail to make presents and donations in the most generous manner to the principal deity of the sanctuary, Ra, the god of light. A text[2] speaks on this subject in a way not to be misunderstood:—'The objects gained as spoil were offered by the divine benefactor to his father Ra, *after he had returned from the land of Khita*, and had smitten the foreign nations, and crushed the Asiatics ('*Amu*) in their abodes—consisting of silver, gold, blue stone, green stone, and other precious stones.'

Many officers of the king and later visitors to the place have attempted to immortalize themselves by inscriptions on the outside walls of the temple and the rock: as, to cite some examples, *Setan*, the king's son of Kush (in the time of Ramses II.); *Meri*, the deputy governor of the province of Wawa (in the time of Seti II. Mineptah III.); the chief priest *Aahmes*, surnamed *Turo*; the scribes *Horemhib* and *R'anofer*; the sculptor of the images of king Ramses Miamun, named *Piaoi*; another artist *Pa-nofer*, and others.

27. *Page 99, line 4.*

The new worships founded by Ramses II., which were connected with his name, had their own priests. For example, a 'chief priest of Amon of Ramses' is frequently mentioned. Among others invested with such an office were the two brothers, *Nu-ta-maten* and *Amen-uah-su*.[3]

28. *Page 112, line 20.*

Read: 'Thy girdle of the finest cotton, thou givest it for a vile rag.'

[1] On the erroneous identification of the remains at this mound of Maskhoutah with the city of Raamses or Rameses (Exod. i. 11, xii. 37), more is said below, pp. 424-5.
[2] Comp. Champollion, *Notices Descriptives*, p. 66.
[3] See Lieblein, *Namen-Lexicon*, No. 1002.

29. *Page* 113, *end*.

The daughter of the king of Khita bore, according to the statement on the great Ramses-stêlê of Ibsamboul, the Egyptian name of *M'a-ur-nofru*. In Tanis also, E. de Rougé discovered her name as 'the great queen and princess of the land, *M'a-nofru-r'a* (*sic*), the daughter of the great king of Khita.'[4] She was, without doubt, the mother of the princess *Bint-antha*, the favourite daughter of the king, mentioned on page 117.

30. *Page* 120, *at beginning of the new reign*.

During the lifetime of his aged father, the new king bore the title of 'an hereditary prince (*i.e.* successor to the throne) on the seat of the earth-god Set, who ruled the lands of his father.'[5]

31. *Pages* 122-8.

On the basis of the latest publication of this important historical text, by J. de Rougé and Mariette, we are in a position to correct some passages in our version. We would note the following (the *lines* are those of the *inscription*, not of the *page*).

Page 122, line 9. *For* 'cities' *read* 'city.'

Page 123, line 14. *For* 'Qauasha' *read* 'Aquasha.'

Line 16. *Read:* 'I give you to know *that* I the king am your shepherd.'

Line 17. *Read:* 'He is *for* you like *a father who* preserves the life of his children.'

Line 18. *Read:* 'The foreigners plunder its borders.'

Pages 123-4, line 20. *Read:* 'in sight of the lowland (*Ta-ahu*, the most ancient designation of the Libyan Oasis, now called Farafrah).'[6]

Page 125, line 37. *Read:* '[with him]. Also the herds of his country, consisting of cattle, goats, and asses, all were,' &c.

Lines 38-39. *Read:* 'Then these were given over to the cavalry, who were behind them on horses. [The enemies] fled (39) [in haste, but the horsemen overtook them, and] a great battle [took place]. They brought hither the killed [in great numbers]. No man,' &c.

[4] See *Mélanges d'Arch. ég. et assyr.* vol. ii. p. 285.
[5] Comp. J. de Rougé, *Inscr. hiérogl.* pl. 74.
[6] See the author's *Appendix VIII.* to Dr. Schliemann's *Ilios*, 'On Hera Boöpis.'—ED.

Line 40. *Read:* '[would render no assistance]. They were not able to keep them at a distance. But it was done,' &c.

Page 125, line 41. *Read:* 'In order to announce *the strength of the divine benefactor.* Then,' &c.

Page 127, line 53.   J. de Rougé gives   752,   instead of   750.
„   „   „ 55.   „   „   6103   „   6111.
„   „   „ 56.   „   „   2362   „   2370.
„   128 „ 60.   „   „   1307   „   1308.
„   „   „ „   „   „   64   „   54.
„   „   „ „   „   „   3175   „   3174.

32. *Page* 130, *last two lines of first paragraph.*

Read: 'Whose name is again reflected in the Greek designation of the town Dardanis in the region mentioned.'

33. *Page* 136, *beginning.*

Read: 'Pinehas, a former governor of Thebes, an Egyptian namesake,' &c.

34. *Page* 160, *after first paragraph.*

Add: 'After such fortunate results and glorious campaigns against countries and peoples, which the lust of plunder had conducted to the boundaries of Egypt by land and water, it should not excite surprise if the poets on the banks of the holy river hastened to magnify the renown and greatness of the king in rhythmic language. Many samples of their performances are preserved to us on the stone walls of the temple of Medinet-Abou. A great stélé on the first pylon of this temple,[7] with the date of the 12th year of the king, appears to me worthy of special notice. From the 28th line onwards, Amon is introduced speaking thus: "I have bestowed on thee courage and victory, and thy strength, which remains in the memory of foreign nations. I have prostrated the peoples of Asia at thy feet for all times even to eternity. Thou art enthroned as king, to receive each day as thy possessions the spoil of thy hands. The kings of all countries and of all peoples bring their children before thy face. I have surrendered them altogether into thy hand, to do with them what pleases thee.

'"I caused thy war-cry to resound in the countries of thine enemies, and fear of thee to fill the valleys. Princes tremble at the remembrance of thee, for thy battle-axe swings over their head.

[7] See J. de Rougé, *Inscr. Hiérogl.* pl. 131, &c.

They come to thee as at one call, to beseech mercy from thee. Thou givest life according to thy pleasure, and thou killest according to thy will. The throne of all nations is thine.

'" I have made all peoples subjects of thy dynasty. I make them come to place themselves as inferiors in the service of thy person. They carry their presents, which their kings have won as booty, and they offer them to thee as tribute of the country for thy Majesty. Their son and their daughter are servants in thy royal house to incline thy soul to mercy."

' The long address of the god concludes with the words: " I raise thee to be sole lord, that thou mayest establish the land of Egypt." '

35. *Page* 160, *line* 16.

The buildings, offerings, and other benefits which Ramses III. caused to be shared among the temples and sanctuaries of the gods of the country, extended, according to the statements of the great Harris Papyrus, to the following places both in and out of Egypt.[8]

A. *In Nubia (To-Khont).*

The building of a special sanctuary dedicated to Amon, named *Pi-r'amses Haq-Ôn 'A-nakht* (*i.e.* 'the well-fortified town of R'amses Haq-Ôn ').

B. *In Upper Egypt.*

Nubti, the Greek Ombi, Ombos, now called Koum-Ombou (situated in Nome I.). Here the *Pi-R'amses Haq-Ôn* ('Temple of Ramses III.') was erected in the *Pi-Sutekh* ('Temple of Sutekh'), and the latter was protected by a wall.

Pi Amun, ' the city of Amon,' the Greek Diospolis, metropolis of Nome IV. Here the following buildings were erected :—

1. *Ta-Hut suten-Kanit R'a-user-m'at Mi-amun* (' the house of king *R'a-user-m'at Mi-amun* ') on the hill of the necropolis of *Neb-'ankh*. At the present day the temple of Medinet-Abou.

2. *Pi-R'amses Haq-Ôn* (' the temple of Ramses III.') Situation uncertain.

3. *Ta-Hut R'amses Haq-Ôn* (' the house of Ramses III.'), with the additional name *Nemu-* (or *Khnemu*) *reshut* in Amon's city of *Apet*. This is the temple of Ramses III. still standing at

[8] In this list of Ramessea, the names of the cities in different nomes are reproduced according to the writing of the period. As each city bore several names, it is not surprising to find them written sometimes in one form, sometimes in another.

Karnak, which opens in a northerly direction on the great entrance court of this national sanctuary. It is the temple M on the general plan of Karnak in Mariette's publication.

4. *Pi-R'a-user-m'at Mi-amun* ('the temple of Ramses III.'); situation unknown.

5. *Pi-R'amses Haq-Ôn* ('the temple of Ramses III.') in the *Pi-Khonsu*, or town of Khonsu, is the designation of the temple of Khonsu at Karnak founded by this king; T on the general plan of Mariette.

Kobti (Coptos), metropolis of Nome V., with the temple of *Khim* (Pan), Horus and Isis.

Hut-sokhem (Diospolis Parva), metropolis of Nome VII.

In the next Nome, VIII., with its metropolis *Tini* (This, Thinis), the following towns with their sanctuaries are mentioned:—

1. In *Abud* (Abydus) a special sanctuary was erected in the interior of the great temple of Osiris, under the designation *Ta-Hut-Ra'mses Haq-Ôn* ('the house of Ramses III.'), and the whole quarter of this god (and his co-deities Horus and Isis) was protected by a wall.

2. In *Tini* (Thinis, This) a sanctuary was founded in the temple of the god Anhur (Onuris according to Greek transcription, the Egyptian Mars) under the same designation as the preceding, but also with the additional name *Uta-tod* (*Uz'a-zod*), to the service of which 457 persons were dedicated.

3. In *Neshi* (Ptolemaïs), with a *Pi-Sebek* or 'temple of the crocodile-headed *Sebek*.'

Apu (Panopolis), metropolis of Nome IX., with a temple of *Khim* (Pan), of Horus and of Isis. A 'house of Ramses III.' was added here in like manner.

Debui (Aphroditopolis), metropolis of Nome X.

Shas-hotep (Hypselé), metropolis of Nome XI., with a temple of the ram-headed god *Khnum*.

Siajout (Lycopolis, the modern Ossiout), metropolis of Nome XIII. Here two sanctuaries were founded in honour of the god Ap-maten 'of the South' (a special local form of the jackal-headed Anubis), and his temple was protected by a wall.

Khimunu (Hermopolis Magna), metropolis of Nome XV. Two sanctuaries of *Thot* were founded, one being designated *ta-Hut* ('the house'), the other *Pi* ('town,' 'temple'), of king Ramses III. The temple of Thot was protected by a wall.

Hut-uër (Hibennu, Hibis), metropolis of Nome XVI., with a temple of the local god *Khnum*.[9]

A-rud (situated in the district of the same nome), with a local worship of the god *Amon-r'a*.

The three following places lay within the district of Nome XVII. (the Cynopolites of the Greeks):

Pa-utui, with a sanctuary of Thot, the Egyptian Hermes;

Matu-Khont, with a worship of Amon;

A-Musha ('island of Musha=Moses'), called by the Greeks Musæ or Musôn, with a worship and temple of the god *Sebek*. At the present day Surarieh. [Spelt *I-en-Moshé* at p. 117.—ED.]

Saptu, metropolis of Nome XVIII., with a temple of Anubis.

Sapt-moru (Oxyrhynchus), metropolis of Nome XIX., with a temple of the (Typhonic) *Sutekh*.

Pi-her-shefni (Heracleopolis Magna), metropolis of Nome XX., with a temple of Her-shafni (with a ram's head), the Harsaphes of the Greeks.

In the next Nome, XXI., the Arsinoites of the Greek classics (now called Fayoum), with its metropolis, Crocodilopolis, the following places are mentioned as favoured by Ramses III.:

1. *Pi-sebek*, Crocodilopolis, with the sanctuary of Horus of Lake Mœris.

2. *Pi-sutekh*, 'the town of Sutekh,' called by its common name *Sessu*. Situation uncertain.

3. *Pehuu* (position unknown), with a temple of the Theban *Amon-r'a*, a kind of Diospolis in the Fayoum.

Tep-ah (Aphroditopolis), the modern Atfih, metropolis of Nome XXII., with a temple of the goddess Hathor—Aphrodite.[1]

C. *In Lower Egypt.*

Men-nofer (Memphis), metropolis of Nome I.

Two sanctuaries were founded within the great temple of *Ptah* (Vulcan), named after the king thus:

1. *Ta-Hut-R'amses-Haq-Ôn*, and
2. *Pi-R'amses-Haq-Ôn*. Besides

---

[9] The note on p. 415 applies here; but my latest studies (see the *Dictionnaire Géographique*) have proved to me that the place *Hut-uër*, otherwise called *Hibennu, Hebennu*, answers to the town Ibis (Ἶβις, Ibennu) of the Greek geographers.

[1] Compare the Author's *Appendix VIII.* to Dr. Schliemann's *Ilios*, 'On Hera Boöpis.'—ED.

3. *Pi-user-m'at Mi-amun,* 'the town on the road to the west of *A-ament* (or *p-a-ament*).'

(*Hut-to-thar-ab*), the Athribis of the Greeks, metropolis of Nome X., with offerings to Horus, the god of the country, whose temple was surrounded with walls.

Ôn (the Biblical Ôn), metropolis of Nome XIII., with the great deity *Tum-R'a-Hormakhu* and his ancient temple. Ramses III. had this temple cleansed, and the ruined sanctuaries restored to a good condition. *Different* from it is *Pi-R'a* ('City of the Sun'), Heliopolis, the temple-buildings of which are named according to their position as 'situated to the north of On,' probably the same place, of which the ruins have been discovered quite lately in the neighbourhood of the so-called *Tel-el-Yahudi*.[2] Here Ramses III. built a circuit-wall, a temple under the name *Ta-Hut-R'amses-Haq-Ôn*, and another sanctuary designated *Pi-R'amses-Haq-Ôn*. He also raised a sanctuary to *Ius'as*, the divine wife of Tum, on the west side of the canal *Ati* (of Heliopolis). In the neighbourhood of this temple there was a place called *Ropi* or *Erpi*, with the local worship of a Horus. This place also the king fortified and surrounded with a wall.

North of On and the above-mentioned towns or temple-buildings one came to the town of *Pi-balos* (the Byblos of the ancients? now called Bilbeis), which was situated 'on the water of R'a,' the Sun-god. Within it was a sanctuary of the goddess *Bast* (easily explained by the proximity of the city called after her Bubastus), to which the care of the king likewise extended.

The case was the same with regard to the place *'Abui-nuter*, near On, in the territory of the province 'An or 'Ain (in later times the Nomos Heroöpolites), towards whose goddess the same king showed his beneficence.

I have now, in conclusion, to specify certain buildings, in places the importance of which, in their historical significance, must specially interest the reader.

In the north of the Delta there was a second Thebes, a second city of Amon, which bears the whole set of names that are employed in the south of Egypt—in *Patoris*—but especially *Na-amon* or *Pi-amon*, 'Diospolis,' the city of Amon, *Apet* and *Us* or *Uas*. It is called besides *Na-mehit*, 'the city (*par excellence*) of the North,'

---

[2] See my observations on this subject in the Berlin *Zeitschrift für Aegyptologie,* 1871, p. 86, &c.

as Thebes is called *Na-ris*, 'the city of the South.' Its territory bore the corresponding designation *pa-to-mehit*, 'the country of the North,' just as *pa-to-ris*, 'the country of the South,' denoted the so-called Thebaïs in Upper Egypt. The Phathmetic branch of the Nile (*pa-to-mehit*) owed the origin of its name among the Greek geographers to this designation, as on the other hand the form *to-mehit*, 'country of the North,' is the mother of the modern town of Damietta (which has taken the place of Diospolis), called by the Copts *Tamiati*, by the Arabs *Damiât*, and which is already mentioned by Stephanus Byzantinus as *Tamiathis*. The importance of the Lower Egyptian city of Diospolis, close to the sea, was pre-eminent in ancient times as at the present day. It is the same *Na-amon*, 'city of Amon,' which is spoken of in the Bible as *No*[3] or as No-amon.[4] It satisfies, both topographically and historically, in fact in every respect, what the latter place named in Holy Scripture requires of it. It is the Diospolis Parva of Strabo (xviii. p. 802).

The magnificent buildings of Ramses III. in this northern city of Amon are mentioned in the Harris Papyrus together with those of Thebes in Upper Egypt, and by the same designations. Thus we find there: 1. *ta-Hut-suten-kauit-R'a-user-m'at-Mi-amon*, or 'the house of king Ramses III.;' 2. *Pi-R'amses-Haq-Ôn*, 'the temple of Ramses III.;' and 3. *Pi-R'a user-m'at Mi-amon*, ' the temple of Ramses III.,' designated thus after his official name.

In this *Na-pa-to-mehi* or 'town of the *To-mehi*' (whence comes evidently the designation of the Biblical Naphtuhim),[5] Ramses III. founded, according to the great Harris Papyrus, an entire quarter of the town, which bore the name *Pi-R'amses-Haq-Ôn-â-nakht*, 'the well-fortified town of Ramses,' and is once (x. 2) denoted expressly as *pa-dema*, that is 'the town.' In it was *ta-hut*, that is 'the sanctuary, the temple' of a local form of Amon, whose image was called in addition 'that of Amon of Ramses Haq-Ôn.'

[3] Ezek. xxx. 14; Jer. xlvi. 25. [4] Nahum iii. 8.
[5] In case any of my readers, in comparing the Hebrew form of the word *naphtuhim* (with the plural termination *im*) with the Egyptian *na-pa-to-mehi* or *na-pha-to-mehi*, should find a stumbling-block in the omission of the *m* in *mehi*, I observe that there happens to be a second designation of the same place, *Na-pa-athv*, 'the town of the Papyrus lake,' which helps us over all difficulties in the comparison. This derivation of the Naphtuhim of SS. appears to me far preferable to that which I formerly proposed (Vol. I. p. 327), connecting them with the nation of the *Thuhen* (Marmaridæ).

The last place, in which Ramses III. sought to immortalize himself by buildings, bears in the same noble Harris Papyrus the name, certainly a very strange one, of *Pi-Sutekh n R'amessu Mi-amon*, 'the city of Sutekh of Ramses II.,' for that this king is intended is shown by the spelling *Ramessu* instead of the spelling *R'amses* for the name of the third king Ramses. The latter, as appears from the text, enlarged the 'Sutekh-city' by a separate building, called *Pi-R'amses Haq-Ôn em pi-Sutekh*, 'the temple of Ramses III. in the town of Sutekh.' That this building bore yet another designation is proved by another passage referring to it in the same papyrus, which runs thus:—*Pi-R'amses-Haq-Ôn em Pi-Sutekh em Pi-R'amessu Mi-amon*, that is 'the temple of Ramses III. in the city of *Sutekh* in the city of *Ramses II.*'

In other words: Ramses III. raised a temple after his own name, in the quarter of the temple of *Sutekh* in the city of *Ramses II.*, a designation borne, as I long ago proved, by a new quarter of the well-known city of Tanis.

As will be perceived from the foregoing contributions, Ramses III., in his buildings in Lower Egypt, confined his attention to those sanctuaries which lay on the east side of the Delta, nearly in the direction of a straight line drawn from Heliopolis northwards to Diospolis (Damietta). This is just the side which was most exposed to the attacks of enemies from the East. Even without special comment this fact is very remarkable.

D. *In Palestine,*

or, as the country is called in the papyrus, in the *to-n-Zaha*, 'country of Zaha,' Ramses III. likewise founded a special sanctuary, which the text denotes by the lengthy name *ta-Hut-R'amses Haq-Ôn em pa-Kan'ana*, 'the house of Ramses III. in the land of Canaan.' We are not informed as to its exact position, but at least we owe to the papyrus the information, that in the sanctuary thus designated an image of the god 'Amon of king Ramses III.' was worshipped.

36. *Page 202, after line 11.*

In the temple of *Khonsu* at Karnak a memorial has been preserved, though, alas! in a very fragmentary condition, of the members of the family of king HIRHOR, remarkable from the fact that several of his sons bore names entirely Semitic. Thus the seventh was called *Masahartha*, and the eighth *Masaqahartha*. The name of the former appears again on a statue now in Brussels, on which he is designated as 'Crown Prince and first Prophet of Amon.'

37. Page 202, line 13, and *Genealogical Table IV.*

According to the very probable results of the researches of M. Naville (see *Berliner ägypt. Zeitschrift*, 1878, pp. 29, f.) the succession of the queens of the Twenty-first Dynasty was as follows:

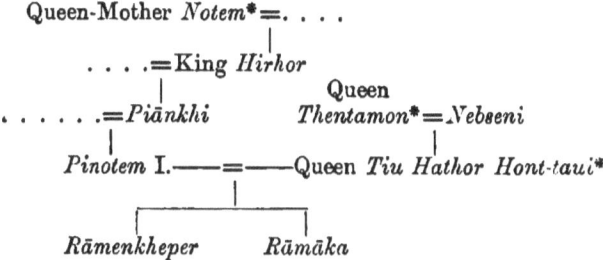

38. NOTES ON THE EXODUS.

1. The geographical studies, to which my attention has been devoted of late years, and the results of which are contained in my great *Geographical Dictionary*, have proved to me most convincingly that I have not deceived myself, and that the *general* direction of the march of the Jews out of Egypt answers to all the geographical conditions revealed to us by the papyri and the monuments regarding the principal stations on the route.

I do not at all dissemble the difficulties in the way of my views, which arise out of several passages in Holy Scripture concerning the Exodus; but I constantly ask myself—Where is the *city of Ramses*, if it is not *Tanis*, whose name of *Pi-Ramses* is demonstrated by the monuments, and whose gigantic ruins are visible at our day? I ask myself—Where is *Etham*, the *Khetam* of the monuments?—Where, especially, is *Migdol*, the name of which has no other meaning than the northern fortress on the eastern side of Lower Egypt? Above all, I ask myself how we are to explain the fact, that the towns named occur in the same geographical order in which the Scripture narrative makes them follow one another. The difficulty, moreover, in identifying the station of *Succoth* with the monumental name of *Thuko* or *Thukot* disappears as soon as we observe (what I have proved in an article in the *Aegyptische Zeitschrift*) that the Egyptian *th* ($=\theta$) answers in many instances to the letter ס (*s*) of the corresponding words in Hebrew.

2. A *monumental difficulty* exists only regarding the exact position of the place called *Pitum*, situated, according to the indications of the papyri, in the country of Succoth, and on that account named, in several documents, the town of Succoth. This town, as is proved by the lists of nomes, formed the centre of a nome. I have made the remark (on p. 377) that a *serpent*, called by the name of *Kereh*, was worshipped at *Pitum*, or *Pitom*, as the living symbol of the god of that place. As the result of new researches, I am now in a position to establish the fact, that the said 'serpent' is rather a *fish*, which still serves, in the Coptic language, to designate *the electric fish*, whose name of *Kereh* is derived from a root signifying to *strike*, to *give a blow*. Its Egyptian name Kereh, prefaced by the masculine article, *pa* or *pha—Pha-Kereh*—gave rise to the Greek designation of *Phagros* or *Phagrorios*, whence must be derived (if I do not deceive myself) the appellation of *Phagroriopolis*, assigned to the capital of the like-named nome. The position of this latter, according to the scanty information preserved to us from antiquity, is very uncertain. All that we are warranted in saying is confined to the notice, that the place was situated on the east side of the Delta, in the neighbourhood of the Arabian Nome, and of the modern valley of Toumeilât.[6] There is no doubt that the name of the sanctuary, where, according to the great geographical list of Edfou, the fish *Kereh* was worshipped— that is to say, *Pa-Kereh*—gave rise to the Greek denomination of the town, Phagroriopolis, which was certainly in the neighbourhood of *Pitom*, and appears to have been identical with the latter.

Another question respecting the position of *Pitom*. If we were to suppose its identity with the town of Patumos, mentioned by Herodotus (ii. 158), the question would become very simple. According to this author, Patumos was not far from Bubastus. As a papyrus in the British Museum speaks of lakes in the neighbourhood of *Pitom*, it would be necessary to seek the ancient

---

[6] Thus Strabo (xvii. p. 804) places Phagroriopolis and the Phagroriopolite nome near the city of Arsinoë and the head of the Red Sea. The Wady-et-Toumeilât is the valley running west and east from the (old) Pelusiac branch of the Nile to Lake Timsah, having along its course the canal of Sesostris and Necho, and the present railway to Suez.—ED.

position of this place on the west side of the valley of Toumeilât, where there are still traces of lakes at the present day. In other words, it would then be necessary to suppose the ancient situation of the country of *Thukot* (Succoth) to have been in the part of Lower Egypt now referred to; and it would consequently be necessary to take this point for the first station of the Hebrews after their departure from Egypt.

Such is what I have called above the *monumental difficulty*, to which I draw the attention of the reader, in order to omit nothing that can serve to illustrate the route of the Jews, fleeing from Ramses to betake themselves to the Desert. But it is by no means proved that the town of Pitom, mentioned as the capital of a nome, was the same as the place cited by Herodotus as *Patumos*; nor is it any more certain that Phagroriopolis was identical with Patumos, for the simple reason that we know nothing about the true position of Phagroriopolis.

3. I repeat, that all the researches I have made, up to the most recent date, have suggested to me no proof founded on the monumental geography, which could tell in favour of a route which would have led along this southern course through the valley of *Toumeilât* to the Red Sea. On the contrary, the stations mentioned in the Bible are met with in the lists of the nomes as places belonging to the North, in the quarter where I have fixed them in my 'Discourse on the Exodus.'[7] The question will be cleared up, in my opinion, as soon as the opportunity shall be afforded *of making excavations in the valley of Toumeilât*, in order to discover monuments which, inscribed with geographical names, would reveal to us at a stroke the mysteries which to the present day cover this part of the geography of Lower Egypt.

---

[7] For example, the argument just referred to would affect the position of the *Sethroite nome*, as a consequence of that of *Pitom*; and, in fact, it has been attempted to place this nome in the Wady-Toumeilât, and to find an etymology to suit this position, instead of Dr. Brugsch's derivation from *set-ro-hatu* (Vol. II. p. 370). But, passing from guesses to *evidence*, we have the testimony of Strabo (xvii. p. 803) that the Sethroite nome extended along one of the two lakes on the left of the Pelusiac arm of the Nile; and its capital, Heracleopolis Parva (Brugsch's 'Pitom'), which the Antonine *Itinerary* places halfway between Tanis and Pelusium, is called *Sethrum* (Σέθρον) by Stephanus Byzantinus. This is but one example of the difference between the *geographical determination* of the places in question and the *invention* of sites to suit a preconceived theory of the Exodus.—ED.

4. The most important point that remains for the beginning of these researches will be the place now called *Maskoutah*[8] (near the railway station called 'Ramses'), which Lepsius, De Lesseps, Linant-Bey, and others regard as the city of Ramses of the Book of Exodus. The existence of a fractured group of the figures of king Ramses II. and two Heliopolitan divinities, as well as the discovery of a great stêlé of the same epoch,[9] may suffice to guarantee the promise of discoveries still more precious both for the geography and the history of ancient Egypt. These discoveries will furnish the starting-point for all further researches which it may be desired to make into the neighbouring sites.

Meanwhile, in the very act of writing these Notes, I have unexpectedly received from Dr. Schweinfurth—so celebrated for his journey into the heart of Africa—a communication of the highest importance in its bearing on the question of the Exodus and the claim of this mound to be the famous city of Ramses. Having made a journey to this place with the object of discovering among the numerous building-bricks, which are met with on the site of Maskoutah, traces of the stalks of straw and of other plants, in order to determine their exact botanical character (Dr. Schweinfurth being a botanist of the highest order), he took the opportunity to study and examine with the greatest care all the ancient bricks at this place, *without having been able to find the least trace of straw*. Without my having asked him the question, or indeed made any answer, he spontaneously sent me the following declaration :—' This place, where the bricks are made only of the mud of the Nile, *cannot be Ramses*; for otherwise we ought to have found

[8] The mound *Tel-el-Maskoutah*, otherwise called *Masroota*. It has been lately asserted that the name 'Ramses' was not given to the railway station by the French engineers, but is a genuine 'Pharaonic survival,' because the *Guide Johanne*, while admitting that the name Ramses is '*passée sous silence par les historiens profanes*,' strangely enough adds that Tel-Masroota ' répond, *d'après les distances de l'Itinéraire d'Antonin, à l'emplacement de l'antique Ramesès construite par les Hébreux*.' But in the route of the *Itinerary* through this valley (pp. 169, 170, Wesseling), there is no *Ramses* nor any name the least like it. The station which *may* correspond to *Tel-el Masroota* is Thou, 12 Roman miles west of Hero, i.e. Heroöpolis, a distance which (as has been pointed out by Mr. Stuart Poole, himself an advocate of the Wady-Toumcilât route) makes a *reductio ad absurdum* of the three days' march of the flying Israelites over *this* distance, and consequently of *this* as the site of Rameses. (*Dict. of the Bible*, art. RAMESES.)—ED.

[9] See above, p. 411.

ON THE EXODUS. 425

there stalks of straw, since, according to the Bible, the Israelites were obliged to scatter themselves over the whole land of Egypt to seek for straw, in order to use it to make bricks.'[1] This avowal is important, as it furnishes another proof that the city of Ramses cannot have been situated at Maskhoutah, near the present railway station of Ramses.[2]

5. There remains an observation for me to make on a point of detail, which seems to me of less importance, but which has been made an objection in order to raise doubts as to the probability of my theory of the Exodus. If, it is said, the Hebrews set out from

[1] Exod. v. 12. The context removes all possibility of supposing that on the withdrawal of the supply of straw the bricks were made without it —an evasion of the order which would have made the task lighter instead of heavier, and which (absurd to suppose in itself) is expressly precluded by the words of Pharaoh's order to the taskmasters (ver. 7): 'Ye shall no more give the people straw to make brick as heretofore: *let them go and gather straw for themselves,*' and so the taskmasters say (vv. 10–12), 'Thus saith Pharaoh, I will not give you straw. *Go ye, get straw where ye can find it;* yet not aught of your work shall be diminished. So the people were scattered abroad throughout all the land of Egypt to gather stubble for straw,' not 'instead of straw,' as in the A. V., but to be used as the chopped straw was, for binding the friable mud of which the sun-dried bricks were made. Of course 'all the land of Egypt' means the country districts round the city they were building.—ED.

[2] The identification of this site with Ramses is, in short, an *assumption* without any positive evidence, but with abundant evidence against it.' The memorials of Ramses II. found on the spot are no evidence for the *name*, unless every place in Egypt similarly marked were also a *Pi-ramses*, and in this case why should *this* be chosen for *the* Ramses of the book of Exodus? But, in fact, that king's memorials are found elsewhere through the valley, as we might have specially expected on account of his canal (which, by the way, furnishes an argument against the residence of the Israelites in this spot from the absence of any mention of their working on it, but only in brickmaking, and building, and field labour). Again, this small *Tel* can hardly have been the 'Temple-city' built for Pharaoh, much less the great and splendid and wealthy Pi-ramses described by Panbesa (Vol. II. pp. 100, f.); and that the Rameses whence the Israelites started had a large and wealthy Egyptian population is proved by the rich spoil which the Hebrews borrowed from their Egyptian neighbours. Now put in the other scale the *positive evidence that Rameses was Zoan-Tanis*, cited abundantly by Dr. Brugsch. The strangest feature in the whole argument is that some eminent commentators, fully admitting that Tanis in 'the field of Zoan' was the residence of Pharaoh, and the scene of his contest with Moses, suddenly and unaccountably transfer him, with his court and army, *to this (imaginary) Rameses*, in order to have him present (as of course he was) at the place whence the Israelites started!—ED.

the city of Tanis, which was situated between the Tanitic and the Pelusiac arms of the Nile, how can we explain the silence of the Bible about the passage of such a great body of emigrants, accompanied by their herds, over the Pelusiac Nile? To this I answer, that Holy Scripture might well dispense with the relation of that which is understood of itself; and, further, that the monuments have even preserved *the drawing of the bridge* which, in the neighbourhood of *Khetam* (the Etham of the Bible), led from one side of this place to the other.[3] On the original monument we see the bridge which joins the two quarters of the town, and by which Seti I. must have crossed with his army in order to return to the territory of Egypt, properly so called. The existence of this bridge has left its trace in the modern name of Qantara-el-*Khazneh*,[4] 'the bridge of the treasure,' the first part of which immediately recals the bridge of the Pharaohs near this site, while the second part, *el-Khazneh*, at once leads our thoughts to the name of *Hazna* or *Hazina*, given by the texts of the papyri and the monuments to the whole country situated to the east of the Pelusiac arm, and rendered by the Greek geographers by the name of *Cassium, Cassiotis*.

6. *Site of Migdol.*—*Tel-es-Samout* is a name which exists at the present day, and which is known by all the authors. The ancient name concealed under it is *Samhud*, and this name serves in another manner to designate the position of the place. No doubt can exist on the subject of this identification.[5]

[3] See above, Vol. II. pp. 12, 19, 387, 388.

[4] But the bridge across the Pelusiac Nile at Khetam (Etham, Daphnæ, now *Defenneh*) must not be confounded with the present station of El-Kantarah (ten miles further east), at the intersection of the great highway with the Suez Canal. Mr. Greville Chester's interesting description of *Tel Dephneh* (as he spells it) shows how well it suits the position of *Etham* ' on the edge of the wilderness ' (Numbers xxxiii. 6), and he adds that 'it could easily be reached in two days from Sán (Tanis), and that, supposing Lake Menzaleh had, as is probable, a lower level in ancient times than at present, Tel Dephneh would probably not be more than a day's journey from *Tel-el-Hîr*' (Mr. Chester's *Migdol*, and Brugsch's *Araris* and *Baal-zephon*). We may add that the season was just after the vernal equinox, when the inundation has long subsided.—ED.

[5] This note was communicated by Dr. Brugsch in reply to Mr. Greville Chester's statement, that the name of *Samout* is unknown to the Arabs. (For the ancient use of it, see Vol. I. pp. 237-8.) Mr. Chester would identify Migdol with *Tel-el-Hîr*; but the question between these two neighbouring mounds is perfectly insignificant in comparison with the fact of its

ON THE EXODUS. 427

7. *Baal-zephon.*—The identification of *Mons Casius* with the place called *Baal-zephon*, that is 'Baal of the North,' or 'Lord of the North,' is not proved by monumental evidence. The word *Casius* is derived from the (Semitic) name *Hazina* or *Hazian* for all the country to the east of the Pelusiac branch;[6] and it is preserved clearly enough in the modern appellation of *Qantarah-el-Hazneh*.

Baal-zephon, which I have *supposed* to be Mons Casius, allows of two explanations: either it is the *translation* of the Egyptian title *neb-mehi*, 'Lord of the North,' given to the god Amon worshipped in this country, and surnamed likewise *neb-Khirot*, 'lord of the lagoons,'—or it is the *transcription* of the Egyptian name of the city *Hauar* (or *-ual*), the first element of which (*Ha* = 'house') has been suppressed, just as in the Hebrew name *R'amses* in place of the Egyptian *Pi-r'amses* ('abode of R'amses'). The corre-

position *in this locality*, which furnishes a pivot for the whole question, inasmuch as we only know of *one Migdol*, that which is placed on the *N.E. frontier of Egypt* by the concurrent testimony of the monuments of Seti I. at Karnak, depicting his march to Palestine (Vol. II. p. 12); of the Harris papyrus, describing Ramses III. encamped (like Israel) 'between Migdol and the sea' to witness the victory of his fleet (Vol. II. pp. 153-5); of the prophets who include the whole length of Egypt, 'from Syene to Migdol' (Vol. I. pp. 237-8), just as it was described under Amenhotep IV. (Vol. I. p. 498); and of the Antonine Itinerary, which places *Magdolum* 12 Roman miles in a S. direction from Pelusium. *A Migdol near the Gulf of Suez is a purely imaginary site invented to suit that theory;* and the same may be said of any *Baalzephon, Etham,* or *Succoth* in that neighbourhood. The sites assigned by Brugsch, on the other hand, are determined (whether rightly or wrongly) by *strict geographical evidence.*—ED.

[6] The distinction between the uses of the word *Casius*, for a definite spot and in a wider sense, forms an important element in the whole question. Herodotus (ii. 6, iii. 5) first mentions it as a mountain extending beside Lake Sirbonis *to the sea*, which may mean a range of hills or a mere promontory. In some passages of Strabo, &c., the name seems to apply to the region S. of the lake. On the other hand *Mons Casius* is distinctly defined as a hill, forming a promontory on the sea-coast (answering precisely to the headland called *Ras Katieh* or *El Gelse*), 40 Roman miles east of Pelusium, and 24 west of Ostracena (Strab. i. p. 58; xvi. p. 759; *Itin. Ant.* p. 152). There would also seem to have been a place *Casium* distinct from Mount Casius. But, in whichever sense, the name *Casius* is taken from the Egyptian name of the district *Hazian*, and has no *direct* connection with Baal-zephon. Strong as is the evidence furnished by the temple of Jupiter Casius for regarding the place as *a* 'Baal-zephon,' the argument applies to *any* sanctuary of that god, and most of all to *Araris*, the chief seat of the Hyksos, whose special deity he was.—ED.

spondence of the Hebrew word *Ba'al* (בעל) with the Egyptian *u'ar* or *u'al* (meaning 'leg;' see my *Dict. Geogr.* App. s. v. *u'ar*) presents no stumbling-block, when we call to mind that the Hebrew *Ba'al* is rendered in Egyptian sometimes by *b'ar*, sometimes by *u'ar*.[7]

From this would follow the important result, that the place *Ba'al-zephon*, 'the city of Ba'al of the North,' would be the same as *Ha-u'ar*, that is to say, as the AVARIS of Manetho. And, as there were several places named *u'ar* in the geographical nomenclature of Egypt, there is every probability that the one designated in the Bible as *Baal*-ZEPHON answers to the '*Avaris* OF THE NORTH' of the Egyptian texts, situated to the east of the Pelusiac branch of the Nile. Lepsius, who has travelled over this part of Lower Egypt, has established by full proof that the long ruins (ramparts now covered with sand) at the place called *Tel-el-Her* (or *Hir*) mark the site of the ancient *Ha-u'ar*.[8]

8. *The Site of the Hebrew Camp.*—In summing up my latest researches, it appears to me that the Hebrews, on quitting *Etham*, directed their march towards *Migdol*, where they encamped opposite to Avaris (*Baal-zephon*). With this interpretation all becomes clear.[9]

---

[7] Readers who do not know Hebrew should be informed that the second letter of the alphabet (ב, *Beth*) represents both B and U or V.

[8] See the interesting description of these ruins by Mr. Greville Chester (*ut sup. cit.* p. 148) :—' *Tel-el-Hir* marks the site of a town of large extent and considerable importance, and its surface is strewn with innumerable sherds of pottery, ancient glass of fine quality, and bits of hewn stone ' (some of which seem to be window frames). ' On the west side of the Tel, the side farthest from the desert, rise *the remains of a massive square tower*, each of whose sides measures about 94 paces. The north, south, and western sides of this fortress descend into *an immense desiccated lake or marsh*. The eastern side of the tower, which is built of crude brick, is joined to the rest of the sandy Tel, which extends eastwards to the desert. . . . It is at once evident to the eye that this was an important frontier fortress.' This answers in all respects to the Hyksos' frontier fortress of *Hau'ar* (Avaris), which has been already described in the History (Vol. I. pp. 236-7). It stood at the N.E. frontier of Egypt, on the right side of the Pelusiac arm of the Nile, and had on its *west* side either a lake or estuary (the ' Pa-zetku of Avaris ') on which the sailor Aahmes fought under the king his namesake in a naval battle with the Hyksos, and also water on its *south* side. (Vol. I. pp. 284–5.) Finally, its distance (about 7 or 8 miles) from Brugsch's site of Migdol (*Tel-es-Sammut*, Mr. Chester's *Tel-Habooa*) gives a fit site for the camp of the Israelites ' between Migdol and the sea ' (the estuary of the Pelusiac Nile) ' in face of Baal-zephon.'—ED.

[9] In these new remarks Dr. Brugsch does not proceed to offer any definite idea as to the manner of the catastrophe, but what follows will

9. *The Gulfs of Pi-hahiroth.*—As to the *Khirot*, the 'gulfs' or 'lagunes,' it is Pliny especially who speaks of them at length in the chapter of his *Historia Naturalis* relating to Lower Egypt.[1]

10. '*The Sea*' *in Exodus xiv.*—You are perfectly right[2] in recognizing the *Mediterranean* in 'the Sea' of the Exodus. Schleiden, in his remarkable work on 'The Isthmus of Suez' (*Die*

show that there were marshes, lagoons, and treacherous pits about the sites of Pelusium and Avaris, which made the passage between them and the sea as difficult and dangerous as that along the causeway between Sirbonis and the Mediterranean.—ED.

[1] Dr. Brugsch wrote this note at Cairo, away from his sources of reference, and we have failed to find the passage in Pliny; but Strabo has statements about the *gulfs* (βάραθρα) *near Pelusium* quite as striking as those of Diodorus about Lake Sirbonis (pp. 391-3). After describing the hill and promontory of Mount Casius, with its tomb of Pompey, he proceeds (xvi. p. 759): 'Next is the road to Pelusium, on which is situated *Gerrha*' (the *Anbu and Shur* of Brugsch, about the west end of Lake Sirbonis). . . . 'and the pits (βάραθρα) near Pelusium, formed by the overflowing of the Nile in places naturally hollow and marshy.' Again (xvii. p. 802): 'Pelusium itself has many marshes lying around it, which some call *barathra* (βάραθρα) or water-holes, and swamps. On this quarter Egypt is difficult of access, that is, from the eastern side towards Phœnicia and Judæa.' Compare this with Mr. Greville Chester's striking account of the immense marshes on the east of the old Pelusiac arm of the Nile, between the sites of Pelusium and Avaris or Baal-zephon at Tel-el-Hir.

If the transference of the catastrophe to this region loses much of that wonderful appropriateness which we have seen in the causeway between Lake Sirbonis and the sea, Strabo supplies us with another striking parallel to show that we are not limited to this or that spot on the Mediterranean shore for sudden movements of wind and water such as overwhelmed the Egyptian host. The geographer relates (xvi. p. 758) how, after a battle on the coast between Tyre and Ptolemais (Acre), 'a wave from the sea, like the rising tide, overwhelmed the fugitives; some were carried out to sea and drowned, others perished in the hollows; then again the ebb succeeding *uncovered and displayed to sight the bodies lying in confusion among dead fish*' (comp. Exod. xiv. 30).—ED.

[2] This note refers to the remark made at the end of p. 400, since writing which we find the same point strongly insisted on in *The Migration of the Hebrews from Egypt* (1879), a very able anonymous work, which no one who wishes to study the subject ought to neglect, in spite of faults which this is not the place to discuss. The absence of any mention of the *Yâm Sûf* in Exod. xiv. is equally remarkable in the summary list of journeys in Numbers xxxiii., where it is said that from the camp before Pihahiroth the Israelites 'passed through the midst of *the Sea* into the wilderness of *Etham*' (v. 8); and it is only after the stages of *Marah and Elim* that they 'encamped by the *Yâm Sûf*' (v. 10). *What* and *where* that *Yâm Sûf* is, we have already observed, is a question too wide to be discussed here.—ED.

Landenje von Suez), has arrived at the same result from his researches, and has critically established by the best proofs the later interpolation of *Yâm Sûph* (the *Red Sea* of the Versions). The Red Sea in all the Egyptian texts (among others, those of the time of Ramses III.) has no other name than *Yuma Kot* or *Yuma Sekot*. But nowhere do we meet with an expression analogous to the Hebrew *Yâm Sûph*. *Sûph* is a plant which grows in lakes, but not in the sea.[3]

11. *The Region and City of Sûph.*—The name Θuf (*thuf*)—in Hebrew *Sûph*—indicates, according to the text, *a whole navigable country, covered with aquatic plants*, especially with papyrus. These are undoubtedly the *lakes* in the North and East of the Delta. There was likewise a *city of Sûph*, named in the Egyptian texts and in the Bible, where it marks the eastern end of a long route leading to Palestine.

12. *The Way of the Land of the Philistines* (Exod. xiii. 17).— The 'Road of the Philistines' of Holy Scripture is not that which commenced at *Khetam*, the *Etham* of the Bible, or no matter what other town in its neighbourhood, but that which touched the country of *Zahi* (Palestine), near Mount Casius. This is *expressly stated* in the inscriptions—consult my *Dict. Géogr.* s. voc. *Khnum* (χnum, 'pits.')[4]

13. *The Geography of Lake Sirbonis and its Neighbourhood.*[5]— While fully acknowledging, without expressly saying so, the two principal points of the route of the Exodus, namely, Ramses=Tanis, and Migdol, Mr. Chester's researches tend to prove that my map of the Lake Sirbonis, in respect of the isthmus, is 'imaginative'

---

[3] The leading passage to determine the original meaning of the word is Exod. ii. 3, where the 'ark' of the infant Moses is made of *sûph*.—ED.

[4] Comp. Vol. I. p. 239, II. 12, 397. The exact point at which Philistia began is placed either at Mount Casius or at Ostracene, which, under the Roman Empire, was reckoned as the point from which Idumæa and Palestine began (Plin. *H. N.* v. 12, s. 14). The best commentators (whatever their view of the Exodus) are generally agreed that the passage in Exod. xiii. 17, 18, describes the *final*, not the *initial*, direction of the march.—ED.

[5] The following remarks are made in a letter to the Editor, with reference to Mr. Greville Chester's paper (see p. 400), which, owing to accidental circumstances, did not reach Dr. Brugsch till the foregoing notes had been despatched. We are able to add the high authority of Captain Burton as to the absurdity of assuming that the ground has not changed in 3000 years; as, for example, if a thread of Nile water from the Pelusiac branch ever found its way to Lake Sirbonis.—ED.

and 'highly imaginative,' and that I have so far abandoned myself to fancies as to invent localities which had no real existence. 'Imaginative' is, in fact, what one invents ; but Mr. Chester seems not to be aware that, for the neighbourhood of Lake Sirbonis, I have only followed the chartographic indications of almost all who have constructed and published maps of Lower Egypt. He has equally overlooked all that Schleiden has said in his work *On the Isthmus of Suez*, and above all he has overlooked the long article in the Appendix to my *Dictionnaire Géographique*, which I have devoted to the geographical name Ouf (= Sûph), to illustrate, in another way, the point where the catastrophe took place. Mr. Chester has forgotten (*et qu'il me pardonne si je prends la liberté de le lui reprocher*) that my labour has not consisted in demonstrating topographically, and beyond the risk of error, the exact localities of the Exodus (that is to say, the sites of their ruins— such as Succoth, Etham, Migdol), but rather in discussing the views which have been held on the subject of the direction of the Exodus, and determining it, on the basis of the monuments, along the road from Tanis to Migdol. Far from having desired to establish a topographic map of an accuracy above reproach, I have had no other purpose than to direct public attention to the historical consequences of the monumental records and the writings on papyrus bearing on the subject of the Exodus.

Mr. Chester is also unaware that *Tel-es-Samout* was already known to the Arabs in the 14th century, and that it marks the site of the ancient *Migdol*; and likewise that Lepsius, after his journey to these regions, proved, in a clear and perfect manner, the identity of *Tel-el-Hir* with the *Hau'ar* or *Avaris* of the Egyptian texts. I must also remind him that the name *Româneh* is very ancient, and that I have discovered it in its ancient form of writing. (See my *Dict. Géogr.* Appendix, s. v. *Roman.*)

In researches of this kind, especially when it is a question of attacking a literary opponent, it is absolutely necessary to be acquainted also with the opinions of other scholars, who have occupied themselves with the same researches in which I have been engaged as the consequence of my geographical studies. In conclusion, the one lesson which I have learnt from the reading of Mr. Chester's paper is that, if *Pi-hahiroth* is to be taken as where I have placed it, it corresponds, and must of necessity correspond, to another spot in the *Barathra* which extended over the region up to the neighbourhood of *Lake Sirbonis*, the name of which, if I am not mistaken, is derived from the Egyptian words *shir bon*, that is, 'the lake of bad salt, salt of bad quality.'

With regard to the present state of the whole question, Dr. Brugsch insists on *the absolute necessity of a survey of the region from the east of the Delta to the frontier of Palestine*. 'If I could afford the means,' he writes, 'I would go and examine the district anew, and make excavations on the sites. *I feel sure of finding on them ancient remains, and I should be able to solve once for all this most interesting question of the Exodus.* But whoever may undertake or be charged with these researches ought to know: (1) the *monumental geography* of this part of Lower Egypt; (2) the *hieroglyphic writing*, so as to be able to read the texts that he might discover; (3) the *Arabic language*, to avoid being ill informed by the Bedouins who inhabit those parts. Perhaps one of your learned societies engaged in Biblical researches would devote the small sum needful to accomplish this object, by sending one of its members to explore this region anew. For my part, I would willingly place myself at his disposal, to serve as his guide and interpreter as occasion might arise.'

['The question of the Exodus is not yet solved,' wrote Dr. Brugsch when he began to communicate these 'Additions,' in the midst of which he was interrupted by dangerous illness; but one remark as to its present position must not be withheld. Whatever may be the ultimate verdict of Biblical, historical, and geographical criticism (for the question involves all three), we cannot but observe the remarkable difference in the *methods* pursued by Dr. Brugsch and others. Starting from the assumption that the 'passage' took place at or about the head of the Gulf of Suez, they *feel back* for *probable* sites for the stations of the journey, 'if haply they may find them.' He alone begins at the beginning, namely the starting-point at Rameses in the field of Zoan, identified with Tanis by overwhelming proofs; and he follows the march along the well-known road marked by the stations which are determined *each by independent geographical evidence*, to whatever end this strict critical method may lead him, though his guide, like that followed by the Israelites, may have its obscure as well as its bright side, trusting to the issue of all honest discussion—'*Lux e tenebris*.'—ED.]

INDEX.

AAH-HOTEP

AAH-HOTEP, queen of Kames, i. 289; treasures found in her coffin, 290, 314, 315; meaning of the name, 318; q. of Amenhotep I., 328, 345
Aahmes I. (Amosis), king, i. 290; conqueror of the Hyksos, 295; founds the 18th dynasty, 315, 317; his campaigns, 318; line of fortresses, 320; wars against the Phœnicians and negroes, 320; restores the temples and buildings, 295, 321; name inscribed on the quarries of Tourah and Massaarah, 322; his pedigree, 345
—queen of Thutmes I., i. 343
—son of Baba-Abana, i. 226; in the war against the Hyksos, 237; tomb at El-Kab, 280, *f.*, 303; pedigree, 281; great historical inscription, 283, *f.*, 326, 329
—Pen-nukheb, memorial stone at El-Kab, i. 287, 319, 326
—courtier of Amen-hotep IV., his prayer to the sun, i. 501
—surnamed Turo, chief priest, *temp.* Ramses II., ii. 412
—II., king of Dyn. XXVI. (Amasis), ii. 286, 326
Aa-kheper-en-ra. *See* Thutmes II.
Aa-kheper-ka-ra. *See* Thutmes I.
Aa-khepru-ra. *See* Amenhotep IV.
Aalim, ii. 398. *See* Elim
Aa-nekht, the Bekhen ('tower') of Ostracene, border-fortress between Egypt and Zahi, at entrance to road of the Philistines, i. 239
Ab, ii. 347. *See* Elephantiné

ADULAM

Abd-el-Qurnah, pictorial representation of brick-making at, i. 417; tomb of Amenhotep II. at, 459
Abdu, ii. 347. *See* Abydus
Abd-ul-Latif, Arabian physician, his account of Memphis, i. 57
Abeha (Behan, Boôn, Semneh), i. 470
Ab-en-pira-o, 'councillor of Pharaoh,' i. 253, 307 *n.*; ii. 146, 188, 379
Abesha, i. 178, 266
Aboulhol, Arabic name of the Sphinx, i. 97
Abousimbel, ii. 70. *See* Ibsamboul
Abousir, pyramid at, i. 106
Abraham, an indication of his being contemporary with Dyn. XII., ii. 405
Ab-sakabu, i. 239; water of, ii. 13
Abydus (Abdu, Abud), capital of Nome VIII. (Up. Eg.), ii. 347; table of kings, i. 44–46, ii. 29; well at, i. 162; temple at, 441; tablet, 441; chief seat in Upper Egypt of the worship of Osiris, 441; temple completed by Ramses II., ii. 36, 46; inscription on wall, 36–44; pictures of the battle of Kadesh, 48–54; Nimrod's tomb, 207; remarkable inscription, 208–211: sanctuary and wall of Ramses III. in the temple of Osiris, 416
Acco (Aak, Acre), i. 392
Achæans, ii. 129
Achæmenes, satrap, ii. 332; killed by Inaros, 332
Achoris (Hagar) king, ii. 287, 335
Adon, title, i. 253, 307, 311, 312, 363, 398, 517; ii. 26, 71, 181, 182, 183
Adulam (Adullam), i. 400; ii. 110, 217

VOL. II. F F

ADULIS

Adulis, i. 406, 408
Aduma (Edom), i. 248, 336; ii. 217
Africa, coast opp. Arabia. *See* Punt
Africanus on the Hyksos, i. 266
Agabot (Libyans), i. 331
Agesilaus, ii. 335, 337, 338
Agriculture, i. 23
Ahnas, i. 201; ii. 224. *See* Heracleopolis Magna
Ai, the holy father, i. 512; restores the worship of Amon, prepares his tomb at Biban-el-Molouk, 513; his titles of honour, supremacy in the south, 514; his sarcophagus and names, 514 *n.*, ii. 408
Aina, or Aian (Aean), the Heroöpolite nome, i. 16, 252; fortress and well, ii. 148; temple, 418
Ajalon, ii. 217
Aken (Acina), ancient name for Nubia, i. 183, 199
Akerith, i. 456; ii. 47, 56, 58
Akharru, the 'hinder land,' Phœnicia, i. 337
A-kheper-ra. *See* Shashanq IV.
Akherkin, i. 159
Akhmun, ii. 246. *See* Hermopolis Magna
Alabastrônpolis. *See* Ha-Suten
Alexander the Great, ii. 287, 288, 308, 309, 318, 319, 339
—Ægus, ii. 315, 339
Alexandria, ii. 289
Alisu, ii. 142. *See* Arisu
Aliurta, ii. 312, 314
Alphabet, old Egyptian, ii. 351
Aluna, i. 369, 370
'Am ('people') for the Israelites, ii. 219
Ama, Mentu-hotep's mother, i. 134
Amada, Nubian temple of, memorial tablet, i. 457, 459; inscription of Thutmes IV., 462
Amalekites, i. 266
Amanus, mountain range, i. 338
Amasis, ii. 298. *See* Aahmes II.
Amazons, band of, ii. 25
Ameneman, architect of Thutmes III., i. 448:—of Ramses II., ii. 91; pro-

AMENHOTEP

bably the oppressor of the children of Israel, 91; his full titles, ii. 411
Amen-em-ape, governor of the South under Ramses II., ii. 79, 81
Amen-em-apet, chief of the young men of Thebes, under Amenhotep III., ii. 408
Amenemhat I., i. 143; instructions to his son, 144; conquers the inhabitants of Wawa-t, 144; founds the temple of Amon at Thebes, 145; his pyramid, 146; king of all Egypt, 146; attempted assassination, 148; reigns with his son Usurtasen, 148; war with the Menthu, Hersh'a, and Hittites, ii. 404–5
Amenemhat II., extends the southern boundary, i. 165; statue of his wife, 167; inscription at Beni-Hassan, 170, 171
—III., constructs the lake Mœris, i. 187; careful about the rise of the Nile, 188, 189; builds the Labyrinth, 191; inscriptions on the rocks of Sinai, 195; at Wady Magharah, 196
—IV., i. 140; his sister-queen, 198
—royal functionary under Mentuhotep, i. 134
Amenemhib, captain, i. 395; inscription of, 395–398, 455, ii. 405–6
—viceroy of Kush, ii. 81
Amen-hi-khopeshef. *See* Ramses V., VI., X., XII.
Amen-hi-unamif, prince, ii. 79, 80
Amenhotep I., memorial stone, i. 291; campaigns, 326–328; war with the Thuhen or Marmaridæ, 327; care in building the great temple of Thebes, 328; statue of, at Karnak, restored by Thutmes III., 433
—II., war in the 'Red Land,' i. 455; revolt in Asia, 456; memorial tablet in the temple of Amada, 458, 459; picture and inscription at Abd-el-Qurnah, 459; temples in Egypt and Nubia, 460; records of, by the scribe Za-anni, ii. 407
—III., rebuilds and restores temples,

INDEX.

AMENHOTEP
i. 295; *scarabæi* as memorials, 468; lion hunts, 468; campaigns in Ethiopia, 469; progress up the Nile, 470; hands of slain foes cut off, 471; penetrates into the Soudan, 471; list of conquered tribes, 471, 472; wealth, governors, 472; inscription, 473-475; colossal statues of, called 'Memnon,' 475, 479, 480; opens new quarries at Mokattam for temple-buildings at Thebes, 476, 477; memorial tablet at Medinet Abou, 478; finishes and adorns the temple on the Island of Elephantiné, 486; thirty years' jubilee, 487; rewards to voluntary tax-payers, 488; thefts committed on his coronation-day, 489; length of his reign, 489; his queen, 490; his sons and daughters, 491; records of, on scarabæi, ii. 406, 407; his Asiatic wife and numerous harem, 407; his lake in the city of Z'aru, 408
Amenhotep IV., his foreign blood, i. 491; aversion to the worship of Amon, 492; new doctrines, 492; peculiar features and figure, 492; obliterates the names of Amon and Mut; rebellion of the priests and people; adopts the name of Khunaten, 494; question about identity, 493 *n.*; founds a new capital; builds a temple to the sun-god, Aten, 494; inscriptions at Silsilis, 498; domestic life, 503; pictures and inscription at Tel-el-Amarna, 503-506; victories over Syrians and Kushites, 506; death without male issue, 507; sons-in-law, 508
—first seer of Amon, his buildings at Thebes, i. 154, 155
—son of Hapu, governor under Amenhotep III., i. 472; special statue dedicated to him, 473; inscription, 473-475; his colossal statues of the king, 474, 475, 481; his parentage, 482; founds the tem-

AMUNENSHA
ple of Ha-kak, 483-485; deified as a god of learning, 485; his works in Egypt and Nubia, 486
—chief priest of Amon under Ramses IX.; presentation of his reward, ii. 186, 187; his restoration of the great temple, 188
Ameni (Amen), inscription of, in time of Usurtasen I., i. 156-158
—inscription of, in time of Usurtasen III., ii. 405
Ameniritis, queen, ii. 277; statue of, at Karnak, 281; inscription, 282
Ameni-Seneb, governor of the temple at Abydus, i. 162
Amen-messu, anti-king, ii. 140
Amenti, the under-world, i. 485
Amenu, king, his pyramid, i. 167
Amen-uah-su, painter under Ramses II., records of, ii. 31, 409
—priest of 'Amon of Ramses II.,' ii. 412
Ammonites, i. 403
Amon, Amon-ra, king of the gods, i. 34, *et passim*; origin from Punt (Arabia), ii. 403; cities specially sacred to: 1. In Upper Egypt: *see* Thebes and Diospolis Parva: 2. In Middle Egypt (the Fayoum), at Pehuu, ii. 417: 3. In Lower Egypt; *see* Na-Amon: temple of, at Thebes, begun by Usurtasen I., i. 155; ii. 188; works upon, *passim*; buildings and endowment by Thutmes III., i. 419-424; restored by the chief-priest, Amenhotep, ii. 188. *See* Karnak
Amon-hi-khopesh-ef, son of Ramses II., ii. 69
Amon-seru, dedication of the temple of, i. 359
Amon-Zefes, wife of the architect Sem-nofer, i. 60
Amu ('people'), east of Egypt, i. 13, 118, 177, 248, 275, 356, 398, 462, &c.; name used for banditti, ii. 110
Amu-Kahak, the, i. 326
Amunensha, king of Tennu, i. 147

F F 2

A-MUSHA

A-Musha ('island of Moses'), ii. 417. *See* I-en-Moshé

Amyrtæus, ii. 287, 332, 333

An, i. 447. *See* Tentyra

An, the Kushites, i. 330, 332, 346

Anaït, or Anaïtis, goddess, i. 245. *See* Antha

A-nakhtu, fortress, ii. 13

An-an-ruth, on Lake Nesroan, i. 377

Anastasi III., papyrus, ii. 100, 131

Anaugas (Jenysus), i. 336, 382, 389; ii, 47

Anbu (Shur, Gerrhon), i. 147, 238; ii. 375, 390, 397

Andromeda, local source of her myth at Iöpé (Joppa) on the coast of Palestine, ii. 403

Andrôn-polis, ii. 374

Anentef (Nentef), kings of Dyn. XI., i. 132; their coffins discovered, *ib.*

Anhur (Onuris), the god of war. i. 50, 70; deity of Sebennytus, ii. 337; his temple at This, 416

Ani, royal architect, ii. 34

Anibe, rock-tomb with records respecting the boundaries of land in Nubia, ii. 182

Animal worship, institution of, ascribed to king Kakau, i. 74

Ankh, 'the living one,' the great god worshipped at Pitom; his peculiar priesthood, and symbol, ii. 377, *f.* *See* Kereh

Ankh-nes-Amon, daughter of Khunaten, i. 507

Ankh-Psamethik, priest, ii. 293
—architect, ii. 309

Ankhs-es-Ranofrehet, queen of Amasis, ii. 326

Annas, i. 163

Annu (i.e. 'obelisks'), city, the On of SS., i. 150, 240, 251; ii. 369. *See* Heliopolis

Antæopolis (Ni-ent-bak), capital of Nome XII. (Up. Eg.), ii. 347

'Antar, stable of,' i. 224

Antha, Anaïtis, warrior goddess, ii. 34, 99

APOLLINOPOLIS

Antilibanus, i. 337, 399

Antinoë, city, i. 156

Anubis, god with a jackal's head, i. 73, 223, 224; temples at Lycopolis and Saptu, ii. 416, 417

Apachnan, i. 263

Ape, Api, Thebes E. of the Nile, i. 347, 366, *et passim* (*cf.* Apetu); in Lower Egypt, ii. 418

Aper, Aperiu, Apuirui, an Erythræan people, *not* Hebrews, ii. 91, 134, 148

Ape-tash, i. 193

Apetu (Ape), temple of the empire at, i. 154, *et passim*

Apheru, god, i. 197, 224

Aphobis (or Aphophis, Apophis, Aphosis), shepherd-king, i. 263, 273, *f.*; said to have been contemporary with Joseph, 300

Aphrodite. *See* Hathor

Aphroditopolis (Debui Tebu), capital of Nome X. (Up. Eg.), ii. 347, 375; temple built by Ramses III., 416

— (Tep-ah, 'cow-city,' now Atfih), capital of Nome XXII. (Up. Eg.), with temple of Hathor, ii. 348, 417

Apis (Hapi), the sacred bull of Memphis, i. 39, 74; the tombs of, at Saqqarah, i. 74; inscribed tombstones, ii. 228, 229, 232; solemn translation of the deceased, to the Serapeum, 229; worship of, at Memphis, 229, 232; memorial stones at the Serapeum, 295-298; care bestowed on their burial under the Persian Empire, 298; time occupied in the construction of the tombs, 298; story of Cambyses refuted, 299, 300; honour paid by Darius, 300; sarcophagus with dedicatory inscription by Khabbash, 301; latest tablet of king Nakht-neb-ef, 302

Apis (Ni-ent-Hapi), capital of Nome III. (L. Eg.), ii. 240, 348

Apollinopolis Magna (Teb, now Edfou), capital of Nome II. (Up. Eg.), seat of Hor (as Hud) and Hathor,

INDEX. 437

APOPHIS

ii. 34, 347, 403; temple of the sun, i. 323; geographical and mythological inscription, 235. *See* Edfou
Apophis, the snake of hell, i. 484
Apopi, or Apopa, Hyksos king, i. 273. *See* Aphobis
Apries. *See* Uah-ab-ra
Apu, ii. 347. *See* Panopolis
Apuirui, ii. 91. *See* Aper
A-qa-ua-sha, the, ii. 122, 123, 127
Arabah, the, ii. 14
Arabia, and the opposite coast of Africa, called the 'land of the gods,' ii. 34 *n.*, ii. 403. *See* Punt
Arabian Hills, the, i. 20
Arabian Nome, E. of the Nile, the modern *Sharkieh*, i. 21
Arabs, i. 91; the Shasu, 179; Arab conquest of Mesopotamia, 367
Aradus (Arathu, Aruth), i. 377, 388, 394, 401; ii. 46, &c.
Aram (Syria), i. 339; wine from, 403
Architects, royal (Mur-ket), office of, i. 60; list of, 60; pedigree of, ii. 309
Argo, island, i. 220
Arinath, i. 456
Arisu, or Alisu (Arius or Alius), usurpation of, ii. 140, 141
Armed force, the, i. 64
Arômata Acrôn (C. Guardafui), in the land of Punt, i. 353, 355
Arses, king, ii. 287, 339
Arsinoites Nomos (the Fayoum), Nome XXI. (Up. Eg.), ii. 417
Art, technical, ancient Egyptian, i. 97
—under the 12th dynasty, i. 201-205
Artaxerxes I., ii. 286, 314, 332-3
—II. Mnemon, ii. 334-338
—III. *See* Ochus
A-rud, in Upper Egypt, with temple of Amon-r'a, ii. 417
Arunata (Orontes), R., i. 337
Aryandes, satrap, ii. 329, 330
Asbytæ, ii. 147
Asebi (Cyprus), i. 372; tribute of the king of, 381, 383, 384, 404
Ashdod, ii. 322

ATHU

Asher, Syria, i. 268
Asher, tribe of, ii. 20
Asher(u), lake, i. 477; ii. 71, 189
Ashtaroth-Karnaim, ii. 5
Ashur, Assyria, i. 268
Asia Minor and islands, places and tribes of, on monuments of Ramses II., ii. 57, 410 *n.*; of Ramses III., ii. 158-9
Asia, Western, war of vengeance against, i. 336
Askalon, i. 337; ii. 68, 69
Asmara, electrum, i. 404
Assa, king, i. 110, 111
Assarhaddon (Esarhaddon), ii. 266.*f.*; memorial stone near Beyrout, 276
Assaseef, necropolis of Thebes, i. 132, 448, *n.*
Asseth, i. 263
Assouan, i. 64, 91; rock-tablet, 346
Assur, king of, i. 339; tribute from, 374, 375, 404
Assurbanipal, king of Assyria, ii. 266; record of, 266-274
Assyrian Empire, rise of the, in Mesopotamia, ii. 201; invasion of Egypt, 202; conquest of Egypt, and new foreign dynasty, 208-211
Astarte, worshipped in Egypt, i. 58, 244
Ata, king, i. 69, 72
Ataiuhi (Athiuhi) and Aliurta, Persian governors at Coptos, ii. 312; their inscriptions in the valley of Hammamat, 313, 314
Atargates, ii. 5. *See* Derceto
Atef-crown, the, ii. 144
Aten, sun-god, i. 494; his obelisk at Thebes destroyed, 521
Athaka, mines of, ii. 148
Athenians in Egypt, ii. 332
Athothis (Tota, Atot, Ata), i. 72
Athribis (Ha-ta-hir-ab), capital of Nome X. (L. Eg.), i. 73; ii. 239, 253, 348; temple of Horus at, 418
Athu, lakes in the lowlands, in the extreme N. of Egypt, i. 146; the Egyptian equivalent of the Semitic Souph, ii. 372-3. *Comp.* Nathu

ATHYR

Athyr, month, i. 465, 527; ii. 232, 296
Ati, king, i. 116
Ati, the canal of Heliopolis, ii. 417
Atot, king, i. 69, 72
Atum, i. 150. *See* Tum
Aup (Aupa), i. 256; northern boundary of the Khalu, i. 400, ii. 110
Auputh, eldest son of Shashanq I., his early death, ii. 222; another, 239, 243, 251
Avaris (Ha-u'ar), i. 235, 266, 270; siege and capture of, by Amasis, 285; probably the Baal-zephon of SS., ii. 428; ruins of, at Tel-el-Hir, 428, 431
Azaba (Ozaeb), fortress of, i. 240

BA, name of a pyramid, i. 107
Baal, i. 244, *et passim*
Baal-Mahar, ii. 165, 168, *f.*
Baal-Sutekh, i. 279; temple to, and his wife Astartha-Anatha, ii. 3.
Baal-Zapuna (Baal-zephon, SS.), the special form of the Semitic Baal worshipped in Egypt at Sutekh, i. 277-8; derivation of the name, ii. 427
Baal-Zephon, Mt. Casius, i. 280; ii. 13, 393; or rather Avaris, 427-8
Baba Abana, i. 280; tomb of, at El-Kab, 302; inscription referring to a famine lasting many years, 304, 305
Babel, Babylon, Babylonia, the central point whence the abodes of the most ancient nations were estimated, i. 255 *n.*; 339, 367, 403; tablet in the language of, ii. 209; peopled by Cushites, 402
Babylon, city of Egypt, i. 150, 403; ii. 251
Bainuter, king, i. 69, 75
Bakhatana, land of, ii. 191, *f.*, 194
Barathra. *See* Gulfs *and* Pihahiroth
Barkal, Mt., i. 151, 329; temple-fortress on, 486; meaning of name, ii. 236, 284; memorials of Piankhi and Miamun Nut at, 238, *f.*, 257, *f.*
Bast, goddess, i. 245; ii. 228

BIGEH

Beba, governor of Pepi's city, i. 126
Bedouins on Pharaoh's property, i. 233; wanderings near the town of Pibailos, 251; (Shasu), 263
Begig, obelisk at, i. 153
Behani (Boôn), i. 470; ii. 9
Behereh, Arab name of Lower Egypt, i. 19
Beit-el-Walli, rock-grottoes of, with victories of Ramses II., ii. 78
Bek, architect, i. 495; his tombstone, 496; inscription, 496; genealogy, 497
Bek-en-aten, princess, i. 495, 498
Beken-khonsu, architect, i. 45
—chief priest of Amon, under Amenhotep III., his statue at Berlin, ii. 408; another under Ramses II., inscriptions on his statue at Munich, ii. 117, 119
Bekhen (tower), i. 423; ii. 13
Benben ('obelisk') i. 521; chamber, the, 151, ii. 252
Beni-Hassan, inscription, i. 149; rock-tombs at, 155; long inscription in the Hall of Sacrifice, 169-171
Berenice, ii. 32
Bersheh, tombs at, i. 120
Berytus (Beyrout), i. 337, 392; ii. 110; rock-tablets near, 65, 276
Bes, or Bas, idol peculiar to the land of Punt, i. 136, 245
Beth-anta (Beth-anoth), i. 393; ii. 20, 67, 218
Beth-horon, ii. 217
Beth-shean, i. 393; ii. 217
Biamites, Bimaites, or Bashmurites, the, i. 259
Biban-el-Molouk (tombs of the kings), i. 348; tomb of king Ai, 513; burial-chamber of Ramses II., ii. 119; sepulchre of Seti II., 130; tomb of Ramses VI., astronomical and chronological value of, 180; thefts in the king's tombs, 189, 190
Bicheres, king, i. 84
Bieneches, king, i. 69
Bigeh, island of, names of Amenhotep III.'s governors at, i. 472

BI-IN-DI-DI

Bi-in-di-di, i. 74. *See* Binebded
Bi-ka-ra, ii. 258, 263. *See* Miamun Nut
Bilbeis, i. 469. *See* Philæ
Binebded (Mendes), the sacred ram worshipped at Mendes, i. 74
Binothris, king, i. 69; law of female succession, 75
Bint-antha, favourite daughter of Ramses II. and his Kethite queen, ii. 412
Bint-resh, princess, ii. 192, *f.*
Birket-el-Keroun, i. 190
Bnon, shepherd king, i. 262
Bocchoris, king (Bok-en-ran-ef, Bu-kur-ni-ni-ip), sole Pharaoh of the 24th dynasty, i. 51, ii. 271, 280
Boken-Khonsu. *See* Beken-Khonsu
Bokennifi, ii. 239, 271
Boundary-stones erected between negro-land and Egypt, i. 182
Brass (*usem*), i. 386; ii. 261
Brick-making, picture of, at Abd-el Qurnah, i. 417, 418
Bricks at Maskhoutah, no straw or stubble in, ii. 424-5
Bridge over the Pelusiac Nile at Khetam (Etham, Daphnæ, Tel-Dafenneh), ancient Egyptian picture of, ii. 19, 387, 388, 426
British Museum, inscription in, of the time of Horemhib, i. 525
Bubastic arm of the Nile, i. 262
Bubastids, Hall of the, at Karnak, ii. 217, 219, 222, 226
Bubastus (Pi-bast, 'city of Bast,' Pi-beseth, SS.) capital of Nome XVIII. (L. Eg.), seat of Dyn. XXII., i. 74, 220, 245; ii. 207, 215, 228, 349, 369
Buhan, temple of, opposite Wady Halfah, i. 438
Bull, the sacred, of Memphis, i. 74, *see* Apis: of Heliopolis, 74, *see* Mnevis
Busiris (Pi-usiri), capital of Nome IX. and chief seat of the worship of Osiris in Lower Egypt, i. 37, 441, 467; ii. 229, 239, 243, 254, 348
Butau, king (Boëthos), i. 69, 74
Buto, goddess, i. 519

CARCHEMISH

Buto (Pi-uto, 'city of Uto,' Isis), capital of Nome XIX. (L. Eg.), lake and city, Thutmes III. exiled to, by his sister, i. 361, 426; ii. 13, 240, 316, 349
Byblus, i. 240, ii. 418. *See* Pi-bailos
Byssus, i. 403

CABASUS (Qa-hebes), capital of Nome XI. (L. Eg.), ii. 348
Cabul, ii. 67
Cairo, i. 58, 322, &c.
Calendar, old Egyptian, fixed holidays and festivals, i. 174-5; ii. 162, 163; Table of, i. 527
Cambyses, his alliance with the Arabs, i. 270 *n.*; ii. 93, 286; story of his slaying the Apis-bull refuted, ii. 299, *f.*, 303, *f.*, 307; true date of his conquest of Egypt, 300, 313-315, 329
Canaan, son of Ham, ethnographical signification, ii. 404
—the land of (*pa Kan'ana*), i. 248, 411; ii. 15, 20; war of Ramses II. with, 66, *f.*; Egyptian fortresses in, 131; towns in, 159; Ramses III.'s temple of Amon in, 419, 420. *See* Zaha
Canaanites, i. 31; ii. 4, 68, 77, 80; employed as the bearers of official despatches, 131
Canal of Seti I. and Ramses II., attempted reopening of, by Necho, ii. 323; of Darius I., inscriptions relating to, 310, 311 of M. de Lesseps, 323
Canana, hill town, i. 248
Canopic branch of the Nile, i. 11, 229, 230, 236; ii. 147, 156
Canopus (Zoq'a), capital of Nome IV. (L. Eg.), ii. 147, 267, *f.*, 348
—decree of, i. 268
—the star, i. 416
Caphtor, SS. (Keftha-Hor), an 'island' on the Egyptian coast, the fatherland of the Philistines, ii. 403
Carchemish (Circesium), i. 337; ii. 3,

CARDINAL

154 ; identified with Jerablûs, xxxvi. n.
Cardinal points, N. E. S. W., how estimated by the Semitic nations, and how by the Egyptians, i. 255 n.
Carian-Colchian nations, victory over, ii. 153, 160 (cf. Pref. xx.)
Cartouches, royal, i. 70 n.; of Senoferu, 78; of Ranuser, 108; of Kaankhra, 216; hieroglyphic, passim
Casius, M. with fortified temple (Uti) of Baal, ii. 13 ; also a district (Cassiotis), 426, 427. See Baal-zapuna and Hazina
Cassiopeia, wife of Cepheus, or of Phœnix, a mythical link between Arabia and Phœnicia, ii. 403
Catabathmus, ii. 130
Cataracts of the Nile : the first, boundary of Egypt and Nubia, i. 329 ; the second, the boundary of negro-land, 159, 438 (see Wady Halfah); the third, of Kerman, 331; god of, 438
Caucasians, ii. 128, 129, 147
Cepheïs, Cepheus, and cognate names, in Ethiopia, Arabia, and Phœnicia, corresponding to the Kefa, &c., of Egyptian inscriptions, ii. 402, 403
Chabrias, ii. 336, 337, 338
Chabryes, king, i. 94. See Khafra
Chaldæan dynasty in Mesopotamia overthrown by the Arabs, i. 367
Chariots first introduced from Canaan, i. 340.
Cheops (Khufu, Chembes, Suphis), i. 85; his pyramid, 86
Chester, Mr. Greville, on the Exodus, ii. 400, 431
Chronology of the Pharaonic history uncertain till Dyn. XXVI., Pref. xxiii., i. 41 ; method of genealogies, 42 ; ii. 264, 321, 340-6
Cibyra, ii. 159
Cilicia, i. 460; ii. 153 ; places in, on monument of Ramses III., 158-160
Civilization, Egyptian, not first founded by the priests of Meroë, i. 9 ; course of, up the Nile, 10

DAMIETTA

Cleopatra's Needles, i. 451
Clysma, ii. 239
Cocheiche, the great dyke of, i. 52
Cœle-Syria, i. 337
Colossæ, ii. 159
Commerce, i. 24 ; with Libya, Palestine, &c., 199 ; Phœnician, 254, 403
Conon, ii. 335
Conquests, lists of. See Lists
Conspiracy, the Harem, ii. 164-172
Coptos (Qobt), capital of Nome V. (Up. Eg.), i. 133, 135, ii. 347 ; road from, to Leucos Limen (Qosseir), i. 138 ; to Berenice, ii. 32 ; temple of Ramses III. to Khim, Horus, and Isis, 416
Coracesium, ii. 159
Crocodile worship, i. 192
Crocodilopolis (Pi-sebek, Pi-sekhem-kheper-ra, Shet), capital of Nome XXI. (Up. Eg.), i. 154, 194, 201 ; ii. 240, 248, 256, 374 ; temple of Horus on lake Mœris, 417
Cronos, i. 35. See Seb
Crowns, the two, insignia of Upper and Lower Egypt, i. 20
Crypt at Heliopolis, ii. 249
Cusæ (Qors, Qos), capital of Nome XIV. (Up. Eg.), ii. 347
Cush, son of Ham, migrated from the East to Arabia and Africa, the land of Pun, streams of Cushite migrations thence to Ethiopia, Babylonia, Egypt, and Phœnicia, ii. 401, 402. See Kush
Cynopolis, Cynônpolis (Qa-sa), capital of Nome XVII. (Up. Eg.), i. 170, 179, 515; ii. 348, 417
Cyprus (Asebi), i. 372, 381, 383, 384, 404; places in, on monument of Ramses III., ii. 158-160
Cyrene, ii. 130, 325, 326

D AMASCUS, i. 337, 392, 403
Damietta (Grk. Tamiathis, Coptic Tamiati, Arab. Damiât),

INDEX. 441

DANAU

successor of Na-amon; origin of the name, ii. 419

Danau (Danai), ii. 130, 146, 154

Daphnæ (Tabenet, now Tel-Defenneh), ii. 307–8, 426. *See* Khetam

Daphne (Tunep), i. 399; ii. 3

Dardani or Dandani, Dardanis, ii. 47, 130, 414 (*cf.* Preface, xx.)

Darius I., king, ii. 286, 314; shows honour to the Apis-bulls, 300, 301; fosters Egyptian learning, 307; his temple of Amon at Hibis (El-Khargeh) in the Great Oasis, 307, 330; his canal, 310, 311, 330; his claim to equality with Sesostris, 331

—II., king, ii. 286; record of his works at El-Khargeh, 307

— III., king, ii. 287, 308, 309, 319, 339

Dashour, pyramid of, i. 113

Debui. *See* Aphroditopolis

Delta, the, i. 21, *et passim*

Denderah, temple at, i. 117

Der (Dirr) temple, picture of a razzia on the negroes, ii. 78; sun-city of Pira, 94, 183

Derceto (Atargatis), goddess, ii. 5

Der-el-bahri, royal tombs and stage-temple at, i. 347; pictures and inscriptions, 351

Der-el-Medineh, temple called Hakak at, i. 486

Despatches, official, records of, ii. 131, 132

Did (Didi), king of the Libyans, ii. 123, 153

Didiun or Didun, god, i. 437, 462

Diodorus, i. 85; ii. 391, 395

Dionysus, same as Bes, i. 137

Diospolis, i. 283, 312; *cf.* Thebes

—Parva. 1. In Upper Egypt; *see* Hut-Sokhem and Pehuu. 2. In Lower Egypt (Pi-Khun-en-Amon), capital of Nome XVII., ii. 349, 375. *See* Na-Amon

Dynasties of gods, demi-gods, and manes, i. 34, 35, 36

—of Pharaohs, causes of change of dynasty, i. 75

EGYPT

Dynasties, 1st, 2nd, and 3rd, i. 69

—4th and 5th, Table of kings, i. 84

—6th to 11th, i. 115; connection of 11th, 13th, 17th, and 18th, 314

—12th, Table of kings, i. 140

—13th, imperfect accounts, i. 208; revolts and internal troubles, 211; list of kings in the Turin papyrus, 214–216; in the chamber of Karnak, 222

—14th to 17th, i. 210, 261–315

—18th, i. 316; genealogical tree of the Pharaohs and their wives, 345

—19th, ii. 1

—20th, ii. 145

—21st, ii. 200; queens of, 421

—22nd, ii. 215

—23rd, ii. 233

—24th, ii. 233, 280

—25th, ii. 234

—26th to 31st, ii. 286, 287; character of their monuments, 290, 291

—26th, of Saïs, ii. 321–329

—27th, Persians, ii. 329–333

—28th, of Saïs, ii. 333

—29th and 30th, at Mendes and Sebennytus, ii. 316, 335, 336

—31st, of Persians, ii. 339

—32nd, of Macedonians, ii. 339

—33rd, of the Ptolemies, ii. 340

ECLIPSE of the moon, in Thakeloth II.'s reign, ii. 226, 227

Edesieh, temple of, ii. 21. *See* Redesieh

Edfou (Apollinopolis Magna), temple of, i. 322–3; geographical inscription at, 235, 240; ii. 404

Edom, i. 147, 160, 248, 326

Education, i. 29; ii. 307

Egypt, its native name, i. 16; Asiatic names, 18; two great divisions, 18; influence of nomes on political state of, 22, 173; condition of, under the 12th dynasty, 198, *f.*; the central point of a world-intercourse in the reign of Thutmes III., 366; decline and fall of, ii. 287; death-blow by

EGYPT

the Persians, 288; silence of the monuments, 290; history, from Psammetichus to Ptolemy, 321
Egypt, prehistoric, i. 32; no age of stone, bronze, or iron, 32; mythical inventions, 33
—list of its nomes, ii. 347–349
Egyptians, the race little altered, i. 7; not Africans, 8; origin from Asia, 8; and immediately from Arabia, ii. 403; language akin to Indo-Germanic and Semitic, i. 9; an agricultural people, 24; navigation, 24; mental endowments, 24; character, 25; desire of learning, 340; trade and arts, 341; theory of their Nigritian origin refuted by Lepsius, ii. 401; from the East, and probably from Arabia; a Cushite race, kindred with Ethiopians, Arabians, Babylonians, and Phœnicians, 401, 403; all coloured red on the monuments, 403–4; regarded Arabia as their sacred cradle, 404
Eileithyia (Nekheb), capital of Nome III. (Up. Eg.), i. 279, 440, ii. 347. *See* El-Kab
Electric fish. *See* Kereh
Electrum (Asmara), i. 404. *Comp.* Usem
Elephantiné (Ab), island and city, i. 18, 181, 224, 437; temple to local god, 439, 486; obelisks from, ii. 59; dialect of, i. 19; ii. 114; capital of Nome I. (Up. Eg.), 347, 374
Eleutherus, R., i. 337
Elim (Aa-lim or Tent-lim, 'the town of fish'), ii. 397, 398
El-Kab (Eileithyiapolis), i. 225, 226; inscriptions at, 237, 302; tombs at, 280; Seti I.'s temple, ii. 31
El-Khargeh, ii. 294. *See* Hibis
Ellahoon pyramid, i. 191, 193
Ellesieh, inscription to Nahi, i. 387; rock-tombs, 438
El-Qassarieh, remains of temple, i. 56
Epiphi, the month, i. 181, 439, 458, 527; ii. 32, &c.

FENEKH

Era of King Nub, about 1750 B.C., i. 299
Eratosthenes, i. 85
Erpa, title, i. 62; ii. 312
Esneh (Latopolis), temple, i. 36, 440
Etearchus, ii. 264. *See* Taharaqa
Etham, i. 234, 239, 247; ii. 12, 56, 98, 132, 138, 386,*f.*, 421, 426. *See* Khetam
Ethiopia (*cf.* Kush) first peopled by Cushites, with capital at Meroë, ii. 402; not the primitive home of the Egyptians, i. 9; civilized from Egypt, 10; inferiority of its art, 11; riches of, 333; independence and kingdom of, with capital at Napata, ii. 235, 236; Egyptian manners, language, and customs preserved, 236; position of the women of the royal house, 236; extension of the kingdom, 236, *f.*; threefold division, 264; contest with Assyria, 265,*f.*; end of empire, 281
Ethiopian proper names, etymology of, ii. 282–284
Etruscans, ii. 129
Euphrates, i. 338, 339, 399, &c.
Eusebius, his *Chronicon*, i. 300 *n.*
Exodus, the, i. 233, 238; date of, about 1300 B.C., 296, 299, 300 *n.*; the Pharaoh of, ii. 133
—the, and the Egyptian Monuments, Discourse on, ii. 357,*f.*, 421,*f.*; Dr. Brugsch's method of identifying the sites, 432

F AMINES in Egypt, i. 158, 304, 305
Fayoum, province of, Nome XXI. (Up. Eg.), the Arsinoite, i. 189; crocodile-worship in, 191, &c.; temples in, ii. 417
Feasts, calendars of, i. 175, 176, 225, 388; ii. 162
Fekhir, a region of Pun (Arabia), the Mocritæ of Ptolemy, ii. 404, *n.*
Female succession, law of, i. 75, 76
Fenekh, or Fenikh, the earliest Phœnicians in Egypt, i. 258, 277, 295, 322; ii. 219

FRONTIERS

Frontiers of Egypt, extension of, under the 12th dynasty, i. 198
Fugitive servants, report about, parallel to the Exodus, ii. 138, 389

G ALILEE, i. 403 ; ii. 53
Galla, the, i. 13. *See* Kar
Ganabut, tribute from, i. 378
Gauzanitis (Gozan, Goshen), ii. 3, 46, 75, 410
Gaza, Gazatu, i. 318, 337, 363, 367, 369 ; ii. 131
Gebel Touneh, rock-tablet at, i. 506
Genealogical Tables :—
— Family of Ameni and Khnumhotep, i. 156
— of Aahmes, son of Abana-Baba, i. 281
— of Dynasty XVIII., i. 345
— at end of Vol. II. :—
  I. of a Family, Dyn. XIII.
  II. of the Ramessids
  III. of the architect Ameneman
  IV. Royal Families of Dyn. XX.-XXVI.
Germanicus, Cæsar, his visit to Thebes, i. 365
Ge-ro-a-ro-pi, sister to Miamun Nut, ii. 258
Gerrhon, i. 147. *See* Anbu
Gharbieh, Arabic name of, the region west of the Nile, the ancient Libyan nome, i. 21
Gilead, balm of, i. 403
Girgaui, valley of, inscription of Amenemhat III.'s victory, i. 144
Gizeh, pyramids of, i. 86 ; memorial stone at, 463 ; inscription, 464-466
Gods, land of the (Arabia), i. 411 ; ii. 403 (*cf.* Holy Land)
Gold-mines of Egypt and Nubia, ii. 32, 33 ; in Wady-Alaki, 81
Gold-washing, ii. 33, 82
Gosem (Qosem, Grk. Phacussa, Coptic Qous, Arab. Faqous), capital of the Arabian nome (XX. L. Eg.), the 'land of Goshen' (88.), ii. 349, 369, 410
Guardafui, Cape, i. 416

HARABAT

'Gulfs' or 'pits' (*barathra*) of the lake Sirbonis, ii. 391, near Pelusium, 429, 432
Gynæcôn-polis, ii. 374

H A, ii. 347. *See* Hut-Sokhem
Ha-ben-ben ('house of the obelisk'), ii. 252. *See* Benben
Habennu. *See* Hasuten *and* Hibennu
Hadramaut, i. 139
Hagar, king. *See* Achoris
Haggi Qandil, rock-tablets at, i. 506
Hai, tomb of, i. 525, &c.
Hak (Haq), title ('prince' or 'king'), i. 127, 136, 173, 178, 228, 265, 274 ; ii. 145, *f.*
Hakak, temple at Der-el-Medineh, memorial stone at, i. 483-485
Hak-Shaus, i. 265. *See* Hyksos
Haleb (Khilibu), ii. 3, 46
Hamath, i. 392 ; ii. 110
Hammamat, rocky valley, road through, from Coptos to Red Sea, with quarries, and gold and silver mines, i. 133-7, 201 ; inscriptions of Pepi, 117 ; of Dyn. XI., 134, 135 (borings for water, ii. 87) ; of Dyn. XII., i. 144, 187, 194-5 ; of Dyn. XIII., 221 ; of Seti I., ii. 32-4, and Ramses II., 87 (gold-washing and water-boring) ; of Ramses IV. (great expedition), 174-8 ; of the architect Khnum-ab-ra, 220, 310 ; of Persian satraps, 312, *f.*
Hands of slain foes cut off, i. 471
Hannu, sent by Sankh-ka-ra to the land of Punt, i. 137, 138
Ha-nub, i. 54, 125
Hapi. *See* Apis
Hapi, the Nile-god, ii. 86
Hapu, architect, i. 60
Hapzefa, tomb of, at Lycopolis, i. 224
Haq. *See* Hak
Haq-Mama. *See* Ramses IV.
Haq-On. *See* Ramses III., VI., XIII.
Haq-Us. *See* Thakelath I.
Harabat-el-Madfouneh, i. 44, 50

HAREM

Harem conspiracy in Ramses III.'s time, ii. 164–172
Harincola (Rhinocolura), i. 336, 389
Harris papyrus, the, xxii., i. 230
Hashop, queen, i. 343, 344; assumes a king's titles and dress, 349; erases the name of Thutmes II. from the monuments, 349; her buildings, 351; expedition to the balsam-land of Punt, 351; homage paid to her ambassador, 353; gifts and treasures, 355, 356; her royal attire, 357; dedication of the treasures, 358–360; her peaceful reign, 361; shares the throne with her brother, Thutmes III., 362; their joint tablet at Wady-Magharah, 362; her obelisk of rose granite, 362; obelisks at Thebes, 420–1
Hasuten ('house of the king,' 'royal city;' Alabastrônpolis), capital of Nome XVIII. (Up. Eg.), early residence of Horemhib, i. 515, f., called also Habennu, ii. 348
Hathor, goddess (Grk. Aphrodite), protectress of Mafkat, i. 81; temple of, at Tentyra, inscription, 446, &c.; her origin from Arabia, ii. 403; worshipped in the form of a cow at Tepahe (the 'cow-city') or Aphroditopolis, 292, 417
Hathor, the month, i. 155, 527
Hat-kheper-ra. *See* Shashanq I.; Thakelath II.
Hat-ra. *See* Thakelath I.
Hat-ta-hir-ab, ii. 417. *See* Athribis
Ha-u'ar ('house of the leg'), i. 235, 236, 237; ii. 428, 431. *See* Avaris
Hazi, Hazina, or Hazion, 'land of the asylum' (Kasion, or Casius), the district east of the Pelusiac Nile, i. 239; ii. 13, 394, 426, 427
Hebrews, the, i. 17, 18, 298, f.; ii. 102, f., 134, 365, f.
Hebron, i. 230; ii. 383; Hethites settled at, in time of Abraham, 405
Heh, or Heha, i. 166, 182, 199
Heka, architect, i. 60

HIBIS

Heliopolis (Annu, On), one of the three capitals of Egypt; capital of Nome XIII. (L. Eg.); temple and obelisks at, i. 23, 149, 153, 204, 252, 308, 448, 450–1; ii. 29, 348, 375, *et passim*; works of Ramses III. in the temple of Tum-R'a-Hormakhu, 418
—another, 418
Heliopolitan nome, i. 23, 463; ii. 134, 239, 348, 369
Helmet, royal, or double crown, i. 517, 519
Hephæstus, Ptah, i. 56
Heracleopolis Magna (Khinensu), capital of Nome XX. (Up. Eg.), ii. 224, 239, 241, 245, &c., 348; temple of the ram-headed Her-shafni, 417
—Parva, ii. 373, 423. *See* Pitom
Heracleum (Karbana), i. 229
Hermes, i. 100. *See* Thut
Hermonthis, i. 150, 440
Hermopolis Magna (Khimunu), capital of Nome XV. (Up. Eg.), i. 100, 103, 317, 444; ii. 239, 241, 243, 245, 347; temple of Thot, 416 (*cf.* Khmun)
—Parva (Pi-Thut, 'city of Thut'), capital of Nome XV. (L. Eg.), ii. 239, 243, 254, 292, 349, 375
Herodotus, i. 44, 92, 100, 128, 191, &c.
Heroöpolitan nome, i. 252; ii. 418
Her-sh'a, east of Egypt, destroyed under Dyn. XII., ii. 405
Her-shafni (Grk. Harsaphes), ram-headed god of Heliopolis, ii. 416
Hethites. *See* Kheta
Hi, governor of the South, i. 472, 509
Hi, Hui, sculptor, under Ramses II., records of, ii. 31, 409
— administrator of the temples under Ramses II., ii. 91
Hibennu, Hibonu ('Phœnix-city,' Hipponon, or Habennu, Hut-uër; Hibis), capital of Nome XVI. (Up. Eg.), ii. 241, 245, 319, 348; temple of Khnum by Ramses III., 417
Hibis (El-Khargeh), in the Great Oasis, temple at, ii. 307

HIPPONON

Hipponon, ii. 241. *See* Hibennu
Hibset, festival of, i. 121, 122
Hierapolis (Mabog), ii. 5
Hin, measure, ii. 199
Hinder region, the N. as estimated by the Egyptians, but the W. by Semitic nations, term applied to the Khar in Assyrian inscriptions, i. 255 *n*. *See* Cardinal Points
Hir pyramid, i. 101
Hirhor, the priest-king, his usurpation, ii. 200; previous high position at court, 200, 201; overthrow of his race, 234; they retire to Ethiopia, 234; seat of their future royalty, 235; member of his family, with Semitic names, 420–1
Hirpit, title, i. 253, &c.; ii. 380
Hir-seshta, the secret learning, i. 64
Hirusha, the, i. 118; Pepi's wars with, 119, 145, 161. *Comp.* Her'sha
Hittites, the, of Scripture, i. 338; ii. 2. *See* Khita
Holy Land, the, Arabia, i. 411, &c.
Holy Scripture, agreement of the monuments with, i. 306; ii. 363, 365
Hontsen, king's daughter, pyramid to, i. 98
Hor (Horus, Apollo), god, and prototype of the king, i. 20, 37, 79, *et passim*; connected with Punt (Arabia), ii. 403
Horemhib (Horus), king, i. 515; his relationship to the royal family, 515; retirement at Ha-suten, 515; statues of him and his wife at Turin, 516, ii. 409; with inscription recording his early history, i. 516–520; crown prince and son-in-law to Aï, 519; coronation and titles, 519; voyage to Thebes and coronation, 520–1, ii. 408; enlarges and beautifies the temple of Amon, i. 521; campaign and victories in the South, 522; pictures illustrating his conquests, 522–525
—master of the horse under Amenho-

HYKSOS

tep II., Thutmes IV., and Amenhotep III., ii. 408
Horemhib, scribe under Ramses II., ii. 412
Hor-em-saf, architect, ii. 220, 309
Hormakhu (Grk. Harmachis), the god of light of Heliopolis, i. 370; also of Thebes, ii. 33, 219, 220; the Sun on the meridian, i. 464; the Sphinx his emblem, 99, 464; his festival, 390; special god of the Pharaohs, 473; ii. 63, &c.; the throne of Egypt his seat, 144, 155; his sanctuaries at Ibsamboul, 94–5, and Zoan-Tanis, 98; *et passim*
Horse and chariot, introduced from Asia, first mentioned, i. 340, 342
Hor-shesu, the successors of Horus, i. 40
Horsiise, priest and satrap, ii. 230, 270
Hortotef, prince, i. 103
Horus. *See* Hor *and* Hud
Hotep-hi-ma. *See* Mineptah II.
Hu, name of the Sphinx, i. 99
Hud, of Apollinopolis Magna, a local form of Horus, connected with Punt, ii. 403–4
Huni, king, i. 69, 70, 83
Hunt, Lake Mœris, i. 193
Hut-Sokhem or Ha (Diospolis Parva in Upper Egypt, now Hou), capital of Nome VII., ii. 347; temple of Ramses III. at, 416
Hut-uër. *See* Hibennu
Hyksos, the, a branch of the Cushite migration from Arabia, ii. 402; the dynasty of, i. 261; Josephus's account of, 261, 262; Arab origin, 263; not mentioned in monuments, 264; the name is Hak-Shaus 'King of the Arabs,' 265, 266; also called Phœnicians, 267; conclusions about them, 270–2; names of kings erased, 272; the two surviving, 273 (*see* Apophis, Nubti); rising against them, 279; their expulsion, 285–8; hatred of, confined to the South, 291; they increased the splendour of Zoan-Tanis, 294; their monuments

HYPSELE

destroyed by the kings of the eighteenth dynasty, 294 (*cf.* Menti)
Hypsele (Shas-hotep), capital of Nome XI. (Up. Eg.), temple of Khnum by Ramses III., ii. 347, 416

IBREEM (Primis), fortress of, i. 438; ii. 182
Ibsamboul (Abousimbel), rock-tablet at, ii. 70, 89; memorial-stone of the peoples of Africa conquered by Ramses II., 81; of the relations between Egypt and Khita, 88-90; rock-temple of, 94-97; built after the victories of Ramses II. over the Khita, 412; inscription of Seti II., 140, 141
I-en-Moshé or A-Musha, the 'island' or 'river-bank of Moses' (now Surarieh), ii. 117; temple of Sebek by Ramses III., 417
Incense, the true, from the land of Punt, i. 355; devoted to the temple at Thebes, 359
Inu'amu (Jamnia), i. 337, 373, 389; battle of, ii. 15
Inundation, regulation of the, i. 52-3, 188, 219; festival of the, ii. 408
Ionians, battle of the, ii. 309
Iöpé (Joppa), i. 392; local source of the myth of Andromeda, ii. 403
Ise (Isis), Ramses III.'s wife, ii. 172
Isi-Anhur, ii. 336. *See* Nakht-hor-ib
Isis, goddess, i. 37, 98, 99, 361, 446, 465; ii. 29, *et passim*
Israel, the children of, pursuit of, ii. 389, 390:—kingdom of, 216
Israelites, chronological relation to the Hyksos kings, i. 296; date of migration into Egypt, about 1730 B.C., 299; no mention of them in the inscriptions, explained, ii. 103
I-ther-nofirt, chief treasurer of Usurtasen III., ii. 405

JACOB, his migration into Egypt, i. 299

KAL

Jeroboam at the court of Shashanq, ii. 216
Jerusalem taken by Shashanq, ii. 216
Jezireh, i. 52.
Jobakchoi, the, i. 327
Joppa, i. 337, 392, 403; ii. 112, 403
Jordan (Iurduna), i. 337; the ford of, ii. 111
Joseph, i. 158, 278; his sale into Egypt placed by tradition under the Hyksos king Apophis, 300; contemporary record of a famine for many years, 302, 304; his offices of Adon and Ab-en-pirao, 307, ii. 146, 379; meaning of his name of Zaphnatpaneakh, i. 307, ii. 378; names of his wife and her father, and of his master, Putiphar, i. 308; striking parallel in the tale of the Two Brothers, 309, *f.*; ii. 139, *n.*
Josephus, i. 235; his account of the origin of the Hyksos, 262, 263
Jua (-aa, -ao), father of Thi, queen of Amenhotep III., i. 345, 490; ii. 407
Jubilee of Amenhotep III., i. 487
— the thirty years', of Ramses II.'s reign, ii. 114; others, *passim*
Judah invaded by Shashanq I., ii. 216; cities, &c., conquered, 217
Judah-Malek ('the royal') in the list of Shashanq's conquests, ii. 217
Judges of ancient Egypt, i. 64
Jupiter, i. 327. *See* Amon *and* Oasis

KADESH, king of, leader of the league in Palestine, i. 394: fortress of, taken by Seti I., ii. 16; pictures of the battle of Ramses II. against, at Abydus, 48-54
Kadosh, goddess, i. 245
Kahani, i. 241
Kaiechos, king (Kakau), i. 69, 70; worship of Apis and Mnevis established in his reign, 74
Kakami, pyramid of the black bull, i. 73 (*cf.* Kochome)
Kakau, king. *See* Kaiechos
Kal, Kar (the Galla), i. 13

INDEX.

KAMBATHET

Kambathet, ii. 304. *See* Cambyses
Kames, king, i. 289, 290
Kanaah, i. 371
Kan'ana, or Kan'aan, fort, i. 248; ii. 12, 14; Ramesseum at, 164, 420
Kanbuza, ii. 304. *See* Cambyses
Ka-ra-ma, Usarkon II.'s wife, ii. 224
Karamat, Shashanq I.'s wife, ii. 212; inscription concerning her property in Egypt, 213, 214
Karba, Karbana, Karbanit (Heracleum), i. 229 (*cf.* Canopus)
Karbelmati, i. 327. *See* Saïs
Kari, or Kali (the land furthest S.), i. 437, 462, 474; ii. 84
Karnak, monuments at, i. 142; village, 154; list of kings in the chamber of, 222; temple of, commencement, 322; inscriptions at, 366; the Hall of Pillars, 390, 410; list of towns, 392; gardens and arable land given to temple, 421; doors and gates of Thutmes III., 422, 423; thanksgiving of the priests, 423, 424; table of kings, 430; Hall of Ancestors, 433; representation of Amenhotep II. on southern gate, 459; of Ramses I.'s coronation, ii. 9; Great Hall of Columns, 10, 21, 92; Mineptah II.'s inscription, 122–128; record of Shashanq I.'s invasion of Judah, 216; list of conquered countries, 217, 218; Hall of the Bubastids, 219
Karu, Kalu, i. 437. *See* Kari
Kas, a district of Kush, i. 159
Kash, i. 183. *See* Kush
Kati (Galilee), ii. 77; beer from, 102, 154
Kefa, Keft, Kefeth, Kefthu (Caphtor, SS.), the land and people of Phœnicia, and afterwards of the Philistines, i. 256, 381, 385, 386; ii. 402, 403; tributes of, 406
Keftha-Hor (the 'Keftha of Horus'), with a special priesthood, ii. 403. *See* Caphtor
Kemi, or Kami (black land), ancient

KHARTOT

name of Egypt, i. 16; ii. 265; *et passim*
Kepkep. *See* Kipkip
Kereh ('the smooth'), the symbol of the 'living' god worshipped at Pitom, ii. 377, 422
Kerkasorus, i. 236
Kerkesh, or Keshkesh (the Girgesites), ii. 47
Kerman, near Tombos, list of victories at, i. 331
Ket, weight, ii. 199
Khnankhra. *See* Sebek-hotep VI.
Khabbash, anti-king to Xerxes, ii. 301, 331; his sarcophagus for the Apis-bull, 302; named in an inscription of Ptolemy I., 315
Khafra, king (Cephren or Chabryes), i. 84, 94; his pyramid, 94; statues, 96, 204; name on the Sphinx, 98, 464, 466; his prophet and wife, 100
Kha-ka-ra. *See* Usurtasen II.
Kha-kau-ra. *See* Usurtasen III.
Khaleb (Khalybon), i. 337, 398, &c.
Khamhat, inscription in tomb of, i. 487
Khamus, Amenhotep II.'s son, and chief priest, i. 461
— Ramses II.'s favourite son, ii. 69; high-priest of Ptah, 116; buildings in Memphis, 116; death, 116
— governor of Thebes, ii. 190
— *See* Ramses IX. and XIII.
Kha-nofer, pyramid, i. 124, 146
Khar or Khal, Kharu or Khalu, the Phœnicians, i. 14, 267, 320, 337, 367, 369, 381, 394, 400, 403–4, 510–11; ii. 14, 15, 80, 142, 157; on the sea-coast of Zaha, from Egypt to the Canaanites, i. 319, 320; and in Egypt, as far as Zoan-Tanis, 254-6, 267; their influence, 257; language, 258; remnant of, about lake Menzaleh, 14, 258–9; employed as bearers of despatches, ii. 131
Khartot (Khartumim), 'warrior-priests,' at Pi-ramses, Zoan-Tanis,

KHEM-AMUN

the 'magicians' who withstood Moses, ii. 384
Khem-Amun, Ramses I.'s temple of, at Wady-Halfah, ii. 9 (as corrected at 409)
Khemmis. *See* Panopolis
Kheper-ka-ra. *See* Usurtasen I.
Kheper-ma-ra. *See* Ramses X.
Khesea, district of Kush, i. 159
Khesef-Thamhue, fortress of Ramses III., Libyans defeated at, ii. 153
Khesuu, ii. 348. *See* Xoïs
Kheta, the, i. 14. *See* Khita
Khetam ('the fortress') of Sukot, near Pelusium, ii. 380
—(Etham), at Tabenet (Daphnæ) on the great Pharaonic road to Palestine, drawing of, at Karnak, ii. 12, 19, 386-8, 389, 390, 426
Kheti, wife of Khnumhotep, i. 179
Khilibu (Haleb), ii. 3, 46, 109; king of, at the battle of Kadesh, 51
Khim (Pan), i. 390; ii. 177, 313, 408
Khimunu. *See* Hermopolis Magna
Khinensu (Ahnas), ii. 224, 308, 309, 348. *See* Heracleopolis Magna
Khita, Kheta (the Khethites or Hittites of SS.), 'the great land of,' i. 384; wars of kings of Dyn. XII. with, ii. 404; settled close to Egypt in the time of Abraham, 405; a great division of the Ruthen, i. 338; tribute from, 379, 384, 404; rise of, ii. 2; locality and supremacy, 3; deities, towns, 3; military array, 4; non-Semitic names, 5; list of their peoples and cities, 5-7; supremacy in Western Asia before the Assyrians, 7; war with Egypt, 46; treaty of alliance, 71, *f.*, 410; relations of Mineptah II. with, 130
Khitasar, or Khitasir, king of Khita, ii. 3, 4; treaty with Ramses II. written on a silver tablet, 70-76, 410; marriage alliance, 78, 413
Khmun (Hermopolis Magna), worship of the moon at, i. 317

KIP-KIP

Khnum, Khnum-ra, god of Elephantiné, i. 36, 185; temple to, at Koummeh, 438, 444; ii. 225, 260
Khnum-ab-r'a, king, burial of the Apis-bull, ii. 297. *See* Amasis
— architect, i. 43, 45; ii. 220; his pedigree, 309; inscription at Hammamat, 310
Khnum-Amon. *See* Hashop
Khnumhotep, i. 156; his tomb at Beni-Hassan, long inscription, 169; paintings, 177; honours accorded to his descendants, 179, 180
Khoiakh, month, i. 187, 524; ii. 296
Khonsu, Khonsu-em-us ('the good and friendly'), son of Amon and Mut, god of Thebes, ii. 22, 71, 119, 163, 178, 191, 213, *f.*, 214; his temple at Thebes, the chapel of the Ramessids, 195, 416, 420
—'the administrator' of Thebes, journey of his image to Bakhatana, and contest with a demon, ii. 193, *f.*
Khonsu-Thut, i. 73. *See* Thut
Khont 'forwards,' *i.e.* the South, ii. 255 *n.* *See* Cardinal Points
Khont-Hon-nofer, a general name for all inner Africa; wars against, i. 285, 286, 329, 330, 346; ii. 41
Khu-aten, new city built by king Khun-aten, i. 494
Khufu, i. 85, 93. *See* Cheops
Khu-mennu, the Hall of Pillars at Karnak, i. 389, 430
Khunaten, name adopted by Amenhotep IV., i. 494; question of their identity, 493 *n.*
Khu-setu, pyramid, i. 135
King, the, of Upper and Lower Egypt, his titles, &c., i. 61
Kings of Egypt, list of, with their epochs, ii. 341-346
Kings and satraps in Lower Egypt, list of, ii. 239, 243
King's sons of Tini, i. 51; of Kush, 51, 332, *et passim*
Kip-kip, or Kepkep, capital of Takhont (Nubia), ii. 264, 265

INDEX.

KIRGIPA

Kirgipa, Asiatic wife of Amenhotep III., ii. 407
Kissing the ground before Pharaoh, i. 104
Kiti (Chittim), i. 394
Kobti, ii. 416. *See* Coptos
Kochome, necropolis of Memphis, i. 73
Kolöe, i. 437
Konosso, island of, bas-relief of Mentuhotep at, i. 133; inscription, 462
Korusko, i. 144
Kouban, stone with inscription to Ramses II. at, ii. 83–87
Koummeh, temple-fortress at, i. 181, 189, 199, 220, 438, 460
Kurdistan, ii. 47
Kush (Kash), Ethiopia, Usurtasen's expedition against, i. 159; names of the races on a memorial stone at Wady-Halfab,159; final subjugation by Usurtasen III., 182; the governor of, first mentioned, 332; tribute, 381, 384, ii. 406; seat of a new kingdom, 236; subdivision of the kingdom, with capital at Napata, 264

LABYRINTH, built by king Amenemhat III., i. 191; meaning of the name, Lape-ro-hunt, 193
Lakes and waters with Semitic names, i. 232
Language, Egyptian, akin to both Aryan and Semitic, i. 9; of the Khethites, its peculiarities, ii. 5
Latopolis, i. 440. *See* Esneh
Lebanon, Libanon, Mount, i. 337, 388, 393, 401. *Comp.* Limanon
Lee and Rollin papyrus, ii. 170, *f.*
Leka, Liku (the Ligyes), ii. 47, 57,*f.*, 122,*f.*, 129
Leontes R., i. 337
Leontopolis, ii. 12, 374. *See* Ta'a-pamau
Letopolis, nome of, i. 467. *See* Sokhem
Letter of an Egyptian, describing the city of Ramses-Miamun (Zoan-Tanis), ii. 100; of a priest on the

MAH

new literature of Ramses II.'s time, 108–114; autograph of Ramses XIII., 196–7
Leucos Limen (Qosseir), i. 138; ii. 87
Libu, the, i. 11, 229. *See* Libyans
Libyan Desert, the, i. 20
Libyan nome, west of the Nile, the modern Gharbieh, i. 21
Libyans, the, i. 11, 12; revolt of, 77; irruption of, 230; wars of Seti I. against, ii. 21; their invasion and defeat by Mineptah II., 121; war of Ramses III. with, 147; &c.
Limanon (Limenen, Rimenen, the region of Lebanon), tribute of, i. 379, 383, 404; fortress in, 388; the inhabitants submit to Seti I., ii. 18; trees felled for ship-building, 18
Lion, fighting, of Ramses II., ii. 80
Lists of countries, peoples, and places conquered by Thutmes III. in Upper Ruthen, i. 392, 393; in the S., 405–9; by Amenhotep III., 471–2; by Ramses III., ii. 158–9; by Shashanq I. in Palestine, 217–8; of names of the Khita, 5–7
Lowlands, the Egyptian, i. 228
Lui (Levi, Roi, or Loi), high-priest and architect, ii. 136, 139
Luqsor, list of prisoners, ii. 69; temple, obelisks, &c., 92
Luten. *See* Ruten
Lycians, ii. 129
Lycopolis, Lycôn-polis (Siajout, now Ossiout), capital of Nome XIII. (Up. Eg.), ii. 347, 374; records in the tombs of, i. 223, 224; temple of Anubis, ii. 416

MAFKAT (green-stone, turquoise), and land of, i. 81, 160, 196, 489; ii. 149
Magdolum. *See* Migdol
Magharah, i. 80. *See* Wady-Magharah
Magicians of *Exodus*, ii. 384. *See* Khartot
Mah, a captain in the reign of Thutmes III., i. 398, 461

MAH

Mah, the nome of, i. 156–8, 180
Mai, architect of Ramses II., ii. 98 *n*.
—scribe and judge, ii. 168, *f*.
Maiu, a district of Nubia, i. 406; ii. 81 *n*., 181
Ma-ka-ra. *See* Hashop
Makitha, ii. 21. *See* Megiddo
Maktol or Magdol, ii. 237. *See* Migdol
Malunna, ii. 47, 56, *f*.
Mama. *See* Ramses IV.
Ma-men-ra. *See* Seti I.
Ma-neb-ra. *See* Amenhotep III.
Manetho, i. 23, 39, 42, *et passim*
Manufactures, i. 26
Map, old Egyptian, at Turin, ii. 81
Marah (the Bitter Lakes), ii. 397–8
Marajui, Mauri, Libyan king, ii. 123, 126, 153
Mareotic nome, ii. 130
Marina, title (lord), i. 374, 376, &c.
Marmarica, i. 327; ii. 21, 242
Marmaridæ, i. 327–8, 460, 507; ii. 21, 79, 123, 404. *See* Thuhen
Mas, viceroy in Ethiopia, ii. 135
Masahartha and Masaqahartha, 7th and 8th sons of Hirhor, ii. 419, 420
Masen, region of Punt in Arabia, the Masonitæ of Ptolemy, ii. 404
Mashashal, Massala, king of the Maxyes, ii. 155
Massaarah, i. 91; quarries of, with rock-tablets of Aahmes, 322
Maskhoutah, in Wady-Toumeilât, memorials of Ramses II. at, ii. 411, 424; but *not* the city of Ramses, 412, 425
Mastabat-el-Faraoun, pyramid, i. 113. *See* Dashour
Mastemut, paint, i. 177, 178
Mastura. *See* Cambyses
Masu (Masius M.), ii. 47
Masui, viceroy, ii. 81
Mat, the (Assyrians), successors to the Khita, ii. 202
Matarieh village, i. 149, 448
M'a-ur-nofru, or M'a-nofru-r'a, queen of Ramses II., daughter of the king of Khita, ii. 413

MEMPHIS

Maurosar, king of Khita, ii. 3
Mauthanar, king of Khita, ii. 3, 16
Maxyes, the, of Libya, irruption of, under Mineptah II., i. 230; war of Ramses III. with, ii. 147, 155
Mazai, police, i. 254; ii. 91, 380, &c.
Mazor ('fortified'), origin of Mizraim, properly a part of Lower Egypt, i. 18, 231, 244; ii. 237, 383 *n*.
Measures, ii. 199
Medinet-Abou, temple of, i. 347, 435; new temple of Amenhotep III., 477; his memorial tablet, 478; monuments of the reign of Ramses III. in his Ramesseum, ii. 150, 415; inscriptions, 151, 157, 159; pictures, 157; names of conquered cities, 158, 159; temple at, on the Nebankh, with inscriptions of the Egyptian calendar and holidays, 162; festivals, 163; list of Ramses III.'s sons, 173
Medinet-el-Fayoum, i. 194
Megabyzus, satrap, ii. 332
Megiddo, battle of, i. 269, 370, 371; account of the harvest reaped by Thutmes III., 373; battle of Necho with Josiah, ii. 322
Mehet-en-usekh, mother of Nimrod, ii. 206
Meidoum (Mitum), i. 59; pyramid near, pictures discovered in, 82
Mekhir, the month, i. 55, 175, 363, 440, 489, 527; ii. 296
'Memnon,' statues of, i. 475, 478; the vocal, 479–482
Memnonium at Abydus, i. 162; of Seti I., dedicated to his father, ii. 28; inscription in, 29
Memphis (Mennofer, Telmonf), one of the three capitals of Egypt, i. 23; capital of Nome I. (L. Eg.), ii. 348, 417; founded by Mena, i. 53; its names, temples, and necropolis, 54, 55; ruins at Mit-Rahineh, 56; stones used for building Cairo, 58; importance of the high-priests, 58; necropolis, 59; worship of the sacred

MEN

bull (Apis), 74, ii. 229; temple of Ptah, 29, 90; capital of the last Bubastids, 228; siege by Piankhi, 249-251; sanctuaries of Ramses III. at, 417

Men and Menti, regions of Punt in Arabia, the Minæi and Manitæ of Ptolemy, ii. 404 n.

Mena (Menes), date of his accession, i. 41; calculations based on Manetho, 42; the first Pharaoh, 51; cursed by Tnephachthus, 52; his ordinances and works, 52; changes the course of the Nile, 52; builds Memphis, 53; killed by a crocodile, 67; meaning of the name, 70

Menankh, pyramid, i. 126

Menat-Khufu, town, i. 170, 171

Mendes, the sacred ram, i. 74

Mendes (Pi-bi-neb-dad, 'city of the sacred ram'), capital of Nome XVI. (L. Eg.), i. 74, 240; ii. 349; seat of Dyn. XXIX., 316, 335

Men-kau-hor (Mencheres), Dyn. V., i. 110

Menkaura (Mencheres), Dyn. IV., i. 101-103; builder of the third pyramid, 101; coffin-lid and inscription, 101; his character, deification, and religious studies, 102

Men-kheper-ra. *See* Thutmes III.

Men-kheper-ra succeeds his father, Pinotem, ii. 208; recalls the banished Ramessids, 203

Men-khepru-ra. *See* Thutmes IV.

Men-ma-ra. *See* Ramses XIII.

Mennofer ('the good place'), i. 55. *See* Memphis

Men-nofer, Pepi's pyramid, i. 120

Men-pehuti-ra. *See* Ramses I.

Men-setu, pyramid, i. 108

Menthu, an Asiatic people, destroyed under Dyn. XII., ii. 405

Menthu, Montbu, god, i. 372, 440

Menthu-khopeshef, chief of the police, ii. 190

Menthu-nesu, under Dyn. XII., monument of, ii. 404

MEROË

Menti, foreign non-Egyptian kings (the Hyksos), i. 268, 269; called 'inhabitants of the land of Asher' (Syria), 268; their capital, 270; adopted the customs, &c., of the Egyptians, 270; patrons of art;271; their names erased from their monuments, 272; two preserved, 273. *See* Hyksos

Mentu-hotep I. Ranebtaui, i. 127, 131, 134, 143

Mentu-hotep II., his pyramid, i. 134

Mentu-hotep, royal architect to Usurtasen I., inscription at Boulaq, i. 161, 162; character and accomplishments, 163

Menzaleh, lake, i. 14, 120, 232, 238, 258; ii. 372

Mer-en-ra, king, i. 123; preparations for his burial, 124; name on the wall of the temple at Abydus, 130

Meri, royal architect to Usurtasen I., inscription at the Louvre, i. 164

—governor of Wawa under Seti II., ii. 412

—Adon, in Ramses IX.'s reign, ii. 183

—(Merris), daughter of Ramses II., named by tradition as the rescuer of Moses, ii. 117

Meribast, chief priest of Amon, ii. 173

Merimes, governor of Kush in Amenhotep III.'s reign, i. 472

Meri-ra, king. *See* Pepi

Merira, Meri-patah-ankh, chief of the public works under Pepi, i. 121

Meri-ra, chief prophet of the Sun, i 500

Meri-ra-ankh, tomb of, i. 60, 121

Meri-ra-ankh-nes, Pepi's wife, her tomb. i. 122

Merisankh, Khafra's wife, i. 100

Meritum, king, ii. 180

Merkaura, or Meri-ka-ra, king, i. 223

Meroë, the priests of, not the founders of Egyptian civilization, i. 9; the Meluḫḫa of the Assyrian inscriptions, ii. 264, *f.*, 273: centre of a primeval Cushite kingdom, 402

MERTISEN

Mertisen, artists of the family of, i. 143; his pedigree, 205, 206
Merur, i. 74. *See* Mnevis
Mesha, young soldiers, i. 64
Mesket (Meskenet), 'treasure,' or rather 'temple' cities, ii. 102, 308
Mesopotamia, monumental records of foreign wars in, i. 15, &c.; Arab conquest of, 367. *See* Naharain
Mesori, the month, i. 247, 296, 527; ii. 156, 227, 295
Mesphres, king, i. 450
Metelis (Sonti-Nofer), capital of Nome VII. (L. Eg.), ii. 348
Miamun, 'friend of Amun.' *See* Ramses II.; Setnakht; Ramses IV., V.; Meritum; Ramses VI., IX., XI., XII., XIII.; Shashanq I., II.; Usarkon I., II.; Thakelath I., II.; Pimai
Miamun Nut, successor to Piankhi, ii. 257; his dream and campaign against Lower Egypt, 257; official designation, 258; memorial stone, 258; sisters, 258; inscription, 259-263; his success not lasting, 264
Miamun-ra, name of Darius II., ii. 333
Migdol 'the tower' (Tel-es-Samout), the northernmost point of Egypt, i. 237, 238; ii. 12, 381, 382, 389, 390, 421, 426, 431; its position the key to the question of the Exodus, 427; naval engagement at, 153, 154
Mineptah I., ii. 10. *See* Seti I.
——II. (Menephthes), hereditary prince in his father's lifetime, ii. 120, 413; mean character of his architectural works, 120; his inscription in the temple of Amon, 121-128; corrections in, 413; invasion by and defeat of the Libyans, 121; battle of Prosopis, 126; relations with the Khita, 130; despatches, 131; the Pharaoh of the Exodus, 133; his court at Zoan-Ramses, 134; troubles of his reign, 135; men of letters, 137; his end unrecorded, 135 *n.*; his dirge, 136 *n.*

NABU-SEZIBANNI

Mineptah Siptah, anti-king to Setnakht, ii. 140; inscription of his supporter, Seti, at Ibsamboul, 141
Minerals, i. 201
Misraim, Muzur, Mudraya, Asiatic names for Egypt, derived probably from Mazor (*q. v.*), i. 18, 231
Mit-Rahineh (Mitrahenne), ruins of Memphis at, i. 56; prostrate colossus of Ramses II., ii. 90; remains of a house, 292
Mitum (Meidoum), ii. 240, 248
Mnevis, the sacred bull of Heliopolis, i. 39, 74; ii. 293
Mob, the, or lowest classes, i. 26
Mœris, lake (She, She-uer, Mi-uer), constructed by Amenemhat'III., i. 187; derivation of name, 190; discovery of the site, 190; different names, 192
Mokattam, hills of, quarries in, i. 91; new quarries opened, 476
Mont, Monthu (Mars), i. 34, *et passim*
Month-em-ha, ally and friend of Taharaqa, ii. 278
Moses, his name preserved in [-en-Moshé, ii. 117
Mushanath, ii. 47
Mut-em-ua ('Mother in the boat'), queen of Thutmes IV., i. 468
Mut-Nofer-t, daughter of Thutmes I., her statue, i. 433
Mut-ut-ankhes, wife of Usarkon, ii. 224
Muzur, Lower Egypt, under the Assyrians, ii. 237
Mycerinus, i. 101. *See* Mencheres

NA-AMON or PI-AMON, 'the city of Amon' (No and No-Amon, SS.; Diospolis Parva, *q.v.*), a second Thebes in Lower Egypt, called by all the same titles, also *Na-mehit* '*the city* of the North,' on the Phatnitic mouth of the Nile, at or near Damietta; magnificent buildings of Ramses III. at, ii. 418-9
Nabu-Sezibanni, son of Necho, ii. 272, 274

NAHARAIN

Naharain, or Naharina (Aram, Mesopotamia), i. 338; memorial tablet set up by Thutmes III., 378; booty from, 381; prisoners, 385; tribute, 404; &c.
Nahasi Negroes, the, i. 12; language of, 258; race, 330
Nahi, Egyptian governor of the south country, i. 343, 387; his inscription at Ellesieh, 387, 438
Nahr-el-Kelb, river, Egyptian monuments at the mouth of, ii. 276
Naifaurot (Nepherites) I. and II., ii. 287, 335
Nakht-hor-hib(Nectarebes, Nectanebo I.), king, ii. 287, 308, 317, 336
Nakht-Khim, priest of Khim, in time of king Ai, ii. 408
Nahkt-neb-ef (Nectanebo II.), the last Pharaoh, his pair of lions, ii. 287, 292; a famous magician, 294; burial of an Apis-bull, 302, 317, 338
Nahkt-neb-ef, chief captain, sarcophagus of, ii. 317
Nakhtu, viceroy of Kush, ii. 81
Nap, or Napata, at Mt. Barkal, i. 329; the capital of the new kingdom of Ethiopia, ii. 235, 236; inscriptions of Ethiopian kings at, *see* Barkal
Na-pa-to-mehi, or Na-pa-athu (Naphtuhim, SS.), buildings of Ramses III. at, ii. 419
Naph, or Noph (Napata), the princes of, in Scripture, ii. 237
Naphtuhim, origin of name, i. 327; ii. 419
Na-ris, '*the city* of the South,' a name of Thebes (*q. v.*), ii. 418
Naromath, ii. 207. *See* Nimrod
—son of Usarkon II., chief priest of Amon, &c., ii. 224; his descendants hereditary priests of Khnum, 225
Nasruna, river, i. 399
Nathu, Natho, the marsh-land of the Delta, i. 520; on the Phatnitic arm of the Nile and the sea-board, ii. 316. *Comp.* Athu
Navigation, i. 139

NI-ENT-BAK

Neb-aiu, high-priest, i. 445; inscription of, 446
Neb-ankh ('the coffin mountain'), i. 347; ii. 161-2
Neb-kher-ra, i. 131. *See* Mentuhotep I.
Neb-pehuti-ra. *See* Aahmes I.
Nebuchadnezzar, ii. 322-8
Neb-unon-f, chief priest of Amon, in time of Ramses II., inscription of, ii. 410
Necherophes, king, i. 69, 77
Necho. *See* Neku
Negeb, the land S. of Palestine, i. 392, 398; ii. 13
Negro peoples, list of, conquered by Amenhotep III., i. 471, 472; tributes of, 509, 510; their excellent workmanship, 511, 512
Negroes, the, in Pepi's army, i. 119; razzias on, 184, ii. 78; song of, i. 335, 523
Nehera, i. 171
Nehi, the first 'king's son of Kush,' i. 332-3. *Comp.* Nahi
Nekheb, ii. 347. *See* Eileithyia
Nekht, son of Khnumhotep, governor of Cynopolis, i. 179, 180
Neku (Nikuu, Neco, Nechao, Necho)
—I., king of Memphis and Saïs, father of Psamethik I., ii. 270, 272, 273; carried prisoner to Nineveh and pardoned, 277
—II., son of Psamethik I., Apis-tablet of, ii. 296, 297; his reign, 322, 323
Nentef, kings, i. 131. *See* Anentef
Nephercheres, king, i. 69, 76, 84, 107
Nepherites I. and II. *See* Naifaurot
Neshi (Ptolemaïs), Ramses III.'s temple of Sebek at, ii. 416
Nes-ro-an, lake, i. 377
Nes-su-Amon, royal councillor, ii. 187, 190
Ni, in Mesopotamia, stêlé set up by Thutmes III., i. 379; not Nineveh, 400; taken by Amenhotep II., 456
Ni-'a, Ni', Ni (the 'great city;' Ni-Amon, Thebes), i. 435; ii. 236, 270, 271, 275, 278, 272, 347. *See* Thebes
Ni-ent-bak. *See* Antæopolis

NI-ENT-HAPI

Ni-ent-Hapi, ii. 348. *See* Apis
Nikuu. *See* Neku
Nile, the (Nil, Nahar, Nahal), meaning of the word, i. 20; its course changed by Mena, 52; inundations of, 188; height recorded in the reigns of Amenemhat III., 189; and Sebekhotep III., 219
Nimrod leads a branch of Cushites from Pun to the Euphrates, confirmed by Babylonian tradition, ii. 402
Nimrod, king of Assyria, invades Egypt, ii. 203; his death and burial at Abydus, 206; statue of, at Florence, 212; meaning of the name, 284. *See* Naromath
Nineveh, i. 400; ii. 7, 202, 267, 268, 271, 274, 275
Nitocris (Nitaker), queen, Dyn. VI., tradition of, i. 127, 128; enlarges the pyramid of Menkara, 129
—princess of XXVIth Dynasty, her Babylonian marriage, ii. 326
No ('*the* city '), Noa ('the great city '), in SS. No-Amon ('city of Amun '), capital of Patoris, i. 278, 282, 288; necropolis of, 289. *See* Thebes
Nobles, the ancient Egyptian, i. 28
Nofer ('good,' 'beautiful '), pyramid, i. 110
Noferabra, prophet, i. 99
Nofer-ar-ka-ra, king, his pyramid, i. 107; officers, 108; several kings of the name, 131
Noferhotep, physician, i. 73
—wife of Ti, i. 110
—surname of the god Khonsu, ii. 410
Nofer-i-Thi, wife of Amenhotep IV., i. 501; her address to the sun, 502
Nofer-ka-ra, king, i. 76; his pyramid, 126; several kings of the name, 131
—*See* Ramses IX.
Noferkara-em-piamon, secretary and councillor, ii. 187, 190
Nofer-ka-Sokari, king, i. 69, 70
Nofer-kheper-ra. *See* Amenhotep IV.
Nofer-setu, pyramid, i. 113

OBELISKS

Nofert, wife of Rahotep, i. 83
Nofert, queen of Amenemhat II., her life-size statue at Tanis, i. 167-8
Nofert-ari Aahmes, queen, i. 323-325; deified as the ancestress of the Eighteenth Dynasty, 324
Nofer-tum-khu-ra. *See* Tabaraqa
Noferu-Ra, daughter of the king of Bakhatana, wife of Ramses XII., ii. 191
Nofre-Ma, tomb of, at Meidoum, i.83*n*.
Nofrus, fortress, ii. 241
Nokheb, god, i. 440
Nomes, the ancient, of Egypt, i. 21; number of, 21; their capitals, 22; governors, temples, &c., 22; boundary stones, 22; lists of, 22, ii. 347
Noph, ii. 260. *See* Naph
Notem, queen-mother of Dyn. XXI., ii. 421
Notem-mut, wife of king Horemhib, her statue, i. 507, 514, 515; ii. 409
Nthariush (-uth). *See* Darius
Nub ('gold '), surname of the god Set, i. 244, 271; ii. 125, 255
Nub, Nubti, Hyksos king, i. 273; era of, 231, 246, 296, 297; ii. 99
Nubia, gold from, i. 160; riches of, 333; the works of Ramses II. in, ii. 94; (Ta-Khont) a division of Ethiopia, 264; temple of Amon by Ramses III., 415
Nubkas, queen, i. 218
Nubkaura. *See* Amenemhat II.
Nubti, ii. 415. *See* Ombos
Nukheb, prince of, i. 461
Nu-ta-maten, priest of 'Amon of Ramses II.' at Tanis, ii. 412
Nuter ('god '). *See* Ramses III., VI., XIII., Thakeloth I.
Nuter-setu, pyramid, i. 110

OASIS of Amon, i. 327
—the Great, ii. 201, 203, *f.*, 307. *See* Hibis *and* El-Khargeh
Obelisks of Eleventh Dynasty, i. 135 *n.*; of Usurtasen I. at Heliopolis and in the Fayoum, 149, 152, 204; of

OCHUS
queen Hashop, 362; of Thutmes III. at Thebes, 448, 449; at Heliopolis, 450-1
Ochus, king, ii. 287, 338, 339; disaster to his army at Lake Sirbonis, 392, 395
Ollaqi, valley of, i. 145
Ombos (Nubti), i. 440; temple of Ramses III., ii. 415
On, i. 74, *et passim.* See Heliopolis
Onka (Anka), Phœnician goddess, i. 245
Onnos (Unas), king, i. 84, 113
Onuris, ii. 416. *See* Anhur
Ophir, the, of the Egyptians, i. 136
Oppert, M., his comments on the record of Assurbanipal, ii. 272
Orbiney papyrus, the, i. 309-311
Orontes, river, i. 337, 398; ii. 46
Osiris (Bacchus), son of Seb, i. 37; his temple at Abydus, 196; two arms of the Nile regarded as his legs, 235, 236; chief seat of his worship in Lower Egypt, Busiris, 441; in Upper Egypt, Abydus, 441
Osiris and Isis, statues of, ii. 292
Osorkhon, king, ii. 233
Ossiout, rock-tomb near, i. 223
Ostracene (-cine), i. 239; tower of Seti I. at, the boundary of Egypt and Zahi, ii. 13; tower of Mineptah II., 132. *See* Aanekht
Othoës, king, i. 115. *See* Teta
Overseers, i. 63
Oxyrhynchus (Pi-maza, Sapt-moru), capital of Nome XVIII. (Up. Eg.), the city of Typhon, i. 180, 515; ii. 348, 417
Ozaeb, i. 240

PAHIR, genealogy of, i. 280, 281, 283, 342
Painting in ancient Egypt, i. 203
Paintings in tombs, i. 88, *et passim*; on walls, *passim*
Pakhons, the month, i. 186, 247, 362, 421, 440, 456, 490, 527; ii. 163
Palestine. *See* Ruthen *and* Zaha
Pa-nakhtu, tower of, ii. 13

PATAH-SHEPSES
Pa-Kereh ('city of the electric fish'), ii. 422, 423. *See* Phagroriopolis
Panbesa, the scribe, his letter describing the city of Ramses, ii. 100
Panofer, artist, under Ramses II., ii. 412
Panopolis (Apu, Khemmis), capital of Nome IX. (Up. Eg.), ii. 347, 408; temple of Horus and Isis built by Ramses III., 416
Panrshns, Assyrian king, ii. 202
Paoni, the month, i. 186, 438, 527
Paophi, the month, i. 134, 157, 331, 346, 390, 401, 527
Papyrus, the Abbot, i. 282; record of Aahmes, 283-287
—Anastasi III., letter of Panbesa, describing the city of Ramses, ii. 100; records of despatches, 131, 132
—the Harris, i. 249; summary of the reign of Setnakht, ii. 143, 144; account of the reign of Ramses III., 145; list of Ramessea, 161, 415, *f.*
—the Lee and Rollin, account of the harem conspiracy, ii. 170; use of magic, 170-172
—the medical, discovered at Memphis, i. 73
—the Orbiney, parallel to the story of Joseph, i. 309-311
—of Patah Hotep, i. 111, 112
—the Sallier, historical, in British Museum, i. 274-279
—the Turin, i. 39, 47, 48; list of kings, 214-216
—probable autograph letter of Ramses XIII., ii. 197
—with the geography of Lake Mœris, i. 192
—rolls of the Nineteenth Dynasty, i. 231
Parihu, prince of Punt, i. 355
Pa-Sahura, i. 107
Pastophorus of the Vatican, the, ii. 291, 304 *n. See* Uzahorenpiris
Patah (Vulcan), the god of Memphis, i. 35, 36; worship of, 54, 58, 145
Patah-hotep, papyrus of, i. 111, 112
Patah-shepses, tomb of, i. 103; steward

PATOMHIT

of the provision stores, like Joseph, 104; prophet of the pyramids of Unas and Teta, 116

Patomhit (Pa-to-me-hit, 'the country of the North'), the Delta, i. 317, ii. 419

Pa-to-ris ('the country of the South,' Pathros, Patrosim, SS., the Thebaïd), i. 278, 316, ii. 419; a province under the Ethiopians, 237

Patumos, ii. 422, 423

Pauër, governor of Thebes, under Seti I. and Ramses II.; his tomb at Thebes, ii. 31, 81, 409
—a 'sculptor from the life,' ii. 98 *n*

Paur, governor of the south, memorial of, at Shetaui, i. 514·

Payni, the month, i. 456, 527; ii. 56, 164, 219, 296

Pa-zetku, or Zeku, lake beside Avaris, i. 237, 284

Pedigree of the architect Khnum-abr'a, ii. 309

Pehenuka, officer of Nofer-ar-ka-ra, i. 108

Pehuu, a Diospolis in the Fayoum, ii. 417

Pelusiac branch of the Nile, i. 229, 232, 236, 270, 336; bridge over, at Etham, ii. 12, 387–8, 426; crossing of, not mentioned in 'Exodus,' explained, 425–6

Penni, Adon of Wawa, tomb at Anibe, ii. 183, 184

Pentaur, the priest, heroic poem of, i. 277, 416; ii. 47, 56–65, 410

Pepi Merira, king, i. 116, 126; inscriptions at Wady-Magharah and elsewhere, 117; his servant, Una, 117; monolith, 118; wars, 118, 119; pyramid, 120; plan of a temple, on leather, found in his time, 447

Pepi-na, guardian of Pepi's pyramid, i. 121

Pepi-nakht, functionary under Pepi, i. 121

Peraara, cartouche of, i. 61 *n*.

Perao, i. 61. *See* Pharaoh

PIAOI

Persians, the, in Egypt, ii. 303, 329, 339

Pet-baal, i. 292

Petise, high-priest and satrap, ii. 231, 251, 253

Petubastes, king, ii. 233

Phacoussa (-æ, -an), chief city of the Arabian nome, the Gosem (Guesem, Goshen) of the monuments, ii. 369

Phagroriopolis, ii. 422, 423

Phamenoth, the month, i. 175, 363, 442, 527; ii. 297

Pharaoh, his titles, i. 61; wife, daughters, harem, children, 62; court, 62; officials, 63; ii. 133. *Comp* Pir'ao

Pharaohs, visits of, to Nubia, i. 335; causes of the fall of, ii. 289; the last, 316; fall of the kingdom of, 319

Pharmuthi, the month, i. 186, 363, 368

Phathmetic (Phatnitic) branch of the Nile (*pa-to-mehit*), origin of the name, ii. 419

Philæ, I., i. 35, 133, 218, 469, 472; ii. 141, 283

Philip Arrhidæus, ii. 339

Philistia. *See* Zaha

Philistines, land of, its boundary towards Egypt, ii. 13 :—'road of,' i. 239, 336, ii. 12, 397, 430

Philosophers, Egyptian, i. 25, 26

Phœnicia, i. 460. *See* Khar

Phœnician usurper in Egypt, i. 257, ii. 142

Phœnicians, Cushite emigrants from Arabia, ii. 402; Caphtor their fatherland, 403; their maritime commerce, i. 254, 255, 403; articles imported by, 403, 404; high style of art in their works, 510, 511; language, 257. *See* Fenekh, Kefa, *and especially* Khar

Pi-Amon, 'the city of Amon,' ii. 415, 418. *See* Thebes *and* Na-Amon

Piankhi, king, his offering at On, i. 150; conquest of Egypt recorded in his great inscription at Mount Barkal, ii. 239–257, 421

Piaoi, sculptor of the images of Ramses II., ii. 412

PIBAILOS

Pibailos (Byblos, now Bilbeïs), i. 240, 251; sanctuary of the goddess Bast at, ii. 418
Pi-bast (Pibeseth, SS.), i. 74; ii. 369. *See* Bubastus
Pi-Bi-neb-dad, ii. 349. *See* Mendes
Pidasa (Pidasis), ii. 47
Pi-hahiroth, ii. 393, 429, 432
Pi-Hathor ('the city of Hathor'), ii. 375. *See* Aphroditopolis
Pi-her-shefni, ii. 417. *See* Heracleopolis Magna
Pi-khun-en-Amon, ii. 349. *See* Diospolis Parva *and* Na-Amon
Pimai, king, ii. 228, 232; name, 284
Pimaz (Oxyrhynchus), ii. 241, 348
Pinehas, noble, ii. 136, 414
Pinotem I., king and high-priest, ii. 190, 203, 421
— secretary and councillor, ii. 190
Pi-nub (Momemphis), ii. 240
Pi-qe-ro-ro, prince of Pisaptu, ii. 262, 263, 276
Pi-R'a, 'city of the Sun' (a second On or Heliopolis), 'to the north of On,' probably at Tel-el-Yahudi, in the Wady-Toumeilât, ii. 418
Pi-ramessu (city of Ramses II.), i. 231; ii. 100, 370, 383, 420. *See* Raamses *and* Zoan-Tanis
Pi-Ramses, cities, temples, and other buildings of Ramses III., ii. 415–419. *Comp.* Ramessea
Pir'ao (Pharaoh), meaning; special title of Mineptah II., ii. 133
Pir-em-heru, a sacred book, i. 103
Pi-sebek. *See* Crocodilopolis
Pisebkhan I., under-king at Tanis, in the time of Shashanq I., ii. 207
Pi-Sutekh of Ramses II., ii. 419. *See* Zoan
Pi-tebhu, statues of, ii. 291
Pi-Thut, ii. 349. *See* Hermopolis Parva
Pi-tom, 'city of Tom,' the Sun-god (Pithom SS., Heracleopolis Parva), chief town of the region of Sukot, the Sethroite nome, i. 233, 234;

PUN

ii. 370, 372, 373, 375, 376, 378, 382, 386, 422
Pitshu, country (Midian), i. 179
Pi-user, ii. 348. *See* Busiris
Pi-Uto, ii. 349. *See* Buto
Pliny, i. 183; ii. 397
Poems, in praise of Thutmes III., i. 412, *f.*, ii. 406; of Seti I., ii. 406; of Ramses II. by Pentaur, 56, *f.*, 410; of Ramses III., 414
Potiphar, i. 308, 311
Potsherds, inscriptions on, i. 488, 489
Prahiunamif, son of Ramses II., ii. 50
Primi (Qasr Ibreem), i. 183, 438
Princes, the, of Kush, and of Hineb, i. 51
Prisoners, hostages, slaves, i. 27; employed on public works, 417; their labour like that of the Israelites in Egypt, 417
Prophet of the pyramid of Pharaoh, the office, i. 60
Prosopis, battle of, ii. 124, 128
Psamethik I., founder of the 26th dynasty, ii. 281; unites the rival dynastic claims, 281; builds new sepulchral chambers for the Apis-bulls, 295; his reign, 322
— II. Psammis, ii. 323
— III., Psammenitus, ii. 329
Psametik, prophet, i. 99, 100
Psampolis (Pimas, Pimases, Pimsa), ancient name for Ibsamboul, ii. 96
Psamus (Psamut, Psamuthis), king, ii. 287, 335
Ptah, temple of, at Memphis, i. 441, ii. 417, *et passim* (*cf.* Patah)
Ptolemaïs, ii. 348, 416. *See* Smen-hor *and* Neshi
Puam, royal architect at the court of Thutmes III., i. 417
Pun, Punt ('the East country'), in Arabia and the opposite coast of Africa (Ophir, Somauli), i. 135; peopled by Cushites, ii. 401; the 'land of God,' and cradle of the Egyptians, 403, 404; first expedition to, i. 137, 138; Queen Hashop's expedition to, 352–357; precious things

PUT

from, 379; tributes from, 383, 386, ii. 406

Put (Phut), son of Ham, the Libyan Tehennu (or Marmaridæ), W. of the Delta, ii. 404

Putha, sculptor, pictures of, i. 498

Pyramids:—i. 31; Abousir, 106; Absetu, 106; Ba, 107; Bai-u, 116; Black bull, 73; Dashour, 113; Ellahoon, 191; Gizeh, 86; Hir, 101; Kha-nofer, 124, 146; Khorp, 167; Khu-setu, 135; Menankh, 126; Menkara, 129; Menkau-ra, 101; Men-nofer, 120; Men-setu, 108; Mentu-hotep, 135; Mer-en-ra, 121; Nofer, 110; Nofer-ar-kara, 107; Nofer-ka-ra, 126; Nofer-setu, 113; Nuter-setu, 110; Qebeh, 105; Tat-setu, 116

—construction of, by each king, i. 89; origin of the word, 89; particular names, 90; materials for, 90

Q

QA-HEBES, ii. 348. *See* Cabasus

Qanta a-el-Hazneh, ii. 426, 427

Qa-sa, ii. 348. *See* Cynopolis

Qasr Agerud, i. 252

—Ibreem, i. 183. *See* Primi

Qasrieh, ii. 90

Qazautana (Gozan, Gauzanites), ii. 3, 46

Qebeh, pyramid, i. 105

Qel'an, slingers, ii. 50

Qinaa (Kanah), the brook, i. 371

Qir-kamosh, the Carchemish of the Bible (now Jerablûs), i. 337, 399; ii. 47

Qobti, ii. 347. *See* Coptos

Qors, Qos, ii. 347. *See* Cusæ

Qosseir, i. 138. *See* Leucos Limen

Qosem. *See* Gosem

Qurnah, i. 347; inscription on tomb at, 523

—old, ii. 28; Seti I.'s sepulchral temple at, 92

R

RA, the sun-god, i. 36; the sign of, 70; worship, 87, &c.

—high-priest of, i. 461

RAMSES

Ra-aa-qenen, i. 273. *See* Apopi

Raamses, Ramses, city of, ii. 45, 100, 365, 370, 399; not at Maskhoutah, 412, 421, 424–5. *See* Pi-ramessu *and* Zoan

Ra-bi-tha, ii. 217

Ra-haa-ab. *See* Uah-ab-ra

Rahotep and his wife, the oldest statues known, i. 82, 83

Ra-kheper-ka. *See* Nakhtnebef

Ra-khu-taui, king, i. 213

Ram, the sacred, i. 74. *See* Binebded, Mendes

Ramaka, son of Pinotem I., ii. 421

Ramenkheper, ii. 421. *See* Menkheper-ra

Ramessea of Ramses III., ii. 164, 415

Ramesseum, at Thebes, ii. 66, 93; at Heliopolis, 97; at Medinet Abou, 25 n., 150, 157; at Kan'ana, 164

Ramessids, the, i. 45; banished to the Great Oasis, ii. 201; recalled by Menkheper-ra, 203-206; Table II.

Ramessu. *See* Ramses

Ramses I., ii. 8; his family doubtful, 8; memorial of his coronation at Karnak, 9; war and treaty with the Khita, 9; monument at Wady Halfah, death, 9

—II. (Sesostris), his date about 1350 B.C., i. 299; rebuilds the temple at Abydus, 163; associated with his father Seti I., ii. 25; his right through his mother, 25; inscription at Abydus, 25; number of his monuments, 35; completes the temple at Abydus, 36, 46; his journey to Thebes, 34, 45, 410; inferiority of his buildings and sculptures, 46; war with the Khita, 46; previous campaigns, 65; war with Tunep, 66; with Canaan, 66; storming of Askalon, 68; list of prisoners inscribed at Luqsor, 69; his maritime wars, 70; treaty with the king of Khita, 71-76, 410; marries a daughter of the king of Khita, 78; her name, 413; razzia on the ne-

RAMSES

groes, 78; wars with Kush and the Libyans, 79; pictures of his court, 79, 80; gold-washing, 81-83; temples built by, 87, 88; temple of Ptah at Memphis, 90; various buildings, 91; works in Nubia, 94; rock-temple of Ibsamboul, 94; his special residence at Zoan-Tanis, 98; new temple city, and worship of gods there with himself, 98, 384, 412; his 'city of Sutekh of Ramses Miamun,' 419; the *Pharaoh of the oppression*, 103; number of prisoners, and their various employments, 105; his long reign, 114; thirty years' jubilee, 114; his family, 115; contemporaries, 117; tomb at Biban-el-Molouk, 119; stélé with inscriptions at Maskhoutah in Wady-Toumeilât; extent of his conquests, 411, 424

Ramses III. (Rhampsinitus), i. 211, 238; his campaigns against the Shasu, 249; protects his frontiers, 252; troubles on his accession, ii. 142, 152; account of his reign in the Harris papyrus, 145; restores the several ranks in the state, 146; war with the Libyans and Maxyes, 147; fortress and well in the land of the Aperiu, 148; fleet on the Red Sea, 148; voyages to the Indian Ocean, 148; the copper mines of 'Athaka discovered, 148; treasures from the peninsula of Sinai, 148; plants, trees, and shrubs, 149; peaceful state of his kingdom, 149; memorials in the Ramesseum at Medinet Abou, 150; treasures dedicated to Amon, 151; boundless generosity, 152; victory over the Carian-Colchian nations, 153; over the Maxyes, 155, 156; pictures of defeated kings, 157; list of conquered cities and countries, 158, 159; booty and captives devoted to the temples, 160; list of his Ramessea, 161; works at Thebes, 163; erects a Ramesseum at Kanaan, 164; the

RANEBMA

harem conspiracy, 164-172; his sons and the order of their succession, 172; his rock-hewn tomb and its pictures, 174; song of praise for his victories, at Medinet-Abou, 414; his buildings, in Nubia, 415; in Upper Egypt, 415; in Lower Egypt, 417; in Palestine, 419

Ramses IV., ii. 174; rock-tablet relating the expedition to Hammamat, 174-178; additions to the temple of Khonsu at Thebes, 178

—V., ii. 178; his tomb at Biban-el-Molouk appropriated by Ramses VI., 178; rock-tablet at Silsilis, 178, 179

—Meritum (*q. v.*), ii. 180

—VI., ii. 180; astronomical and chronological value of his tomb, 180; record respecting boundaries of lands in Nubia, 181, 182

—VII., ii. 185

—VIII., ii. 185

—IX., ii. 185; growing power of the priests of Amon, 186; presentation of rewards to them, 186, 187; burglaries in the royal tombs at Biban-el-Molouk, 189

—X., ii. 190

—XI., ii. 190

—XII., ii. 190; curious inscription, 191-194; the king's visit to Naharain, and marriage, 101; cure of the queen's sister, 193

—XIII., ii. 195; finishes the temple of Khonsu, 195; deposed by the priest Hirhor, 196; his probable autograph letter, 197; banished, 201; his descendants, 202, *f.*

—XVI., marriage with an Assyrian princess, ii. 202; recognized as king at Thebes, 207

Ramses, city of. *See* Raamses and Pi-ramessu

Ramses, railway station of, not an ancient name, ii. 424, 425

Ramses-Nekht, seer, i. 154

Ranebma. *See* Ramses VI.

RANEBMA-NAKHT

Ranebma-Nakht, governor of Thebes, ii. 190
Ranebtaui. *See* Mentuhotep I.
Ra-n-maat. *See* Amenemhat III.
R'anofer, scribe, in time of Ramses II., ii. 412
Ranseneb, commander at Sokhemkhakaura, i. 219
Ranuser, king (Rathures), i. 84; his pyramid, 108; tablet of, 109
Ra-sekenen, Hak or sub-king of Thebes, i. 274–279, 282, 283. *See* Taa
Rashid, i. 11. *See* Rosetta
Rasnotsemhet. *See* Nakht-hor-ib
Ra-sokhem-sut-taui. *See* Sebekhotep IV.
Ratatf, king, i. 84, 94
Rathures, i. 108. *See* Ranuser
Ra-uah-ab. *See* Psamethik I.
Ra-uah-em-ab. *See* Neku II.
Ra-user-ma. *See* Ramses II.
Red land, the, i. 16, 455
Red Sea, its Egyptian name, ii. 430. *Comp.* Yâm Sûph
Redesieh, temple, ii. 21, 32
Registers, value of, i. 174
Rekhi-khet, the, experts, i. 278
Rekhmar'a, inscription of; collector of tributes under Thutmes III.,ii.406
Religion, innovations in, ii. 292; demons, genii, and witchcraft, 293
Reshpu, idol, i. 245
Resurrection of the body, belief of the ancient Egyptians in the, i. 87
Rhampsinitus (Ramessu-pa-Nuter, 'R. the god'), ii. 145. *See* Ramses III.
Rhinocolura, or Rhinocorura, i. 239. *See* Ab-sakabu
Ribatha (Rohoboth), water of, ii. 13, 109
Ribu, or Libu, i. 11. *See* Libyans
Roads from Egypt to Syria and the Euphrates, i. 338; the Northern from Tanis to Pelusium, through Pitom, ii. 382, 386; the great Pharaonic (Sikkeh-es-Soultanich) from Tanis to Palestine, 387; its four

SANGAR

stations, Ramses (Tanis), the barrier of Sukot, Khetam, and Migdol, 387–391; through the desert of Shur to the Gulf of Suez, 398. *Comp.* Philistines
Rohan, valley of, inscriptions, i. 187, 195
Rohannu, Mt., i. 146
Rosetta (Rashid), i. 11
Rosetta stone, the, i. 122
Rudamon. *See* Urdamaneh
Ruten, or Luten, Rutennu, or Lutennu, the, i. 14; first appearance of the name, 268, 269, 286; the Upper, territory coincident with that of the Twelve Tribes, 269, 338; conquered by Thutmes III., 367; list of places in, 392, 393; tributes of, 374, 377, 380, 404, 509, &c.; ii. 406; extreme north of Egyptian empire under Ramses II., 411
Ruthen and Khita, connection between, ii. 23

SA'A-NEKHT, king, i. 345, 508
Sahura (Sephres), king, i. 84, 106; his pyramid and effigy, 106
Said, Arabic name of Upper Egypt, i. 18
Sair (Seir), i. 249
Sais, Saï, Sa, the city of Nit or Neith (Athena), capital of Nome V. (L. Eg.), i. 327; ii. 239, 240, *f.*, 255, 256, 286, 287, 288, *f.*, 304, *f.*, 348
Saïte dignitaries, stone sarcophagi of, ii. 291
Sakhau, or Khasau, i. 227. *See* Xoïs
Salatis, Hyksos king, i. 262
Sallier papyrus, i. 274–279
Samta, Samtaui, 'lord of both worlds,' name of Thutmes III., i. 425; of Cambyses, ii. 299, 329.
Samtaui-taf-nakht, inscription of, under Darius III. and Alexander the Great, ii. 319, 320
Samud, Samout, i. 238, 498. *See* Migdol
Sangar, tribute of, i. 379

SANKH-KA-RA

Sankh-ka-ra, king, i. 131, 135; inscription at Hammamat, 135
Sa-pa-li-li, king of Khita, ii. 3, 9
Sapti, king, i. 69, 73
Sapt-moru. *See* Oxyrhynchus
Saptu, capital of Nome XVIII. (Up. Eg.), with temple of Anubis by Ramses III., ii. 417
Saqqarah, Serapeum at, tombs of the Apis-bulls, i. 74
Sarbut-el-khadem, inscription of the joint reign of queen Hashop and Thutmes III., i. 451; inscription of the time of Amenhotep III., 489
Sardanapalus. *See* Assur-bani-pal
Sargon, ii. 224. *See* Usarkon
Satarona, king of Naharana, sends his daughter and a whole harem to Amenhotep III., ii. 407
Satrap, Ptolemy so called, ii. 289, 315
Satraps, Assyrian, in Lower Egypt, ii. 231, 232, 267, *f*.
Scarabæi, as amulets and memorials, i. 452, 468; interesting records of Amenhotep III. on, ii. 408
Schleiden on the Exodus, ii. 360, 366, 430, 431
Schools, i. 200; ii. 307
Scribes, the, i. 66; temple-scribes in Mineptah II.'s time, ii. 137
Sculpture, i. 203
Sea, the (Exod. xiv.), and the Yam Suf (Red Sea), ii. 400, 429-430
Seb, or Zeb (Cronos, Saturn), god of the earth, i. 35, 36
Sebek, the god, i. 70; the crocodile his emblem, 192; temples to, 194, 213, 440
—city of, i. 201. *See* Crocodilopolis
Sebekhotep, name of the greater number of kings of the 13th dynasty, i. 213
—III., the height of the Nile in his day, i. 218, 219
—IV., his statues, i. 220
—V., his monuments, i. 220; colossal statue at Tanis, ii. 405
—VI., i. 216; his memorial stone, 221

SENTA

Sebek-nofru-ra, queen, i. 191, 198, 208, 213
Sebercheres (Shepseskaf), king, i. 84
Sebennytus (Theb-nuten), capital of Nome XII. (L. Eg.), ii. 348; seat of Dyn. XXX., 316, 336
Segot or Segol, 'the barrier of Sukot,' ii. 380, 387
Se-hathor, official under king Nub-ka-ra, inscription, i. 166; re-erects public monuments, 167
Sehêl, island of, ii. 141
Sehotep-ab-ra. *See* Amenemhat I.
—guardian of the temple at Abydus, i. 196; inscription, 197
Seir, mount, ii. 249
Sekha-en-ra. *See* Ramses XI.
Sekhem-kheper-ra. *See* Shashanq II., Usarkon I.
Sekhuu, i. 317. *See* Xoïs
Semempses, king, i. 69; miracles and plagues in his reign, 74
Semitic race, its generic types, i. 14; immigrants, picture of, 177, 178; colonists, 240; natives in Egypt, 241; names, 241; words used by priests and scribes, 243; worship of their gods adopted by the Egyptians, 244; influence on religion, manners and language, ii. 105-107
Semitism, i. 230-247; power of, shown by the stone of Tanis, 246
Semneh, inscription on boundary stone at, i. 166, 182; border fortress, 181, 437; height of the Nile inscribed on rock, 189; temple to Usurtasen III., 437; memorial tablet and list of prisoners, 470
Senebef and his son Hor-heb, memorial stone, ii. 229
Senen-Tanen. *See* Khabbash
Senmut, architect to queen Hashop, i. 350, 351
Senoferu, king, i. 69, 78; his cartouche, 78; titles of honour, 79; tomb, 81
Senta, king, i. 69, 70, 73

SERAPEUM

Serapeum, the, at Memphis, Apis tablets in, ii. 229, 232
Ser-ka-ra. *See* Amenhotep I.
Ser-khepru-ra. *See* Horemhib
Serpent, the symbol of 'the living' god worshipped at Pitom, ii. 377; or rather the electric fish, 422
Servants, i. 27
Sesochris, king, i. 69, 77
Sesostris (Sestura, Settura), surname of Ramses II., ii. 35, 65; of Darius I., 307, 329, 331 *n.*
Set (Typhon), i. 37, &c.
Set (or Sutekh) Nub, god, his temples at Zoan and Avaris, i. 271
Set-aa-pehuti, Hyksos king. *See* Nub
Setau'an, viceroy of Kush, with the care of the gold-mines, ii. 81, 412
Sethroë, ii. 348. *See* Thuku
Sethroite nome, the, 'region of the river mouths,' i. 235, 237, ii. 370; Joseph the nomarch of, i. 307, ii. 378, 423
Seti I., Mineptah I. (Sethos), ii. 10; his Great Hall of Columns at Karnak, 10; representations of his wars, 10; campaign against the Shasu, 11; route from Khetam to Kan'aan, 12-14; inscriptions recording his victory, 14-16; triumphal return, 19; list of nations conquered, 20; wars against the Libyans, 21; record of prisoners and spoils, 22, 23; services to the temple of Amon, 23; his wife of the royal line of Dynasty XVIII., 24; worships Baal-Sutekh, 24; associates his infant son, Ramses II., as king in his own right, 25; wars with Kush and Punt, 26; artistic works, 27; his tomb, pictures, and inscriptions, 28; his Memnonium, to Ramses I., 28; his name of Usiri, 28; inscription to, by Ramses II., 29; table of kings at Abydus, 29; temples at Memphis, Heliopolis, El-Kab, and Speos Artemidos, 29, 31; sculptors of his reign, 31; tributes and taxes, 32; gold mines

SHASHANQ

in Egypt and Nubia, 32, 33; journey to the gold mines, 32; inscriptions at the temple of Redesieh, 33; poem in honour of Thutmes III. plagiarized for him, 406
Seti II. Mineptah III., ii. 137; records of the first two years of his reign, 137; report concerning his fugitive servants, 138, 389; temple at Thebes, 139; sepulchre at Biban-el-Molouk, 139
Setnakht, king, ii. 140; the anti-king Mineptah Siptah, 140; a Phœnician usurper, 142, 143; restores order, 143; account of his reign by his son Ramses III., 143, 144
Settura. *See* Sesostris.
Shabak (Sabaco), king, ii. 275 *n.*, 277, *f.*; meaning of his name, 284
Shabatak (Sebichus), king, ii. 277; his statue, 278; meaning of name, 284
Shabatun (Sabbaticus), R., i. 337; ii. 54
Shakana, lake, i. 240; ii. 122
Sharkieh, Arabic name of the region east of the Nile, the ancient Arabian nome, i. 21
Shashanq, king of Assyria, father of Nimrod, conqueror of Egypt, ii. 207 (*cf.* 203); visits his son's tomb at Abydus, 207; inscription, 208
Shashanq I. (Shishak of the Bible), son of Nimrod, made king of Egypt, ii. 207, 212; his Egyptian wife Karamat, and her inheritance, 212-214; his royal residence at Bubastus, 215; receives the fugitive Jeroboam, 216; his invasion of Judah recorded at Karnak, 217; list of conquered towns, 217, 218; Hall of the Bubastids at Karnak, 219; record of its building, 219; memorial tablet, 221
—Shashanq II., king, ii. 225
—III., king, ii. 228
—IV., king, ii. 228
Shashanq, son of Usarkon I., high-priest of Amon, and grandfather of Shashanq II., ii. 223, 225

SHASHANQ

Shashanq, son of Usarkon II., chief priest of Ptah, ii. 224; the office hereditary in his family, 225
Shas-hotep, ii. 347. *See* Hypsele
Shasu (Shasa, Shaus, Shauas), the, i. 263; attracted to the Delta, 248, 250; extent of their territory in the reign of Seti I., 256; booty from, 383; campaigns against, ii. 12–14; name used for robbers, 110; received into the Delta, 132, &c.
Sheat, a district of Kush, i. 159
Sheddâd, son of Ad, his irruption into Egypt, i. 266
Sheikh-el-Belled, the, i. 96, 204
Shemik, a district of Kush, i. 159
Shepseskaf, king, i. 103; inscription at Saqqarah, 103, 104
Shepseskaf-ankh, prophet, i. 105
Sherohan, city, i. 285, 288, 369
Shet (Sheti, Shat), i. 155, 193
Shetat, feast of, i. 171, 175
Shishak, ii. 216. *See* Shashanq I.
Shu (Agathodæmon), the god of the air, i. 35, &c.
Shur, i. 147; ii. 389, 390, 391; desert of, 397. *See* Anbu
Si-Amon ('son of Amon'). *See* Hirhor
Si-Bast. *See* Usarkon II.
Siajout, Siaut, ii. 347. *See* Lycopolis
Sidon, i. 337; ii. 324
Si-Ise ('son of Isis'). *See* Thakelath I., II.; Nakht-hor-hib
Silsilis, rock-grotto at, song of praise in, i. 335; quarries, inscription of a stonemason, 490, 498; of king Horemhib, 522, 523; rock-tablet of Ramses V., ii. 178, 179; inscription recording the building of the Hall of the Bubastids, 219, 220; memorial tablet to Shashanq I. and his son Auputh, 221, 222
Silver tablet, treaty on, ii. 71–76, 410
Simyra (Zamira), i. 388
Sinai, peninsula of, turquoise and copper mines worked, conquests, and inscriptions, by Senoferu, i. 80; Khufu, 93; Ranuser, 109;

SPHINX

Usurtasen I., 160; Amenemhat III., 195, 196, 201; Thutmes II., 346; Hashop and Thutmes III., 451; Amenhotep III., 418; called the 'land of the gods,' 411 *n.*; treasures from, ii. 148; &c.
Sineh, his flight from Egypt to Edom, illustrating the route of the Exodus, i. 146, *f.*; his exploits and marriage, 147; his return, 148
Singara (Sinear), i. 401, 404; ii. 20, 67
Si-Nit ('son of Nit'). *See* Amasis
Siptah. *See* Mineptah
Sirbonis, lake, i. 147, 238; ii. 391, *f.*, 400, 430-2
Smam-kheftu-f, Ramses II.'s fighting lion, ii. 80
Smen-hor (Ptolemaïs?), capital of Nome XXI. (Up. Eg.), ii. 348
Smonkhkara, king (Mermesha, Mermentiu), colossal statues of, i. 219
Sokar (Osiris), worship of, i. 54
Sokhem (Letopolis), capital of Nome II. (L. Eg.), i. 73; ii. 239, 254, 348
—(Sekhem, Khesem) the Holy of Holies in the temples, i. 419, 429, 435
Sokhem-khakaura, fortress, i. 219
Sokhet, worship of, i. 54
Soleb, inscriptions at, i. 507
Song of praise to Thutmes III., i. 412–415
Sonti-Nofer, ii. 348. *See* Motelis
Sotep-en-Amon. *See* Thakelath I.; Usarkon II.; Shashanq II.; Pimai
Sotep-en-Anhur. *See* Nakht-hor-hib
Sotep-en-Ptah. *See* Ramses XIII.; Khabbash
Sotep-en-ra. *See* Ramses II., IX., X., XII.; Setnakht; Shashanq I., III.; Thakelath II.
—daughter of Amenhotep IV., i. 495
Sothis star, rising of, i. 175, 439
Souph. *See* Suf
Speos Artemidos, rock-grotto erected by Seti I., ii. 31
Sphinx, the great, at Gizeh, i. 95, 97; temples of and near, 97, 98; older

SPHINXES

than Khufu, 98, 99; an emblem of Hormakhu, 99, 464; cleared of sand by Thutmes IV.; his chapel and inscription between its paws, 97, 98, 463-466; inscriptions of visitors, 97

Sphinxes before temples, i. 271; of the Louvre, 272; one female (the Egyptian sphinx being generally male), ii. 409

Strabo, i. 151, 162, 191; ii. 311, 395, 429

Suan (Syene, Assouan), i. 19, 91, &c.; the southernmost point of Egypt, ii. 381-2

Succoth, i. 233, 373. *See* Sukot

Suchos (sacred crocodile), i. 194

Suf, Sufi, Souph, i. 232; 'sea of,' ii. 376, *f.*, 389; 'city and region of,' i. 138; ii. 176, 430

Suhen, i. 391

Sukot, Suko, Suku (Succoth), i. 233, 248, 250; ii. 138, 370; region of the Sethroïte nome, 373, 421, 422, 423; its foreign population, 380. *Cf.* Thuku

Sukot, the barrier of, station on the great Pharaonic road, ii. 380, 387, 389, 390

Sun, the, personified in the deities, Ra (the rising sun in the East), Tum (the setting sun in the West), Hormakhu (the sun at its meridian height), Khepra (the sun at midnight), i. 494; temple of, at Edfou, 322; at Khu-aten, 498

Suphis, king, i. 69, 84, 85. *See* Cheops

Sutekh, surnamed Nub, also Set, Egyptian name of the Semitic Baal, especially Baal-Zapuna, a foreign Semitic (Hyksos) deity of evil, worshipped also in Egypt, especially by the Ramessids, i. 244, 271, 275, 277, 278; ii. 3, 49, 60, 63, 71, 75; his likeness on the silver plate of the treaty between Ramses II. and the king of Khita, 76, 411; his worship at Tanis, 99; temples of, 417; Ramses II.'s city of, at Zoan-Tanis, 419

TANTERER

Suten-rekh, title of king's grandchildren, i. 28; ii. 303

Syene, i. 12, 19, 184, *et passim*

Syncellus, i. 300, &c.

Syrians, the, their irruptions, aided by the Shasu-Arabs, i. 270

TAA, kings of Dyn. XVII.; their tombs at Thebes, i. 282, 283
—I. *See* Ra-sekenen
—II. A or Ao, 'the Great,' i. 282, 283
—III. Ken, 'the brave,' i. 282, 283, 288

Ta'a-pa-mau (Leontopolis), ii. 12

Tabenet, ii. 388. *See* Daphnæ

Tachos, king. *See* Teos

Tafnakhth(Tnephachthus, Technatis), king of Saïs and Memphis, ii. 238; father of Bocchoris, i. 51; grandfather of Neku, and great-grandfather of Psamethik, 277, 281 (*see* Geneal. Table IV.); his renunciation of luxury and curse on Menes, 51, 52; his revolt against Egypt, and submission to Piankhi, 238, *f.*

Ta-ha-ra-qa (Tirhakah, Tearco, Etearchus, Tarachus, Tarkus), ii. 264, *f.*; his memorials at Thebes, 278

Ta-Hut ('the house of') Ramses III., several temples built by that king, ii. 415-420

Tai-uzai, ii. 241

Takhis or Tekhis, city of Upper Ruthen, on R. Nasruna, i. 399, 400

Ta-Khont (Nubia), the regions bordering on Egypt from the First Cataract to the south of Mt. Barkal, i. 321, 329; ii. 264

Tamahu, the Libyan, i. 229; warlike dances of, 360

Tamera, name of Lower Egypt, i. 17

Tamiathis, Tamiati, ii. 419. *See* Damietta

Tanis, i. 160. *See* Zoan

Tanitic branch of Nile, i. 230; ii. 372
—nome (14th), the seat of Semitic races, i. 231; ii. 12

Tanterer, ii. 347. *See* Tentyra

INDEX.

TA-NUTER

Ta-nuter, the land of the gods, i. 136, 410
Taroau, Tarufu (Lat. Troja, the 'Egyptian Troy,' now Tourah), quarries of, i. 63, 91, 118, 165, 322, 476; ii. 91; deities of, i. 295 n.; rock-tablet in, 322
Ta-setu, pyramid, i. 116
Tatehan (Teneh), ii. 244
Tat-ka-ra, king, i. 110. *See* Assa
Taurus, M., i. 338
Ta-user, queen, ii. 140, 141
Tax-payers, voluntary, presents to, i. 487, 488
Teb. *See* Apollinopolis Magna
Tebu, ii. 347. *See* Aphroditopolis
Technatis. *See* Tafnakhth
Tefab, rock-tomb of, near Ossiout, i. 223
Tehen, the, i. 229. *See* Thuhen
Tel-el-Amarna (Khu-aten), i. 494, 495; prayer of Aahmes, 501; queen Nofer-i-Thi's address to the sun, 502; rock-pictures and inscriptions of Khunaten's family, 503-506
Tel-el-Maskhoutab. *See* Maskhoutah
Tel-el-Yahudi ('mound of the Jews') in the Wady-Toumeilât, probably site of Pi-R'a, a second On or Heliopolis, ii. 418
Tel-es-Samout, the ancient Migdol, ii. 426, 431
Tel-Mukhdam, statue at, i. 272
Tel-monf, modern name of Memphis, i. 55
Ten, weight, ii. 199
Tennu, kingdom of, i. 147
Tentyra (Tanterer, now Denderah), capital of Nome VI. (Up. Eg.), temple at, i. 446, ii. 347
Teos, Tachos (Ziho), king, ii. 287, 337
Tep-ah, 'the cow-city,' ii. 348, 417. *See* Aphroditopolis
Tesher (Erythræans), i. 16; ii. 265
Teta, king, i. 72; his hair-ointment, 72, 76, 115; his pyramid, 116
Thakelath I. (Tiglath), ii. 224
—II., ii. 225; record of an eclipse

THUHEN

of the moon, 226, 228; irruptions of the Ethiopians and Assyrians, 226
Thamask (Damascus), i. 337
Thamhu, ii. 124, 126, 152; another name of the Thuhen, *q.v.*
Thebes, capital of Upper Egypt, i. 20; and of Nome IV., ii. 347, 415 (called Ni, No, '*the city*,' Ni'a, No'a, 'the great city,' Ni-Amon, No-Amon, 'city of Amon;' Na-ris, '*the city* of the South,' ii. 418; *A-pet*, the sacred city E. of the Nile, i. 286); seat of Dyn. XI., i. 131; of Dyn. XIII. and XVII., 210, 221, 277, *f.*, 282, 288, *f.*; tombs of these Dynasties at, 283; capital of Egypt under Dyn. XVIII., 317, *f., et passim*; priests of, expel Ramessids, and usurp the crown as Dyn. XXI., ii. 196, 200; expelled by the Assyrians, 206; Ramses XVI. acknowledged at, 207; subdued by the Ethiopians, 236; twice captured by Assurbanipal, 268-9, 273-4;— great temple of, *see* Amon; *see* also Memnonium, Ramesseum, &c.; temples of Ramses III. at, 415; necropolis of, i. 524-5, *et passim*
Theb-nuter, ii. 348. *See* Sebennytus
Thentamon, ii. 421
Thi, queen, wife of Amenhotep III., i. 479, 490; her connection with Z'aru in the North country, ii. 408
—nurse to king Khunaten, i. 512
This or Thinis (Tini), capital of Nome VIII. (Up. Eg.), its situation and vast necropolis, i. 50; cradle of the Egyptian monarchy, 51; seat of the earliest dynasties, i. 71; sanctuary of Ramses III. in the temple of Anhur, ii. 347, 416
Thot, Thoth, the month, i. 175, 225, 226, 527; ii. 247, 442
Thua (-aa, -ao), mother of Thi, queen of Amenhotep III., i. 345, 490; ii. 407
Thuhen, Thuhi, Thubeni, Thuhennu, Tehen, Tehennu, Thamhu (Naphtuhim, SS.), i. 327, 414; ii. 21, 79,

VOL. II. H H

THUKU

80, 123, 126, 152, 404. *See* Marmaridæ

Thuku, Thukot, Tuku, capital of Nome VIII. (L. Eg.), i. 233 *n.*, 248 *n.*, 250 *n.*; ii. 132, 133, 138, 348; identified with Sukot, 421-2

Thut (Hermes), the scribe of the gods, i. 38; worship of, 100; *et passim*

Thutmes I. ('child of Thut;' Thothmes, Thotmosis), i. 286, 318, 319, 328; his victories, 331, 332; 'war of vengeance,' 336; campaign against the Ruthen, 339; erects a tablet of victory, 342, ii. 405; great temple at Karnak, i. 343; short life and reign, 343; tomb, 348; statue destroyed by queen Hashop, 432; re-erected by Thutmes III., 432

— II., his name erased from the monuments by queen Hashop, i. 344; campaign against the Shasu-Arabs, 346; rock-tablet near Assouan, 346; buildings at Thebes, 347; tomb, 348

— III., secluded by his sister at Buto, i. 361; admitted to the throne with her, 362; their joint tablet at Wady-Magharah, 362; his long reign, 364; numerous monuments, 365; riches in the treasuries of the temples, 365; wars and victories, 366; number of campaigns, 366; against Ruthen and Zahi, 367; record of campaigns and tributes, 368-375; further victories, tributes, and booty, 375-386; registration of the tributes, 386, 387; return to Egypt, 387, 388; thanksgiving and homage to the gods, 387; feasts of victory, 388; buildings and obelisks as memorials, 389; catalogues of peoples of Up. Ruthen, 391-393; confederacy in Palestine, 394; his captain Amenemhib, 395-398; wars in Naharain, 398; summary of campaigns, 401, 402; tributes and treatment of hostile towns, 402;

TIU

articles brought from Phœnicia and Palestine, 403; from other places, 404, 405; pictures of plants and animals from Ruthen, 409, 410; poem in praise of the king and Amon, 412-415; prisoners employed on public works, 417-419; gifts to the temple, 420, 421; meaning of the king's name, 425; relations to his sister, queen Hashop, 426; inscription of his 24th year, 426-428; his important share as founder of the temple precincts, 429; re-erects the statues of former kings, 432; endeavours to preserve the monuments of his forefathers, 433, 434; architectural works, 435; numerous monuments executed by prisoners, 436; rock-tombs, temples, 437-439; temple and inscription at Abydus, 442-445; temple to the goddess Hathor, 446; to the god Ptah at Memphis, 448; beautifies the temple of the sun at Heliopolis, 448; obelisks, 448, 449; his deification during his lifetime, 450; numerous memorials of, 452; chronological summary of his reign, 453; tributes from Ethiopia, Arabia, Syria, and Phœnicia, ii. 406; conquest of Zahi, 406; his victories recorded by the scribe Za-anni, 406-7

Thutmes IV., his surnames, i. 461; campaigns, 462; memorial stone in front of the Sphinx, 97, 463; inscription about the vision of Hormakhu, 464-466; removes the sand from the Sphinx, 466; his records by the scribe Za-anni, ii. 407

Thutmes, governor of the South under Amenhotep III., i. 472

Thutmesu, burgomaster of Thebes, i. 525, 526

Ti, royal architect, i. 60; his tomb, 109

Timaius, king, i. 262

Tini, i. 50. *See* This

Tiu Hathor Hont-taui, queen of Pinotem I., ii. 421

TNEPHACHTHUS

Tnephachthus, Technatis, renounces luxury; his curse on Menes, i. 51, 52. *See* Tafnakhth

To-khont, ii. 415. *See* Nubia

Tom, the sun-god of Heliopolis, tutelar deity of Pitom and Sukot, ii. 376, 377. *Comp.* Tum

Tombos, island, i. 331

Tombs, construction of, i. 87

To-mehit, 'country of the North,' name preserved in the Coptic Tamiati, Arab. Damiat, Damietta, ii. 418

Torso of Ramses II. from the temple of Ptah at Memphis, ii. 90, 331

Tosorthos, king, i. 69; the physician-god, 77

Tota, king, i. 69, 70, 72

Totun, the god, i. 185, 186

Toumeilât, the valley of, ii. 422, *f.*

Tourah. *See* Taroau

'Treasure cities,' or rather temple-cities, built by the Israelites, ii. 102

Treaty of Ramses II. and king of Khita, ii. 71, 410

Tributes and taxes of Thutmes III., i. 374, *f.*; marked, weighed, and registered, 386

Tritonis, lake, i. 229

Troja. *See* Taroau

Tua, or Tui, queen of Seti I., mother of Ramses II., grand-daughter of Khunaten, ii. 24

Tuher, chosen ones, ii. 50

Tuku. *See* Thuku

Tum, the sun-god, the sun in the West, i. 150, 464, *et passim. Comp.* Tom

Tunep (Daphne), catalogue of the booty carried from, i. 376; tribute, 404; Ramses II.'s wars with, ii. 66

Turin papyrus, i. 39, 47, 48; ii. 165

Turquoises, i. 196

Tut 'ankh-amon, king, i. 508; his memorial at Thebes, 508, 509; offerings from the South and the Ruthen, 509, 510; short reign, 512

Tutesher, or red mount, i. 91

USERCHERES

Two Brothers, tale of the, i. 309-311; written for Seti II., ii. 139

Tybi, the month, i. 55, 442, 505, 527

Tyre, i. 337

U A-EN-RA. *See* Amenhotep IV.
Uah-ab-ra, king (Pharaoh-Hophra, Apries, Vaphres), son of Psamethik II., his Apis-tablet, ii. 296; his reign, arrogance, and prosperity, 323, 324; league with Zedekiah, 324; conquered by Nebuchadnezzar, 325; the story of his fall, 325-6

Uak, feast of, i. 225

Uas. *See* Us

Uenephes I., i. 69; his pyramid of the black bull, 73

—II., i. 69

Uit, fortress of, i. 239

Una, i. 116; brings a sarcophagus for Pepi from Troja, 118; his wars and expeditions, 119, 120; historical text in his tomb at Memphis, 123; governor of Upper Egypt, 123; brings materials for the Khanofer pyramid, 124; brings alabaster slab from Ha-nub, 124, 125

Unas (Onnos), king, i. 113

Unnofer, a name of Osiris, ii. 36, 41, 44

Uot-kheper-ra. *See* Kames

Urdamaneh (Rudamon), Assyrian campaign against, ii. 272, 273; his parentage, 275 *n*

Urkhuru, tomb of, i. 107

Ur-maa Nofiru-ra, queen of Ramses II., ii. 78

Usarkon I. (Sargon), ii. 223; contest between his two sons for the crown, 223

—II., his wives, ii. 224

— prince, high-priest of Amon, ii. 225-227

Us, Uas, *see* Thebes: in Lower Egypt, ii. 418

Usem, brass, rather than electrum, i. 386

Usercheres (Uskaf), king, his pyramid, i. 106

USER-KHA-RA

User-kha-ra. *See* Setnakht
User-khepru-ra. *See* Seti II.
User-ma-ra. *See* Ramses XII., Usarkon II., Shashanq III., Pimai
Usiri, tomb of, ii. 27, 28. *See* Seti
Uskhopesh, the Theban Amon, ii. 308
Usurtasen I., inscription at Heliopolis, i. 149, 152; fragments of obelisk near lake Mœris, 153; works on the temple of Amon at Thebes, 155, ii. 188; not the Pharaoh of Joseph, i. 158; inscriptions at Beni-Hassan, 155, 171; his statue at Tanis, 203; inscription of Khnumhotep, 169; victories over the Hittites, &c., ii. 404-5
Usurtasen II., his prosperous reign; inscription at Syene, i. 168
—III., his power and wisdom, i. 180; inscription at Elephantiné, 181, two inscribed pillars at Wady-Halfah; 182, ii. 352-355; builds sanctuaries and fortresses, i. 181; final subjection of Kush, 182; war with the Menthu, Hersh'a, and Hittites, ii. 404; in Ethiopia, 405; his statue at Tanis, 405
—artist, i. 206
Uten (Vedan, SS.), a region of Pun, in Arabia, the Udeni of Ptolemy, ii. 404 *n.*
Uti or Uit (Buto), frontier fortress at M. Casius, i. 239, ii. 13
Utur, the great sea, ii. 403
Uza-hor-en-pi-ris, commander of the fleet under Amasis, ii. 303; serves Cambyses and Darius, 303; inscription on his shrine-bearing statue, 3-306

V ALUES and prices, list of, about B.C. 1000, ii. 198, 199
Vaphres. *See* Uah-ab-ra

W ADY ALAKI (Al-aki, Akita), gold mines, ii. 81
—Arabah, i. 248
—Halfah, memorial of Usurtasen I.

ZAHA

near, i. 159; fortress, temples, and inscriptions of Usurtasen III. at, 181-3, ii. 352; memorial stone of Ramses I. at, 9
—Magharah, in the peninsula of Sinai, rock inscription of Senoferu, i. 80; tablet of Khufu's victories, 92; tablet of Ranuser, 109; mining works of Tatkara, 110; inscription of king Nofer-ka-ra, 126; of Amenemhat III., 195; joint tablet of queen Hashop and Thutmes III., 362
Wawa, Wawa-t, land of, i. 144, 145, 333; tribute from, 378, 380, 382, 384; temple lands in, ii. 181-2
Weights, ii. 199
Wells, at Abydus, i. 162; sunk at Akita, ii. 32, 33, 81, 86; four on the old road from Coptos to Qosseir, 87

X ERXES I. (Kshiarsh or Khsherish) and the anti-king Khabbash, ii. 314, 315; his tyranny in Egypt, 332
—II., ii. 333
Xoïs (Sakhau, Khesuu), capital of Nome VI. (L. Eg.), seat of Dyn. XIV., i. 210, 227, 317

Y AM-SOUPH, 'Sea of Weeds' (the 'Red Sea' of the Versions), i. 232; ii. 376, *f.*, 429, 430
Year, the ancient Egyptian, different forms of, i. 176; of 365¼ days, 440
Yuma Kot, or Yuma Sekot, Egyptian name of the Red Sea, ii. 430

Z AANNI, royal scribe and general staff officer, recorded the victories of Thutmes III., Amenhotep II., and Thutmes IV., ii. 406-7
Zaha, Zahi (to-en-Zaha, 'the country of Zaha,'), land of the Phœnicians, on the sea-coast from Egypt to the Canaanites, aft. of the Philistines, i. 319, 320, 367, ii. 13; boundary with Egypt, i. 239, ii. 13, 154, 430; war of Aahmes in, i. 319; subdued

ZA-PATAH
by Thutmes III., 368, 376, 401, 402, 414; kings taken captive, ii. 406; places taken, booty, and tribute, i. 379, 380, 384; products of, 403; vessels of gold and silver wrought in, 379; wars of Seti I., ii. 13; of Ramses II., 52, 57; a city of Ramses II. in, 57; a Ramesseum of Ramses III. in the city of Kanaan, 164, 420

Za-Patah, i. 54

Zar, Zal, Zaru, i. 160; ii. 408. *See* Zoan

Zarduna (Zarthon, Zaretan, SS.), ii. 132

Zar-Tyrus, i. 399

Z'aru, city, lake made in, by Amenhotep III., ii. 408; *probably* Zoan

Ziho, king. *See* Teos

Zoan (Egyptian and Hebrew), Tanis (Greek), also Zor, Zar, Zal (pl. Zoru, Zaru, Zalu), 'strong place,' and Pi-Ramessu ('the city of Ramses'), now Sân, the 'great and splendid city of Lower Egypt,' in the midst of a Semitic population, i. 160; ii. 382-3; an essentially foreign city, on the eastern border of Egypt, 231; capital of Nome XIV., i. 230, ii. 349; meaning of the name, 383; its oldest monuments of Pepi's time, i. 117; works of Dyn. XII., 160, 167, 168, 203; of Dyn. XIII., 212, 219, 220; date compared with Hebron, 230; ii. 383; stone of Ramses II., with inscription dated from the era of Nub, i. 245, *f.*, 296, ii. 99; beginning of the land of the Shasu from the west eastwards, i. 248; also of the Khar (Phœnicians), 256, 257, 267, 399; administrative centre of eastern provinces under the Ramessids, 253; trilingual stone called the Decree of Canopus, 268; seat of the Hyksos kings, 271; adorned by them with new temples

ZOR
and monuments, 271, 294; starting-point for campaigns towards the East, 368; and of the great roads to Palestine, ii. 98, 386, *f.*; the special residence of Ramses II., 45, 77, 98; importance of its position—*the key of Egypt*, 98; abandoned by the kings of Dyn. XVIII., 100; new temple-city of Ramses II. to gods associated with himself, 98, 384, 412; henceforth called Pi-Ramessu, 100, 384; a quarter of it called 'the city of Sutekh of Ramses Miamun,' 419; records of oppression in its building, 385; abundant notices by the scribes, 100; full description in a letter, 100-102; *here is the seat of the court*, 100; one of the 'treasure cities,' or rather 'temple-cities,' built by the Israelites for Pharaoh, 102; importance of its history, 103, *f.*, 385; despatches sent out from it, 132; the royal seat of Mineptah II., the Pharaoh of the Exodus, of which it was the starting-point, 133, 386; and of Mineptah III., 138; report on fugitive servants, an exact parallel to the Exodus, 138 *n.*, 389-390; its college of priests, 201; buildings of Ramses III. in, 419; seat of the 23rd dynasty, 233; an unnamed satrap of, 254; subdued by Assurbanipal, 270; its site still strewn with monuments and statues, i. 212, 220; ii. 99

Zoan, plain or 'field of' (Ps. lxxviii. 12, 43, so called also in Egyptian, Sokhot-Zoan), the muster-place and exercise ground of Egyptian armies and the scene of the miracles of Moses, i. 212; ii. 104, 133, 383; its present aspect, 99

Zoar, i. 257

Zodiac on ceiling at Denderah, i. 447

Zoq'a, ii. 348. *See* Canopus

Zor (Zor-Tyrus), i. 257

Spottiswoode & Co., Printers, New-street Square, and Parliament-street.

RS OF THE THIRTEENTH DYNASTY.

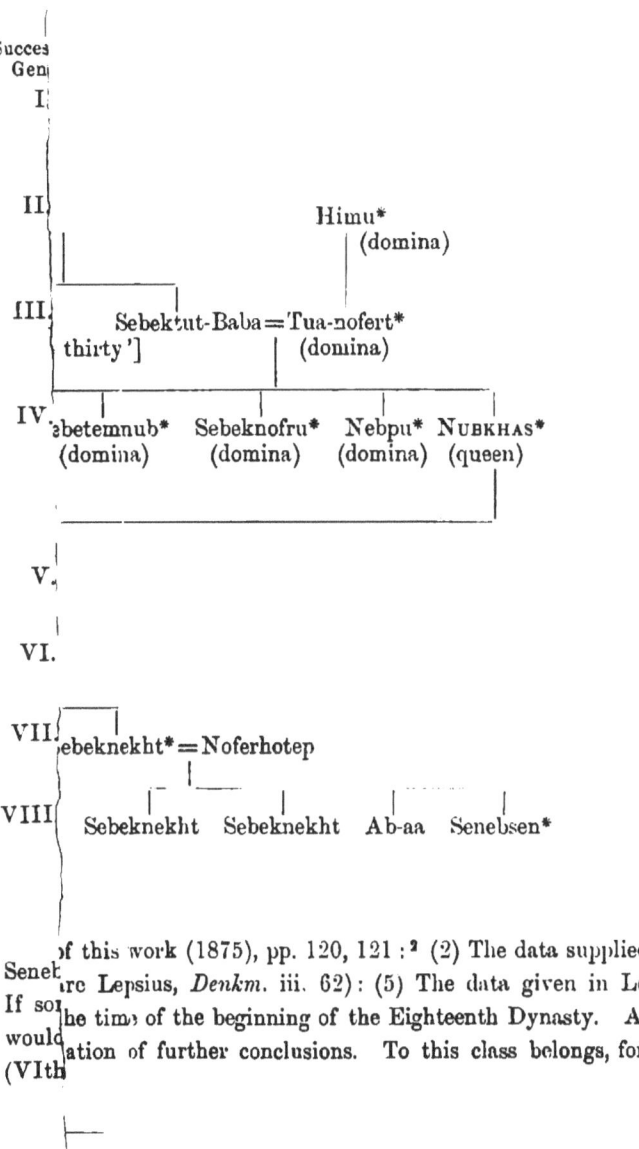

)f this work (1875), pp. 120, 121 :² (2) The data supplied
Senet ire Lepsius, *Denkm*. iii. 62): (5) The data given in Le
If so he time of the beginning of the Eighteenth Dynasty. A
would ation of further conclusions. To this class belongs, for
(VIth

121, 122.—ED.

'SSIDS.

King of Khita
|
=Nofirura Urmaa *

Son ira. Horhiunamif. 4. MINEP
Dau . . Meri, etc.

Hebuanrozanath
|
Isi Hemarozatha *=7. F

11.   1
mun V. Meritum   At(

with * are those of women.

See Vol. II. p.

RAMSES.

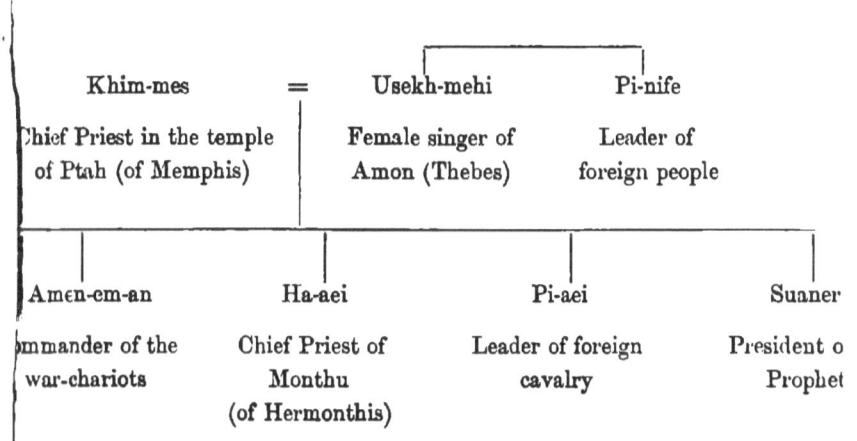

	Khim-mes	=	Usekh-mehi	Pi-nife	
	Chief Priest in the temple of Ptah (of Memphis)		Female singer of Amon (Thebes)	Leader of foreign people	
Amen-em-an	Ha-aei		Pi-aei		Suaner
Commander of the war-chariots	Chief Priest of Monthu (of Hermonthis)		Leader of foreign cavalry		President o Prophet

www.ingramcontent.com/pod-product-compliance
Lightning Source LLC
Chambersburg PA
CBHW021416300426
44114CB00010B/524